>>> 改訂版

完全攻略！
TOEFL ITP® テスト
模試4回分

TOEFL ITP® is a registered trademark of ETS.
This publication is not endorsed or approved by ETS.

ポール・ワーデン
ロバート・ヒルキ
藤井哲郎 共著

著者からのメッセージ

●TOEFLスコアアップのためにすべきこと

TOEFL ITPのスコアアップのために大切なこと ―― それは一にテスト演習、二にテスト演習、そして三にテスト演習です。特別なテスト対策をしなくても、実際の試験を何度か事前に受験するだけでスコアが伸びるというのは、他でもない、TOEFLを作成しているETS（ニュージャージー州プリンストンに所在）が認めるところでもあります。

●Test first, then understand.

とは言え、実際のTOEFLを何度も受験するのがベストの対策というわけではありません。これでは第一、費用がかかりすぎます。それに受験をいくら繰り返しても、わかるのはスコアだけです。スコアだけでは、スコアアップは望めません。大切なのは、問題を復習して解法を確かめること、和訳と照らし合わせて理解の精度を確認すること、頻出分野や必修語彙を知り実戦的な対策を行うこと、つまり "Test first, then understand." ――「まずは演習、そして分析・学習」の手順に従って、合理的な対策を行うことです。この意味で、良質な問題集を使ってTOEFL対策を行うことは、実際のTOEFLを繰り返し受験するよりもはるかに効果的で効率がよいと言えるのです。

●最も効率的な対策を立てられる本書

本書が最高品質の問題ばかりを集めたTOEFL問題集であることに、著者一同、誇りと自信を持っています。本書に収録したテスト4回分の模試問題は、いずれも長年にわたるTOEFL研究に基づくものであり、実際のTOEFL ITPテストに限りなく近いものとなっています。問題作成に当たり分析対象としたテストは、実に60回分以上。またその研究成果は、私たちがこれまでさまざまな機会に、専門的な学術研究誌や国際学会で発表してきたものです。

実際のTOEFLを受験したり、TOEFL対策予備校に通ったりするのも、確かにひとつの対策ではあるかもしれません。しかし、皆さんが、本当に効果的で効率のよいTOEFL対策を願っているのであれば、ぜひ本書を使って「演習」と「復習」を繰り返してみてください。その成果はすぐにスコアとして表れるはずです。

本書が、最短最速での効果的なTOEFL対策と、長く使える本当の英語力を鍛えるための一助となれば幸いです。

Paul Wadden,　Robert A. Hilke

● 「字幕式学習法」からの脱却

　今まで洋画を何本見ましたか？　かなりの本数になるでしょう。ところで、映画で英語は上達しましたか？　もし答えが "NO" なら、それはあなたが吹き替えや字幕に頼り、日本語で意味を取ってきたからです。人は主に意味を取るのに使った言語を習得します。英単語のすぐ近くに日本語を書いて字幕をつけるのはやめましょう。まず英語から直接意味を取り、日本語より英語に取り組む時間を長く取ります。その後、どうしても意味がわからない箇所は日本語で確認します。本書の全訳が別冊にあるのはそのためです。

● 「訳」よりも「言い換え」が上達の秘訣

　同時に、日頃から「言い換え」に慣れましょう。これも日本語に訳すのではなく、英語で英語を理解することを指します。TOEFLの本文と問題、選択肢の関係のほとんどが、実はこの「言い換え」です。ですから英語で語義を知っていることが大事です。日頃から英英辞典やシソーラスを使って英語で言い換える訓練をしましょう。また、同じ事柄を別の言葉で表す訓練もしてみてください。例えば、"How are you?" 一本槍でなく、"How are you doing?"、"How's it going?"、"What's up?" など、多彩な英語表現で言い換えられるとよいでしょう。

● 「模試、模試、カメ作戦」── 本書の３倍活用法

　まず、本書の模試１を本番と同じ制限時間１時間55分、休憩なしで受けます。これで、あなたの時間管理能力を含むTOEFLスコアが出ます。次に時間制限なしで同じ模試を解きます。これで、時間さえかければ正解できる今の英語力が測れます。最後は本書を英語の底力を付ける教材として利用します。模試の正答や日本語訳を覚えても、同じ問題が本試験に出ない限り効果はありません。では何を学ぶのか。それは解答に至る思考プロセスです。例えば、リスニングは音声について何度もリピートし、会話文は音読筆写し、トランスクリプトを見て一字一句確認し、全てが聞けて言えるまで口頭練習します。文法セクションは出題パターンがひと目で見破れるまで学びます。だから正答を見た後が大切です。なぜ正答に至ったのか解法の手順を考えます。リーディングは設問と選択肢に知らない語句がないほどに学び、遅くとも着実にカメの歩みのように英語力を付けていきます。ここまでやったら、模試２を制限時間付きで受けます。スコアはきっと上がります。同じ学習法で模試３と４にも挑戦します。このように本書を３倍活用すれば、TOEFLスコアの上昇のみならず、大学教育に必須な英語力の土台を築くことも可能だと信じています。

藤井哲郎

目次 CONTENTS

おことわり：収録している英文・問題には学術的・専門的な内容が含まれますが、一部最新の情報ではないものや事実と異なるものも含まれています。また、内容の真偽を問うたり、特別な意図を含んだりすることは一切ありません。

本書の効果的な使い方

　本書の構成は以下のようになっています。活用法を確認し、効率よく学習を進めていきましょう。

■本書の構成

本誌　❶ 巻頭にTOEFLの概要と出題傾向を収録
　　　　❷ 模験4回分を収録
　　　　❸ 模試4回分の解答・解説を収録

別冊　❶ 問題の対訳を収録
　　　　❷ 巻末に解答用マークシート

■本書の活用法

❶ 巻頭の「出題傾向と対策」を読み、問題のパターンを学ぶ
　　　————各セクションの問題パターンをひととおり頭に入れてから模試に取り組みましょう。
❷ 模試（Practice Test）を解く
　　　————解答の際は、別冊巻末のマークシートを使用しましょう。
　　　————模試を解く際、リスニング・セクションの音声を途中で止めないでください。
　　　————リスニング・セクションと文法／リーディング・セクションの間に休憩を入れたりせず、約2時間の制限時間内に全問題を解くようにしてください。
　　　————リスニング・セクションの所要時間、文法／リーディング・セクションの制限時間は次の通りです。

リスニング・セクション	約35分
文法セクション	25分
リーディング・セクション	55分

❸ 換算点を算出する

――――全問題の解答が終わったら、「解答・解説」で答え合わせを
し、正答数を数えましょう。それを基にスコア換算表 (p.37)
を参照して換算点を導き出してください。

❹ 復習し、弱点を克服する

――――リスニング・セクション：意味が取れなかった箇所は、別
冊の訳文を参考にしながら音声を聞き直し、再確認しましょ
う。

――――文法セクション：解説を読んだり、文法書で確認したりして、
本番前に弱点を潰しておきましょう。

――――リーディング・セクション：解説と別冊の訳文を読んで、
本文の意味や設問の意図を再確認しておきましょう。

――――問題の英文はシャドーイングや速読の訓練にも使えます。
自分なりの勉強法を工夫して活用してください。

付属音声の内容と使い方

●音声ダウンロードについて

本書の学習に必要な音声はすべて MP3 ファイル形式です。以下の手順でダウンロードしてご使用ください。

※パソコンでダウンロードする場合
以下のURLで「アルク・ダウンロードセンター」にアクセスの上、画面の指示に従って、音声ファイルをダウンロードしてください。
URL　https://portal-dlc.alc.co.jp

※スマートフォンでダウンロードする場合
QR コードから学習用アプリ「booco」をインストール（無料）の上、ホーム画面下「さがす」から本書を検索し、音声ファイルをダウンロードしてください。
（本書の書籍コードは 7022064）
詳しくはこちら：https://booco.page.link/4zHd

●収録内容について

模試1〜4のリスニング・セクションで使用する音声が収録されています。Part A の Directions（指示文）から最後の Part C までは、音声を止めずに解答してください。音声ファイルは全部で232ファイルあります。

Practice Test 1＞001.mp3〜058.mp3
Practice Test 2＞059.mp3〜116.mp3
Practice Test 3＞117.mp3〜174.mp3
Practice Test 4＞175.mp3〜232.mp3

QRコードを読み取って
boocoをインストールしよう！

TOEFL ITPとは

まずは TOEFL ITP の概要を確認しておきましょう。ここではテストの構成や時間配分、頻出問題のタイプ、スコア算出法などを解説します。

TOEFL ITPの概要

TOEFL（Test of English as a Foreign Language）は、英語を母語としない人のアカデミックな英語能力を測る試験です。アメリカの教育機関であるETS（Educational Testing Service）が実施しています。

TOEFL ITP（Institutional Testing Program）は、学校やその他教育機関で行われる団体向けのテストで、主に大学のクラス分けや単位認定、大学院入試などに利用されています。交換留学や海外研修の選考に使われることもあります。

ただし、ITPのスコアは試験実地団体内でのみ有効で、公的には認められていません。交換留学以外で留学を希望する際は、TOEFL iBT（Internet-Based Testing）を受験しましょう。

また、TOEFL ITPは団体が実施する試験なので、個人で申し込むことはできません。受験については、学校や企業など所属団体に問い合わせてください。

●構成と流れ

TOEFL ITPにはLevel 1 TOEFLとLevel 2 Pre-TOEFLの2種類があります。Level 1はPBT（Paper-Based Testing）の過去問題から出題され、Level 2はLevel 1と比べて難易度の低い問題が出題されます。本書はこのLevel 1 TOEFLに対応しています。

TOEFL ITPは、リスニング、文法、リーディングの3つのセクションから成ります。以下が、試験全体の流れです。

---

① 準備時間……………………………………………………………………… 約20分
   ↓
② セクション1：リスニング・セクション ………………………………… 約35分
   ↓
③ セクション2：文法セクション ……………………………………………… 25分
   ↓
④ セクション3：リーディング・セクション ………………………………… 55分
   ↓
⑤ 解答用紙と問題用紙の回収および確認……………………………………… 約20分

※全体で約155分（約2時間半）かかります。

試験時間は約2時間ですが、氏名の記入や問題・解答用紙の回収などを含めると、試験終了まで2時間半ほどかかるとみてよいでしょう。途中休憩はありません。

　試験は四者択一のマークシート方式です。

　解答用紙への書き込みは禁止されています。書き込みが発見されると採点してもらえない可能性があるので、注意してください。

　また、試験監督の指示に従って、指定されたセクションだけを解いてください。他のセクションを無断で解いていると判断された場合は、スコアが無効になることがあります。

　※2016年1月より書き込み（Note Taking）に関する方針が変更となり、リスニング試験中の問題冊子の余白への書き込みが可能になりました。ただし、別途のメモ用紙やTOEFL iBT® で使用されているScratch Paperの使用は許可されていません。最新の情報は、日本でTOEFLの運営を行っているETS Japanのウェブサイトで確認しましょう。

ETS Japan
https://www.etsjapan.jp

●問題数とスコア

　各セクションの内容と問題数、時間配分、最高/最低スコアは以下の通りです。

		内容	問題数	最低点	最高点
Section 1 リスニング	Part A Short Conversations	短い会話を聞き、その内容に関する質問に答える	30 問	31	68
	Part B Long Conversations	長めの会話文を2つ聞き、その内容に関する質問に答える	8 問 （2題×4問）		
	Part C Talks	長めの話や講義の一部などを聞き、その内容に関する質問に答える	12 問 （3題×3〜5問）		
Section 2 文法	Structure	英文の空所に適切な語句を補充する	15 問	31	68
	Written Expression	英文中の間違いを指摘する	25 問		
Section 3 リーディング	（5つのパッセージ）	350 語程度の英文を読み、その内容及び本文中の語彙に関する質問に答える	50 問 （5題×10問）	31	67
合計			140 問	310 点	677 点

出題傾向と対策

TOEFL ITPの問題は、アカデミックな題材を扱っているものの、特定分野の専門知識は必要とされません。内容的には**高校2年生以上の教科に関する知識が必要**です。

また、さまざまな英語レベルの受験者が全世界で同じテストを受けるため、難問から易しい問題まで混在しています。とはいえ、全問題に対する難問の割合は決して多くありません。難問でもあまり悩まずに、とりあえずマークシートを塗りつぶし、後で時間が余ったら確認しましょう。その際、解答用紙の余白などに小さな点を打って、再確認する問題を覚えておくとよいでしょう。ただし、**解答用紙をメモ代わりに使うのは禁止**されているので、セクションを移る前に印を消すのを忘れないようにしてください。

では、実際にセクション別に出題傾向を分析し、その対策を見ていきます。

Section 1 Listening Comprehension
リスニング・セクション

リスニング・セクションで重要なのは、設問から次の設問に移る「12秒のリズム」をつかむことです。音声は待ってくれません。12秒たったら容赦なく次の問題に移り、テスト終了後に再確認することもできません。大切なのは、「聞き逃したらあきらめる、くよくよ悩まない」という姿勢です。たとえ選択に迷っても、さっと直感でマークし、次の問題に備えましょう。

Part A Short Conversations （短い会話）
〜第二話者の発言が聞き取りのポイント〜

Part Aの設問は、ほぼ以下の**5タイプに分類**できます。いずれの出題パターンも第二話者の発話に関連していることが多いため、その発言内容に注意し、文を頭の中で言い換えてみることが大切です。選択肢には、音の似た単語が引っかけとして入っているケース（音声でacceptが登場し、選択肢にexceptが入っている場合など）も多くあるので気をつけてください。

TYPE ① 発言の意味や意図を問う設問 Mean 出題比率：40%

このタイプの設問は多くの場合、第一話者の発言をヒントに第二話者の発言について答えます。場合によっては、第二話者の発言だけを聞いても答えられます。

■問題例

Woman: The original price of this car was ridiculous.
Man: Wasn't it, though?

Question: What does the man mean?
Answer: He also thinks that the car was expensive.

女性：この車の元値はありえなかったわ。
男性：そうだったね。

設問：男性は何を言いたいのか？
解答：男性もその車は高かったと思っている。

TYPE ② 言外の意味を尋ねる設問 Imply 出題比率：30%

言外にほのめかしている意味を聞き取ります。これもほとんどが第二話者の発言に関する設問です。以下の例のように皮肉をこめた表現には要注意。文字通り取らないようにしましょう。

■問題例

W: I'm not sure whether to ask Michael or Robert to proofread my essay.
M: What difference does it make? Neither of them can read English.

Q: What does the man imply about Michael and Robert?
A: They are both incompetent proofreaders.

女性：マイケルとロバート、どちらにリポートの校正を頼むか迷ってるの。
男性：どんな違いがあるというんだい？　2人とも英語が読めないじゃないか。

13

設問：男性はマイケルとロバートについて何をほのめかしているか？
解答： 2人とも校正者として役に立たない。

TYPE (3) 推測して答える設問 [Infer] 出題比率：10%

　男女の会話から推測できることを答える問題です。会話内容を踏まえ、その状況に適切な選択肢を選びます。

■問題例

M: What a relief. All we have to do is finish our research papers and we're totally done with our Introduction to Economics class.

W: Yes, I'm so grateful Professor Conrad decided to cancel our final exam.

Q: What can be **inferred** from this conversation?

A: The students will not have to take a test for their class.

男性：ほっとしたよ。僕たちは調査リポートを完成させれば、それだけで経済入門のクラスは完全にやり終えたことになるんだ。

女性：ええ、コンラッド教授が期末試験を取りやめにすると決めたことにとても感謝しているわ。

設問：この会話から何が推測できるか？

解答：学生たちはクラスのためにテストを受ける必要がない。

TYPE (4) 提案やアドバイスに関する設問 [Suggest] 出題比率：5%

　このタイプの設問では、第二話者が第一話者に「〜したら？」とアドバイスします。第一話者が不平をこぼしているようだったら、このタイプの設問がくると思って間違いありません。第二話者が用いる「動詞」に注意して聞きましょう。

■問題例

W: This is a terrible computer. It always crashes in the middle of important work.

M: Why don't you take it back to the shop where you got it?

Q: What does the man **suggest**?
A: The woman should return the computer.

女性：このパソコン、ひどいわ。いつも大事な仕事の最中にクラッシュするの。
男性：そのパソコンを買った店に持って行ったらどうだい？

設問：男性は何を提案しているか？
解答：女性はパソコンを返品すべきだ。

TYPE 5 未来の行動を予測する設問 Future 出題比率：5%

　会話から、話者がこれからするであろう行動を予測します。以下の例のように会話の中で、話者自らがこれからすることを述べる場合もありますが、選択肢は別の言葉で言い換えられます。

■問題例

W: Are you happy with your new math professor?
M: Sure. As a matter of fact, I'm on my way to an appointment with her now.

Q: What is the man **going to do**?
A: He will meet his teacher.

女性：新しい数学の教授に満足している？
男性：もちろんさ。実は、ちょうど彼女との面会に行く途中なんだ。

設問：男性は何をするつもりか？
解答：彼は先生に会うだろう。

まれに登場する問題

Rare (A) 推量 Assume

■問題例

What had the man/woman **assumed**?
（男性／女性は［会話の前に］何を推測していたか？）

Rare (B) Want 問題 Want

■問題例

What does the man/woman **want** to know?
（男性／女性は何を知りたいのか？）
What does the man/woman **want**?（男性／女性は何を欲しているか？）

Rare (C) Say About 問題 Say About

■問題例

What does the man/woman **say about** XXX?
（男性／女性はXXXについて何と言っているか？）

Rare (D) Happen 問題 Happen

■問題例

What will probably **happen** next?（おそらく次に何が起こるか？）
What will **happen** to XXX?（XXXに何が起こるか？）

Rare (E) Problem 問題 Problem

■問題例

What is the man/woman's **problem**?（男性／女性の問題は何か？）

● Part B Longer Conversations（長い会話）
● Part C Longer Talks（長めのトーク）
〜聞き取りのポイントは5W1H〜

　このパートでは、事前に選択肢に目を通し、話の流れをつかみながら聞きましょう。「話の流れ」とは、Why（なぜ）、When（いつ）、Where（どこで）、Who（だれが）、What（何を）、How（どうやって）という5W1Hにポイントをしぼることです。また、リスニングの前に、設問と選択肢の文頭に素早く目を走らせましょう。
　このパートの問題は、以下の7つのタイプに分類することができます。

TYPE ⑥ 原因・理由を尋ねる設問 　Why

　設問はWhy ...? で始まります。また、会話の中で、理由や目的を述べていたら注意が必要です。選択肢によっては、文頭に In order to 〜（〜するために）という目的を表すto不定詞や、Because ... などの理由を表す表現が含まれます。

■問題例

Q: Why does the speaker mention a story about a monkey and man?
　(A) To describe the differences between them
　(B) To indicate their shortcomings
　(C) To point out the importance of their brain
　(D) To illustrate that both can learn language

なぜ、話者はサルと人間に関する話を述べているのか？
　(A) 両者の違いを説明するため
　(B) 彼らの短所を示すため
　(C) 彼らの脳の重要性を指摘するため
　(D) 両者とも言語を学べると説明するため

TYPE (7) 時間・期間を尋ねる設問 When

リスニングの前に素早く選択肢に目を通しましょう。選択肢がAt、On、In、During などの前置詞で始まっていたら、選択肢にある時間や期間を表す言葉に注意して聞くとよいでしょう。

■問題例

Q: When was the United States Constitution finally ratified?

　(A) **In** 1620
　(B) **In** 1776
　(C) **In** 1787
　(D) **In** 1812

アメリカ合衆国憲法が最終的に批准されたのはいつか？

　(A) 1620年
　(B) 1776年
　(C) 1787年
　(D) 1812年

TYPE (8) 場所を尋ねる設問 Where

設問はwhereで始まります。このタイプの設問も、選択肢の先読みでが大切です。例えば、At、On、In、Toなどの前置詞と場所を表す言葉の組み合わせになっています。駅や図書館などの名詞が並んでいる場合もあります。

■問題例

Q: Where does it take place?

　(A) The school library
　(B) The social science department
　(C) The college cafeteria
　(D) The university hall

それはどこで行われるか？
- (A) 学校の図書館
- (B) 社会学部
- (C) 大学の食堂
- (D) 大学の講堂

TYPE 9 事実・意見・項目について尋ねる設問 What

このタイプは多くの場合、会話に登場した語句を別の表現で言い換えたものが選択肢にあります。つまり、同意語の知識が必要になってきます。

リスニングの練習をする際は、同意語や反意語などに置き換えて聞く訓練をしてください。例えば、Everybody came to ... という表現を聞いたら、All attended ... や Nobody missed ... などの表現がすぐに頭に浮かべられるようになるとよいでしょう。また、選択肢によっては以下のように、5W1Hを使って内容を言い換えたものもあります。

■問題例

Q: **What aspect** of a telephone does the lecture discuss?
- (A) What it is made of
- (B) Where it was invented
- (C) How it works
- (D) Why it is useful

講義では、電話のどんな側面について議論しているか？
- (A) それが何でできているか
- (B) それがどこで発明されているか
- (C) それがどのように動作するか
- (D) それがなぜ便利か

TYPE (10) 「誰が」「誰に」を問う設問 Who/Whom

「誰が話しているか」「誰に向かって話されているか」などに関する問題。選択肢の中に人を表す言葉、役職名や職業名などが入っていれば、WHO does what to WHOMに気をつけて聞けばいいのです。

■問題例

Q: **Who** is the audience for this talk?

   (A) Medical assistants

   (B) Painters

   (C) College students

   (D) Computer programmers

このトークを聞いているのは誰か？

   (A) 医療アシスタント

   (B) 画家

   (C) 大学生

   (D) コンピューター・プログラマー

TYPE (11) 「どれが」を問う設問 Which

Which（どちらが〜、どれが〜）を使った設問はそれほど多くありません。本文の内容を理解できていれば正解できる問題ですが、選択肢に迷う場合は、選択肢の内容に適合するかどうか、本文を読み直してみる必要があります。

■問題例

Q: **Which** of the following best describes XXX?

   (A) It was dirty.

   (B) It was long.

   (C) It was hard.

   (D) It was slow.

次のうちXXXを最もよく表わしているのはどれか？
- (A) 汚れていた。
- (B) 長かった。
- (C) 硬かった。
- (D) ゆっくりだった。

TYPE⑫ 方法・手段を問う設問 How

　How XXX feel ...？ など〈状態〉を聞く問題や、How many、How muchなど「どのくらい～？」という〈程度〉を尋ねる問題があります。前もって選択肢を読み、もしそこに数の表現が出ていたなら、数に注意して聞き取る必要があります。

　また以下の例のように選択肢の文頭に手段を表すBy ... があれば、「どんなふうに～？」、「いかに～？」、「どうやって～？」などが問われています。

■問題例

Q: According to the woman, how did Arlene study Spanish?
- (A) By listening to music
- (B) By watching movies
- (C) By memorizing idioms
- (D) By taking classes

この女性によれば、アーリーンはどのようにしてスペイン語を学んだか？
- (A) 音楽を聞いて
- (B) 映画を見て
- (C) イディオムを暗記して
- (D) 授業を受けて

Section 2

Structure and Written Expression
文法セクション

　文法問題は、ある意味では英語のコミュニケーション能力というよりむしろ、決まった型を文中で応用できるかが試されます。リスニング・セクションが終わったら頭を切り替え、単語の意味そのものよりも、単語の品詞が何であるかを見極めてください。

Structure (Fill in the Blank：空所補充問題)
～動詞を探せ！～

　まず、大前提として「正しい表現は４つの選択肢の中に必ずある。つまり消去法が使える」ということを覚えておきましょう。そして、文を見たら必ず「動詞を見つけ、次に主語が何か」を確かめてください。
　このパートの問題は以下の５つのタイプに分類できます。

TYPE 13 文の構造に関する設問 WIAS (What Is A Sentence)

　文に必要な要素がそろっているかを試す問題です。大前提は〈文や節には主語(S)がひとつ、動詞(V)がひとつ必要〉だということ。文は、例えば〈S＋V〉、〈S＋V＋that (S＋V)〉、〈(S＋V) and (S＋V)〉というような構造になっています。問題文を見たらすぐに動詞を見つけ、もし２つ以上の動詞が見つかったら、そのひとつが、that、which、although、because などを伴って節に入っていることを確認しましょう。

■問題例

Q: ---------- who was the first black woman to run for the office of President of the United States in 1972.
(A) Shirley S. Chisolm
(B) It was Shirley S. Chisolm
(C) Shirley S. Chisolm was

(D) When Shirley S. Chisolm

[正解：B]
1972年にアメリカ大統領選に出た初の黒人女性がシャーリー・S・チゾムだった。

TYPE⑭ 語の選択に関する設問 Word Choice

　熟語や構文を理解して、適切な言葉を空所に入れる問題です。熟語はリスニングでもよく出題されるので、日頃からセットになっている表現を学んでおきましょう。

■問題例

Q: Parasitic roundworms have ⋯⋯⋯⋯ problem of drying out once they have
located a host, which furnishes them a moist environment.
(A) no any
(B) never the
(C) not
(D) **no**

[正解：D]
寄生回虫は、湿っぽい環境を提供する宿主をひとたび見つけると、干からびる問題がなくなる。

TYPE⑮ 語順に関する設問 Word Order

　〈冠詞＋形容詞＋名詞〉や、〈冠詞＋副詞＋形容詞＋名詞〉といった語順に関する問題（例えば a pretty girl や a really pretty girl）です。
　語順に関する問題はこの他にも、〈動詞＋主語〉という順になる倒置表現が出題されます。場所を表す語There、Here、In、On、At や否定語Not、Never、Seldom、Rarelyが文頭に来た場合（On the wall are some pictures.や Never have I met such a pretty girl.など）、〈場所／否定語＋動詞＋主語〉という語順になります。
　こうしたタイプの設問の選択肢は、次のように同じいくつかの語の語順を変えただけの場合が多くあります。

■問題例

Q: Bellevue, the oldest town in Nebraska, was founded in the nineteenth century as a ⸻ .

(A) center fur-trading

(B) fur center-trading

(C) trading fur-center

(D) fur-trading center

［正解：D］

ネブラスカ州で最も古い町ベルビューは、毛皮の売買所として19世紀に作られた。

TYPE 16 動詞の形に関する設問 Verb Form

　時制の一致や態（受動態be＋〜 ed）に関する問題です。出題率はあまり高くありませんが、英語の「時間の概念」がきちんと理解できていないと答えられないので、日本人学習者にとっては難しい設問のひとつと言えるでしょう。

　選択肢には、同じ動詞が違う形で並んでいることが多くあります。

■問題例

Q: Playwright Lillian Hellman ⸻ noted for the mixture of strength and sensitivity she gave to her female characters.

(A) was

(B) had

(C) been

(D) being

［正解：A］

劇作家のリリアン・ヘルマンは、女性の登場人物たちに与えた強さと繊細さが入り交じった描写で有名だった。

TYPE ⑰ 並列に関する設問 Parallelism

　カンマやand、butなどで単語や句が連なっている場合、品詞を統一する必要があります。例えば、faster, higher, and stronger ...〈比較級、比較級、and比較級〉や、waking up, washing my face and brushing my teeth〈動名詞、動名詞、and動名詞〉というようなパターンがあります。

　この形式の問題の出題率は近年上がってきました。練習問題をこなすとき、カンマやand、butを○で囲んで注意する癖をつけましょう。

■問題例

Q: Cobalt resembles iron and nickel in tensile strength, appearance, ---------- .

(A) is hard
(B) although hard
(C) has hardness
(D) and hardness

[正解：D]
コバルトは張力、見た目、硬度の点で鉄やニッケルに似ている。

まれに登場する問題

Rare Ⓕ 前置詞 Preposition

■問題例

Q: He plays tennis ---------- the park every weekend.

(A) in
(B) at
(C) of
(D) on

[正解：A]
彼は毎週末、公園でテニスをする。

Written Expression (Error Analysis：誤文訂正問題)
〜下線部以外の語にも注目〜

　このパートで大切なのは「下線のない所にヒントがある」ということです。ある項目が間違いかどうかは、絶対的なものではなく、下線部と下線のない所の相関関係で決まります。言い換えれば、下線部そのものが大切なのではなく、下線以外の部分との「関係」が大切なのです。よって、下線部だけに目を凝らしていても正答は導き出せません。

　このパートの問題は、12のタイプに分類することができます。この12タイプで、過去10年間に実際に出題された問題の実に97パーセントをカバーしています。

TYPE 18 品詞の誤りに関する設問 Part of Speech

　この形式で最も多いのは、「形容詞と副詞の混同」です。形容詞は名詞を修飾し、副詞は名詞以外（動詞、形容詞、他の副詞、文全体など）を修飾します。

■問題例
He writes good.　　（誤）⇒　well（正・副詞）

TYPE 19 数の一致に関する設問 Agreement

　1）主語と動詞の数の一致、2）代名詞とそれが指す名詞の数の一致などに関する問題です。

■問題例
Every one of us have …	（誤）⇒	has	（正）
A number of students is …	（誤）⇒	are	（正）
Since some animals are … , its …	（誤）⇒	their	（正）
The color of this table is … those of …	（誤）⇒	that	（正）

TYPE 20 複数形に関する設問 Plural

名詞が正しく複数形、または単数形になっているかを問う問題です。

■問題例

... twenty percent of the student ...　（誤）⇒　students（正）
... a lot of fruits ...　　　　　　　　（誤）⇒　fruit（正）

TYPE 21 並列に関する設問 Parallelism

　単語や句がいくつか連なっている場合、カンマやand、butなどを含む文では品詞を統一します。形容詞を使うべき所に副詞を入れた誤りはTOEFLに非常によく出題されます。この形式の問題は練習問題をこなす時、カンマやand、butを○で囲んで注意する癖をつければ、比較的楽に正解できるでしょう。

■問題例

... red, green, and bluish ...　（誤）⇒　blue（正）

TYPE 22 代名詞、関係代名詞の誤りに関する設問 Pronoun Errors

　代名詞と、代名詞が受ける名詞の形を一致させる問題です。代名詞が文中に出てきたら、何を指しているかを確認しながら読むようにしましょう。

■問題例

Washington, D.C., that is the capital of the United States, ...

（誤）⇒　which（正）

Johnny Appleseed planted apple trees during him travels ...

（誤）⇒　his（正）

TYPE 23 前置詞の誤りに関する設問 Prepositional Error

in、on、at、aside、with、without などの前置詞が適切かどうかを問う問題です。前置詞句、動詞句などの使い方も日頃から注意して学んでおきましょう。

■問題例

Recent studies have shown that air <u>into</u> a house …　（誤）⇒　in（正）

TYPE 24 重複に関する設問 Redundancy

　同じ意味を表す言葉の重複に関する問題。日本語で言えば「危険が危ない」「頭痛が痛い」というようなもの。TOEFLでは、特に代名詞が重複しているパターンが多く出題されます。

■問題例

<u>less</u> easier　　　　　　　　　　　　（誤）⇒　lessを除く（正）

Mr. White <u>he</u> spoke …　　　　　　　　（誤）⇒　heを除く（正）

TYPE 25 動詞の形に関する設問 Verb Form

　Structure問題のTYPE⑯と同様、時制の一致や態（受動態be＋〜ed）に関する問題です。英語の時間の概念が理解できていないと答えられません。出題率は高くないものの、日本人学習者に難しい設問タイプのひとつと言えます。

■問題例

When a tree <u>to die</u>,　　　　　　　　（誤）⇒　dies（正）

He was often <u>call</u> Sam …　　　　　　（誤）⇒　called（正）

TYPE 26 語の脱落に関する設問 Deleted Word

　必要な単語が欠如している箇所を見つける問題です。

■問題例

This can <u>proved</u> …（受け身の文脈で）　（誤）⇒　can be proved（正）

I don't know how <u>spell</u> the word.　　（誤）⇒　how to spell（正）

<u>Because</u> the rain, we couldn't go for a picnic.（誤）⇒　Because of（正）

TYPE 27 語順に関する設問 Word Order

Part Bで出題される「語順」の問題は、通常、2つの単語の語順が入れ替わっています。急いで読んでいると見逃してしまいがちなので注意しましょう。

■問題例

from <u>away</u> the Earth	（誤）⇒	away from（正）
a lot <u>than bigger</u>	（誤）⇒	bigger than（正）

TYPE 28 冠詞に関する設問 Article

a、an、theなどの冠詞の脱落、不要な冠詞、誤った冠詞の用法などに関する問題です。前述の語の「重複」「語の脱落」と重なる場合もありますが、日本人学習者が不得意な分野なので、別項目として挙げておきます。

■問題例

only <u>few</u> weeks	（誤）⇒	only a few（正）
A <u>singing</u> is ...	（誤）⇒	Singing（正）
by <u>a</u> eighteenth century	（誤）⇒	the（正）

TYPE 29 接続詞に関する設問 Conjunction

誤った接続詞を使ったものや、他の品詞が必要な所に接続詞を入れたものなどを問う問題です。

■問題例

<u>either</u> male and female ...	（誤）⇒	both（正）
... from 1941 <u>and</u> 1946	（誤）⇒	to（正）

Section 3 Reading Comprehension
リーディング・セクション

　Reading Comprehensionに出題されるパッセージのトピックは、アメリカに関するものがほとんどです。内容に関する背景知識があるかどうかで、理解の程度も違ってくるもの。日頃からアメリカに関する伝記、歴史などの文を読んでおくといいでしょう。

　また、このセクションの特徴として「パッセージの流れに沿って問題が出題される」ということを知っておくといいかもしれません。それぞれのパッセージに関する問題は、まずその主旨や筆者の主張といった文全体に関わる設問がおかれ、その後の設問はパッセージの流れに沿っています。

　従って、例えば5問目に「10行目にあるXXという単語の意味は?」という設問があったとすれば、それ以前の設問の答えは10行目より前に記述があり、また、6問目以降の設問の答えは10行目以降に記述があるのです。

　語彙に関する問題では、その語が登場する行が示されています。まず設問全体に目を通して、どこに注意を配りながら解答を探せばいいか手掛かりをつかみましょう。

　ただし、パッセージの中に書かれている内容がそのまま選択肢にあることはめったにありません。その内容を言い換えたものやその内容から推測できることが問われるので、語彙に関する知識はもちろん、論理的思考を養っておくことが大切です。

　全部で5つのパッセージを55分で解くということは、1パッセージを11分で終了しなければならないということです。時間配分を考えて臨みましょう。

　このパートの問題は以下の11のタイプに分類することができます。

TYPE 30 要旨を問う設問 Main Idea

　この設問タイプはほぼ全パッセージに、しかも最初に登場します。要旨やトピックに関する問題で、設問文中にmainという言葉がよく用いられます。

　英文のパラグラフは、まず一番主張したいことが最初に書かれ（トピックセンテンス）、それを補足する項目（サポート情報）が続く構造になっていることが多くあります。こうした英文構造の知識は、解答を導き出す手掛かりになるでしょう。

What does the passage **mainly** discuss?（主に何を議論しているか？）

What is the author's **main** point?（筆者の趣旨は何か？）

What is the **main** purpose of the passage?（文章の主な目的は何か？）

What is the **main** topic of the passage?（主題は何か？）

The passage supports which of the following statements/conclusions?
（次のどの発言／結論を支持しているか？）

▶▶▶**解法のポイント** パッセージの最初に登場するトピックセンテンスや、何度も繰り返される単語が鍵になります。また、具体的な選択肢よりも、比較的一般的な概要が答えになる場合も多くあります。

TYPE ③1 事実を問う設問 Factual

　本文に述べられた事実、本文に登場する特定の情報に関する設問です。このタイプは、他のタイプに比べ、特に出題率が高くなっています。答えは本文に直接、「具体的に」書かれていることが多いです。また、選択肢は本文と全く同じ表現ではなく、paraphrase（言い換え）されていることがほとんどです。

■問題例

According to the passage, what .../where .../who .../when .../ what is true of ...?（この文によれば、何が／どこで／誰が／いつ／何が本当の……）

▶▶▶**解法のポイント** まず、選択肢の表現が本文のどの部分の言い換えにあたるかを見つけること。また、たとえ自分の知識（常識）と違ったとしても、本文に基づいて解答することが大切です。

TYPE ③2 推論・示唆を問う設問 Inference

　本文の内容に基づいて推論できるもの、または文中で示唆されたもの、筆者の視点、意見などに関する設問です。本文中に明示されていないので、行間を読んで答えることが要求されます。

■問題例

It can be inferred from the passage that ...（この文章から推論できるのは）

The author implies that ...（筆者が示唆しているのは）

It can be concluded from the passage that ...（この文章から結論づけられるのは）

▶▶▶ **解法のポイント** 本文中にある具体的事実のいくつかを組み合わせると、正しい答えが導き出せます。「結局、著者は何を主張したいの?」と自問しながら本文を読むとよいでしょう。

TYPE (33) 語彙を問う設問 Vocabulary

単語や句の意味に関する問題。以下の例のように「〜行目 "XX" という単語」のように聞かれます。下の例のように文脈から判断することを求められています。

■問題例

The word "interest" in line 8 is closest in meaning to ...（8行目 "interest" に最も意味が近いのは）

The phrase "lame duck" in line 7 suggests that ...（7行目 "lame duck" が示しているのは）

▶▶▶ **解法のポイント** ひとつの単語にはいくつもの意味があります。文脈に一番適した単語を推測してください。ただし問われている単語の意味をまったく知らなければ解答が出せないようになっていますから、難しい語の場合は消去法でいくといいでしょう。

TYPE (34) 語法を問う設問 Usage

代名詞の指すものを問う問題であったり、句読点のひとつであるquotation marks（" "）が使われる理由を尋ねたりする場合もあります。

■問題例

The word "they" in line 12 refers to ...（12行目 "they" が指しているのは）

➤➤➤ **解法のポイント** 代名詞の問題では多くの場合、すぐ前の文に答えがあるもの
です。可算・不可算、単数・複数形などの違いに気をつけて、
名詞を探してみましょう。

TYPE 35 Not で問う設問 Negative Factual

これは本文の内容に反するもの、本文で触れていないものに関する問題です。設問にNOT、EXCEPT、LEAST（〈最も〉〜でないものは?）というように、否定の単語が大文字で出てきたらこのパターンの問題です。

■問題例

Which of the following is **NOT** mentioned ... ?（以下のうち述べられていないものはどれか？）

➤➤➤ **解法のポイント** 本文中に、いくつもの項目を列挙している文があれば、そこにないものが正解。あとは、拾い読みと消去法で解答を導きましょう。

TYPE 36 段落の要旨を問う設問 Minor Idea

TYPE㉚がパッセージ全体の要旨を尋ねるのに対し、これはある特定の段落の要旨を尋ねる問題です。

■問題例

In the second paragraph, the author primarily discusses ...（第2段落で、筆者が主に論じているのは）
Which of the following is most extensively discussed **in the last paragraph?**（最終段落では、以下のどれが最も長く論じられているか？）

➤➤➤ **解法のポイント** 文全体の構成要素として、指定された段落が詳しく掘り下げている内容に目を向けます。また、指定されていない段落に述べられた内容を基に、消去法で解答を導き出せる場合もあります。

TYPE (37) 理由を問う設問 Rhetorical Questions

筆者がなぜ特定の話題やテーマを取り上げたのかを問う問題です。

■問題例

Why does the author mention .../call ...?（なぜ、筆者は～を述べている／呼んでいるのか？）

▶▶▶ **解法のポイント** 筆者が何を述べたのか、その理由を知るにはそのテーマが登場する前後の文章の論旨をつかむことが大切です。テーマが特定の事実などであれば、その前後に理由や経緯が書かれていることが多くあります。

TYPE (38) 構成に関する設問 Organization

「この文章の前／後で何が論じられるか」が問われます。論旨を理解する力が試されると言えるでしょう。

■問題例

The paragraph preceding this passage probably discusses ...（この文章の前のパラグラフでおそらく論じているのは）

▶▶▶ **解法のポイント** 直前または直後のパラグラフで何が話題になっているかを確認しましょう。例えば何かの事象について触れているパラグラフであれば、その前後ではその原因、理由、結果などが書かれている、といったパターンがありえます。

TYPE (39) 場所を問う設問 Location

問題文のどの箇所で筆者が特定の話題を論じているかが問われます。

■問題例

Where in the passage does the author discuss XXX?（筆者はこの文章の

どこでXXXを論じているか？）

>>> **解法のポイント** 文章のどこでXXXが取り上げられているかを探します。たい
ていは関連語や類義語が含まれている箇所、あるいは言い換
えている箇所が該当します。

TYPE 40 視点を問う設問 View point / Tone

筆者の視点や論調に関する問題。筆者のものの見方、あるいはどういったニュア
ンスで述べているのか、などを考える問題です。

■問題例

The tone of the last paragraph could best be described as ...（最後のパ
ラグラフの論調を最もよく表現すると）

>>> **解法のポイント** 何らかの事柄に対し、批判的なのか、賛同しているのか、協
力的なのかなど、筆者のスタンスを読み取ります。

自己採点のためのスコア換算表

この換算表について

　本書の模試は、実際のTOEFL ITPよりも少し高めのレベル設定で作成しています。打席に向かうバッターはまず重いバットで素振りをして、いざピッチャーを前にしたときにはバットが軽く感じられるようにするものです。

　そういった当初のねらい通りに模試が標準よりも多少難しいものになっているかどうかを確かめるため、40人にこのテストを受けてもらいました。彼らが持っている実際のTOEFLのスコアと本書の模試のスコアを比較し、結果得られたのが右の換算表です。この換算表を使って、模試で得た得点が実際のTOEFLでどのくらいの成績になるのかを割り出すことができます。

　ただし、そのときの体調や状況によっても得点は上下するということを心に留めておいてください。実際のTOEFLテスト自体、いつも難易度は一定とは限らないのです。また個人のスコアも、実力は変わっていないのに変動することもあります。TOEFLは±14点の誤差が生じると言われています。毎回正確に実力を測定できるテストなど、この世に存在しないのです。模試は本試験でどれくらいの成績が取れるのか、現在の実力および弱点を知る上での参考と考えましょう。

換算スコアの出し方

　次ページのスコア換算表を参照しながら予想得点を算出してみましょう。

- (1) まず自己採点をし、各セクションの正解数を調べる。
- (2) 換算表を見て、正解数からスコアの最小値・最大値を見つける（この最小値と最大値の間に、各セクションの予想得点が位置することになる）。
- (3) 各セクションの最小値・最大値をそれぞれ合計する。
- (4) 2つの合計点に10をかけ、その数字を3で割る。
- (5) こうして得られた2つの数字の間に、あなたの予想得点が入ることになる。

スコア換算表

正解数	Section 1	Section 2	Section 3
46〜50	67〜68		61〜67
43〜45	65〜66		59〜60
41〜42	63〜64		57〜58
38〜40	60〜62	65〜68	55〜56
35〜37	58〜59	61〜64	53〜54
31〜34	55〜57	57〜60	50〜52
28〜30	52〜54	53〜56	47〜49
25〜27	50〜51	50〜52	45〜46
22〜24	47〜49	47〜49	43〜44
18〜21	45〜46	43〜46	39〜42
15〜17	43〜44	41〜42	36〜38
13〜14	40〜42	38〜40	33〜35
10〜12	36〜39	34〜37	30〜32
7〜9	33〜35	28〜33	28〜29
5〜6	29〜32	26〜27	26〜27
3〜4	26〜28	23〜25	24〜25
0〜2	24〜25	20〜22	21〜23

計算例

〈Section 1、2、3の正解数がそれぞれ30、30、34の場合〉

	最小値	最大値
Section 1	52	54
Section 2	53	56
Section 3	50	52
合　　計	155	162
×10÷3	516.6	540

※ 予想得点は［517〜540］の間、ということになります。

なお、500、550、600点を取るための目安は下のようになります。

Section 1	Section 2	Section 3	スコア
46	54	50	500
52	58	55	550
58	62	60	600

memo

Practice Test 1

Section 1
Listening Comprehension

In this section of the test, you will have an opportunity to demonstrate your ability to understand conversations and talks in English. There are three parts to this section with special directions for each part. Answer all the questions on the basis of what is stated or implied by the speakers in this test. Do **not** turn the pages until you are told to do so.

Part A

Section 1
Part A
Part B
Part C

Directions: In Part A you will hear short conversations between two people. After each conversation, you will hear a question about the conversation. The conversations and questions will not be repeated. After you hear a question, read the four possible answers in your book and choose the best answer. Then, on your answer sheet, find the number of the question and fill in the space that corresponds to the letter of the answer you have chosen.

Listen to an example.

On the recording, you hear:
What does the woman say about Bill?
In your book, you read: (A) He bought a new car.
            (B) He had his car painted blue.
            (C) He fixed his old car.
            (D) He is having his car repaired.

Sample Answer
Ⓐ Ⓑ Ⓒ ●

You learn from the conversation that Bill's car is being repaired. The best answer to the question, "What does the woman say about Bill?" is (D), "He is having his car repaired." Therefore, the correct choice is (D).

Wait

41

mp3 002-006

1. What does the man mean?
   (A) He met some interesting people on his trip.
   (B) He wishes he had gone to Britain instead.
   (C) He wonders why more people did not go.
   (D) He saw some beautiful scenery in Canada.

2. What does the woman imply?
   (A) She will take chemistry on Wednesday.
   (B) She could not register for chemistry.
   (C) Her first choice was not available.
   (D) The Friday lab was already full.

3. What does the woman imply about country music?
   (A) She does not have time to listen to it.
   (B) She finds it very practical.
   (C) She enjoys it a great deal.
   (D) She used to like it more than she does now.

4. What does the man mean?
   (A) He is feeling much better.
   (B) He would like some more to drink.
   (C) He can pour it by himself.
   (D) He has already had enough coffee.

5. What does the woman imply?
   (A) It may start raining again.
   (B) She would rather not go for such a long walk.
   (C) They should not park their car there.
   (D) The man often forgets his umbrella.

Go on to the next page

mp3 **007-011**

6. What does the woman mean?
   (A) She pulled every weed in her garden.
   (B) She is very tired from working so hard.
   (C) She needs to make a better garden.
   (D) She works in her garden every afternoon.

7. What does the man imply about Patricia's journal article?
   (A) It did not meet his standards.
   (B) He thought the vocabulary was too difficult.
   (C) He could not find it in the library.
   (D) It was very well written.

8. What does the woman mean?
   (A) Linda does not listen to what she says.
   (B) Linda does not seem to like her job.
   (C) Linda has been busy looking for work.
   (D) Linda will still graduate on time.

9. What does the woman imply?
   (A) The bus is about fifteen minutes late.
   (B) The man had better start walking.
   (C) The man should get out of the taxi.
   (D) The buses are not running.

10. What does the man mean?
   (A) The woman is being overly critical.
   (B) He agrees that the sculpture is ugly.
   (C) He has not finished working on the sculpture yet.
   (D) The woman should take an art class.

Practice Test 1

Section 1
Part A
Part B
Part C

Go on to the next page ⟹

mp3 012-016

11. What can be inferred from this conversation?

(A) The man and woman are ready to place their order.

(B) The woman is still waiting to be served.

(C) Some customers are talking loudly.

(D) The server is very busy at the moment.

12. What does the woman suggest about Veronica?

(A) She has not brought the boxes downstairs yet.

(B) She apparently is not feeling very well today.

(C) She has not finished packing for her trip yet.

(D) She will not fly in until later tomorrow.

13. What does the man mean?

(A) He will help to move the file cabinet.

(B) He will be back after lunch.

(C) He also does not know where the file is.

(D) He no longer has the file.

14. What does the woman imply about Rachel?

(A) She gave a flawless performance.

(B) She will become a better musician.

(C) She is a very considerate person.

(D) She needs to practice more often.

15. What does the woman mean?

(A) She is a teacher at the elementary school.

(B) She has a part-time job at the zoo.

(C) She is taking care of a group of children.

(D) She rarely visits the local zoo.

Go on to the next page ⟹

mp3 **017-021**

16. What does the man mean?
    (A) He has other plans this week.
    (B) He is declining the woman's invitation.
    (C) He will not join the ski club.
    (D) Skiing is his favorite sport.

17. What does the woman want to know?
    (A) What the man means by his comment
    (B) What the man is giving her
    (C) What the man will do next
    (D) What the man did last night

18. What does the man imply?
    (A) Tuition is expected to drop.
    (B) The loan will not be enough.
    (C) He is applying for a new job.
    (D) He loaned his bucket to the woman.

19. What does the woman mean?
    (A) She does not like to practice basketball.
    (B) They will not be able to play basketball later.
    (C) She would rather play volleyball instead.
    (D) The man should go to volleyball practice.

20. What does the woman imply about Bob?
    (A) He often does his work at the last minute.
    (B) He is not very good at typing.
    (C) He was not the first one to hand in his paper.
    (D) He rarely submits his work on time.

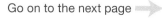

mp3 022-026

21. What does the man mean?

(A) He would really like to meet Margaret.

(B) He wonders why Margaret did not ring the doorbell.

(C) He hopes Margaret will give him a call soon.

(D) He does not know anyone named Margaret.

22. What does the woman mean?

(A) She will attend the play in the auditorium.

(B) She plans to practice over the weekend.

(C) She needs to have her ears examined.

(D) She will wait and see what happens.

23. What had the man assumed?

(A) She wondered where David went.

(B) David was already married.

(C) David would not get married.

(D) She and David have never met.

24. What does the woman suggest the man should do?

(A) Visit the professor's office

(B) Drop his professor a line

(C) Work hard to improve his grade

(D) Accept what happened

25. What does the man imply about Jan?

(A) She is hard to work for.

(B) She is certain not to come back.

(C) She is a good manager.

(D) She hired a new manager.

Go on to the next page ⟹

mp3 027-031

26. What does the man mean?
    (A) The landlord's action was unexpected.
    (B) The woman's apartment is reasonably priced.
    (C) The woman should find a quieter apartment.
    (D) Many landlords are now raising rents.

27. What does the woman imply?
    (A) Terry's sister is not good at math.
    (B) Terry's sister helps him with his homework.
    (C) Both Terry and his sister are shy.
    (D) Terry does not talk to his sister.

28. What had the man assumed?
    (A) The woman's plan would not be approved.
    (B) The meeting with the advisor would be successful.
    (C) The advisor would be unable to see the woman.
    (D) The woman would need to visit the advisor's office.

29. What does the woman imply about Tom?
    (A) He should not criticize his roommate.
    (B) He should try to compromise with his roommate.
    (C) He should find a different roommate.
    (D) He is a very considerate person.

30. What does the man mean?
    (A) He would like another glass of punch.
    (B) He disagrees with the woman's opinion.
    (C) He does not like the taste of the punch.
    (D) He thinks the punch tastes good.

Practice Test 1

Section 1
Part A
Part B
Part C

NO TEST MATERIAL ON THIS PAGE.

Part B

Directions: In this part, you will hear longer conversations. After each conversation, you will hear several questions. The conversations and questions will not be repeated.

After you hear a question, read the four possible answers in your book and choose the best answer. Then, on your answer sheet, find the number of the question and fill in the space that corresponds to the letter of the answer you have chosen.

Wait

mp3 **033-037**

31. Who proposed the new honor's program?
    (A) The president
    (B) The dean
    (C) The incoming freshman
    (D) The best professors

32. What is the main reason the university is establishing the honor's program?
    (A) To increase enrollment
    (B) To attract better students
    (C) To encourage better teaching
    (D) To award more scholarships

33. How do students qualify to be in the program?
    (A) They must receive high test scores.
    (B) They should have excellent recommendations.
    (C) They need to have performed well in high school.
    (D) They have to win an award.

34. Who are the two people having this conversation?
    (A) Faculty members
    (B) College students
    (C) High school applicants
    (D) University administrators

mp3 **038-042**

35. Where does this conversation probably take place?
    (A) The political science department
    (B) The student union
    (C) The university library
    (D) The college bookstore

36. According to the woman, why aren't the journals that the man wants available?
    (A) They have been checked out.
    (B) They are no longer published.
    (C) They are seldom needed.
    (D) They were cut from the budget.

37. What is the charge for ordering an article?
    (A) Nothing at all
    (B) Just a few pennies
    (C) Ten cents a page
    (D) Two dollars

38. According to the woman, how long does it take to receive an article once it's been ordered?
    (A) About two days
    (B) About a week
    (C) No time at all
    (D) Around two weeks

Go on to the next page

Part C

Directions: In this part, you will hear several talks. After each talk, you will hear some questions. The talks and questions will not be repeated. After you hear a question, read the four possible answers in your book and choose the best answer. Then, on your answer sheet, find the number of the question and fill in the space that corresponds to the letter of the answer you have chosen.

Here is an example.
On the recording, you hear:

Now listen to a sample question.

Sample Answer

Ⓐ Ⓑ ● Ⓓ

In your book, you read: What is this talk about?
         (A) Air pollution
         (B) A new type of silicon
         (C) A new type of solar panel
         (D) The cost of solar panels

The best answer to the question, "What is this talk about?" is (C), "A new type of solar panel." Therefore, the correct choice is (C).

Now listen to another sample question.

Sample Answer

● Ⓑ Ⓒ Ⓓ

In your book, you read: Why is the new type of solar panel better than the current one?
         (A) It is cheaper to produce.
         (B) It is easier to manufacture.
         (C) It is more efficient.
         (D) It pollutes less.

The best answer to the question, "Why is the new type of solar panel better than the current one?" is (A), "It is cheaper to produce." Therefore, the correct choice is (A).

Wait

Section 1
Listening Comprehension

mp3 044-048

39. When is this talk most likely being given?
    (A) At the beginning of the term
    (B) During the fifth week
    (C) Just before exam week
    (D) Near the end of the semester

40. What should students who have not taken the prerequisite course do?
    (A) Speak with the professor
    (B) Leave the classroom
    (C) Enroll in another history class
    (D) Ask their friends for help

41. What types of questions will appear on the final exam?
    (A) Mainly multiple-choice questions
    (B) Both objective and subjective questions
    (C) Only essay questions
    (D) A series of short-answer questions

42. What will count the most in determining the course grade?
    (A) The research paper
    (B) The student's attendance
    (C) The mid-term exams
    (D) The final test

mp3 049-052

43. For whom is this announcement primarily intended?
    (A) Senior citizens
    (B) City workers
    (C) Health care professionals
    (D) Student volunteers

44. What is the main reason that this program has been created?
    (A) To take care of a shortage of medical personnel
    (B) To alleviate the loneliness and boredom of elderly people
    (C) To help people better understand the concerns of the elderly
    (D) To provide future nurses with valuable experience

45. Where should people who need more information go?
    (A) Any local nursing home
    (B) The municipal health clinic
    (C) The university medical center
    (D) The city administrative offices

Go on to the next page ➡

Section 1
Listening Comprehension

mp3 **053-058**

46. What is the main subject of this talk?
    (A) Foods of the first humans
    (B) Types of early agriculture
    (C) The relationship between culture and food
    (D) The development of trade routes

47. What was the main diet of Paleolithic peoples?
    (A) Fish and small animals
    (B) Wild plants
    (C) Livestock
    (D) Cultivated crops

48. According to the speaker, what important transition occurred in the Mesolithic and Neolithic periods?
    (A) People learned to walk standing up straight.
    (B) Large groups of people began to migrate.
    (C) More people began to survive childhood.
    (D) People shifted from gathering to producing food.

49. What important effect did the invention of agricultural tools have on human civilization?
    (A) They created food surpluses and thus commerce.
    (B) They started the process of industrialization.
    (C) They made it possible to keep large herds of animals.
    (D) They led to the creation of borders and thus land ownership.

50. What was one result of the increased contact between different groups of people?
    (A) Greater consumption of meat
    (B) The extinction of agricultural societies
    (C) Better methods for hunting animals
    (D) The emergence of new cultures

This is the end of Section 1.
Stop work on Section 1.

Do NOT read or work on any other section of the test.
Your supervisor will tell you when to begin working on Section 2.

NO TEST MATERIAL ON THIS PAGE.

Section 2
Structure and Written Expression
Time: 25 minutes

This section is designed to measure your ability to recognize language that is appropriate for standard written English. There are two types of questions in this section, with special directions for each type.

Structure

Directions: Questions 1-15 are incomplete sentences. Beneath each sentence you will see four words or phrases, marked (A), (B), (C), and (D). Choose the one word or phrase that best completes the sentence. Then, on your answer sheet, find the number of the question and fill in the space that corresponds to the letter of the answer you have chosen.

Example I

---------- band music of John Philip Souza that established his reputation as one of America's leading composers.

(A) The
(B) That the
(C) Because the
(D) It was the

Sample Answer

The sentence should read, "It was the band music of John Philip Souza that established his reputation as one of America's leading composers." Therefore, you should choose answer (D).

Example II

John Steinbeck was 55 years old ---------- he finished the novel *East of Eden*.

(A) then
(B) finally
(C) at last
(D) when

Sample Answer

The sentence should read, "John Steinbeck was 55 years old when he finished the novel *East of Eden*." Therefore, you should choose (D).

Now begin work on the questions.

 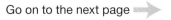

1. Mold obtained from a particular kind of cheese yields a compound vital to the ---------- of bacterial infections.

    (A) treats
    (B) treatings
    (C) treatment
    (D) treat

2. The physicist Richard Feynman, using space-time diagrams rather than mathematics, ---------- the notion that subatomic particles could move backward in time.

    (A) he conceived
    (B) conceived
    (C) conceive
    (D) had conceived

3. ---------- , known as bear markets, when the stock market has lost more than ten percent of its value.

    (A) During regular periods
    (B) Regular periods have
    (C) There have been regular periods
    (D) Regular periods

4. Gertrude Stein was considered a writer of "the lost generation," ---------- themes such as identity and alienation.

    (A) whose focus on
    (B) which focused on
    (C) they focused on
    (D) she was focusing

5. A spring tide occurs only ---------- the moon is in one of two phases: full or new.

    (A) on
    (B) during
    (C) when
    (D) whether

6. Norman Mailer's *The Naked and the Dead* received ---------- almost immediately upon publication.

    (A) critical acclaim enormously
    (B) enormous critical acclaim
    (C) critical enormous acclaim
    (D) enormously acclaim critical

7. The cockroach ---------- the most disliked, city-dwelling insect in the world.

    (A) it is probably
    (B) that is probably
    (C) is probably
    (D) probably

8. The muscles in a frog's legs ---------- to jump many times its own body height.

    (A) enable it
    (B) enabling
    (C) enable
    (D) it enables

9. On a typical winter night during the new moon, the Dog Star, Sirius, is the ---------- in the sky after Venus.

    (A) brightest second object
    (B) second brightest object
    (C) second object bright
    (D) bright is the second object

10. Linking power grids makes ---------- for cities to lend each other electricity at times of peak demand.

(A) it possible
(B) it possibly
(C) that possible
(D) possible

11. The pre-Civil War economies of the southern states to some extent depended upon the manufacturing of textiles and ---------- light goods, but mainly relied upon income generated from agriculture.

(A) another
(B) other
(C) the others
(D) other also

12. Because of its scenic beauty and ---------- , Marin County has some of the most valuable real estate in all of California.

(A) it is close proximity to San Francisco
(B) San Francisco is in close proximity
(C) its close to San Francisco in proximity
(D) its close proximity to San Francisco

13. The skin, contrary to popular belief, ---------- of the human body.

(A) is the largest organ
(B) the largest organ
(C) it is the largest organ
(D) a large organ

14. Child psychologists believe ---------- between the ages of one and five increases a child's skill at spatial reasoning.

(A) music is listened to
(B) that listening to music
(C) that in music listening
(D) listen to music

15. ---------- major cosmological theory is that the universe originated in a colossal explosion called the "Big Bang."

(A) One
(B) Despite
(C) That
(D) Unlike

Section 2
Structure
Written
Expression

NO TEST MATERIAL ON THIS PAGE.

Written Expression

Directions: In questions 16-40 each sentence has four underlined words or phrases. The four underlined parts of the sentence are marked (A), (B), (C), and (D). Identify the one underlined word or phrase that must be changed in order for the sentence to be correct. Then, on your answer sheet, find the number of the question and fill in the space that corresponds to the letter of the answer you have chosen.

Example I

Changes in atmospheric pressure affects human behavior.
 A   B   C   D

Sample Answer

Ⓐ Ⓑ ● Ⓓ

The sentence should read, "Changes in atmospheric pressure <u>affect</u> human behavior." Therefore, you should choose (C).

Example II

An equilateral triangle it has equal interior angles and
A   B   C

Sample Answer

Ⓐ ● Ⓒ Ⓓ

equal sides.
 D

The sentence should read, "An equilateral triangle <u>has</u> equal interior angles and equal sides." Therefore, you should choose answer (B).

Now begin work on the questions.

16. Present in large amounts between 10 and 50 kilometers above the earth, ozone
    ___A___   B
    is a gas with molecules consisting and made up of three atoms of oxygen.
                           C   D

17. By 1950, J. Edgar Hoover, long-time director of the Federal Bureau of
                                                      A
    Investigation, had become one of a most powerful men in Washington.
                   B   C   D

18. Imagism was a movement in American poetry which influence exerted from
            A   B   C   D
    the early- to mid-20th century.

19. Paints were first made from vegetable and mineral sources, but are now
    A   B
    manufactured from many differ substances.
                 C   D

20. Angleworms, a main source of bait for fishermen, use their mouths to dig, eat,
                                      A   B   C
    and feeling.
        D

21. Archaeologists have established that art has probably existed as long human
                   A   B   C
    culture has.
            D

22. Maple syrup, distilled from the sap of the sugar maple, is one of the sweetest
                          A   B   C
    natural sweetener known to humans.
            D

23. The Museum of Modern Art has traditionally showcased the best available
                                 A   B
    contemporary art in it exhibitions.
    C   D

24. Despite their reputation, pigs are of the most intelligent of all domesticated
    A   B   C
    animals.
    D

Go on to the next page ⟹

25. Erosion <u>can be</u> <u>caused</u> either by wind <u>and</u> <u>by</u> water.
          A   B   C D

26. When <u>the</u> first settlers <u>arrive</u> in North America, the <u>plains</u> buffalo numbered
          A   B   C
    <u>nearly</u> 60 million.
      D

27. Arthur Ashe, after his <u>retire</u> from professional tennis, <u>became</u> a <u>prominent</u>
                     A   B   C
    spokesman <u>for a number</u> of charitable organizations.
              D

28. Research <u>has</u> shown <u>but</u> most cold germs are <u>transmitted by</u> touching the
           A   B   C
    hands to the mucous membranes <u>of the nose</u> and eyes.
                              D

29. A body of air <u>form</u> a cloud <u>when</u> it cools <u>below</u> its <u>dew</u> point.
              A   B   C   D

30. Management Science <u>refers</u> to <u>the</u> study of organizing, directing, and
                  A   B
    <u>also to sustain</u> social and <u>economic</u> institutions.
        C   D

31. One <u>of</u> the <u>most</u> important natural <u>resources</u> of Oklahoma is <u>their</u> oil.
          A   B   C   D

32. Geysers <u>they</u> are a type of hot spring <u>that</u> at regular intervals <u>emits</u> steam
             A   B   C
    <u>and water</u> into the air.
      D

33. *Moby Dick*, perhaps the <u>finest</u> novel of the 19th century, <u>was</u> <u>large</u> <u>ignored</u> for
                     A   B   C
    <u>more than</u> 50 years after its publication.
      D

34. Passenger pigeons <u>had become</u> rare by the end of the 19th century, <u>and</u> <u>soon</u>
                     A   B   C
    after <u>becoming</u> extinct.
          D

Go on to the next page ⟹

35. Thermal power stations tap <u>the heat</u> of hot springs and geysers in those <u>place</u>
                                           A   B
   <u>where</u> geothermally heated water is found near the <u>Earth's</u> surface.
    C   D

36. The crow, <u>like</u> the dove and many other birds, <u>mate</u> for <u>the duration</u> of <u>its life</u>.
               A   B   C   D

37. <u>The acceleration</u> of the jaguar over 30 yards is <u>too</u> great that it can catch
            A   B
   <u>nearly any</u> prey it <u>successfully</u> stalks.
      C   D

38. The husks of <u>unpolished</u> brown rice are composed of fibrous material <u>that</u>
                   A   B
   makes <u>they</u> only <u>partly</u> digestible.
         C   D

39. At the Alamo, the defenders of the fort found <u>itself</u> <u>outnumbered</u> by a superior
    A   B   C
   army of <u>better armed</u> Mexican soldiers.
          D

40. The Air and Space Museum in Washington, D.C., <u>exhibits</u> some of the <u>most</u>
                                                 A   B
   primitive and most <u>sophisticate</u> machines related to the history of human
                       C
   <u>flight</u>.
    D

This is the end of Section 2.
If you finish before time is called, check your work on Section 2 only.

| Stop | Stop | Stop | **Stop** | Stop | Stop | Stop |

Do NOT read or work on any other section of the test.
Your supervisor will tell you when to begin working on Section 3.

Section 3
Reading Comprehension
Time: 55 minutes

Directions: In this section you will read several passages. Each one is followed by several questions about it. For questions 1-50, you are to choose the one best answer, (A), (B), (C), or (D), to each question. Then, on your answer sheet, find the number of the question and fill in the space that corresponds to the letter of the answer you have chosen.

Answer all questions following a passage on the basis of what is stated or implied in that passage.

Read the following passage:

> Many animals pass the winter in a state of severely decreased activity known as hibernation. This kind of long-term winter sleep allows them to survive severe cold and scarcity of food. The bodily activities of hibernating animals are lowered to such an extent that even their breathing is extremely slow and they appear to be
> 5 near death. Among the animals best known for their ability to hibernate are bears, squirrels, mice, and bats.
>   In some regions of the world, animals need to similarly adapt to survive high heat and lack of water during the summer. During this time, certain frogs and fish, for example, burrow into mud and suspend all activity until the hot season ends.
> 10 This kind of inactivity is known as estivation, and, like winter hibernation, helps them to avoid death due to extreme temperatures and lack of nourishment.

Example I
What happens to the bodily functions of animals during hibernation?
(A) They slowly speed up.
(B) They continue as usual.
(C) They greatly slow down.
(D) They come to a complete halt.

Sample Answer

The passage states that hibernation is a state of "severely decreased activity" and that the "bodily activities of hibernating animals are lowered." Therefore you should choose (C).

Example II
The word "nourishment" in line 11 is closest in meaning to
(A) oxygen
(B) food
(C) water
(D) protection

Sample Answer

The word "nourishment," as used in line 11, is closest in meaning to "food." Therefore, you should choose (B). Now begin work on the questions.

Questions 1-9

Although the Plains Indians in North America were perhaps not as
astronomically sophisticated as some of the native peoples of Central and South
America, they also studied the heavens and made astronomical observations. One site
that demonstrates the interest they took in the movement of the heavenly bodies is
5 the Medicine Wheel, which stands on an exposed shoulder of the Bighorn Mountains
in Wyoming. Located at longitude 107° 55'W and latitude 44° 50'N, at an altitude
of 9,640 feet, this structure consists of 28 lines of stones set out like the spokes of a
wheel. A central pile of stones about four meters in diameter forms the hub; there is
a large circle 25 meters in diameter around the edge. Six additional stone cairns are
10 located just outside the rim.

In the oral tradition of the Crow tribe whose ancestors built it, the Bighorn
Wheel is said to have been "created before the light came," which suggests great
antiquity. In Crow language, the structure is called the "Sun's House," and
superficially, the wheel does resemble the floor plan of a round ceremonial lodge.
15 This linguistic connection of the sun to the Medicine Wheel, however, very
likely originated from later visitors who had no part in the design of the original
structure. Certainly the site is not a practical place for a teepee or for an architectural
monument. It is uninhabitable, well above the tree line in the Bighorn National
Forest, and even in mid-June can be struck by blizzards.

1. The main topic of the passage is

(A) astronomical observation of early
peoples
(B) the traditions of the Crow tribe
(C) the so-called Medicine Wheel
(D) the Bighorn National Forest

2. The word "they" in line 4 refers to

(A) native peoples of Central and
South America
(B) heavenly bodies
(C) astronomical observation
(D) Plains Indians

3. The Medicine Wheel is located in which
of the following types of terrain?

(A) Valley
(B) Plain
(C) Forest
(D) Mountain

4. Why does the author mention in line 5 that the Medicine Wheel is located on "an exposed shoulder" of the Bighorn Mountains?

(A) To describe the shape of the structure
(B) To emphasize the inhospitability of the site
(C) To indicate the view possible from the site
(D) To stress the availability of stone to build the structure

5. The word "pile" in line 8 is closest in meaning to

(A) circle
(B) post
(C) structure
(D) heap

6. The word "antiquity" in line 13 is closest in meaning to

(A) strength
(B) ingenuity
(C) fragility
(D) age

7. The word "superficially" in line 14 is closest in meaning to

(A) at first glance
(B) in every respect
(C) with great power
(D) upon careful study

8. Who were probably the first people to use the name "the Sun's House"?

(A) Ancient predecessors of the Crow tribe
(B) The structure's original architects
(C) Crow Indians who visited the site after its completion
(D) American anthropologists who discovered the site

9. It can be concluded from the passage that the main function of the Bighorn Wheel was to serve as a place to

(A) watch over the surrounding area
(B) conduct traditional rituals
(C) establish safe living quarters
(D) perform astronomical observation

Go on to the next page

Questions 10-19

Crocodiles are tropical reptiles belonging to the family Crocodylidae. There are about 20 species of living crocodilians, among them alligators, caimans, and gavials, as well as true crocodiles. They are usually found near swamps, lakes, and rivers in Asia, Australia, Africa, Madagascar, and the Americas. The best known species is the
5   Nile crocodile, found mainly on the African continent. Like the saltwater crocodile from the coastal marshes of southern India and Malaysia, it can be a man-eater.

Alligators, which belong to the family Alligatoridae, are found in two freshwater locales. The American alligator inhabits the southeastern United States from North Carolina to Florida and west to the lower Rio Grande. The Chinese alligator is found
10   in the Yangtze River valley of China.

All crocodilians, including alligators, are characterized by a lizard-like shape and a thick skin composed of close-set overlapping bony plates. They can grow to very large sizes. Adult crocodiles range from 2 to 9 meters long, and alligators have been known to reach 6 meters, though 1.8 to 2.4 meters is the average. Crocodiles are the largest
15   modern reptiles and with their distant cousins the Komodo dragons, they constitute the last living link to the dinosaur-like reptiles of prehistoric times.

Crocodiles and alligators are by far most at home in the water but are able to travel on land by sliding on their bellies, stepping along with their legs extended, or galloping awkwardly. Large adults can stay underwater for over an hour without
20   breathing. Particularly when hunting for food, they swim by using the snakelike movements of their bodies and by powerful strokes of their muscular, oar-like tails, which are also effective weapons.

10. What is the main purpose of this passage?

(A) To describe in detail specific kinds of crocodiles and alligators
(B) To trace the evolution of crocodiles
(C) To present an overview of the characteristics of crocodilians
(D) To indicate where in the world crocodiles live

11. The word "them" in line 2 refers to

(A) tropical reptiles
(B) 20 species of living crocodilians
(C) crocodiles
(D) alligators

12. Which of the following is NOT referred to in the passage as a crocodilian species?

(A) Komodo dragons
(B) Caimans
(C) Gavials
(D) Alligators

13. The word "swamps" in line 3 is closest in meaning to

(A) marshes
(B) jungles
(C) bays
(D) streams

14. According to the passage, which of the following is true of the Nile crocodile?

(A) It lives only in Africa.
(B) It sometimes eats humans.
(C) It is the largest of crocodiles.
(D) It lives mainly in saltwater.

15. The word "locales" in line 8 is closest in meaning to

(A) lakes
(B) sources
(C) rivers
(D) areas

16. The author implies that one difference between crocodiles and alligators is that

(A) alligators are larger than crocodiles
(B) only crocodiles live on both land and water
(C) alligators tend to live in freshwater
(D) crocodiles' skin is composed of bonier plates

17. According to the passage, the average size of alligators is

(A) less than 1.8 meters
(B) approximately 2 meters
(C) around 6 meters
(D) up to 9 meters

18. The word "awkwardly" in line 19 is closest in meaning to

(A) sharply
(B) quickly
(C) clumsily
(D) aggressively

19. According to the passage, what is one common characteristic of both crocodiles and alligators?

(A) They are anatomically very similar to dinosaurs.
(B) They give birth to their young like snakes.
(C) They are incapable of running.
(D) They strongly prefer an aquatic environment.

Go on to the next page

Questions 20-30

When the hipster comedian Lenny Bruce was arrested for obscenity in New York City in 1964, he was publicly defended as a social satirist "in the tradition of Swift, Rabelais, and Twain" and as a Savonarola of black humor. Bruce himself noted, "All my humor is based on destruction and despair." His irreverence fostered the cynical
5   routines used by almost all the stand-up comics who developed after his death.

This highly controversial entertainer revolutionized show business in that his freewheeling improvisations were intended to shock rather than amuse the audience. His staccato delivery was salted with lewd vulgarities — both in speech and in concept. Though he was certainly not apathetic when it came to politics,
10   they were not his main focus. Instead, his favored targets were Jews, blacks, religion, drugs, and sex. However, in his later years, after he had been repeatedly arrested for indecent performances or for narcotics possession, his rambling monologues usually deteriorated into diatribes about his court trials and audiences eventually lost interest.

Lenny Bruce was born Leonard Alfred Schneider on October 13, 1925, the only
15   child of Myron Schneider, a Jewish shoe clerk, and Sadie Kitchenberg. His parents were divorced when he was five, and he lived with relatives while his mother looked for jobs as a dancer under such stage names as Sally Man and Boots Malloy, trying to conceal her own Jewish heritage.

The wit and cleverness of Bruce's monologues did not come through any formal
20   schooling. After dropping out of high school in 1942, Lenny enlisted in the Navy. After his discharge in 1946, he attended a Hollywood acting school under the GI Bill. He began his career as a mediocre impressionist. While working the nightclub circuit, which he regarded as the "last frontier" of uninhibited entertainment, he married an exotic dancer, Harriet Lloyd, in 1951. Bruce died on August 3, 1966, in
25   his Hollywood home, presumably from an accidental overdose of heroin. Ironically, had he not died, he likely would have faded into obscurity. His premature death then ultimately allowed his declining reputation to be posthumously resuscitated and his great contribution to be recognized by future generations.

Go on to the next page ⇒

20. What does this passage mainly discuss?

(A) The career of an important American entertainer
(B) The history of American stand-up comedy
(C) The eventual decline of Lenny Bruce's influence
(D) The revolution in show business during the 1960's

21. The author suggests which of the following is true of Lenny Bruce?

(A) He was universally condemned for his obscenity.
(B) He took much of his material from Mark Twain.
(C) Careful preparation was the key to his success.
(D) Current comic performers owe him a great debt.

22. The word "despair" in line 4 is closest in meaning to

(A) cynicism
(B) despondency
(C) violence
(D) insolence

23. The word "intended" in line 7 is closest in meaning to

(A) employed
(B) created
(C) expected
(D) designed

24. According to the passage, in what way did Lenny Bruce revolutionize show business?

(A) He dealt with subjects that had been previously taboo.
(B) He was the first person to do stand-up comedy.
(C) He was not primarily concerned with entertaining his audience.
(D) He did not attempt to conceal his extensive drug use.

25. The author would probably liken Lenny Bruce's speaking style to

(A) lyrical melodies sung by an opera star
(B) short bursts from a machine gun
(C) the inundating force of a tidal wave
(D) the taste of very salty fish

26. The author implies that near the end of his career Lenny Bruce had

(A) lost contact with what his audiences were interested in
(B) become the most famous comedian of all time
(C) become much less cynical than he had been previously
(D) stopped doing stand-up comedy entirely

Go on to the next page ➡

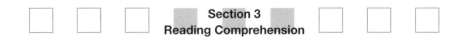

27. The word "deteriorated" in line 13 is closest in meaning to

    (A) progressed
    (B) shifted
    (C) disintegrated
    (D) digressed

28. In what way could Lenny Bruce's monologues about Jews be considered ironic?

    (A) He was married to a Jewish woman.
    (B) He himself was raised as a Jew.
    (C) Many famous entertainers are Jewish.
    (D) A Jew helped him to get his first job.

29. The author implies that the intelligence present in the routines of Lenny Bruce was all the more amazing because he

    (A) never finished his secondary education
    (B) never knew his own parents
    (C) grew up in a poverty-stricken environment
    (D) had only mediocre acting skills

30. Which of the following is NOT mentioned in the passage as a reason for the controversy surrounding Lenny Bruce?

    (A) The obscene language he used in his routines
    (B) The iconoclastic attitude he displayed
    (C) The revolutionary political change he advocated
    (D) The manner in which he attacked the Church

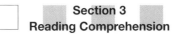
Questions 31-40

Although people's handwriting was once considered the very reflection of their character and personality, cursive script is gradually disappearing throughout the United States. The main cause of its decline is the assault by technology: first the typewriter and then the computer. As a result, when a message, essay, or application

5 form must be written by hand, more and more Americans now opt for printing, the form of writing they were taught at the start of elementary school, rather than the more flowing, interconnected script they learned later. Some graphologists — that is, specialists in handwriting — believe that the shift from written to printed letters suggests a transition from community to selfishness. Unlike the interconnected

10 letters of cursive, the separate printed ones consist of vertical strokes that, as one graphologist put it, "stand on their own and reflect the single self." The return to printing also perhaps indicates a lack of time in the nation's classrooms. Schools may still teach cursive handwriting, but they rarely make time to practice it the old-fashioned way with copybooks and extended repetition. The modern curriculum is

15 too crowded, and demands on teachers too pressing.

With so many adults printing like grade schoolers, the nation's handwriting speed is slowing to a crawl; ironically, this decline in handwriting speed has resulted in no measurable gains in legibility. The U.S. Post Office supplies one of the best illustrations of this nation-wide handwriting trend. Despite considerable

20 improvements in its automated address reading systems, postal workers must still individually and personally process 60 percent of all handwritten addresses because they are unreadable by machine. Some larger post offices send illegible addresses to specialists for decoding. Even so, every year about 10 million pieces of mail end up undelivered because their addresses cannot be read.

25 Perhaps it is too early to write off handwriting, however. Now that standardized tests for college entrance exam are requiring essays, readable cursive script may make a comeback, since no one wants to risk a college rejection by wasting time printing an entire essay exam. Also, since fewer people can now write elegantly in their own hand, cursive writing could once again emerge as the hallmark of the educated and

30 the elite.

31. What is the main topic of this passage?

   (A) The superiority of printing to writing
   (B) The failure of schools to teach writing
   (C) The U.S. Post Office's difficulty in reading addresses
   (D) The decline of cursive handwriting

32. According to the passage, the principal cause for the decrease in cursive handwriting is which of the following?

   (A) The greater clarity of printing
   (B) The slowness of writing cursive script
   (C) Technological innovation
   (D) A crowded curriculum.

33. According to the author, Americans learn printing

   (A) through computer programs
   (B) at the beginning of grade school
   (C) from copybooks
   (D) when they first use typewriters

34. In the first paragraph the author refers to specialists who think that the change from cursive to printed script suggests that

   (A) Americans have become more self-centered
   (B) schools do not have time to teach cursive script
   (C) teachers are no longer trained to teach writing
   (D) printing is more attractive than writing

35. In line 10, the word "vertical" is closest in meaning to

   (A) attractive
   (B) legible
   (C) appealing
   (D) upright

36. In line 22, the word "they" refers to

   (A) considerable improvements
   (B) postal workers
   (C) handwritten addresses
   (D) automated address reading systems

37. Which of the following points does the author use the U.S. Post Office to illustrate?

   (A) The inadequacy of address-reading machines
   (B) The decrease in handwriting speed
   (C) The need for specialists to decode bad printing
   (D) The poor legibility of American handwriting

38. The phrase "make a comeback" in line 26 can best be replaced by which of the following?

   (A) return to popularity
   (B) undergo a transformation
   (C) serve a purpose
   (D) come to be abandoned

39. Paragraph 3 is mainly about

    (A) the writing tests now part of
        college entrance exams
    (B) reasons why handwriting may
        again become prevalent
    (C) the refined handwriting used by
        the upper-class
    (D) the purpose of handwriting in
        the next decade

40. Which of the following generalizations
    is best supported by the passage?

    (A) Computers will increasingly
        replace the handwritten word.
    (B) Schools ought to spend more
        time teaching children to print.
    (C) A person's character is distinctly
        reflected in his or her cursive
        script.
    (D) Use of handwriting is influenced
        by a wide variety of factors.

Go on to the next page

Questions 41-50

As early as 1928, theories in physics posited that each kind of particle has its "anti" counterpart: a reverse twin of the same mass but opposite characteristics. "Antimatter," as this substance came to be called, caught the imagination of not only scientists but also science fiction writers. In novels and films, soon antimatter engines
5 propelled space ships and antimatter weapons annihilated their targets. As a result, the notion of matter and antimatter ironically became among the few concepts of particle physics widely understood by the general public.

Meanwhile, in serious science, one of the central questions of antimatter theories has been whether nature treats normal matter and antimatter the same way. For half
10 a century, the hopeful response has been "yes," and it has shaped the now standard view of cosmology. According to current thinking, around 12 billion years ago, only a few seconds after the Big Bang that created the cosmos, there were nearly identical amounts of matter and antimatter. These promptly obliterated each other. For some reason, however, this destruction left a tiny preponderance of ordinary matter
15 (around 1 part in 100 million), and it is these remains of ordinary matter that make up the universe as we know it today. Since that early time just after the origination of the universe, nearly all the antimatter in existence has been produced artificially in the lab.

Unfortunately, the lifetime of antimatter produced in labs is of extremely short
20 duration since whenever a particle of antimatter is produced it promptly collides with matter and is destroyed. Of course, this creation and extinction of antimatter particles is a phenomenon that can be observed only in the most costly of labs; that is, particle accelerators that raise particles to very high speeds and then smash them together. The antiparticles created in these collisions typically last only 10 to 40
25 billionths of a second. One of the most far-reaching new projects of physics is to create and capture antimatter for longer periods as well as to put antimatter particles together to form whole atoms of antimatter. New theories and new technology now suggest that it may be possible to create "jars" of antimatter that can be studied for months or even years.

Go on to the next page ➡

41. What is the main topic of this passage?

(A) The origin of antimatter
(B) Antimatter in the field of physics
(C) New possible uses of antimatter
(D) How science fiction portrays antimatter

42. The word "posited" in line 1 is closest in meaning to which of the following?

(A) proposed
(B) assumed
(C) investigated
(D) disputed

43. The author uses the word "ironically" in line 6 to imply that

(A) non-scientists have little knowledge of physics
(B) the notion of antimatter is relatively uncomplicated
(C) ideas portrayed by science fiction often become widely accepted
(D) the general public prefers science fiction based on actual science

44. According to the first paragraph, what are the qualities of a particle's antimatter twin?

(A) Identical characteristics but different mass
(B) Greater speed but less mass
(C) The same mass but opposite characteristics
(D) Longer life but less stability

45. In line 10, the word "it" refers to

(A) half a century
(B) nature
(C) one of the central questions
(D) hopeful response

46. The word "far-reaching" in line 25 is closest in meaning to

(A) ambitious
(B) long-lasting
(C) innovative
(D) uncommon

47. It can be concluded from the second paragraph that

(A) large amounts of antimatter are being produced in laboratories
(B) more antimatter existed just after the Big Bang than does now
(C) antimatter may eventually destroy much of the current universe
(D) the standard view of cosmology may be wrong

48. The word "promptly" in line 20 is closest in meaning to

(A) inevitably
(B) quickly
(C) violently
(D) remarkably

49. According to the paragraph three, where can antimatter particles typically be observed?

(A) In specially created "jars"
(B) At distant points in the universe
(C) In particle accelerators
(D) In chemical laboratories

50. Which of the following statements can be inferred from the passage?

(A) Antimatter will be used someday to power spaceships.
(B) The existence of antimatter is not accepted by all physicists.
(C) Antimatter will soon be studied even more carefully and closely.
(D) Research on antimatter is being funded mainly by governments.

Practice Test 2

Section 1
Listening Comprehension

In this section of the test, you will have an opportunity to demonstrate your ability to understand conversations and talks in English. There are three parts to this section with special directions for each part. Answer all of the questions on the basis of what is stated or implied by the speakers in this test. Do **not** turn the pages until you are told to do so.

Part A

Directions: In Part A you will hear short conversations between two people. After each conversation, you will hear a question about the conversation. The conversations and questions will not be repeated. After you hear a question, read the four possible answers in your book and choose the best answer. Then, on your answer sheet, find the number of the question and fill in the space that corresponds to the letter of the answer you have chosen.

Listen to an example.

On the recording, you hear: **Sample Answer**
What does the woman want the man to do?   Ⓐ Ⓑ Ⓒ ●
In your book, you read: (A) Look at her ID
(B) Let her pass
(C) Listen to her excuse
(D) Repeat what he said

You learn from the conversation that the woman couldn't catch what the man said. The best answer to the question, "What does the woman want the man to do?" is (D), "Repeat what he said." Therefore, the correct choice is (D).

Part A
Part B
Part C

Wait

Section 1
Listening Comprehension

mp3 060-064

1. What does the woman mean?
   (A) Class ends on the last day of the month.
   (B) No late reports will be accepted.
   (C) She plans to assign a lot of homework.
   (D) The lab assignment is due at the end of the month.

2. What does the man mean?
   (A) He is sorry his wife could not come.
   (B) The seat is already occupied.
   (C) The woman is welcome to sit down.
   (D) The seat is not expensive.

3. What does the man imply?
   (A) The woman should study harder.
   (B) It is possible to take the course again.
   (C) It is necessary to go to graduate school.
   (D) The professor's exams are usually difficult.

4. What does the woman mean?
   (A) She feels that the paper was pretty good.
   (B) She does not know how to type.
   (C) She is not good at checking for errors.
   (D) She appreciates the man's compliment.

5. What does the man suggest?
   (A) To hold off on the assignment
   (B) To contact another student
   (C) To sign up for the class later
   (D) To be sure to cover the reading

Go on to the next page ⇒

Section 1
Listening Comprehension

6. What does the man mean?

(A) He is happy to see the woman.

(B) The woman should be careful where she is walking.

(C) The woman has not changed at all.

(D) He can not talk to the woman very long.

7. What can be inferred from this conversation?

(A) The woman has made a mistake with her reservations.

(B) The computers sometimes fail to work.

(C) Ms. Jones has changed her mind about the reservations.

(D) Ms. Jones would like advice on possible destinations.

8. What will happen to the apartment?

(A) John's girlfriend will move in.

(B) John will look for someone to stay there.

(C) John plans to be gone for only a short time.

(D) John's brother will take care of it.

9. What does the man imply?

(A) The woman has done this before.

(B) He does not believe what the woman said.

(C) He has not gained anything.

(D) The woman has made a mistake.

10. What can be inferred from this conversation?

(A) The bookstore is usually closed at this time.

(B) The woman does not understand why the bookstore is not open.

(C) The bookstore's selection of books is too limited.

(D) The woman needs to shop at the bookstore before the end of term.

Section 1
Part A
Part B
Part C

Section 1
Listening Comprehension

mp3 **070-074**

11. What does the woman mean?

(A) Her parents think the tuition is expensive.

(B) She does not understand the situation.

(C) Her parents gave her a recent present.

(D) Tuition will soon increase.

12. What does the man want to know?

(A) When the woman is going to arrive

(B) Whether or not he can help

(C) If the woman likes her apartment

(D) Why the woman wants to move

13. What does the man mean?

(A) He has been a very careful driver.

(B) The road is rather dangerous.

(C) He has received several speeding tickets.

(D) This road is the fastest way home.

14. What does the woman imply about the magazine?

(A) The library no longer receives it.

(B) It is no longer required for the economics course.

(C) It can be obtained only by subscription.

(D) It is not worth reading.

15. What does the woman suggest that Dave should do?

(A) Use his friend's computer

(B) Consult the manual

(C) Take a computer class

(D) Use different software

 Go on to the next page ➡

Section 1
Listening Comprehension

 mp3 **075-079**

16. What does the man mean?

(A) He forgot to do what she asked.

(B) He likes that blend of coffee.

(C) He plans to meet his friend.

(D) He had someone do it for him.

17. What does the woman mean?

(A) She would like the man to repeat what he said.

(B) She usually does not eat at the cafeteria.

(C) She agrees with the man's opinion.

(D) She would rather come back again later.

18. What can be inferred about Tom?

(A) The woman wants to cheer him up.

(B) The woman has not seen him, either.

(C) He tends to talk too much.

(D) He is very pleased about winning.

19. What does the woman imply?

(A) The man is taking too many classes.

(B) The man should not lift so much.

(C) The man ought to go home as soon as possible.

(D) The man needs to get some exercise.

20. What does the man suggest that the woman should do?

(A) Keep working on the paper

(B) Ask someone else to finish the last part

(C) Ignore the section she has not finished

(D) Take a break for a while

Practice Test 2

Section 1

Part A

Part B

Part C

Go on to the next page ➡ **83**

Section 1
Listening Comprehension

mp3 080-084

21. What does the professor mean?

(A) She does not think the man's topic is appropriate.

(B) The man must submit his paper by Friday.

(C) She cannot meet the man tomorrow.

(D) The man should come to her office in the afternoon.

22. What does the man imply about Bill?

(A) He often loses things.

(B) He should have taken a taxi.

(C) He is a very reliable person.

(D) He neglected to pay for the taxi.

23. Where will the man probably go?

(A) To a department store

(B) To a specialty shop

(C) To a different shopping mall

(D) To a dressmaker

24. What does the woman mean?

(A) Somebody else must know the spelling.

(B) The professor's name is difficult to spell.

(C) She is not sure what the professor's name is.

(D) Her name is also hard to spell.

25. What does the man imply about George?

(A) He is busy doing many different things.

(B) He is looking for something else to do.

(C) He is working very hard.

(D) He and the man will meet soon.

Go on to the next page ⇒

mp3 085-089

26. What does the woman mean?

  (A) She thinks the man is mistaken.

  (B) She did not know Marilyn took the exam.

  (C) She is surprised about Marilyn's grade.

  (D) She considers Marilyn an excellent student.

27. What does the man imply about the film festival?

  (A) He had to stand up to watch it.

  (B) It is extremely popular.

  (C) There are no more tickets available.

  (D) He thinks it was too long.

28. What had the man assumed?

  (A) The woman was going to pick him up.

  (B) The picnic was canceled.

  (C) The woman was not planning to go.

  (D) He was supposed to prepare some food.

29. What does the woman imply?

  (A) She has to pay her own tuition.

  (B) She contacted the dean quite a while ago.

  (C) She has to drop out of school.

  (D) She has not spoken to the dean yet.

30. What can be inferred from the man's comment?

  (A) He is waiting for a bus.

  (B) The housing office has not returned his keys.

  (C) He left the door open.

  (D) His keys are still lost.

Section 1
Part A
Part B
Part C

Go on to the next page ⟹   85

Section 1
Listening Comprehension

NO TEST MATERIAL ON THIS PAGE.

Part B

Directions: In this part, you will hear longer conversations. After each conversation, you will hear several questions. The conversations and questions will not be repeated.

After you hear a question, read the four possible answers in your book and choose the best answer. Then, on your answer sheet, find the number of the question and fill in the space that corresponds to the letter of the answer you have chosen.

Wait

Practice Test 2

Section 1
Part A
Part B
Part C

mp3 **091-095**

31. How did the man and woman find out about the exhibit?
    (A) It appeared on a TV news program.
    (B) They heard it on the radio.
    (C) It was mentioned in the newspaper.
    (D) They saw an advertisement.

32. In the past, what kinds of crafts did the man make?
    (A) Silver jewelry
    (B) Ceramic cups and bowls
    (C) Handmade paper
    (D) Wooden furniture

33. What do the speakers suggest is the best thing about handmade crafts?
    (A) They are fun to make.
    (B) They can be excellent gifts.
    (C) They can be widely sold.
    (D) They are unusually valuable.

34. What will the speakers probably do when they leave the exhibit?
    (A) Return home
    (B) Go to the park
    (C) Do some shopping
    (D) Eat at a restaurant

mp3 **096-100**

35. Why is John tired?
    (A) He went to a party last night.
    (B) He had a late night class.
    (C) He stayed up all night writing a paper.
    (D) He got up early to work.

36. What did John write about?
    (A) Efficient study methods
    (B) High school education
    (C) Research techniques
    (D) His major field

37. What field do the memorization techniques John referred to seem most suited for?
    (A) Science
    (B) Humanities
    (C) Sociology
    (D) Education

38. Where did John go after he talked with Patty?
    (A) To a coffee shop
    (B) To bed
    (C) To class
    (D) To eat

Go on to the next page ➡

Part C

Directions: In this part, you will hear several talks. After each talk, you will hear some questions. The talks and questions will not be repeated.

After you hear a question, read the four possible answers in your book and choose the best answer. Then, on your answer sheet, find the number of the question and fill in the space that corresponds to the letter of the answer you have chosen.

Here is an example.
On the recording, you hear:

Now listen to a sample question.

Sample Answer

In your test book, you read: Who should register at the south end?
  (A) Engineering students
  (B) Graduate students
  (C) Humanity students
  (D) Science students

The best answer to the question, "Who should register at the south end?" is (B), "Graduate students." Therefore, the correct choice is (B).

Now listen to another sample question.

Sample Answer

In your test book, you read: Where is the exit?
  (A) On the north side
  (B) On the south side
  (C) On the east side
  (D) On the west side

The best answer to the question, "Where is the exit?" is (C), "On the east side." Therefore, the correct choice is (C).

Practice Test 2

Section 1
Part A
Part B
Part C

89

Section 1

Listening Comprehension

mp3 **102-106**

39. In what class is this lecture probably being given?
    (A) Philosophy
    (B) Geology
    (C) Geography
    (D) Biology

40. Which "missing link" does the newly discovered creature fill?
    (A) The one between apes and humans
    (B) The one between dinosaurs and mammals
    (C) The one between early primates and later primates
    (D) The one between fish and reptiles

41. Which of the following best describes the animal's physical characteristics?
    (A) It was small.
    (B) It was strong.
    (C) It was fast.
    (D) It was quiet.

42. According to the speaker, what did the creature probably eat?
    (A) Only plants
    (B) Fruits and insects
    (C) Other animals
    (D) Nuts and berries

mp3 **107-111**

43. Where is this talk being given?
    (A) A university
    (B) A health club
    (C) A hospital
    (D) A diet center

44. What does the speaker say about "fat-free" products?
    (A) They are excellent health foods.
    (B) They actually contain a lot of fat.
    (C) They may be high in calories.
    (D) They should always be avoided.

45. According to the speaker, what is one of the little-known effects of exercise?
    (A) Greater chance of injury
    (B) Increased burning of calories throughout the day
    (C) Better physical fitness
    (D) Deeper and sounder sleep at night

46. What is the speaker going to do next?
    (A) Use a visual illustration
    (B) Demonstrate a work-out technique
    (C) Recommend a diet
    (D) Give some examples of healthy foods

90

Go on to the next page

mp3 **112-116**

47. Where are the greatest number of meteorites found?
    (A) In Europe
    (B) In the southwest United States
    (C) In Antarctica
    (D) In Japan

48. Why do many scientists believe that some small meteorites may have originated from comets?
    (A) They have highly irregular orbits.
    (B) They are located in the asteroid belt.
    (C) They are quickly disintegrating.
    (D) They are extremely volatile.

49. How can the age of a meteorite best be determined?
    (A) By comparing it to the surrounding rock
    (B) By analyzing its metallic composition
    (C) By looking at its shape and size
    (D) By measuring the decay of its radioactive elements

50. What will the students do next?
    (A) Finish their homework
    (B) Ask questions to the professor
    (C) Go over an assignment
    (D) Take notes on the lecture

Practice Test 2

Section 1
Part A
Part B
Part C

This is the end of Section 1.
Stop work on Section 1.

Stop   Stop   Stop   **Stop**   Stop   Stop   Stop

Do NOT read or work on any other section of the test.
Your supervisor will tell you when to begin working on Section 2.

NO TEST MATERIAL ON THIS PAGE.

Section 2
Structure and Written Expression
Time: 25 minutes

This section is designed to measure your ability to recognize language that is appropriate for standard written English. There are two types of questions in this section, with special directions for each type.

Structure

Directions: Questions 1-15 are incomplete sentences. Beneath each sentence you will see four words or phrases, marked (A), (B), (C), and (D). Choose the one word or phrase that best completes the sentence. Then, on your answer sheet, find the number of the question and fill in the space that corresponds to the letter of the answer you have chosen.

Example I

-------- mammals, whales nurse their young.
(A) Since
(B) For
(C) To be
(D) Being

Sample Answer
Ⓐ Ⓑ Ⓒ ●

The sentence should read, "<u>Being</u> mammals, whales nurse their young." Therefore, you should choose (D).

Example II

The Civil War had just ended -------- was shot.
(A) when Lincoln
(B) that Lincoln
(C) while Lincoln
(D) Lincoln

Sample Answer
● Ⓑ Ⓒ Ⓓ

The sentence should read, "The Civil War had just ended <u>when Lincoln</u> was shot." Therefore, you should choose (A).

Now begin work on the questions.

1. Genetic engineering --------- to first understand and then manipulate the process of genetic coding.

   (A) it aims
   (B) its aiming
   (C) aiming
   (D) aims

2. As a poet, novelist, and critic, Robert Penn Warren exerted considerable influence on the --------- of 20th century American literature.

   (A) developing
   (B) develop
   (C) development
   (D) developed

3. It is commonly accepted by economists --------- exists a strong relationship between interest rates and inflation.

   (A) when it
   (B) that it
   (C) that there
   (D) which

4. The iron range of northern Minnesota comprises --------- iron ore deposits found in North America.

   (A) the largest one of the
   (B) a larger of the
   (C) the larger one of
   (D) one of the largest

5. With its many beaches, marshes, and estuaries, the Gulf Coast --------- prized as an environmental sanctuary until recently.

   (A) had
   (B) was
   (C) is
   (D) being

6. The power --------- a body outward from a circular orbit is centrifugal force.

   (A) draws
   (B) which it draws
   (C) that draws
   (D) it draws

7. --------- of two female senators from one state, California, which marked the beginning of a new era for women in politics.

   (A) It was the election
   (B) The election
   (C) The election it was
   (D) Was the election

8. --------- many experiments have been performed, the exact cause of baldness has yet to be identified.

   (A) Despite
   (B) Even though
   (C) There are
   (D) Regardless of

Go on to the next page ➡

9. Though himself ---------- imaginative statesman, James Polk was unusually successful in accomplishing his goals during his term.

(A) not an
(B) without an
(C) he was not
(D) was not an

10. Blends of spices have been created by spice manufacturers to make the art of seasoning ----------.

(A) a quick and easy one
(B) easy and quick a one
(C) a quick one and easy
(D) one easy and quick

11. During the 1950s, proponents of linguistic relativity believed that thought ---------- to language or representational functioning.

(A) can reduce
(B) could be reduced
(C) reducing
(D) could be reducing

12. ---------- that nearly all households would have broadband internet within the first few years of the 2000s.

(A) Expecting
(B) Many expecting
(C) In expectation
(D) It was expected

13. In contrast to popular opinion, measures of intelligence have ---------- reliable predictors of future success.

(A) never been
(B) not any
(C) no
(D) seldom

14. The name "porpoise" sometimes ---------- to some members of the dolphin family.

(A) it is extended
(B) is an extension
(C) extended
(D) is extended

15. In old age, the immune system gradually becomes less resistant to viral, fungal, and ----------.

(A) infection by bacteria
(B) bacteria's infection
(C) bacterial infection
(D) infectious bacteria

Practice Test 2

Section 2
Structure
Written
Expression

NO TEST MATERIAL ON THIS PAGE.

Written Expression

Directions: In questions 16-40 each sentence has four underlined words or phrases. The four underlined parts of the sentence are marked (A), (B), (C), and (D). Identify the one underlined word or phrase that must be changed in order for the sentence to be correct. Then, on your answer sheet, find the number of the question and fill in the space that corresponds to the letter of the answer you have chosen.

Example I

San Diego, California, was <u>originally</u> founded <u>as</u>
                      A   B

a mission <u>through</u> Junipero Serra <u>in</u> 1769.
           C   D

Sample Answer

Ⓐ Ⓑ ● Ⓓ

The sentence should read, "San Diego, California, was originally founded as a mission by Junipero Serra in 1769." Therefore, you should choose answer (C).

Example II

<u>Many people</u> <u>consider Einstein</u> to be
      A   B

the most brilliant scientist who lived ever.
           C   D

Sample Answer

Ⓐ Ⓑ Ⓒ ●

The sentence should read, "Many people consider Einstein to be the most brilliant scientist who ever lived." Therefore, you should choose (D).

Now begin work on the questions.

16. <u>Mail ordering</u> is <u>economic</u> feasible when <u>it serves</u> widely scattered <u>but</u>
        A   B   C   D
    numerous customers.

17. Massachusetts <u>was one</u> of the <u>original</u> thirteen <u>colonies</u> <u>who</u> formed the United
                      A   B   C D
    States in 1776.

18. The Boston Marathon <u>acts as</u> a yardstick <u>in which</u> the abilities <u>of</u> long distance
                            A   B   C
    runners <u>can be</u> measured.
            D

19. By <u>a</u> mid-20th century, American novelists <u>such as</u> Hemingway, Steinbeck,
       A   B
    and Faulkner <u>finally received</u> the critical acclaim <u>they</u> had long deserved.
                         C   D

20. A zenith telescope <u>contains</u> a fixed-end lens that <u>look</u> directly <u>overhead</u> <u>toward</u>
                       A   B   C   D
    the celestial zenith.

21. George Mason <u>showed</u> his abilities <u>as an</u> aristocratic farmer, a successful
                A   B
    businessman, and <u>he was</u> an original <u>thinker</u>.
                 C   D

22. <u>The</u> Chief Justice of the Supreme Court <u>is</u> responsible for <u>administration</u> the
     A   B   C
    oath of office to <u>newly elected</u> presidents.
                  D

23. <u>When</u> a firm uses strategic layoffs to <u>decrease its losses</u> or increase its
      A   B
    <u>competitiveness</u>, the company <u>said</u> to be "downsizing."
        C   D

24. <u>Much</u> early American lawmen were <u>themselves</u> <u>on</u> the wrong side <u>of the law</u>.
      A   B   C   D

25. Though it has taken various forms and at times retreat, the spread of
        A   B
    democracy as a political system has been constant, progressive, and remarkable.
                                      C   D

26. Despite its aridity, the deserts of southwestern Arizona has been a habitat for a
        A   B   C
    rich variety of animal life.
                   D

27. Coccidiosis is a contagious sick that affects all young domestic animals except
                              A   B   C
    the horse.
     D

28. A quasar, that stands for quasi stellar radio source, is now thought to be the
            A   B   C
    reverse side of a black hole.
             D

29. Speed, powerful, and fierceness are qualities that make the lioness a remarkable
           A   B   C   D
    predator.

30. The theory of evolution, as put forth by Darwin, envisioned the evolution of
                          A   B   C
    humans as a gradually yet constant process.
                D

31. Ceramics are often used as superconductors because they do not need to
              A   B
    be cooled to as low a temperature than other current-bearing compounds.
     C   D

32. The Colorado River, one of the great rivers in North America, it drains an area
                       A   B   C
    of 637,140 square kilometers.
             D

33. The widespread use of social media may soon make not only air mail and also
           A   B   C
    potentially even e-mail obsolete.
                   D

34. George Washington <u>is</u> usually <u>refer</u> to <u>by</u> school children <u>as</u> "the father of the
                A   B   C   D
    country."

35. <u>Certain</u> lower organisms, <u>as such</u> amebas, <u>can</u> replicate <u>themselves</u> through cell
      A   B   C   D
    division.

36. <u>The</u> state of Tennessee has <u>a</u> unusually <u>varied</u> landscape, ranging <u>from</u> rugged
     A   B   C   D
    mountains to low plains.

37. <u>When</u> electrons are <u>in motion</u>, <u>a magnetic</u> field is created around <u>it</u>.
     A   B   C   D

38. <u>The</u> value of a company's stock, in contrast to <u>those</u> of manufactured goods,
     A   B
    depends almost <u>entirely</u> <u>upon</u> the perception of the buyer.
                      C   D

39. The <u>orbital plane</u> of the dwarf planet Pluto is <u>steeply</u> inclined <u>to</u> the orbits of
           A   B   C
    the <u>other planet</u> in the Solar System.
            D

40. <u>Because</u> of its unusual molecular structure, water actually <u>becomes</u> <u>less denser</u>
     A   B   C
    in its solid <u>than in</u> its liquid form.
                  D

This is the end of Section 2.
If you finish before time is called, check your work on Section 2 only.

Stop Stop Stop **Stop** Stop Stop Stop

Do NOT read or work on any other section of the test.
Your supervisor will tell you when to begin working on Section 3.

Section 3
Reading Comprehension
Time: 55 minutes

Directions: In this section you will read several passages. Each one is followed by several questions about it. For questions 1-50, you are to choose the one best answer, (A), (B), (C), or (D), to each question. Then, on your answer sheet, find the number of the question and fill in the space that corresponds to the letter of the answer you have chosen.

Answer all questions following a passage on the basis of what is stated or implied in that passage.

Read the following passage:

> While only a few groups of birds sing, nearly all have the same vocal system by which they communicate. Alarm calls, for example, are used to signal the approach of a predator. In order not to reveal their position, many small birds give a shrill whistling warning call that is like a ventriloquist's voice, and which is hard for the
> 5   predator, such as an owl or a fox, to locate.

Example I
According to the passage, many birds use a "shrill whistling warning call" in order to
(A) locate predators
(B) indicate danger
(C) frighten predators away   **Sample Answer**
(D) reveal their position

According to the passage, in order to signal the approach of a predator such as an owl or a fox, many small birds give a shrill whistling warning call. Therefore, you should choose (B).

Example II
The word "locate" in line 5 is closest in meaning to
(A) perceive
(B) notice
(C) pinpoint   **Sample Answer**
(D) hear

The word " locate," as it is used in line 5 "hard for the predator, such as an owl or a fox, to locate," has the meaning of "determine the location exactly" or "pinpoint." Therefore, you should choose (C).

Now begin work on the questions.

101

Questions 1-9

　　Early immigrants to America viewed the New World not only as a paradise free
of the corruptions of civilized Europe, but also as an uncharted wilderness filled with
terrors and dangers. Unlike Native Americans who had essentially lived in harmony
with nature, the early settlers found it difficult to adjust to their new environment.
5　Those who survived the long sea journey found upon their arrival that they were
destined to suffer from cold, hunger, and disease. Their traditional crops often failed,
and commodities they were accustomed to having, such as sugar and cotton cloth,
were in short supply if available at all. Often the settlers' day-to-day experience in
the New World was a sheer struggle for survival. As a result, it is easy to see why
10　many came to regard nature not as a natural paradise but as a hostile force to be
conquered. Moreover, they also feared the wilderness because it was the opposite of
"civilization." They came to feel that it was their moral mission to tame and civilize
the wild landscape and its inhabitants, bringing the "light" of civilization to the
"darkness" of the unexplored continent. Thus, both their physical existence and their
15　philosophical outlook led the settlers to regard Native Americans not as noble savages
but as subhumans who should either convert to the white man's way of life or be
slaughtered.

1. What is the main topic of the passage?

　(A) How the early immigrants
　　　came to America
　(B) Hardships of the first settlers
　(C) The early settlers' view of
　　　America and its inhabitants
　(D) How America gradually
　　　became civilized

2. Which of the following is NOT
mentioned as a reason for why early
settlers came to regard the wilderness
as a hostile power that needed to be
overcome?

　(A) Indian attacks
　(B) Lack of food
　(C) Shortage of commodities
　(D) Harsh climate

3. The word "paradise" in line 1 is closest
in meaning to

　(A) prison
　(B) arena
　(C) retreat
　(D) utopia

4. According to the passage, which of the
following was true of Native Americans?

　(A) They sometimes supplied the
　　　settlers with food.
　(B) They were well adjusted to
　　　the natural environment.
　(C) They feared the civilizing
　　　influence of the European
　　　immigrants.
　(D) They often suffered from
　　　cold, hunger, and disease.

5. Why does the author mention sugar and cotton cloth?

(A) They were luxuries the settlers expected to have.
(B) They were basic goods the settlers often had to do without.
(C) They were used by the settlers as a form of money.
(D) They were frequently traded with the native Americans.

6. What did European settlers quickly discover about North America?

(A) It was not as beautiful as they had first thought.
(B) It took longer to get there than they had imagined.
(C) It was not easy to raise the crops they knew how to grow.
(D) It was more densely populated than they had anticipated.

7. The author mentions "moral mission" in line 12 to show how

(A) immoral the behavior of many early settlers was
(B) strongly many early settlers respected the sanctity of nature
(C) the mindset of many early settlers was formed
(D) many early settlers felt obligated to befriend the native people

8. The word "outlook" in line 15 is closest in meaning to

(A) point of view
(B) misgivings
(C) way of life
(D) arrogance

9. The word "slaughtered" in line 17 is closest in meaning to

(A) persuaded
(B) captured
(C) terrorized
(D) killed

Practice Test 2

Section 3

Go on to the next page ⟹ **103**

Questions 10-19

Even though it is one of the most commonly used measures of economic activity, Gross National Product (GNP) has some severe limitations. Because it measures only economic output, it does not fully take into account many kinds of economic losses. For instance, if a $100,000 house burns to the ground and is re-built by its owner for
5 the same amount, the GNP increases by $100,000 even though there has been no net gain of wealth. In fact, it could even be argued that a net loss has occurred since the resources the homeowner might have used for genuinely productive purposes have been expended. Environmentalists in particular have been critical of GNP because it fails to deduct costs such as depletion of non-renewable natural resources, loss of
10 agricultural land, and the expense of cleaning up pollution.

One measurement that was proposed as a substitute for GNP during the late 1980's was ISEW (Index of Sustainable Economic Welfare). This index adds up all the goods and services that genuinely contribute to a better quality of life in order to arrive at a figure that includes such things as unpaid household labor as well as public
15 spending on highways, health, and education. The index then subtracts superfluous items that have conventionally been assigned economic value but which do not actually contribute to a better quality of life. Advertising is one example. What insights does a comparison of GNP to ISEW offer? While GNP figures show that the American economy nearly doubled between 1951 and 1986, the ISEW figures show
20 that quality of life during this period only improved 20 percent.

10. What does the passage mainly discuss?

(A) The concept of Gross National Product
(B) A need for a new economics
(C) GNP versus ISEW
(D) The increasing quality of American life

11. The word "it" in line 2 refers to

(A) economic activity
(B) a $100,000 house
(C) economic output
(D) Gross National Product

Go on to the next page ⇒

12. It can be inferred from the passage that the cost of which of the following would be added to the GNP but not to the ISEW?

(A) Building a new public sports center
(B) Cleaning up a hazardous waste site
(C) Paying company employees
(D) Providing subsidies to local schools

13. The word "critical" in line 8 is closest in meaning to

(A) skeptical of
(B) curious about
(C) interested in
(D) serious about

14. The word "deduct" in line 9 is closest in meaning to

(A) subtract
(B) consider
(C) mention
(D) allocate

15. What conclusion can be drawn from using the ISEW as opposed to GNP to measure quality of life in 1986?

(A) Quality of life was twice as good as in 1951.
(B) Quality of life failed to improve since 1951.
(C) Quality of life has mirrored the economic gains since 1951.
(D) Quality of life was only somewhat better than in 1951.

16. The main drawback of GNP in the opinion of environmentalists is that it

(A) includes the cost of replacing something that is damaged or destroyed
(B) fails to consider economic activity in the form of barter
(C) does not deduct resource losses such as polluted land and water
(D) focuses more on public spending than private consumption

17. Why does the author mention "unpaid household labor" in line 14?

(A) To show that gender inequality still exists
(B) To encourage a more equitable division of household labor
(C) To illustrate something that contributes to quality of life
(D) To recommend that the value of this labor should be taxed

Practice Test 2

Section 3

18. The word "superfluous" in line 15 is
    closest in meaning to

    (A) valuable
    (B) nonessential
    (C) traditional
    (D) useless

19. According to the passage, which of the
    following does the Index of Sustainable
    Economic Welfare NOT include?

    (A) Highway construction
    (B) Health spending
    (C) Education expenses
    (D) Advertising budgets

Go on to the next page ⇒

Questions 20-29

Water buffalo are unrelated to bison, which are often mistakenly referred to as buffalo. They are roughly the shape of cattle and almost always gray-black in color. They are noted for their rather unusual horns, which are either swept back or curly. Many water buffalo grow quite large, weighing in at well over one ton. Water buffalo
5 have received little but neglect from American cattle ranchers and animal scientists alike, yet they have recently begun to receive recognition in many parts of the world. Of all domestic animals, the water buffalo may have the greatest unexplored potential for increased meat production, milk yield, and work output.

To most Westerners, water buffalo are alien animals and myths about them
10 abound. It is said, for instance, that they are a vicious breed, especially around other animals, whereas in fact they are probably the gentlest farm animals in the world: sociable, genial, and fond of humans. And though it is widely reported that water buffalo need water in which to wallow, they in fact grow and reproduce normally without it, as long as adequate shade is available. There is also the common
15 misconception that they are exclusively tropical animals; in reality, their adaptability has allowed them to be raised in a number of climates. Despite this adaptability, however, it was felt any experimentation to determine the animal's commercial potential in the United States should first be carried out in a climate similar to the water buffalo's original native environment. For this reason, the University of Florida
20 was chosen to receive America's first herd of water buffalo in 1978. In subsequent experiments, animal scientists from the school's international agriculture program determined that water buffalo do indeed have a definite commercial potential in the United States. In fact, under conditions of poor feed they seem to have a competitive advantage over cattle, growing more quickly and producing more calves. Among
25 other advantages observed by the scientists were the breed's tolerance for heat and humidity and its liking for aquatic weeds that blanket many of Florida's waterways. They also found that the meat of the water buffalo has considerable market potential. Indeed, many subjects in a blind taste test preferred water buffalo meat to a corresponding cut of beef.

Practice Test 2

Section 3

20. What can be inferred about water buffalo?

    (A) Their meat is less tasty than beef.
    (B) They are a highly promising source of protein.
    (C) Their diet is limited to aquatic plants.
    (D) They cannot be bred easily outside their native habitat.

21. Which of the following attributes is characteristic of the water buffalo?

    (A) It has a shape unlike that of cattle.
    (B) It comes from the same family as the bison.
    (C) It comes in a wide variety of colors.
    (D) It has very distinctive horns.

22. The word "roughly" in line 2 is closest in meaning to

    (A) abruptly
    (B) exactly
    (C) approximately
    (D) increasingly

23. The word "they" in line 6 refers to

    (A) cattle
    (B) water buffalo
    (C) ranchers
    (D) animal scientists

24. The first paragraph of the passage most fully discusses which of the following topics?

    (A) Myths about water buffalo
    (B) The climates that water buffalo prefer
    (C) Physical features of water buffalo
    (D) The potential for water buffalo breeding

25. The word "genial" in line 12 is closest in meaning to

    (A) friendly
    (B) active
    (C) genuine
    (D) intelligent

26. What is necessary for the water buffalo to be able to thrive?

    (A) Muddy fields
    (B) An ample supply of water
    (C) High humidity
    (D) Protection from the sun

27. The word "tolerance" in line 25 is closest in meaning to

    (A) adaptability to
    (B) dependence on
    (C) preference for
    (D) apathy toward

Go on to the next page ⟹

28. Which of the following is NOT true about the behavior of the water buffalo?

    (A) It gets along well with other farm animals.
    (B) It can adapt to a number of different climates.
    (C) It tends to be averse to humans.
    (D) It has a mild temperament.

29. Why was Florida the first state to import water buffalo?

    (A) It has weather conditions akin to the animal's native habitat.
    (B) It has the largest agricultural university in the United States.
    (C) It has an abundance of water.
    (D) It has only a small competing cattle industry.

Practice Test 2

Section 3

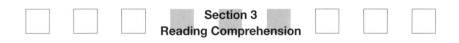
Questions 30-39

A short, plump man, John Adams enjoyed a robust life even in his old age, in contrast to his predecessor, George Washington. Unlike Washington, however, under whom Adams served two terms as vice president, Adams was not one of the United States' wealthiest presidents. He dipped repeatedly into his own modest
5 savings to meet official expenses during his term of office. Perhaps Adams' financial difficulty began as vice president when his salary was a pitiful $5,000 — far too little to live on, he complained. As president, it increased to $25,000, still too little to cover his official expenses. After serving a single term, Adams retired early and passed his last 25 years in seclusion at his Quincy estate, composing his will at age 84. By
10 then, most of his preferred beneficiaries — his wife, two daughters, and one son — were dead. Two of his surviving sons shared his estate. However, Adams had lived so long off his fortune that its worth had dwindled to $30,000. The younger son, Thomas Boylston Adams, inherited a portion of the land property and a share of the cash assets of the estate. The older son, John Quincy Adams, not to be confused with
15 his father, received not only part of the estate but also the presidential library in what perhaps foreshadowed his own destiny — to follow in his father's political footsteps and become the nation's sixth president.

30. What does the passage mainly discuss?

(A) Major events in the life of John Quincy Adams
(B) Early presidents of the United States
(C) The finances of John Adams, the second president
(D) Salaries of the early presidents and vice presidents

31. The word "plump" in line 1 is closest in meaning to

(A) healthy
(B) chubby
(C) sturdy
(D) pleasant

Go on to the next page

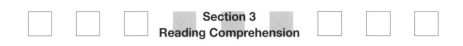

32. It can be inferred from the passage that George Washington was

    (A) a great colonial leader
    (B) not as healthy as Adams
    (C) about the same age as Adams
    (D) Adams' close friend

33. It can be inferred from the passage that during most of Adams' life he probably

    (A) gave most of his money to his sons
    (B) lived in relative poverty
    (C) spent more money than he made
    (D) lived off his wife's earnings

34. When Adams was vice president, his annual salary amounted to

    (A) $5,000
    (B) $15,000
    (C) $25,000
    (D) $30,000

35. In line 7, "it" refers to

    (A) a single term in office
    (B) financial difficulty
    (C) the presidential salary
    (D) Adams' fortune

36. John Adams served as president for

    (A) only one term
    (B) three terms
    (C) two terms
    (D) one-half term

37. The word "seclusion" in line 9 is closest in meaning to

    (A) relative isolation
    (B) active retirement
    (C) periodic consultation
    (D) intermittent depression

38. The word "dwindled" in line 12 is closest in meaning to

    (A) doubled
    (B) increased
    (C) equaled
    (D) declined

39. How did Adams spend much of his life after serving his term as president?

    (A) Grooming his oldest son to be president
    (B) Living alone at his family home
    (C) Establishing several important charities
    (D) Compiling materials for the first presidential library

Practice Test 2

Section 3

Go on to the next page ➡

Questions 40-50

A fiber may be defined as a unit of matter whose length is at least 200 times greater than its width. Natural fibers comprise three categories: cellulose base, protein base, and mineral base. The first, cellulose base, has a vegetable origin. Although more than 2,000 types of fibrous plants have been identified, only around 50 have
5   commercial uses. Cotton is by far the most important of these, both in terms of consumption and the enormous variety of applications, and a wide range of textiles and other products are manufactured from it. Jute, which is produced from the stalks of South Asian plants, is second to cotton in terms of production. However, while the cost of cultivating jute is much lower, it is inferior to cotton in several ways. It is
10 coarse and difficult to bleach or dye, as well as lacking in tensile strength.

Protein base fibers come primarily from animal hair. Sheep wool, beaver pelts, and rabbit furs are all examples of this category. Silk, the only natural animal fiber that does not grow from the skin as a protective covering, is extruded as a continuous filament by the silkworm.
15 The only naturally occurring mineral fiber is asbestos. Although it is very brittle, requiring much care during mining and subsequent processing to avoid crushing its long fibers, until recently asbestos was widely used because of its fire-resistance and its ability to retain heat. However, with the revelation that continued exposure to it can cause cancer, asbestos has given way to other materials.
20 All of the natural fibers, except asbestos, are hydrophilic, i.e. they have an affinity for water in both its liquid and vapor forms. The capacity of these natural fibers to absorb moisture makes them suitable for use in clothing; by absorbing moisture and transferring it to the surrounding atmosphere, they make the wearers more comfortable. Artificial fibers cannot do this as well, because of their inability to
25 absorb moisture.

Go on to the next page ➡

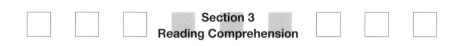
40. What would be the best title for the passage?

    (A) Some Commercial Uses of Cotton and Jute
    (B) A Comparison of Natural and Artificial Fibers
    (C) Fibers: A Concise Definition
    (D) Natural Fibers: Their Classification and Use

41. According to the passage, how many kinds of fibrous plants have been identified?

    (A) At least 200
    (B) More than 2,000
    (C) About 50
    (D) Exactly 3

42. In line 5, the word "these" refers to

    (A) fibrous plants with commercial uses
    (B) fibrous plants in general
    (C) naturally occurring fibers
    (D) categories of natural fibers

43. The word "cultivating" in line 9 is closest in meaning to

    (A) producing
    (B) exporting
    (C) marketing
    (D) growing

44. According to the passage, what is true of the first category of commercially used natural fibers?

    (A) They come from a relatively small percentage of fibrous plants.
    (B) There are many that have yet to be discovered and classified.
    (C) They are derived mainly from animal hair.
    (D) Their length ranges from very short to extremely long.

45. The word "retain" in line 18 is closest in meaning to

    (A) hold
    (B) claim
    (C) transfer
    (D) resist

46. Why has asbestos been replaced by other materials?

    (A) It is difficult to process.
    (B) It is too fragile.
    (C) It constitutes a health hazard.
    (D) It cannot be mined in sufficient quantities.

47. In what way is cotton NOT superior to jute?

    (A) It is smoother to the touch.
    (B) It makes stronger cloth.
    (C) It is easier to dye.
    (D) It is cheaper to produce.

Practice Test 2

Section 3

48. The word "it" in line 18 refers to

    (A) revelation
    (B) asbestos
    (C) heat
    (D) cancer

49. The word "capacity" in line 21 is closest
    in meaning to

    (A) ability
    (B) volume
    (C) tendency
    (D) characteristic

50. It can be inferred from the passage
    that asbestos is unsuitable for clothing
    because it

    (A) is a man-made fiber
    (B) cannot absorb moisture
    (C) is a mineral-based fiber
    (D) irritates the skin

Practice Test 3

Section 1
Listening Comprehension

In this section of the test, you will have an opportunity to demonstrate your ability to understand conversations and talks in English. There are three parts to this section with special directions for each part. Answer all the questions on the basis of what is stated or implied by the speakers in this test. Do **not** turn the pages until you are told to do so.

Part A

Directions: In Part A you will hear short conversations between two people. After each conversation, you will hear a question about the conversation. The conversations and questions will not be repeated. After you hear a question, read the four possible answers in your book and choose the best answer. Then, on your answer sheet, find the number of the question and fill in the space that corresponds to the letter of the answer you have chosen.

Listen to an example.

On the recording, you hear:
How many books can the man check out?
In your book, you read: (A) None
                 (B) One
                 (C) Two
                 (D) Three

Sample Answer

Ⓐ Ⓑ ● Ⓓ

You learn from the conversation that the man cannot check out a reference book. The best answer to the question, "How many books can the man check out?" is (C), "Two." Therefore, the correct choice is (C).

Part A
Part B
Part C

117

mp3 **118-122**

1. What does the man imply about his science project?
   (A) It is proceeding smoothly.
   (B) It will be turned in late.
   (C) He will start working on it soon.
   (D) He wishes it were better.

2. What does the woman mean?
   (A) She enjoys writing about history.
   (B) Her essay is not going very well.
   (C) The paper is required for a course she is taking.
   (D) She is feeling rather depressed lately.

3. What does the man say about the bus?
   (A) It leaves in half an hour.
   (B) There are two each hour.
   (C) It takes an hour to reach the airport.
   (D) The bus has already left.

4. What does the woman mean?
   (A) The man should take some time off work.
   (B) The man will have to study a lot.
   (C) The term will end soon.
   (D) The man should not miss work so often.

5. What is the woman assuming?
   (A) The man has been watching television.
   (B) The rental shop is closed.
   (C) The couple went shopping.
   (D) The man has rented some DVDs.

Go on to the next page ➡

mp3 123-127

6. What does the man mean?
   (A) He wants to know if the woman used the copy machine.
   (B) He planned to write a note to the woman.
   (C) He would like to borrow the woman's notes from class.
   (D) He agrees that the woman's answer is correct.

7. What does the man mean?
   (A) The woman may be trying to do too much.
   (B) Working hard is necessary for success.
   (C) It is important to take an occasional break.
   (D) The woman should ask him for help.

8. What does the woman mean?
   (A) It is better to make reservations early.
   (B) The food was not very good there.
   (C) The service is gradually improving.
   (D) The restaurant closed earlier than usual.

9. What does the man imply about the essay?
   (A) He is almost finished writing it.
   (B) He wants to change his topic.
   (C) He has not even started writing it.
   (D) He did not know it was due tomorrow.

10. What can be inferred about the man from this conversation?
    (A) He cannot seem to locate the contract.
    (B) He is planning to sign the contract next week.
    (C) He needs to contact Mr. Wilson soon.
    (D) He has been busy with other work.

Practice Test 3

Section 1
Part A
Part B
Part C

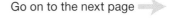 Go on to the next page

119

mp3 128-132

11. What does the woman imply about the members of the anthropology class?

(A) They are working together on class projects.
(B) They are all behind in their reading.
(C) They will do well on their mid-term test.
(D) They will take a field trip together by boat.

12. What will the woman probably do?

(A) Apply for a credit card
(B) Show her identification
(C) Pay with cash
(D) Ask for a receipt

13. What does the woman suggest the man should do?

(A) Board the plane immediately
(B) Book a flight at once
(C) Cancel his trip to San Antonio
(D) Look for a cheaper flight

14. What does the woman imply about the bird?

(A) It is rarely seen in this area.
(B) Its color makes it hard to see.
(C) It is flying south for the winter.
(D) She has never seen one like it.

15. What does the man imply?

(A) The woman should be more patient.
(B) The woman is next in line to be served.
(C) The woman should have made a reservation.
(D) The woman can place her order now.

mp3 133-137

16. What does the woman say about Murray?
    (A) He was delayed because of bad weather.
    (B) He is not feeling very well.
    (C) He has been on vacation the past few days.
    (D) He did not know where to go.

17. What does the woman imply?
    (A) She thought it was quite cold.
    (B) She does not know how to spell it.
    (C) She also had nothing to do over the weekend.
    (D) She agrees with the man's opinion.

18. What does the man imply?
    (A) They should take the subway.
    (B) The clouds will vanish soon.
    (C) Another way might be faster.
    (D) The traffic will let up eventually.

19. What does the man imply the woman should do?
    (A) Stop studying so hard
    (B) Make different friends
    (C) Avoid late-night parties
    (D) Join a study group

20. What can be inferred about the weather?
    (A) It has not been nice lately.
    (B) It is unlikely to change soon.
    (C) It is impossible to predict.
    (D) It has been almost perfect recently.

Practice Test 3

Section 1
Part A
Part B
Part C

 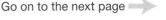

mp3 138-142

21. What does the woman suggest about her performance on the exam?
   (A) She did not score as high as she had hoped.
   (B) She scored the most on the factual questions.
   (C) She had an average result compared to her classmates.
   (D) She performed very well on it.

22. What does the woman mean?
   (A) She only has one class today.
   (B) She does not want any more coffee.
   (C) She will be able to join the man.
   (D) She is not interested in Canadian history.

23. What can be inferred from the woman's question?
   (A) She is busy talking on the telephone.
   (B) She seldom receives calls at work.
   (C) She is just leaving the office.
   (D) She wants to take a message.

24. What does the man mean?
   (A) They should meet immediately.
   (B) There are problems with the budget.
   (C) Now is not a good time to get together.
   (D) The budget is not his responsibility.

25. What does the woman imply?
   (A) She forgot to ask Mark to bring the photos.
   (B) She did not like the photos very much anyway.
   (C) She suspected Mark would let them down.
   (D) She had wanted the present to be a surprise.

Go on to the next page

mp3 **143-147**

26. What does the man imply?
    (A) He does not like sweets.
    (B) He cannot give the woman a ride.
    (C) He is allergic to chocolate.
    (D) He needs to watch his weight.

27. What does the woman want to know?
    (A) What the man said
    (B) What happened to the man
    (C) What the problem with the printer is
    (D) What the man is writing

28. What does the man mean?
    (A) He got the job he really wanted.
    (B) He definitely needs to apply for a job.
    (C) He has decided to work in a bank.
    (D) He already went to the bank yesterday.

29. What does the woman imply about the man?
    (A) He should pick her up earlier.
    (B) He does not often watch football.
    (C) He is going to play in the game.
    (D) He is almost never on time.

30. What can be inferred about the man and woman from the conversation?
    (A) They expected it to rain.
    (B) They are too busy to have a picnic.
    (C) They will have to postpone their picnic.
    (D) They are lucky to have good weather.

Practice Test 3

Section 1
Part A
Part B
Part C

Go on to the next page  **123**

NO TEST MATERIAL ON THIS PAGE.

Part B

Directions: In this part, you will hear longer conversations. After each conversation, you will hear several questions. The conversations and questions will not be repeated.

After you hear a question, read the four possible answers in your book and choose the best answer. Then, on your answer sheet, find the number of the question and fill in the space that corresponds to the letter of the answer you have chosen.

Wait

Practice Test 3

Section 1

Part A
Part B
Part C

Section 1
Listening Comprehension

mp3 149-153

31. When is the tournament going to take place?
    (A) On Sunday
    (B) Later today
    (C) Tomorrow morning
    (D) Early next week

32. Who will judge the debate contest?
    (A) Students from other universities
    (B) Professional debate judges
    (C) Members of the local community
    (D) Professors from area colleges

33. How will the debaters know which topic to debate?
    (A) It will be up to them to choose it by themselves.
    (B) It will be chosen by the opposing team members.
    (C) It will be given to them the day before the debate.
    (D) It will be announced immediately prior to the debate.

34. According to the man, what will NOT be one of the major criteria used in deciding the winner?
    (A) Organization
    (B) Originality
    (C) Style of delivery
    (D) Audience appeal

mp3 154-158

35. Why is the woman so tired?
    (A) She has been painting late at night.
    (B) She is working on an exhibition.
    (C) She has been finishing an assignment for an art class.
    (D) She got up early this morning.

36. Why does the man say he is surprised?
    (A) He did not know an exhibit was going to be held next week.
    (B) He thought the woman already finished her course requirements.
    (C) He did not realize art students prepared their own works for display.
    (D) He thought the woman would graduate the following year.

37. Where will the exhibit be held?
    (A) In the art department
    (B) At the city art museum
    (C) At the performing arts center
    (D) In a private gallery

38. What is the woman looking forward to?
    (A) The opening of the exhibition
    (B) The hanging of her works
    (C) The end of the term
    (D) The close of the exhibition

Go on to the next page

Part C

Directions: In this part, you will hear several talks. After each talk, you will hear some questions. The talks and questions will not be repeated. After you hear a question, read the four possible answers in your book and choose the best answer. Then, on your answer sheet, find the number of the question and fill in the space that corresponds to the letter of the answer you have chosen.

Here is an example.
On the recording, you hear:

Now listen to a sample question.

Sample Answer

In your book, you read: Who is the speaker?
        (A) A student in a psychology class
        (B) A graduate student
        (C) A clinical psychologist
        (D) A psychology professor

The best answer to the question "Who is the speaker?" is (D), "A psychology professor." Therefore, the correct choice is (D).

Now listen to another sample question.

In your book, you read: What does the speaker suggest to those
        people who cannot choose a topic?
        (A) Go to the library
        (B) Talk with their classmates
        (C) Transfer to another class
        (D) Come visit her office

Sample Answer

Practice Test 3

Section 1
Part A
Part B
Part C

The best answer to the question "What does the speaker suggest to those people who cannot choose a topic?" is (B), "Talk with their classmates." Therefore, the correct choice is (B).

Wait

mp3 **160-164**

39. For whom is this talk intended?
    (A) Expecting mothers
    (B) Nurses
    (C) Medical students
    (D) Parents with small children

40. According to the speaker, what percentage of women experience long-term depression after giving birth?
    (A) One percent
    (B) Ten percent
    (C) Twenty percent
    (D) Eighty percent

41. What happens to estrogen in a woman's body after a baby is born?
    (A) It increases drastically.
    (B) It remains higher than before birth.
    (C) It completely disappears.
    (D) It significantly decreases.

42. What is the speaker going to do next?
    (A) Distribute a new medical device
    (B) Display a chart that explains estrogen
    (C) Analyze the cause of post-birth depression
    (D) Ask for volunteers for an experiment

mp3 **165-169**

43. Who is probably giving this talk?
    (A) A professor
    (B) An anthropology student
    (C) A museum employee
    (D) A geologist

44. What important recent discovery was made about the Spirit Cave Man?
    (A) He is much older than previously thought.
    (B) He was probably an accomplished fisherman.
    (C) He lived in a large community.
    (D) He hunted animals with a spear.

45. According to the speaker, what does the cloth found with the mummy suggest about early North American peoples?
    (A) They were skilled at weaving.
    (B) They raised plants to make cloth.
    (C) They wore animal furs to keep warm.
    (D) They had an interest in color dying.

46. What was found in the Cave Man's stomach?
    (A) Animal skin
    (B) Wild berries
    (C) Fish bones
    (D) Medicinal plants

Go on to the next page

`mp3` **170-174**

47. Who is the likely audience for this talk?
    (A) Publishers
    (B) Students
    (C) English teachers
    (D) Book-sellers

48. What does the speaker compare dictionaries to?
    (A) An encyclopedia
    (B) The United States Constitution
    (C) A history book
    (D) The Bible

49. What is the reason Americans were concerned with English usage and correctness?
    (A) They wished to form an identity distinct from the British.
    (B) Many were immigrants insecure about the language.
    (C) They had elitist views of language and its use.
    (D) Most wanted to obtain a basic education.

50. How does the traditional American approach to dictionaries differ from the British?
    (A) It is more sophisticated.
    (B) It is more descriptive.
    (C) It is more scholarly.
    (D) It is more prescriptive.

Practice Test 3

Section 1
Part A
Part B
Part C

This is the end of Section 1.
Stop work on Section 1.

Do NOT read or work on any other section of the test.
Your supervisor will tell you when to begin working on Section 2.

NO TEST MATERIAL ON THIS PAGE.

Section 2
Structure and Written Expression
Time: 25 minutes

This section is designed to measure your ability to recognize language that is appropriate for standard written English. There are two types of questions in this section, with special directions for each type.

Structure

Directions: Questions 1-15 are incomplete sentences. Beneath each sentence you will see four words or phrases, marked (A), (B), (C), and (D). Choose the one word or phrase that best completes the sentence. Then, on your answer sheet, find the number of the question and fill in the space that corresponds to the letter of the answer you have chosen.

Example I

There are ---------- of textbooks utilized in university classrooms.
(A) many different types
(B) a different types
(C) the difference of type
(D) much different in type

Sample Answer
● Ⓑ Ⓒ Ⓓ

The sentence should read, "There are <u>many different types</u> of textbooks utilized in university classrooms." Therefore, you should choose answer (A).

Example II

---------- to save fuel, people are driving smaller cars.
(A) Since
(B) Over
(C) In order
(D) Because of

Sample Answer
Ⓐ Ⓑ ● Ⓓ

The sentence should read, "<u>In order</u> to save fuel, people are driving smaller cars." Therefore, you should choose (C).

Now begin work on the questions.

Section 2
Structure
Written
Expression

1. In his poetry, Robert Hass addresses what ---------- the spiritual deterioration of American life.

   (A) he regards
   (B) he regards as
   (C) he is regarding
   (D) he regarded

2. Plastics ---------- from several varieties of petroleum oil.

   (A) can be made
   (B) made
   (C) they can be made
   (D) are making

3. Beans and rice, ---------- , satisfy most minimum daily requirements for protein intake.

   (A) as eaten together
   (B) if together they are eating
   (C) when eaten together
   (D) together eaten

4. After the Civil War, the federal government encouraged the development of higher education through ---------- of land grant colleges.

   (A) establish
   (B) the establishment
   (C) having establishing
   (D) the established

5. ---------- their superior night vision, owls hunt their prey in the nocturnal hours between dusk and dawn.

   (A) Means of
   (B) The means of
   (C) Of the means by
   (D) By means of

6. A falling barometer generally indicates that bad weather ---------- soon.

   (A) arrive
   (B) arrived
   (C) will arrive
   (D) will have arrived

7. In the Mississippi River Valley, archaeological digs have provided evidence that Native Americans dwelt in the area ---------- thousands of years.

   (A) in
   (B) since
   (C) for
   (D) until

8. Sports trainers have developed a highly scientific basis for estimating the exact level of exertion ---------- cardio-vascular conditioning.

   (A) are an increase of
   (B) that will increase
   (C) which increasing
   (D) to be increased of

Go on to the next page ➡

9. Many comets, ----------, revolve in an elliptical orbit around the sun.

(A) like planets
(B) as planets
(C) planets like
(D) as such planets

10. Ernest Hemingway's novel *The Old Man and the Sea*, which first appeared in *Life Magazine*, ----------.

(A) whose commercial success was enormous
(B) was an enormous commercial success
(C) that enormously had a commercial success
(D) commercially and enormously successful

11. ---------- they are often thought of as vegetables, tomatoes are botanically regarded as fruits.

(A) However
(B) Because
(C) Even though
(D) Instead

12. The temper of steel depends upon its metallic composition and the heat ---------- subjected at the time that it was forged.

(A) to which it was
(B) it was
(C) which was
(D) has been

13. Bank checks require that their monetary value ---------- in both words and numerals.

(A) printed
(B) prints
(C) be printed
(D) were printed

14. ---------- devotion to precision is one of the principal qualities demanded of competent mechanical engineers.

(A) The
(B) A
(C) It is
(D) There is

15. After hibernating all winter, it takes ---------- wake up.

(A) fully several days for bears
(B) bears several days to fully
(C) bears several fully days to
(D) several days fully for bears

NO TEST MATERIAL ON THIS PAGE.

Written Expression

Directions: In questions 16-40 each sentence has four underlined words or phrases. The four underlined parts of the sentence are marked (A), (B), (C), and (D). Identify the one underlined word or phrase that must be changed in order for the sentence to be correct. Then, on your answer sheet, find the number of the question and fill in the space that corresponds to the letter of the answer you have chosen.

Example I

<u>Some</u> novella is a short novel
  A

<u>that</u> can <u>be</u> read <u>in</u> a single sitting.
  B   C   D

Sample Answer

The sentence should read, "A novella is a short novel that can be read in a single sitting." Therefore, you should choose answer (A).

Example II

Lacrosse, <u>a sport</u> that is <u>still played</u>,
      A   B

began <u>as a game</u> <u>played Native Americans</u>.
      C   D

Sample Answer

The sentence should read, "Lacrosse, a sport that is still played, began as a game played by Native Americans." Therefore, you should choose (D).

Now begin work on the questions.

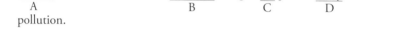

16. <u>Found</u> in <u>large numbers</u> in the American Southwest, the mountain cougar uses
      A   B
    both speed <u>and</u> stealth to attack <u>their</u> prey.
            C   D

17. <u>Among</u> the principal causes of <u>common</u> allergies <u>are</u> pollen, <u>dusty</u>, smoke, and
      A   B   C   D
    pollution.

18. Soil <u>acidity</u> is influenced by <u>vegetation</u> and rainfall and <u>can vary</u> <u>great</u> from
         A   B   C   D
    region to region.

19. <u>Despite of</u> the narrow margin of <u>his election</u>, John F. Kennedy <u>became</u> one of
        A   B   C
    the <u>most admired</u> American presidents.
         D

20. Hydrogen <u>can produced</u> simply by <u>separating</u> the <u>single</u> oxygen atom from the
             A   B   C
    two hydrogen atoms in a molecule <u>of water</u>.
                                 D

21. Size and anatomy are <u>but two</u> of the <u>criteria</u> used for <u>comparing</u> one species to
                    A   B   C
    <u>other</u>.
     D

22. The Great Society programs of the 1960s <u>provided</u> the funds <u>for</u> urban <u>renew</u>
                                      A   B   C
    in major cities <u>across</u> the United States.
               D

23. The behavioral differences between men and women <u>in a</u> society <u>depend</u> not
                                           A   B
    only <u>upon</u> culture <u>and also</u> biology.
         C   D

24. The <u>thickest</u> Arctic ice is <u>close</u> the North Pole, <u>where</u> the temperature remains
          A   B   C
    low <u>throughout</u> the year.
         D

25. An object moving in a weightless vacuum indefinitely maintain its original
    <u>A</u>   <u>B</u>   <u>C</u>
    velocity.
    <u>D</u>

26. Pete Seeger, <u>an</u> American folk singer, <u>he</u> was a writer of popular songs and
                  A   B
    <u>a social activist</u> for <u>more than</u> 50 years.
         C   D

27. Most <u>areas urban</u> in the United States <u>originally</u> had a manufacturing <u>or</u>
            A   B   C
    agricultural <u>base</u>.
                 D

28. <u>A</u> two principal forms of formal <u>reasoning</u> <u>are</u> deductive logic <u>and</u> inductive
    A   B   C   D
    logic.

29. Lighter than <u>others</u> metals, aluminum <u>is</u> extensively <u>used</u> in home construction
                 A   B   C
    <u>for</u> siding and roofing.
    D

30. Silicon wafers <u>are</u> high-tech <u>composites</u> used <u>in</u> the <u>made</u> of computer chips.
                   A   B   C   D

31. The very notion <u>of vacation</u> arose <u>only after</u> the emergence of <u>sizable</u>, affluent
    <u>A</u>   B   C   D
    middle class.

32. The Federal Bureau of Investigation was <u>form</u> to <u>investigate</u> serious federal
                                            A   B
    crimes <u>and</u> to aid local law enforcement <u>officials</u>.
           C   D

33. With modern plastics, <u>car bodies</u> can be built <u>that are</u> lighter, stronger, and
                          A   B
    <u>most</u> durable than those built <u>of</u> metal.
    C   D

34. One of the most important <u>sites</u> for the production of nuclear submarines <u>is</u>
                                A   B
    the <u>shipyard</u> located at Groton, Connecticut, <u>there</u>.
         C   D

35. <u>A</u> formidable opponent of unfair business <u>practices</u>, Ida Tarbell displayed
    A   B
    <u>herself</u> courage by writing articles <u>critical of</u> the Standard Oil Company.
     C   D

36. Alligators have the same <u>bodily</u> structure <u>than</u> crocodiles, except their heads are
                              A   B
    broader and <u>their</u> snouts <u>blunter</u>.
                 C   D

37. Many psychologists <u>argue</u> that <u>excessively</u> control over children's eating may
                        A   B
    cause <u>them</u> to later suffer <u>from</u> eating disorders.
           C   D

38. The loon, <u>whose</u> haunting call was <u>legendary</u> among Native Americans,
              A   B
    <u>are found</u> in lakes throughout <u>northern</u> North America.
     C   D

39. A u-turn <u>in</u> a pipe not only helps <u>to prevent</u> clogging <u>or</u> makes plumbing
             A   B   C
    repairs <u>easier</u>.
             D

40. Transcendental meditation, <u>whom</u> relaxation techniques have been found to
                                A
    <u>markedly</u> reduce stress, <u>first</u> came to <u>prominence</u> in the 1960's.
     B   C   D

This is the end of Section 2.
If you finish before time is called, check your work on Section 2 only.

Do NOT read or work on any other section of the test.
Your supervisor will tell you when to begin working on Section 3.

Section 3
Reading Comprehension
Time: 55 minutes

Directions: In this section you will read several passages. Each one is followed by several questions about it. For questions 1-50, you are to choose the one best answer, (A), (B), (C), or (D), to each question. Then, on your answer sheet, find the number of the question and fill in the space that corresponds to the letter of the answer you have chosen.

Answer all questions following a passage on the basis of what is stated or implied in that passage.

Read the following passage:

> During and after the French Revolution of 1789, French musicians, dancing masters, and actors once employed by the now deposed aristocrats, added a touch of grace to the rustic life of America. They introduced the French art of cooking, the waltz, and the quadrille. The French-Spanish immigrants from the West Indies
> 5 made New Orleans into a great cultural and social center.

Example I
The influence of the French on American society was
(A) prior to the French Revolution
(B) detrimental to the new land
(C) particularly evident in New Orleans **Sample Answer**
(D) only temporary Ⓐ Ⓑ ● Ⓓ

In the passage, it says that New Orleans was a "great cultural and social center." Therefore, you should choose (C).

Example II
The word "rustic" in line 3 is closest in meaning to which of the following?
(A) Rural
(B) Daily
(C) Royal **Sample Answer**
(D) Artistic ● Ⓑ Ⓒ Ⓓ

The word "rustic," as used in line 3 "the rustic life of new America," has the meaning of "rural" or "countryside." Therefore, you should choose (A).

Now begin work on the questions.

Questions 1-10

    Bacteria are among the smallest of living creatures and their identification is often difficult. Among the kinds of information used for their classification are their size, shape, and appearance, the structure of their bacterial "colonies," and the chemical changes they undergo as they multiply. Many kinds of bacteria that have
5 been identified have been studied very little; hundreds of other kinds wait to be discovered.
    Although bacteria are popularly believed to be disease-causing, they are in reality essential to life on earth. Soil, air, and even water are to some extent "produced" by bacteria. In practical terms, because bacteria often use the same vitamins as
10 human beings or animals they are valuable aids in the laboratory. For instance, the amount of vitamin in a given solution can be measured, under carefully controlled conditions, by observing the multiplication of a particular kind of bacterium. In many instances, a few dozen test tubes of growing bacteria can measure in several days what would require many weeks and hundreds of animals to accomplish.
15   To grow bacteria one must use a "culture medium." This is a food prepared usually in liquid form. Bacteria grow on the surface of the culture medium and spread into colonies that can be easily seen under a microscope. The foods provided for bacterial colonies vary depending on the species. Some bacteria grow best on powdered sulfur and other inorganic substances. Other kinds thrive on sugars,
20 amino acids, or vitamins. There is practically no limit to the varieties of food that support bacteria.

1. It can be inferred from the passage that bacteria are difficult to study because they

(A) grow slowly
(B) are tiny
(C) are dangerous
(D) die easily

2. According to paragraph 1, what is true of bacteria?

(A) They are the main cause of disease in humans.
(B) There are many types yet to be discovered.
(C) There are some types that do not reproduce.
(D) They are the primary component of soil.

Go on to the next page ➡

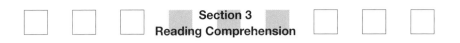
3. The author mentions all of the following characteristics as means used to classify bacteria EXCEPT

(A) their size and shape
(B) their chemical make-up
(C) the organization of their groups
(D) the locations where they live

4. The word "undergo" in line 4 is closest in meaning to

(A) experience
(B) resist
(C) cause
(D) require

5. According to the passage, scientists are able to use bacteria to analyze chemicals such as vitamins by observing

(A) the rate at which the bacteria multiply
(B) the types of bacteria that appear
(C) the shape of the colonies the bacteria form
(D) the length of time the bacteria survive

6. The word "given" in line 11 is closest in meaning to

(A) received
(B) measured
(C) particular
(D) sweet

7. In the second paragraph, the author mainly discusses which of the following?

(A) How bacteria cause sickness
(B) Where bacteria most often grow
(C) Why bacteria are important to human beings
(D) How bacteria are used in the laboratory

8. Why are bacteria of great interest to laboratory scientists?

(A) They often mutate when they multiply.
(B) They frequently use vitamins similar to those used by humans.
(C) They can easily be preserved for later study.
(D) They adapt quickly to a laboratory environment.

9. The phrase "culture medium" in line 15 is put in quotation marks because

(A) it is taken from a direct quotation
(B) it is given special emphasis
(C) it is a particularly defined term
(D) it is used ironically

10. Which of the following is true of the food consumed by bacteria?

(A) Almost any type of food allows bacteria to thrive.
(B) Most bacteria prefer inorganic substances.
(C) The culture medium must be in a liquid form.
(D) Different bacteria need different culture mediums.

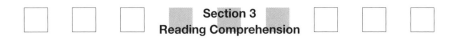
Questions 11-21

Although concerns about instruments of debt exist today (and wisely so), the creation of debt was a practice of government even in colonial times. The Southern colonies — Maryland, Virginia, and "Carolina" as it then was called — based their currencies on the value of tobacco and they greatly deplored any demand for gold or
5 silver as a means of payment. On occasion, they even outlawed the use of precious metals as a means of currency exchange. In Maryland, paper money based on tobacco served as currency for nearly two centuries, longer by a considerable margin than the practice of basing the dollar on gold bullion.

Still, precious metals, silver and gold chief among them, had their lure. In 1690,
10 Sir William Phips led an expedition of irregular soldiers from the Massachusetts Bay Colony all the way to the fortress of Quebec in what is now Canada. They intended to use the gold they would capture from the fort to pay for the cost of their expedition. To their disappointment and surprise, the fortress did not fall, and when the troops returned, there was no hard money — no gold or silver coin — in
15 the colonial treasury to pay them. It then seemed a minor step for the colonial government to issue paper notes promising eventual payment in gold or silver. For two decades thereafter the paper circulated side by side with the metals that were the basis of this promise. In this case, the Massachusetts' debt in the form of paper notes was backed by fewer solid assets (meaning hard money) than were available should
20 all the notes be presented at once for payment.

The wonder of paper currency soon spread to other colonies; paper notes were issued in abundance, indeed with abandon. Rhode Island, for instance, issued huge amounts of unbacked currency. There, as elsewhere, on the eventual day of reckoning, the notes would one day become worthless. The lesson to be drawn from
25 this history is not that debt should always be condemned — after all, Washington's soldiers in the Revolutionary War were paid with paper currency — but rather that debt always carries with it the risk of loss and default.

Go on to the next page ➡

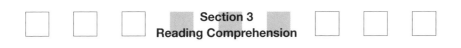
11. What is the main topic of this passage?

(A) Tobacco used for cash
(B) The value of gold and silver
(C) The use of debt in the colonies
(D) The origin of money

12. In the first paragraph the author compares currency based on tobacco with

(A) one based on gold
(B) money in the Southern colonies
(C) silver used by settlers
(D) government promises for repayment

13. According to the author, the Southern colonies at times

(A) traded tobacco rather than paper notes
(B) banned the use of silver and gold for currency
(C) refused to honor their debts
(D) collected large amounts of precious metals

14. The word "deplored" in line 4 is closest in meaning to

(A) envied
(B) invited
(C) accepted
(D) discouraged

15. The word "their" in line 9 refers to

(A) dollar bills
(B) precious metals
(C) silver and gold
(D) irregular soldiers

16. The author mentions the expedition of Sir William Phips in order to give an example of

(A) foolish military ventures during colonial times
(B) the willingness of the early settlers to go to war
(C) the dependence of the early governments on gold
(D) how colonies were forced to issue paper money

17. The word "eventual" in line 16 is closest in meaning to

(A) complete
(B) quick
(C) later
(D) reliable

18. The author would probably most agree with which of the following statements?

(A) Governments should avoid debt at all costs.
(B) The concept of debt is difficult to define precisely.
(C) Creating debt can be potentially risky.
(D) All debt should be backed by some concrete asset.

Practice Test 3

Section 3

Go on to the next page ⟹

19. The phrase "with abandon" in line 22 is closest in meaning to

    (A) in multitude
    (B) recklessly
    (C) stealthily
    (D) with regularity

20. In the final paragraph, the author implies that

    (A) a number of colonies gave up the use of paper money
    (B) gold ultimately became the common form of currency
    (C) sometimes paper money completely lost its value
    (D) many colonies tried to achieve the success of Rhode Island

21. The author would probably agree with which of the following statements?

    (A) Debt can be potentially hazardous.
    (B) The concept of debt is difficult to define.
    (C) Debt should be avoided at all costs.
    (D) All debt should be backed by concrete assets.

Go on to the next page ⇒

Questions 22-30

In the American Civil War, raiders swept through southwestern Missouri and seized a slave mother and her baby on Moses Carver's farm. Moses Carver was able to buy the baby back in exchange for a $300 racehorse, but the child's mother was never returned. Carver gave the motherless child his own family name, "Carver,"
5 and the name of the first American president, George Washington.

Young George Washington Carver was not strong or robust enough to labor in the hot fields, but he did perform household chores. Moreover, in the garden he seemed to have a gift for making the plants grow. He soon left the Carver family in order to get an education and worked his way through high school in Kansas by
10 cooking, washing clothes, and doing odd jobs. When he graduated from high school he did not stop his education but earned his way through college and through agriculture school, receiving a bachelor's and master's degree from the Iowa State College of Agriculture and Mechanic Arts in 1896.

Carver's achievements in the laboratory and in the fields with plants brought
15 him to the attention of Booker T. Washington, founder of Tuskegee Institute in Alabama. Carver became head of Tuskegee's agriculture department in 1896. In his 47 years there the great plant scientist did notable work in scientific agriculture and chemurgy (the industrial use of raw products from plants). He made hundreds of useful products from peanuts and sweet potatoes alone.

22. What is the main topic of this passage?

(A) The scientific accomplishments of George Washington Carver
(B) George Washington Carver's humble beginnings
(C) The life of George Washington Carver
(D) George Washington Carver's struggle for success

23. According to the passage, Moses Carver obtained the infant George Washington Carver by

(A) paying $300
(B) trading a horse
(C) giving away the boy's mother
(D) promising to be a good father

24. The word "seized" in line 2 is closest in meaning to

    (A) rescued
    (B) kidnapped
    (C) purchased
    (D) assaulted

25. The word "robust" in line 6 is closest in meaning to

    (A) motivated
    (B) obedient
    (C) large
    (D) healthy

26. According to the passage, how did George Washington Carver support himself in high school?

    (A) He grew plants and worked in the fields.
    (B) He received help from Moses Carver.
    (C) He did various small jobs.
    (D) He cleaned houses.

27. According to the passage, where did George Washington Carver attend college?

    (A) Missouri
    (B) Iowa
    (C) Alabama
    (D) Kansas

28. The word "there" in line 17 refers to

    (A) in the fields
    (B) Alabama
    (C) Tuskegee's agriculture department
    (D) scientific agriculture

29. The word "notable" in line 17 is closest in meaning to

    (A) original
    (B) important
    (C) award-winning
    (D) necessary

30. It can be concluded from the passage that George Washington Carver

    (A) never knew his mother
    (B) was treated poorly by Moses Carver
    (C) was a superb teacher
    (D) taught himself to read

Go on to the next page ➡

Questions 31-40

It has generally been assumed that fairy tales were first created for children and are largely the domain of children. But nothing could be further from the truth.

From the very beginning, thousands of years ago when tales were told to create communal bonds in the face of the powerful forces of nature, to the present, when
5 fairy tales are written and told to provide hope in a world seemingly on the brink of catastrophe, mature men and women have been the creators and cultivators of the fairy tale tradition. When introduced to fairy tales, children welcome them mainly because they nurture their great desire for change and independence. On the whole, the Western literary fairy tale has become an established genre within a process of
10 Western civilization that cuts across all ages. Even though numerous critics and shamans have mystified and misinterpreted the fairy tale because of their spiritual quest for universal archetypes or their need to save the world through religion, both the oral and the literary forms of the fairy tale are grounded in history: they emerge from specific struggles to humanize bestial and barbaric forces which have terrorized
15 our minds and communities in concrete ways, threatening to destroy free will and human compassion. The fairy tale thus sets out to conquer this concrete terror mainly through the use of metaphors.

Though it is difficult to determine when the first "literary" fairy tales were conceived, and also extremely difficult to define exactly what a fairy tale is, we do
20 know that oral folk tales, which contain wondrous and marvelous elements, have existed for thousands of years and were told largely by adults for adults. Motifs from these, memorized and passed on by word of mouth, made their way into the Bible and the Western classics. The early oral tales that served as the basis for the development of the literary fairy tales were closely tied to the rituals and beliefs of
25 tribes, communities, and trades. They fostered a sense of belonging. They instructed amused, warned, initiated, and enlightened. They were to be shared and exchanged, and unlike the literary tales they subsequently spawned, used and modified according to the needs of the tellers and listeners.

Practice Test 3

Section 3

31. What is the main topic of the passage?

(A) The difference between literary and oral folk tales
(B) The origin and purpose of fairy tales
(C) The modern need for fairy tales
(D) The universal themes of fairy tales

32. According to the author, which of the following is one common misunderstanding of fairy tales?

(A) They were oral before they were written.
(B) They are an unreliable guide to history.
(C) They are intended for children.
(D) They were passed from generation to generation.

33. Which of the following is NOT mentioned as one of the purposes of fairy tales?

(A) To overcome fear of dark, natural forces
(B) To create shared human bonds
(C) To explain the origin of the physical world
(D) To instruct and amuse

34. The word "communal" in line 4 is closest in meaning to

(A) social
(B) valuable
(C) tight
(D) individual

35. The word "catastrophe" in line 6 is closest in meaning to

(A) despair
(B) breakthrough
(C) revelation
(D) disaster

36. In the third paragraph the author implies that

(A) the first fairy tales were written down
(B) some early fairy tales may be found in the Bible
(C) themes from the earliest folk tales have been lost
(D) tellers of folk tales fight over the tales' meanings

37. In the discussion of fairy tales, why does the author mention "metaphor" in line 17?

(A) It is easily understood by adults and children alike.
(B) It is the primary tool utilized to overcome fear.
(C) It conveys concepts more explicitly than usual language.
(D) It is the main means of communicating in Western civilization.

Go on to the next page ⟹

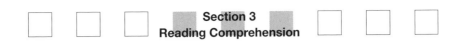

38. The word "conceived" in line 19 is
    closest in meaning to

    (A) invented
    (B) told
    (C) witnessed
    (D) recorded

39. The word "these" in line 22 refers to

    (A) literary fairy tales
    (B) oral folk tales
    (C) elements
    (D) adults

40. With which of the following statements
    would the author most likely agree?

    (A) Folk tales are a form of the
        earliest fine art.
    (B) Fairy tales are essential to
        religious teachings.
    (C) Fairy tales arise from specific
        human conditions.
    (D) Folk tales have largely lost their
        meaning and value.

Practice Test 3

Section 3

Questions 41-50

A dramatic change is underway in the scientific understanding of schizophrenia, a devastating mental illness with 2.5 million victims in the United States alone. The first signs of this disease usually appear when people are in their late 20s, but neuroscientists now believe that the origin of the disorder may actually lie in fetal
5 development during the time when the brain forms and the first nerve cells grow and divide.

The basic flaw in the brains of many schizophrenics seems to be that certain nerve cells migrate to the wrong areas when the brain is first taking shape, leaving small regions of the brain permanently out of place or mis-wired. The out-of-
10 place nerve cells are especially found in the neural subplate, a structure that guides other neurons to their proper sites. The subplate forms about the fourth month of pregnancy and disappears soon after the child is born. These errors in neural architecture may have one or more causes, which remain to be discovered. One speculation, however, is that brain misconnections may occur when the mother
15 catches a virus early in pregnancy.

The chief symptoms of schizophrenia include apathy, a blunting of emotions, delusions, and the hearing of internal voices. Once these appear, they typically wax and wane for the rest of a person's life. The origins of the disorder have long been mysterious. Once attributed to poor communication within families, the
20 condition is now recognized as a disease of the brain. The basis for the changing view of schizophrenia lies in laboratory analysis of tissue samples from the brain. In one recent study, for instance, brain dissections found neurons out of place in the prefrontal areas of 7 out of 20 brains from schizophrenic patients, and none out of place in the 20 brains from normal people.

25 One bothersome question for proponents of the new conception of schizophrenia is why no symptoms of the disease appear for two decades or more if the brain abnormalities are present from birth. One possible answer is that there are indeed signs of coming trouble throughout the early lives of schizophrenics, but that they are commonly overlooked.

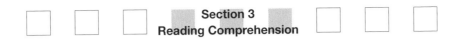

41. What does the passage mainly discuss?

    (A) The symptoms of schizophrenia
    (B) Treatment of schizophrenia
    (C) A new theory of schizophrenia
    (D) The discovery of schizophrenia

42. According to the passage, when do the symptoms of schizophrenia first appear?

    (A) At birth
    (B) Before birth
    (C) In childhood
    (D) During early adulthood

43. Which of the following is most extensively discussed in the second paragraph?

    (A) The structure of the normal human brain
    (B) The ability of the brain to re-locate nerve cells
    (C) The development of a schizophrenic's brain
    (D) The role of heredity in brain formation

44. The word "speculation" in line 14 is closest in meaning to

    (A) conclusion
    (B) hypothesis
    (C) argument
    (D) picture

45. The word "these" in line 17 refers to

    (A) symptoms
    (B) delusions
    (C) voices
    (D) origins

46. The author mentions all of the following as manifestations of schizophrenia EXCEPT

    (A) hearing of internal voices
    (B) apathy
    (C) violent impulses
    (D) delusions

47. In paragraph three the author refers to a laboratory study to illustrate that

    (A) the origins of schizophrenia are mysterious
    (B) victims of schizophrenia have troubled family lives
    (C) schizophrenia is a physical sickness
    (D) healthy people can also develop schizophrenia

48. The phrase "wax and wane" in line 18 can best be replaced by which of the following?

    (A) increase and decrease
    (B) proceed
    (C) grow worse
    (D) appear and disappear

Practice Test 3

Section 3

49. The word "proponents" in line 25 is
   closest in meaning to

   (A) opponents
   (B) critics
   (C) advocates
   (D) victims

50. Which of the following statements is
   best supported by the passage?

   (A) With proper treatment
      schizophrenics can lead
      productive lives.
   (B) Researchers now understand the
      true cause of schizophrenia.
   (C) Schizophrenia will likely become
      more common in the future.
   (D) Mothers may someday be
      screened for schizophrenia-
      causing sicknesses.

Practice Test 4

Section 1
Listening Comprehension

In this section of the test, you will have an opportunity to demonstrate your ability to understand conversations and talks in English. There are three parts to this section with special directions for each part. Answer all the questions on the basis of what is stated or implied by the speakers in this test. Do not turn the pages until you are told to do so.

Part A

Directions: In Part A you will hear short conversations between two people. After each conversation, you will hear a question about the conversation. The conversations and questions will not be repeated. After you hear a question, read the four possible answers in your book and choose the best answer. Then, on your answer sheet, find the number of the question and fill in the space that corresponds to the letter of the answer you have chosen.

Listen to an example.

On the recording, you hear:
What does the woman think the class should do?
In your book, you read: (A) Present Professor Smith with a picture
　　　　　　　　　　(B) Photograph Professor Smith
　　　　　　　　　　(C) Put glass over the photograph
　　　　　　　　　　(D) Replace the broken headlight

Sample Answer

　　From the conversation you learn that the woman thinks Professor Smith would like a photograph of the class. The best answer to the question, "What does the woman think the class should do?" is (A), "Present Professor Smith with a picture." Therefore, the correct choice is (A).

Practice Test 4

Section 1
Part A
Part B
Part C

Wait

155

mp3 **176-180**

1. What does the man imply about Kathy?
   (A) She is opening a new business.
   (B) She hopes to get two degrees.
   (C) She is no longer studying psychology.
   (D) She has given up on college.

2. What can be inferred from this conversation?
   (A) The woman has already loaned money to the man.
   (B) The woman is not available this weekend.
   (C) The man would like to pay the woman back.
   (D) The man is very careful about his budget.

3. What does the man mean?
   (A) The woman should not talk about that now.
   (B) The woman should apply for a different job.
   (C) He would like the woman to tell him about it later.
   (D) He is pleased about what the woman told him.

4. What does the man want?
   (A) To look at the newspaper
   (B) To speak with the woman
   (C) To help the woman fill in the form
   (D) To borrow the woman's dictionary

5. What does the man imply about Susan?
   (A) She decided to drop out of school.
   (B) She is working more than before.
   (C) She is not a very dedicated student.
   (D) She is applying for another scholarship.

mp3 **181-185**

6. What does the woman mean?
    (A) The renovation has not started.
    (B) She did not read the report.
    (C) The dorm has not been built yet.
    (D) She has moved to the ground floor.

7. What does the man mean?
    (A) There is only one student recreation center.
    (B) He is not the right person to ask.
    (C) The center probably opens at 1 o'clock.
    (D) This is the only recreation center open on Sunday.

8. What does the man mean?
    (A) He is ahead in his course reading.
    (B) He is pleased with his decision.
    (C) He did not change his major.
    (D) He regrets what he did.

9. What does the man imply?
    (A) He will be happy to give the woman a hand.
    (B) Men cannot enter the women's dormitory.
    (C) The woman should follow the housing policies.
    (D) The refrigerator is too heavy to carry.

10. What does the woman imply?
    (A) The man should check his pockets again.
    (B) The car should not be parked in that place.
    (C) The man forgot the keys in the car.
    (D) She will help the man find what he is looking for.

Practice Test 4

Section 1
Part A
Part B
Part C

mp3 186-190

11. What does the man imply?

 (A) He is rather busy.
 (B) He forgot about the picnic.
 (C) He will accept the woman's invitation.
 (D) He will be out of town this weekend.

12. What does the woman imply?

 (A) The man does not believe she has a chemistry lab.
 (B) She already told the man about the course.
 (C) She does not care for chemistry.
 (D) Many labs are required for her class.

13. What does the woman mean?

 (A) She will continue to drive very carefully.
 (B) They will still arrive in time.
 (C) She would like the man to drive.
 (D) The weather conditions will improve soon.

14. What can be inferred about Jack?

 (A) He is still rather upset.
 (B) He is running a temperature.
 (C) He has not been to work lately.
 (D) He is feeling a lot better.

15. What does the man imply about the woman?

 (A) She does not help out much around the house.
 (B) She cannot study when it's too noisy.
 (C) She needs to get the vacuum cleaner fixed.
 (D) She can do her studying later in the day.

                    Go on to the next page ➡

16. What does the woman mean?

  (A) She agrees to go there together.
  (B) She usually eats at another restaurant.
  (C) She shares the man's opinion.
  (D) She thinks the regular chef is a poor cook.

17. What does the man mean?

  (A) All the CD's were sold out.
  (B) He has become a fan of that artist.
  (C) He prefers listening to music live.
  (D) The artist has released no new albums.

18. What does the woman imply?

  (A) They should turn up the heater.
  (B) It is time to eat breakfast now.
  (C) It is very hot outside.
  (D) The man should check the frying pan.

19. What can be inferred about the man's lecture notes?

  (A) The woman should return them.
  (B) He cannot seem to find them.
  (C) Tim's notes are better than his.
  (D) Another student is using them now.

20. What does the man imply about the woman?

  (A) She is lucky she could take the class.
  (B) She should think about changing her major.
  (C) She is enrolled in an unusually difficult course.
  (D) She should try to meet more people.

Practice Test 4

Section 1

Part A
Part B
Part C

Go on to the next page **159**

mp3 196-200

21. What does the woman imply about the man?
    (A) He recently inherited a lot of money.
    (B) He usually does not offer to pay for dinner.
    (C) He does not often cook dinner for her.
    (D) He spends too much money on the lottery.

22. What will the man probably do?
    (A) Stay home and rest
    (B) Write a letter to his mother
    (C) Visit his family
    (D) Go to the doctor's office

23. What does the man imply?
    (A) The professor is being unreasonable.
    (B) The woman should have been more punctual.
    (C) The professor was not clear about the deadline.
    (D) The woman will not really fail the class.

24. What is the woman's problem?
    (A) She had a fight with her friend.
    (B) Her computer needs to be repaired.
    (C) She lost the file she was working on.
    (D) She cannot decide on a topic for her paper.

25. What will the man probably do?
    (A) Turn on the air conditioner
    (B) Take the car in for servicing
    (C) Get out of the car and walk
    (D) Roll down the windows

                                        Go on to the next page ⇒

mp3 **201-205**

26. What does the woman imply?
    (A) The man does not need to dress so formally.
    (B) The man's interview is not today.
    (C) The man should wear a different necktie.
    (D) The man could find a better job.

27. What had the man assumed?
    (A) The woman did not attend the play.
    (B) The woman arrived late to her theater class.
    (C) The department's production rate has fallen.
    (D) The theater construction is behind schedule.

28. What can be inferred from this conversation about the man and woman?
    (A) They are angry with each other.
    (B) They have never visited this place before.
    (C) They are on vacation in Mexico.
    (D) They are eating in a restaurant.

29. What does the woman imply?
    (A) She canceled her camping trip.
    (B) It was much colder than she had expected.
    (C) She prefers skiing to camping.
    (D) The man does not believe they really went.

30. What does the man mean?
    (A) He does not agree with the woman.
    (B) He will not be able to attend the lecture.
    (C) He wishes they could stay longer.
    (D) He also enjoyed the lecture.

Practice Test 4

Section 1

Part A
Part B
Part C

Go on to the next page

NO TEST MATERIAL ON THIS PAGE.

Part B

Directions: In this part, you will hear longer conversations. After each conversation, you will hear several questions. The conversations and questions will not be repeated.

After you hear a question, read the four possible answers in your book and choose the best answer. Then, on your answer sheet, find the number of the question and fill in the space that corresponds to the letter of the answer you have chosen.

Wait

Practice Test 4

Section 1
Part A
Part B
Part C

mp3 207-211

31. What position is the woman running for?
    (A) Captain of the debate team
    (B) Student representative
    (C) Student council president
    (D) Director of the radio station

32. Where do the man and woman plan to take out advertisements?
    (A) On the college radio
    (B) In the cafeteria
    (C) In the student newspaper
    (D) On the campus TV station

33. When will the woman speak to students outside the cafeteria?
    (A) Before breakfast
    (B) At lunch
    (C) During the afternoon
    (D) After dinner

34. What will the man and woman do next?
    (A) Make a budget
    (B) Draw a poster
    (C) Stop at the student union
    (D) Call the radio station

mp3 212-216

35. Who may live in Cooper Hall?
    (A) Only female students
    (B) Only male students
    (C) Only international students
    (D) Only sophomores, juniors, and seniors

36. What special regulations are in effect for Morris Hall?
    (A) Visitors must register at the front desk.
    (B) There is a curfew on school nights.
    (C) There is a quiet time after midnight.
    (D) No parties are permitted in the dormitory.

37. What advice does the director of Student Housing give to the man?
    (A) He should send in his application as soon as possible.
    (B) He should try to find off-campus housing.
    (C) He should wait to hear from her office before he applies.
    (D) He should send in an application form to each dormitory.

38. Which dormitory is the student eligible to live in?
    (A) Franklin Hall
    (B) Morris Hall
    (C) Fennel Hall
    (D) Cooper Hall

Part C

Directions: In this part, you will hear several talks. After each talk, you will hear some questions. The talks and questions will not be repeated. After you hear a question, read the four possible answers in your book and choose the best answer. Then, on your answer sheet, find the number of the question and fill in the space that corresponds to the letter of the answer you have chosen.

Here is an example.
On the recording, you hear:

Now listen to a sample question.

Sample Answer

In your book, you read: Why are gas balloons considered dangerous?
        (A) They are impossible to guide.
        (B) They may go up in flames.
        (C) They tend to leak gas.
        (D) They are cheaply made.

The best answer to the question, "Why are gas balloons considered dangerous?" is (B), "They may go up in flames." Therefore, the correct choice is (B).

Now listen to another sample question.

Sample Answer

In your book, you read: According to the speaker, what must balloon pilots be
        careful to do?
        (A) Watch for changes in weather
        (B) Watch their altitude
        (C) Check for weak spots in their balloons
        (D) Test the strength of the ropes

The best answer to the question, "According to the speaker, what must balloon pilots be careful to do?" is (A), "Watch for changes in weather." Therefore, the correct choice is (A).

Practice Test 4

Section 1
Part A
Part B
Part C

Wait

165

Section 1
Listening Comprehension

mp3 218-222

39. What was the subject of last week's lecture?

(A) Railway station architecture
(B) The origins of rail travel
(C) Future trends in railroading
(D) Railroads and economic development

40. What period of history does the speaker point to as being the high point in American railroading?

(A) The early 20th century
(B) The late 19th century
(C) The middle 20th century
(D) The late 20th century

41. According to the speaker, why did railroads slide into neglect?

(A) Transcontinental trains were too expensive to operate.
(B) Train stations were uncomfortable and unsafe.
(C) The government discontinued its financial support.
(D) Other forms of transportation were more attractive.

42. How does the speaker view the future of rail travel in the United States?

(A) Mainly pessimistic
(B) Essentially neutral
(C) Cautiously optimistic
(D) Extremely enthusiastic

mp3 223-227

43. For whom is this announcement primarily intended?

(A) High school seniors
(B) University freshmen
(C) College sophomores
(D) Professional musicians

44. What is special about the Brixton College orchestra?

(A) It is entirely run by students.
(B) People in the community can join.
(C) It has a world-famous conductor.
(D) Members receive college credit.

45. How often does the orchestra meet to rehearse?

(A) Every day after class
(B) Only on weekends
(C) Three times a week
(D) Twice a month

46. What type of music will the orchestra mainly play at its next concert?

(A) Traditional classical music
(B) Easy listening selections
(C) Arrangements of popular tunes
(D) Ethnic folk music

Go on to the next page

mp3 228-232

47. Who is giving this talk?
   - (A) A professional beekeeper
   - (B) A zoology professor
   - (C) A student in a biology class
   - (D) A guide in a science museum

48. According to the speaker, what is the most important function of the queen bee?
   - (A) Laying eggs
   - (B) Managing other bees
   - (C) Protecting the hive
   - (D) Making honey

49. What is pheromone?
   - (A) A substance which inhibits reproduction
   - (B) A hormone which promotes rapid growth
   - (C) A hormone which triggers sexual activity
   - (D) A substance which provides basic nutrition

50. What happens to worker bees who have not mated?
   - (A) They stop working in a normal manner.
   - (B) They are unable to produce female offspring.
   - (C) They attempt to attack the queen.
   - (D) They cease laying any more eggs.

This is the end of Section 1.
Stop work on Section 1.

Do NOT read or work on any other section of the test.
Your supervisor will tell you when to begin working on Section 2.

Practice Test 4

Section 1
Part A
Part B
Part C

NO TEST MATERIAL ON THIS PAGE.

Section 2
Structure and Written Expression
Time: 25 minutes

This section is designed to measure your ability to recognize language that is appropriate for standard written English. There are two types of questions in this section, with special directions for each type.

Structure

Directions: Questions 1-15 are incomplete sentences. Beneath each sentence you will see four words or phrases, marked (A), (B), (C), and (D). Choose the one word or phrase that best completes the sentence. Then, on your answer sheet, find the number of the question and fill in the space that corresponds to the letter of the answer you have chosen.

Example I

Vegetables are an excellent source ---------- vitamins.

(A) of
(B) has
(C) where
(D) that

Sample Answer

The sentence should read, "Vegetables are an excellent source of vitamins." Therefore, you should choose (A).

Example II

---------- in history when remarkable progress was made within a relatively short span of time.

(A) Periods
(B) Throughout periods
(C) There have been periods
(D) Periods have been

Sample Answer

The sentence should read, "There have been periods in history when remarkable progress was made within a relatively short span of time." Therefore, you should choose (C).

Now begin work on the questions.

Go on to the next page

Practice Test 4

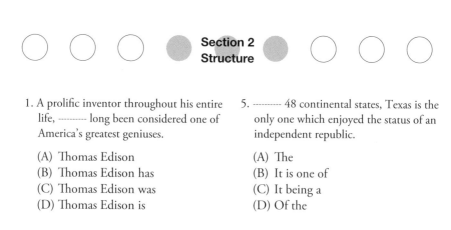

1. A prolific inventor throughout his entire life, ---------- long been considered one of America's greatest geniuses.

(A) Thomas Edison
(B) Thomas Edison has
(C) Thomas Edison was
(D) Thomas Edison is

2. In landscape gardening, the ---------- is created by the careful placement of trees, rocks, and shrubs.

(A) impression of space
(B) space impressing
(C) impressions space
(D) impress of space

3. Although it has not been conclusively proven, many historians believe the first Europeans to arrive in America ---------- .

(A) were the Vikings
(B) had been the Vikings
(C) was Vikings
(D) they were Vikings

4. Born a slave, George Washington Carver worked his way through high school and college and later ---------- as a plant scientist.

(A) gained acclaim international
(B) gained international acclaim
(C) internationally to have gained acclaim
(D) acclaim gained internationally

5. ---------- 48 continental states, Texas is the only one which enjoyed the status of an independent republic.

(A) The
(B) It is one of
(C) It being a
(D) Of the

6. ---------- the tiger is popularly considered a jungle cat, less than a century ago it flourished as far north as Siberia.

(A) Nonetheless
(B) Because
(C) Even though
(D) Despite

7. Red skies in the evening often indicate that the next day ---------- fair.

(A) would be probably
(B) probably be
(C) probably will be
(D) it probably is

8. Uranium does not occur in pure form but ---------- from uranium-rich ore.

(A) it must extracted
(B) must be extracted
(C) must extract
(D) extractable it must be

9. The heavier a gas is, ---------- throughout the entire volume of its container.

(A) it more slowly diffuses
(B) it diffuses more slowly
(C) the more slowly it diffuses
(D) more slowly its diffusing

Go on to the next page ➡

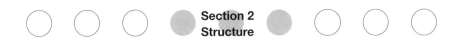
10. The cause of the mass extinction of the dinosaurs is something on which ---------- agreement among scientists.

(A) is little
(B) there is little
(C) little
(D) there is few

11. When the Federal Reserve Bank raises the prime interest rate, ---------- to other banks, interest rates throughout the economy rise.

(A) it is the rate at which money loans
(B) the rate at which it loans money
(C) the rate which money is loaned
(D) the money rate which loans

12. Large primates ---------- human beings are called anthropoids.

(A) resemble
(B) which resembles
(C) they resemble
(D) that resemble

13. A written argument can be made far more ---------- when concrete examples are included to support it.

(A) persuadable
(B) persuaded
(C) persuade
(D) persuasive

14. Most states demand that a citizen ---------- within state boundaries for at least one year in order to be considered a legal resident.

(A) resides
(B) reside
(C) to reside
(D) residing

15. Parasites are chiefly remarkable for their ability ---------- to the conditions of their host.

(A) it adapts them
(B) to their adaptation
(C) to adapt themselves
(D) they adapt

Practice Test 4

Section 2

Structure
Written
Expression

Go on to the next page 171

NO TEST MATERIAL ON THIS PAGE.

Written Expression

Directions: In questions 16-40 each sentence has four underlined words or phrases. The four underlined parts of the sentence are marked (A), (B), (C), and (D). Identify the one underlined word or phrase that must be changed in order for the sentence to be correct. Then, on your answer sheet, find the number of the question and fill in the space that corresponds to the letter of the answer you have chosen.

Example I

A ray of light passing <u>through</u> <u>the center of</u>
                A   B

a thin lens <u>maintain</u> its <u>original</u> direction.
          C   D

Sample Answer

Ⓐ Ⓑ ● Ⓓ

The sentence should read, " A ray of light passing through the center of a thin lens maintains its original direction." Therefore, you should choose (C).

Example II

The mandolin, a musical <u>instrument</u> <u>that has</u> strings,
                           A   B

was probably copied <u>from</u> the lute, a <u>many</u> older instrument.
             C   D

Sample Answer

Ⓐ Ⓑ Ⓒ ●

The sentence should read, "The mandolin, a musical instrument that has strings, was probably copied from the lute, a <u>much</u> older instrument." Therefore, you should choose (D).

Now begin work on the questions.

Practice Test 4

Section 2

Structure

Written
Expression

173

16. Although <u>it</u> may vary slightly during the day, <u>human</u> body temperature
        A   B
remains <u>relative</u> constant <u>at</u> 37.0 degrees Celsius.
        C   D

17. The pineapple is <u>actually</u> a cluster of fruits <u>that unite</u> to form a whole as <u>did</u>
                A   B   C
blackberries <u>and</u> raspberries.
          D

18. The early American realists painted in <u>such a way</u> that <u>their</u> pictures seemed
                                     A   B
<u>if as</u> they were more <u>real than</u> photographs.
  C   D

19. A political convention <u>is</u> a gathering of members of a <u>political party</u> <u>for</u> the
                            A   B   C
purpose of choosing leaders or <u>adopt platforms</u>.
                                    D

20. A blow torch <u>is</u> a high-temperature <u>flames</u> <u>used</u> to melt and <u>fuse</u> metal.
            A   B   C   D

21. Color, <u>transparency</u>, and weight <u>are</u> the qualities <u>by which</u> fine porcelain
            A   B   C
<u>judged</u>.
  D

22. Indian arrowheads, <u>they</u> are still <u>commonly found</u> on <u>sites</u> where Native
                           A   B   C
Americans <u>once lived</u>.
          D

23. The Spanish language <u>provided</u> the common ground <u>for</u> Hispanics to unite
                           A   B
<u>ourselves</u> politically <u>during</u> the 1980's.
    C   D

24. Some <u>varieties</u> of carp can survive <u>until to</u> three months <u>when</u> covered in cold,
         A   B   C
<u>moist</u> mud.
  D

25. Aerobic <u>exercise</u> increases muscle tone, <u>raises</u> the metabolic <u>rate</u>, and <u>strength</u>
         A   B   C   D

    the heart.

26. Without <u>accurate</u> projections of future earnings, <u>a company</u> can expend its
              A   B

    budget such that there <u>was</u> not enough money <u>to cover</u> even fixed expenses.
                               C   D

27. In the <u>latter</u> half of the 20th century, <u>a</u> widespread information was made
            A   B

    <u>available</u> by a highly sophisticated global <u>telecommunications</u> network.
       C   D

28. The Boston Museum of Fine Art, <u>known</u> for its fine modern collections, also
                                   A

    <u>attract</u> many art lovers with <u>its</u> early <u>American paintings</u>.
      B   C   D

29. William Fulbright, Senator of Arkansas, was <u>one of</u> the first of <u>him</u> generation
                                      A   B

    to <u>criticize</u> American <u>foreign</u> policy.
       C   D

30. The <u>ancient</u> Appalachian Mountains of the eastern United States <u>first</u> emerged
         A   B

    <u>before</u> more than 200 million years <u>ago</u> during the Permian period.
      C   D

31. Because of <u>its</u> rhythm and sound, poetry <u>has</u> traditionally been considered one
              A   B

    of the best <u>ways</u> to <u>expression</u> deep feelings.
             C   D

32. The cotton gin, <u>invented</u> just <u>prior</u> to the Civil War, <u>was</u> one of the most
                 A   B   C

    important agricultural <u>breakthrough</u> of the 19th century.
                        D

33. <u>The</u> three types of materials <u>expelled by</u> volcanoes <u>are</u> lava, gases, and
      A   B   C

    <u>there are also</u> solid rock fragments.
      D

34. The cowboy ballad, made popular during the nation's westward expansion,
       A   B   C
    had it origin in medieval songs.
         D

35. The widely respect jurist Thurgood Marshall was a leading civil rights attorney
             A   B   C
    prior to his appointment to the Supreme Court.
                D

36. Clothing made from natural fibers such as cotton and wool are often warmer,
              A   B   C
    stronger, and cheaper than that made from synthetic fibers.
           D

37. A particle accelerator is the indispensable means of which much of the research
    A   B   C
    of quantum physics is now conducted.
                D

38. Gilsonite is an extremely pure form of asphalt that is used in the manufacture
             A   B   C
    of both paints as well as varnishes.
            D

39. Many skin specialists are skeptical of the claim that diet is the main factor in
           A   B   C
    skin healthy.
        D

40. Among the prominent characteristics of scientific discourse are detachment,
     A   B   C
    object, and abstraction.
     D

This is the end of Section 2.
If you finish before time is called, check your work on Section 2 only.

| Stop | Stop | Stop | Stop | Stop | Stop | Stop |

Do NOT read or work on any other section of the test.
Your supervisor will tell you when to begin working on Section 3.

Section 3
Reading Comprehension
Time: 55 minutes

Directions: In this section you will read several passages. Each one is followed by several questions about it. For questions 1-50, you are to choose the one best answer, (A), (B), (C), or (D), to each question. Then, on your answer sheet, find the number of the question and fill in the space that corresponds to the letter of the answer you have chosen.

Answer all questions following a passage on the basis of what is stated or implied in that passage.

Read the following passage:

> The rattles with which a rattlesnake warns of its presence are formed by loosely interlocking hollow rings of hard skin, which make a buzzing sound when its tail is shaken. As a baby, the snake begins to form its rattles from the button at the very tip of its tail. Thereafter, each time it sheds its skin, a new ring is formed. Popular belief holds that a snake's age can be told by counting the rings, but this idea is fallacious. In fact, a snake may lose its old skin as often as four times a year. Also, rattles tend to wear or break off with time.

Example I
A rattlesnake's rattles are made out of
(A) skin
(B) bone
(C) wood
(D) muscle

Sample Answer

 Ⓐ Ⓑ Ⓒ Ⓓ

According to the passage, a rattlesnake's rattles are made out of rings of hard skin. Therefore, you should choose (A).

Example II
How often does a rattlesnake shed its skin?
(A) Once every four years
(B) Once every four months
(C) Up to four times annually
(D) Four times more often than other snakes

Sample Answer

Ⓐ Ⓑ Ⓓ

The phrase states that "a snake may lose its old skin as often as four times a year." Therefore, you should choose (C).

Now begin work on the questions.

177

Questions 1-8

A difference in the ability to tolerate pain is not the only gender myth to be debunked by recent research. A cursory look at the most commonly utilized statistics on gender and crime reveals an enormous imbalance in the ratio of men and women in prison in all industrialized nations. As a result, another commonly accepted
5 dictum is that males are much more likely to commit crimes than are females. In reality, though, the actual gender difference in crime rates may be less than the official statistics show.

"Lost letters" experiments have provided an interesting source of information about gender, opportunity, and crime. In these experiments, letters enclosing
10 money were dropped in public places. Various conditions were altered in differing versions — the amount of money involved, whether it was in cash or another form (like a money order), and the apparent loser (an old lady or an affluent man). The characteristics of the individuals who picked up the letters were observed and the researchers could tell from code numbers whether they were posted or kept. These
15 studies showed that stealing the money was most common when the apparent victim was an affluent man and cash was involved, but females were just as likely to steal as males, except where larger sums of money were concerned, where males were twice as likely to keep the money. It seems possible that pocketing a small amount of cash is not seen as "stealing," while taking a large amount is — and that men are more
20 prepared to profit in this way.

The only crime for which the female rate of conviction approximates that of men is shoplifting. Some have argued that this indicates that women will engage in criminal activities where they find themselves in a public context, for example out shopping, rather than a domestic one. In other words, where the opportunity to
25 commit crime is more or less equal, men and women are equally likely to commit offenses.

Yet, it cannot be disputed that there are some important contrasts between the types of crimes men and women commit, since the reported offenses of women rarely involve violence. As a result, police and other officials might perhaps regard female
30 offenders as less dangerous than men, and consequently let pass certain activities for which males might be arrested.

Go on to the next page ➡

1. What is the main point of this passage?

 (A) Women and men have different notions of what constitutes "stealing."
 (B) Women are by nature less prone to violence than men.
 (C) Gender is the deciding factor in the tendency to commit crime.
 (D) Gender differences are often overstated in accounting for crime.

2. The word "imbalance" in line 3 is closest in meaning to

 (A) disparity
 (B) unfairness
 (C) improbability
 (D) inconsistency

3. Why does the author use the phrase "tolerate pain" in line 1?

 (A) Pain is something that cannot be easily be quantified.
 (B) Men are better able to endure the pain of imprisonment than women.
 (C) The notion that men are more susceptible to pain has been shown to be false.
 (D) Men are more subject to pain in industrialized nations.

4. Which of the following was shown by the "lost letters" experiments?

 (A) Preconceived notions of male and female criminal tendencies were essentially correct.
 (B) The economic status of the apparent victim played an important role.
 (C) Men tend to profit much more from crime than do women.
 (D) Women are more likely to be arrested for shoplifting than are men.

5. The word "altered" in line 10 is closest in meaning to

 (A) modified
 (B) disguised
 (C) avoided
 (D) posited

6. The word "they" in line 14 refers to

 (A) researchers
 (B) code numbers
 (C) letters
 (D) individuals

7. The word "rarely" in line 28 is closest in meaning to

 (A) hardly
 (B) plausibly
 (C) seldom
 (D) unlikely

Practice Test 4

Section 3

8. Which of the following statements is implied by the passage?

(A) Women tend to avoid committing crimes outside the domestic setting.
(B) Men are more likely to admit their offenses than women.
(C) Women are actually more violent than is commonly assumed.
(D) Police tend to be more tolerant of crimes committed by women.

Questions 9-19

During World War II a number of European painters immigrated to the United States, where they had a profound effect on young painters. After the war, a group of these artists initiated a movement that became famous throughout the world and served as a model for artists everywhere. Called abstract expressionists (or sometimes
5   "action painters"), they produced works that were large in scale, energetic in effect, and highly individualistic in character. The movement especially flourished in the 1950s when the United States entered a period of great economic and political expansion. Therefore, the works of the abstract expressionists convey the strength and confidence of a powerful country, and yet they are nonetheless private statements
10   proclaiming the importance of the individual in the face of pressures for uniformity and depersonalization. The advent of abstract expressionism was important for another reason as well: the United States became, for the first time in its history, the center of the Western art world.

Jackson Pollock was one of the first of the abstract expressionists to achieve
15   prominence, and "Blue Poles" is an example of his mature work. A large canvas (about five meters long), it is punctuated by eight dark-blue slender and generally vertical forms. The remainder of the canvas is covered with a tangle of lines of various colors of paint that are thick, thin, light, dark, smooth, jagged, warm, or cool. The picture has no center of interest, unlike most traditional paintings; every part is about
20   as interesting as every other part, and the forms extend with undiminished vigor to the very edge of the canvas. Pollock applied the pigment in an unusual manner: he laid the canvas on the floor and poured the paint on it, changing color, type, and thickness of paint as the work progressed. The lines of the pigment, therefore, reflect the movements of his arm and body as he applied the paint; thus the activity of
25   painting became part of the painting itself. The impression is one of spontaneity and tremendous energy. When Pollock's paintings were first exhibited, his method of painting was greeted with expressions of scorn. But he had supporters as well, and his influence has been enormous.

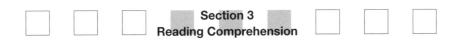
9. What is the author's main point?

(A) America's post-war economy was also reflected in the nation's art.
(B) Jackson Pollock developed into a very talented painter.
(C) Abstract expressionism was a significant art movement.
(D) The method of painting Jackson Pollock used was distinctly original.

10. According to the passage, one of the principal origins of the abstract expressionist movement was

(A) World War I
(B) immigrant painters
(C) economic expansion
(D) artistic rebellion

11. Abstraction expressionism most flourished during which of the following times?

(A) During World War II
(B) Prior to World War II
(C) In the 1960s
(D) In the 1950s

12. The word "profound" in line 2 is closest in meaning to

(A) astonishing
(B) deep
(C) fleeting
(D) sudden

13. The word "uniformity" in line 10 is closest in meaning to

(A) sameness
(B) expression
(C) submission
(D) progress

14. In paragraph one, the author implies that

(A) abstract expressionism was more imaginative than other art movements
(B) art cannot thrive without generous financial support
(C) most abstract expressionist painters were born in the United States
(D) economics and art are related

15. According to the passage, one of the most important consequences of abstract expressionism was that it

(A) limited the influence of Jackson Pollock
(B) made America prominent in the art world
(C) shifted art away from representation
(D) created a whole new world of color

Practice Test 4

Section 3

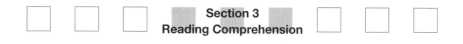
16. Why does the author mention "Blue Poles" in line 15?

   (A) To exemplify Pollock's early attempts at abstract expressionism
   (B) To emphasize the size of paintings of abstract expressionists
   (C) To provide a representative sample of abstract expressionist art
   (D) To show how much Pollock developed as an artist as he matured

17. The word "vertical" in line 17 is closest in meaning to

   (A) glowing
   (B) prominent
   (C) vague
   (D) upright

18. In contrast to traditional paintings, Jackson Pollock's paintings

   (A) are less vigorous in color and form
   (B) have no visual center
   (C) are made from a new kind of paint
   (D) include more distinct images

19. The author organizes the discussion according to what principle?

   (A) An argument supported by a series of examples
   (B) A classification of several types
   (C) General description followed by an illustration
   (D) An explanation that precedes a summary

Go on to the next page ➡

Questions 20-31

Boontling is the name given by its speakers to a deliberately contrived jargon which was spoken extensively between 1880 and 1920 in the upper Anderson Valley of Mendocino County, California. This name, an abbreviated, self-explaining compound, is itself a typical word in the jargon. "Boont" is the local term for
5   Boonville, the largest town in the valley, and "ling" is short for lingo. Boontling, then, is the lingo of Boonville.

This "local language," which reached the zenith of its development during the first decade of the 20th century, contains a basic lexicon of more than one thousand unique words and phrases, in addition to several hundred specialized names for local
10   residents and for prominent geographical features of the area. It was at one time spoken and understood by most of the people in the isolated rural valley of which Boonville was the focal point. Although the grammar and sounds of Boontling are almost identical to English, the extensive use of obscure words makes Boontling virtually incomprehensible to anyone not closely familiar with it. At that time, the
15   local residents took great glee in the fact that those few outsiders who ventured into the Anderson Valley were thoroughly unable to understand them. In fact, Boontling became a symbol of their identity, a badge of membership in a close-knit community. Though the lingo has ceased to play the important role it once had in Anderson Valley life, it is still remembered and spoken among old-timers and
20   is studied and developed by members of more recent generations who enjoy and cultivate the traditions of their valley forebears.

One is tempted to say that for Boontling "context is everything." Certainly, if it is not everything, it is nearly everything. This local dialect is so intimately related to the valley itself and to the people who spoke it that one cannot begin fully to
25   understand and appreciate this special lingo without knowing the social context in some detail. Before taking up this sociological background, however, it is necessary to examine the physical features of the region. The role that the unique topography of the valley has played in shaping the local society cannot be denied. Surrounded by steep-sloped hills, until the 1950s the valley had only one road going in and out.

Practice Test 4

20. What is the purpose of the first paragraph of this passage?

(A) To indicate the origin of the name Boontling
(B) To show the location of Boonville
(C) To introduce the Anderson Valley
(D) To give an example of a word in Boontling

21. The author uses the expression "local language" in line 7 to indicate that Boontling is NOT

(A) so difficult to understand sometimes
(B) really a language in the standard sense
(C) as localized as is commonly thought
(D) so different from standard English

22. The word "lexicon" in line 8 is closest in meaning to

(A) diction
(B) array
(C) complement
(D) vocabulary

23. It can be inferred from the passage that Boontling

(A) developed naturally from native languages spoken in the region
(B) was specifically and purposefully created by local residents
(C) is in jeopardy of dying out due to lack of interest
(D) is symbolic of old traditions that are no longer respected

24. The word "virtually" in line 14 is closest in meaning to

(A) practically
(B) somewhat
(C) partially
(D) certainly

25. It can be inferred from the passage that the most widespread use of Boontling would likely have been in

(A) 1880
(B) 1895
(C) 1905
(D) 1920

26. The word "them" in line 16 refers to

(A) obscure words
(B) local residents
(C) outsiders
(D) sounds

Go on to the next page ➡

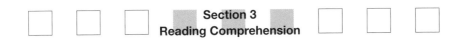

27. The author implies that the main reason why Boontling developed as it did was because

    (A) the Anderson Valley itself was not easily accessible
    (B) people in the Anderson Valley welcomed outsiders
    (C) there were so few people in the Anderson Valley
    (D) most residents of the Anderson Valley were elderly

28. According to the passage, why is Boontling so difficult for most people to understand?

    (A) It contains many non-standard sounds.
    (B) It uses many unfamiliar words.
    (C) It is indirect and contextually based.
    (D) It has an unusual grammatical structure.

29. The word "intimately" in line 23 is closest in meaning to

    (A) falsely
    (B) emotionally
    (C) closely
    (D) apparently

30. Which of the following is true of Boontling?

    (A) It requires a deep knowledge of Boonville's social context.
    (B) It is now spoken even by people outside the Anderson Valley.
    (C) It contains words from original Native American residents.
    (D) It has never been systematically analyzed by linguists.

31. It can be inferred that the land forms of the Anderson Valley contributed to the early development of Boontling because

    (A) they limited the amount of outside influence
    (B) the infertile soil forced local residents to work together closely
    (C) the steep-sloped hills made people live in close proximity
    (D) it was difficult for local residents to get outside supplies

Practice Test 4

Questions 32-41

Over thousands of years, in billions of transactions by millions of people, many commodities have been used as money: stones, salt, cattle, and seashells among them. But wherever gold was available, it tended to surpass other media of exchange. Like any successful currency, gold never needed to be appointed as "legal tender" by a
5   government; it was recognized as the most desirable money by common consent because of its unique properties.

These qualities of money were identified as early as the fifth century B.C. by Aristotle and still remain true today — especially for gold.

First, money must be durable. It must not evaporate, mildew, rust, crumble,
10   break, or rot. Gold, more than any other solid element, is chemically inert. This is why foodstuffs, oil, or artwork can't be used for money. Second, it must be divisible. One ounce of gold — whether bullion, coin, or dust — is worth exactly 1/100th of one hundred ounces. In contrast, when a diamond is split, its value is destroyed, and you can't easily make change from a piece of land. Third, money must be convenient.
15   Gold allows its owners to physically bring the wealth of a lifetime with them. Real estate stays where it is. And an equivalent value of copper, lead, zinc, silver, and most other metals would be too heavy to carry. Fourth, a currency or coin has to be consistent. Only one grade exists for 24 carat gold, so there is no danger of owning 24 carat gold in differing qualities. Twenty-four carat gold is the same in every time
20   and place since gold is a natural element, unlike gems, artwork, land, grain, or other commodities. Fifth, money, at least ideally, should have intrinsic value. Each year there are new industrial uses found for gold. Of all metals, it is the most malleable (able to be shaped) and least reactive (able to withstand sea water, air, and acid without being damaged).
25   Obviously, these qualities make gold very useful, entirely apart from its value as jewelry through the last 5,000 years. It is also important to remember that gold is one of the 92 natural elements and possesses some unique chemical properties, though arguments that its value is therefore "mystical" are hard to regard as anything but silly.

Go on to the next page ⟹

32. What is the main purpose of the passage?

   (A) To describe the specific qualities of gold
   (B) To define various kinds of money
   (C) To outline the evolution of money
   (D) To explain why gold is valuable

33. Which of the following is NOT mentioned as a commodity that has been used as money?

   (A) seashells
   (B) beads
   (C) salt
   (D) livestock

34. According to the author, why has the value of gold remained independent of its designation as an official currency?

   (A) All money has traditionally been based on gold.
   (B) People agree that gold itself is precious.
   (C) The supply of gold is less than the demand.
   (D) Gold has always been needed to make fine jewelry.

35. The word "surpass" in line 3 is closest in meaning to

   (A) replace
   (B) devalue
   (C) exceed
   (D) speed up

36. The word "it" in line 11 refers to

   (A) gold
   (B) money
   (C) artwork
   (D) one ounce

37. According to the passage, why are commodities such as foodstuffs, oil, and artwork unsuitable to be used as money?

   (A) Their value varies widely.
   (B) They cannot be used immediately.
   (C) They do not necessarily last a long time.
   (D) They are unable to be transported.

38. In paragraph three, the author compares diamonds to gold in order to illustrate which of the following points?

   (A) Diamonds are usually overvalued.
   (B) Gold can be divided into smaller quantities.
   (C) Gold is easier to transport than diamonds.
   (D) Diamonds are not as durable as gold.

39. The word "gems" in line 20 is closest in meaning to

   (A) jewelry
   (B) rare ores
   (C) coins
   (D) precious stones

Practice Test 4

40. The word "intrinsic" in line 21 is closest in meaning to

    (A) inherent
    (B) unusual
    (C) obvious
    (D) practical

41. Which of the following statements is best supported by the passage?

    (A) The value of gold is closely related to that of other precious metals.
    (B) Industrial uses of gold are more important than gold's financial uses.
    (C) Gold could serve as a reliable currency even today.
    (D) Land and gold are the two commodities with the most consistent value.

Go on to the next page ⟹

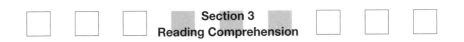
Questions 42-50

According to the National Institute of Dental Research, a federal agency devoted to oral health care, half of the school children in the United States have never had a cavity in a tooth. This claim is based on an extensive survey of oral health performed in 2010. But is this claim really true? And are these alleged findings prompting
5   parents and health-care agencies to overlook the real and often serious dental needs of millions of American children?

Actually, careful examination of the data leads to a different conclusion than that of the National Institute of Dental Research. Experts who have inspected the data of the Institute's study maintain that the agency's 50 percent cavity-free claim is a myth
10   derived by ignoring decay in "primary teeth" — commonly called "baby teeth" — and by averaging the decay in permanent teeth among children from 5 to 17 years old. If decay in primary teeth is included, 42 percent of kindergartners have been affected by tooth decay, half of 7-year-olds have had at least one decayed tooth, and children younger than 9 have an average of four decayed teeth. Moreover, if the progress of
15   decay is tracked through the childhood years, 84 percent rather than 50 percent of the nation's 17-year-olds have had decay in one or more permanent teeth. Only one in six 17-year-olds can legitimately be said to have had no cavities.

The 50-percent-cavity-free statistic of the National Institute was derived by averaging the decay experience of all children who have at least one permanent tooth,
20   from pre-schoolers who have not had their permanent teeth long enough for them to decay to high school seniors who have had plenty of time for decay to develop. The reason why the results of a closer analysis of the data are important is that they suggest dental diseases in children are widespread throughout the population rather than limited to a minority. Recognition of this fact points to the need for particular
25   public health policies, for the problem of tooth decay is almost entirely preventable if parents and society do their jobs right.

42. What is the author's main point?

    (A) Reports from the National
        Institute of Dental Research are
        unreliable.
    (B) Good public health policies are
        gradually reducing cavity rates.
    (C) Dental decay in children is a
        serious and overlooked problem.
    (D) Parents ought to be more
        conscious of dental health care.

43. According to the National Institute of
    Dental Research, what percentage of
    American school children have never
    had a cavity?

    (A) 17 percent
    (B) 50 percent
    (C) 42 percent
    (D) 84 percent

44. Which of the following mistakes do
    experts say the National Institute of
    Dental Research made in conducting
    its study?

    (A) It did not survey a large enough
        sample of the population.
    (B) It neglected to consider the
        dental health of teenagers.
    (C) It did not define "dental decay"
        clearly enough.
    (D) It failed to include cavities found
        in primary teeth.

45. The word "extensive" in line 3 is closest
    in meaning to

    (A) critical
    (B) preliminary
    (C) large
    (D) ongoing

46. The word "inspected" in line 8 is closest
    in meaning to

    (A) compiled
    (B) checked
    (C) computed
    (D) rejected

47. Which of the following statements is
    best supported by the passage?

    (A) More accurate research would be
        helpful in establishing the extent
        of dental diseases.
    (B) Federal agencies are frequently
        poor sources of public health
        information.
    (C) Insurance companies ought to be
        required to help cover the cost of
        dental check-ups.
    (D) Sugar-rich diets are one of
        the major causes of cavities in
        children.

48. The word "tracked" in line 15 is closest in meaning to

(A) curbed
(B) increased
(C) isolated
(D) analyzed

49. The word "they" in line 22 refers to

(A) the results
(B) the data
(C) dental diseases
(D) children

50. Why does the author mention "17-year-olds" in line 16-17?

(A) Age 17 is the accepted standard used for measuring dental disease.
(B) Late adolescent behavior is highly predictive of adult behavior.
(C) Only one-sixth of these teenagers were included in the original study.
(D) Far fewer members of that age group were actually without cavities.

Practice Test 4

Section 3

Practice Test 1
解 答 と 解 説

解答の冒頭にある「TYPE」アイコンは「出題傾向と対策」（pp.12 ～ 35）で解説
した問題タイプを示しています。

はその問題が「難問」であることを示しています。正解できたら自信を持って
ください。

解答済みのマークシート（別冊巻末）と照らし合わせましょう。

正答一覧

Section 1

#	Ans	#	Ans	#	Ans	#	Ans	#	Ans
1	D	11	C	21	D	31	A	41	C
2	C	12	B	22	D	32	B	42	D
3	C	13	D	23	C	33	C	43	B
4	D	14	B	24	D	34	B	44	C
5	A	15	C	25	C	35	C	45	A
6	B	16	B	26	A	36	D	46	C
7	D	17	A	27	A	37	A	47	B
8	A	18	B	28	B	38	D	48	D
9	D	19	B	29	A	39	A	49	A
10	A	20	A	30	D	40	B	50	D

Section 2

#	Ans	#	Ans	#	Ans	#	Ans	#	Ans
1	C	9	B	17	C	25	C	33	C
2	B	10	A	18	C	26	B	34	D
3	C	11	B	19	D	27	A	35	B
4	B	12	D	20	D	28	B	36	B
5	C	13	A	21	C	29	A	37	B
6	B	14	B	22	D	30	C	38	C
7	C	15	A	23	D	31	D	39	B
8	A	16	C	24	B	32	A	40	C

Section 3

#	Ans	#	Ans	#	Ans	#	Ans	#	Ans
1	C	11	B	21	D	31	D	41	B
2	D	12	A	22	B	32	C	42	A
3	D	13	A	23	D	33	B	43	A
4	B	14	B	24	C	34	A	44	C
5	D	15	D	25	B	35	D	45	D
6	D	16	C	26	A	36	C	46	A
7	A	17	B	27	C	37	D	47	B
8	C	18	C	28	B	38	A	48	B
9	D	19	D	29	A	39	B	49	C
10	C	20	A	30	C	40	D	50	C

Practice Test 1　解答と解説

Section 1
Listening Comprehension

Part A

mp3 **002-006**

1. 正解▶ (D)

Woman（以下W）　: Barry, how was your trip to Canada?
Man（以下M）　　: Wonderful. British Columbia is every bit as
　　　　　　　　　 gorgeous as people say it is.
Question（以下Q）: What does the man mean?

TYPE 1 発言の意味　男性のせりふにある「Wonderful.（素晴らしい）」と
「gorgeous（見事な）」が聞き取りのポイント。people say ... に惑わされて(A)
や(C)を選ばないこと。

every bit 隅から隅まで　people say ～ みんなが～と言っている

2. 正解▶ (C)

M: Were you able to register for the Wednesday afternoon chemistry
　 lab you wanted?
W: No, all the sections were full. I had to settle for Friday.
Q: What does the woman imply?

TYPE 2 言外の意味　女性のせりふにある「No」と「I had to settle for Friday.
（とりあえず金曜日にするしかなかった）」が聞き取りのポイント。第一希望が通
らなかったとわかる。Part Aでは月日や曜日に注意して、事実関係を捉えよう。

register for ～ ～に登録する　chemistry lab 化学実験のクラス
settle for ～ とりあえず～にする

3. 正解▶ (C)

M: Isn't that Garth Brooks you're listening to? I didn't know you
　 liked country music.
W: Like it? It's practically all I listen to these days.
Q: What does the woman imply about country music?

195

Practice Test 1

TYPE②言外の意味　女性のせりふにある「It's practically all I listen to these days. (実際、最近私が聞くのはそればかりよ)」が聞き取りのポイント。

> all I listen to ~ ~だけを聞いている (＝I only listen to ~)　a great deal とても、すごく　used to ~ かつて~だった

4. 正解 (D)

W: Can I get you another cup of coffee?
M: I'm fine, thanks.
Q: What does the man mean?

TYPE①発言の意味　男性のせりふ「I'm fine, thanks. (けっこうです。ありがとう)」のニュアンスを正確につかめるかどうかがポイント。「十分にコーヒーを飲んだ」ということである。

5. 正解 (A)

M: It looks like it's clearing up some. You want to go for a walk in the park?
W: Why not? But maybe we'd better take our umbrellas just in case.
Q: What does the woman imply?

TYPE②言外の意味　男性は「晴れ上がってきているように見える」と言ったが、女性は「でも、念のために傘を持っていったほうがいいでしょう」と言っているので、「また降り出すかもしれない」と考えていることがうかがわれる。

> Why not? もちろんだ。ぜひそうしよう。　just in case 念のために

mp3 007-011

6. 正解 (B)

M: Your garden sure looks nice!
W: It'd better. I've been pulling weeds all afternoon. I'm exhausted.
Q: What does the woman mean?

TYPE①発言の意味　女性の「I'm exhausted. (くたくたに疲れた)」がヒント。all はafternoonにかかる。every weedに惑わされて(A)を選ばないこと。

> It'd better. ＝ It had better. (そうでなければいけない)

解答と解説

7. 正解▶ (D)

W: What did you think of Patricia's most recent journal article?
M: I found it to be up to her usual high standards.
Q: What does the man imply about Patricia's journal article?

TYPE 2 言外の意味 「男性はパトリシアの紀要について何をほのめかしている か」という問い。男性が「I found it to be up to her usual high standards.（彼 女のいつもの高い基準に達していると思った）」と言っているので、よく書けて いることが推測できる。

up to ～ ～に達する　journal 定期刊行物　article 記事

8. 正解▶ (A)

M: If Linda doesn't start coming to class, she's not going to be able to graduate this term.
W: I know. I've tried talking to her, but nothing seems to work.
Q: What does the woman mean?

TYPE 1 発言の意味 女性のせりふ「I've tried talking to her, but nothing seems to work.（彼女に話してみたんだけど、何をやってもうまくいかない）」 から「リンダは言うことを聞かない」ことがわかる。

9. 正解▶ (D)

M: I wonder why the bus is so late today. I've been standing here almost 15 minutes.
W: I guess you didn't hear that the bus drivers walked off their jobs earlier this morning. You'd be better off taking a cab to work.
Q: What does the woman imply?

TYPE 2 言外の意味 女性のせりふ「the bus drivers walked off their jobs earlier this morning（バスの運転手が今朝早くストに入った）」、「You'd be better off taking a cab（タクシーを拾ったほうがいい）」から「バスは走ってい ない」ことが推測できる。

walk off one's job ストに入る　be better off doing ～するほうがいい

10. 正解 (A)

W: That new sculpture in front of the administration building is terrible.
M: I don't think you should put it down so much. Many people consider it a true work of art.
Q: What does the man mean?

TYPE 1 発言の意味 まず、男性のせりふにある「I don't think ...」より、女性の意見に同意していないことがわかる。「I don't think you should put it down so much. (そんなにけなすべきではない)」と言っているので「女性が極端に批判的になっている」という意味の(A)が正解になる。

sculpture 彫刻　administration building 本部ビル　put it down けなす、こきおろす

mp3 012-016

11. 正解 (C)

W: The noise from that table is giving me a headache. I thought we came here for a nice, quiet dinner.
M: We did. Let me talk to our server.
Q: What can be inferred from this conversation?

TYPE 3 推論 女性が「I thought we came here for a nice, quiet dinner. (静かにディナーを楽しむためにここへ来たと思っていたのに)」と言うと、男性が「Let me talk to our server. (接客係に話してみる)」と応じているので、「何人かの客が大声で話している」と推測できる。

We did. = We came here for a nice, quiet dinner.
place one's order 料理を注文する

12. 正解 (B)

M: Have you seen Veronica? I thought she was going to help us pack these boxes.
W: I heard she's coming down with the flu.
Q: What does the woman suggest about Veronica?

TYPE 4 提案・示唆 女性のせりふにある「she's coming down with the flu. (彼女はインフルエンザにかかっている)」の意味がわかれば、どうやらベロニカの体調があまり良くないとわかる。

come down with ～ (病気に) かかる　flu インフルエンザ、influenza の短縮語

13. 正解 (D)

W: Gary, have you still got that file I gave you this morning? I didn't see it in the filing cabinet.
M: I put it back on your desk right after lunch.
Q: What does the man mean?

TYPE 1 発言の意味　男性の「I put it back on your desk (君の机に戻したよ)」が聞き取りのポイント。「no longer has the file (もうファイルを持っていない)」とある(D)を選ぶ。

14. 正解 (B)

M: I hardly ever see Rachel any more. Ever since she became a music major, she's always in a practice room playing her clarinet.
W: Good for her. Practice makes perfect.
Q: What does the woman imply about Rachel?

TYPE 2 言外の意味　女性の「Good for her. (いいことよ)」、「Practice makes perfect. (習うより慣れよ)」というせりふから、(練習をたくさんすれば)「レイチェルはよりよい演奏家になるだろう」と考えていることがわかる。

15. 正解 (C)

M: Debbie! What are you doing here at the zoo with all those little kids?
W: I'm working as a volunteer for a local elementary school and we have a field trip today.
Q: What does the woman mean?

TYPE 1 発言の意味　女性のせりふ「I'm working as a volunteer for a local elementary school (地元の小学校でボランティアとして働いている)」が聞き取りのポイント。(A)の教員をしているわけでも、(B)のアルバイトをしているわけでもなく(C)「子どもたちの世話をしている」のである。

`mp3` `017-021`

16. 正解 ▶ (B)

W: A group of us is going skiing this weekend. Why don't you join us?
M: Thanks, Marcy, but skiing's not my favorite sport.
Q: What does the man mean?

TYPE①発言の意味 男性は「Thanks（ありがとう）」と言っているものの、「but skiing's not my favorite sport.（でもスキーは好きなスポーツではない）」と言っているので、これはやんわりと「女性の誘いを断っている」と解釈する。

decline an invitation 招待を断る

17. 正解 ▶ (A)

M: It seems like maybe you stayed up too late last night, Carol.
W: Just what are you implying, Clarence?
Q: What does the woman want to know?

Rare (B) Want問題 女性は「Just what are you implying?（何が言いたいの？）」と少しばかりいら立ちを含んだ聞き方をしている。この質問を換言したのが(A)。

stay up 寝ずに起きている

18. 正解 ▶ (B)

W: Congratulations. I heard you got the student loan you applied for.
M: Yeah, but it's just a drop in the bucket given the new tuition.
Q: What does the man imply?

TYPE②言外の意味 男性のせりふにある「but it's just a drop in the bucket（しかし、それは大海の一滴だ）」が聞き取りのポイント。「学生ローンは十分でない」という意味である。drop in the bucketの音に惑わされて(A)や(D)を選ばないこと。

student loan 学生ローン　apply for ~ ~に申し込む　a drop in the bucket 大海の一滴　given ~ ~を考慮すれば　tuition 学費

19. 正解 (B)

M: What are the chances of us getting into the gym later for a game of basketball?

W: Practically zero. The volleyball team's got a practice scheduled.

Q: What does the woman mean?

TYPE 1 発言の意味 女性は「Practically zero.（事実上ゼロ）」と言っている。「バスケットボールはできないだろう」という意味である。practice に惑わされて(A)を、またvolleyball に惑わされて(C)や(D)を選ばないこと。

What are the chances of A doing ～? Aが～する可能性はあるか?

20. 正解 (A)

M: Did you hear that Bob wrote his whole term paper the night before it was due?

W: That's not the first time he's done that type of thing.

Q: What does the woman imply about Bob?

TYPE 2 言外の意味 女性のせりふ「That's not the first time he's done that type of thing.（彼がそんなことをしたのは初めてじゃない）」から「彼はよくぎりぎりになって物事にかかる」ということがわかる。(D)「期限通りに課題提出するのはまれだ」とまでは言っていないことに注意。

the night before it was due 締め切りの前夜に at the last minute ぎりぎりになって submit 提出する

mp3 022-026

21. 正解 (D)

W: A woman named Margaret called and wants you to get in touch with her right away.

M: Margaret? Really? That name doesn't ring a bell.

Q: What does the man mean?

TYPE 1 発言の意味 男性のせりふ「That name doesn't ring a bell.（その名前にはピンとこないな）」が聞き取りのポイント。ring に惑わされて(B)や(C)を選ばないこと。

get in touch with ～ ～と連絡を取る ring a bell ピンとくる、思い出させる

22. 正解▶ (D)

M: Got any plans for the weekend, Audrey?

W: Not yet. I'm just going to play it by ear, depending on what comes up.

Q: What does the woman mean?

TYPE①発言の意味　女性のせりふにある「I'm just going to play it by ear（成り行きにまかせるわ）」の意味がつかめるかどうかがポイント。

> play it by ear 成り行きにまかせる＝Let's wait and see.（あせらず成り行きにまかせよう）

23. 正解▶ (C)

W: Guess what! David's just got engaged to his girlfriend.

M: Will wonders never cease? I thought he'd be the last person to get married.

Q: What had the man assumed?

Rare Ⓐ推量　デービッドがついに婚約したと聞かされた男性は、「Will wonders never cease?（世に驚きの種は尽きないね）」と言った。思っていたことと正反対のことが起きたのだ。つまり男性は「デービッドは結婚しないだろう」と思い込んでいた。

> Guess what! ちょっと聞いてよ！、ねえ、知ってる？

24. 正解▶ (D)

M: I'm so angry with Dr. Patterson for the grade she gave me in physics. Do you think I should say anything to her about it?

W: If I were you, I'd just let it drop. From what I hear, once her mind is made up, you just can't change it.

Q: What does the woman suggest the man should do?

TYPE④提案・示唆　女性が「If I were you, I'd just let it drop.（私だったらやめにしておくわ）」と助言しているのがポイント。「you just can't change it（とにかくそれは変えられない）」からも、(D)「起きたことを受け入れる」ことを提案しているとわかる。

> let it drop やめにしておく

25. 正解 (C)

W: Did you hear that Jan announced her retirement?

M: Wow. That's a loss. A better manager will certainly be hard to come by.

Q: What does the man imply about Jan?

TYPE ② 言外の意味 男性のせりふにある「A better manager will certainly be hard to come by.（より優れたマネージャーは確かに得にくい）」が聞き取りのポイント。彼女がいい管理職だったことがわかる。

come by 〜 〜を手に入れる

mp3 027-031

26. 正解 (A)

W: When I moved in last month, my landlord assured me there would be no rent increases, but now she tells me I have to pay $50 more for my apartment.

M: What an unpleasant surprise! It certainly sounds as if the landlord misled you, doesn't it?

Q: What does the man mean?

TYPE ① 発言の意味 男性のせりふ「as if the landlord misled you（まるで大家が君を欺いた）」の意味がつかめるかどうか。(A)「大家の行動は想定外だった」のである。

moved in 引っ越してきた

27. 正解 (A)

M: Terry's just as good in math as his sister.

W: That's sure not saying much.

Q: What does the woman imply?

TYPE ② 言外の意味 女性のせりふ「That's sure not saying much.（あまり褒めたことになってないわね）」の意味がつかめただろうか。「テリーの姉（妹）は数学が得意ではない」ということ。

say much (for〜) (〜を) 高く評価する

28. 正解▶ (B)

W: I met with my advisor and he approved the plan for my major.
M: So it did go smoothly, just as I said it would.
Q: What had the man assumed?

Rare Ⓐ 推量　男性のせりふ「So it did go smoothly, just as I said it would. (じゃあうまくいったんだ。まさに僕が言った通りに)」が聞き取りのポイント。「アドバイザーとの面談はうまくいくだろう」と思っていたのである。did にアクセントを置くことで「やっぱり」といったニュアンスを強調している。

go smoothly うまくいく

29. 正解▶ (A)

M: I can't stand my new roommate. She always insists on getting her own way.
W: And you like to compromise, Tom?
Q: What does the woman imply about Tom?

TYPE ② 言外の意味　女性のせりふ「And you like to compromise, Tom? (それであなたは譲ることが好きなわけね、トム？)」は、「あなたも人のことは言えない、ルームメイトを非難すべきではない」という意味。you にアクセントを置いて皮肉っぽく言っている点に注目。

can't stand ～ ～に耐えられない　insist on doing ～することを主張する、固執する
get one's own way 思い通りにやる

30. 正解▶ (D)

W: This fruit punch is delicious.
M: I couldn't agree with you more.
Q: What does the man mean?

TYPE ① 発言の意味　「I couldn't agree with you more.」は「これよりさらに君に同意することはできない」、つまり「まったく同感だ」という意味。従って男性も、「フルーツポンチはおいしい」と思っている。

解答と解説

Part B

mp3 033-037

Questions 31-34

Listen to the following conversation about an honor's program.

W: Hey Richard, have you heard the university is going to start an honor's program?
M: Really? Is that one of the ideas of the new president?
W: That's right. It seems that she believes one way to increase the status of the school and to attract better students is to create a special program for the top students.
M: And how do you get into this new program?
W: Well, the plan hasn't been announced, but from what I've heard, you need to be in the top 10 percent of your high school class. Incoming freshman can apply to be in the program —— no transfer students allowed —— and if they're accepted, they get to take special small classes taught by the university's best professors. Also, when they graduate, they can say that they graduated "with honors."
M: Wow. That sounds pretty impressive. But isn't this program going to cost the school a lot of money?
W: I don't think so. At least not initially, since there aren't any plans to hire new faculty.
M: All in all the proposal sounds great. As far as I can tell, there's only one thing wrong with it.
W: What's that?
M: Since we're already juniors, we can't get in it.

> incoming 入ってくる、後任の　impressive 印象的な、感動的な　initially 当初は、初期は　faculty (大学・高校の) 教授陣、教員たち

Section 1
Part A
Part B
Part C

31. 正解▶ (A)

Q: Who proposed the new honor's program?

TYPE 10 Who/Whom問題　最初に男性が「Is that one of the ideas of the new president?」と聞くと、女性が「That's right. (その通り)」と答えている。学長のアイデアであることがわかる。

32. 正解 (B)

Q: What is the main reason the university is establishing the honor's program?

TYPE 9 What問題 女性が「one way ... to attract better students is to create a special program」と言っているので、「より良い学生を呼び込むため」が正解。

33. 正解 (C)

Q: How do students qualify to be in the program?

TYPE 12 How問題 男性が、「How do you get into this new program?」と聞くと、女性が「you need to be in the top 10 percent of your high school class. (高校で上位10パーセントに入っていること)」と答えている。つまり、高校で「performed well (成績が良かった)」ことが条件。

34. 正解 (B)

Q: Who are the two people having this conversation?

TYPE 10 Who/Whom問題 最後の男性の一言が鍵。「Since we're already juniors, we can't get in it. (もう3年生だからそのプログラムには入れない)」と言っている。

mp3 038-042

Questions 35-38

Listen to a conversation between two people at a university.

M: Excuse me. I have a few questions about some periodicals.
W: Sure. How may I help you?
M: Well, I'm working on a research paper for my political science class, but most of the journals I need aren't in the library.
W: Yes, that's a major problem here these days. We used to have a lot more journals but we've dropped some of our subscriptions because of budget cuts. Still, if you have the complete reference for an article—that is, the author, title, and issue number of the journal in which it appeared—we can order it.

M: Really? You mean even if the journal isn't here I can get a copy?

W: Sure. You just need to fill out an inter-library loan card. There's a whole stack on the counter by the reference desk.

M: This sounds too good to be true. Is it going to cost me anything?

W: Not a penny. It's part of our service budget.

M: That's wonderful. Last question. How long will it take me to get these articles?

W: There you hit upon a drawback. You have to allow approximately two weeks. So if you think you need a particular article, make your request as soon as possible.

periodical 定期刊行物　drop 〜 〜を打ち切る　subscription 購読契約　reference 参照データ　not a penny 一銭もかかりません　approximately およそ　budget 予算　stack 束　drawback 障害

35. 正解 (C)

Q: Where does this conversation probably take place?

TYPE 8 Where問題　男性が「most of the journals I need aren't in the library（必要なジャーナルの大半が図書館にない）」と言うと、女性が「Yes, that's a major problem here（ええ、それがここの大きな問題なんです）」と答えているので、図書館での会話だとわかる。

36. 正解 (D)

Q: According to the woman, why aren't the journals that the man wants available?

TYPE 6 Why問題　女性が「we've dropped some of our subscriptions because of budget cuts.（予算削減のため、いくつかの購読契約を打ち切った）」とはっきり述べている。

37. 正解 (A)

Q: What is the charge for ordering an article?

TYPE 9 What問題　男性が「Is it going to cost me anything?（お金はかかるのか）」と聞くと、女性が「Not a penny.（一銭もかからない）」と答えている。つまり、まったく何もなし、無料だということ。

Practice Test 1

38. 正解▶ (D)

Q: According to the woman, how long does it take to receive an article once it's been ordered?

TYPE⑫How問題 最後に女性が、「You have to allow approximately two weeks. (少なくとも約2週間見ておくべきです)」と言っている。

Part C

mp3 **044-048**

Questions 39-42

Listen to the following announcement made by a history professor.

　Good morning. I'm Dr. Phillips and this is History 320, the history of African-Americans after the Second World War. The prerequisite for this class is History 101, the lower-division introductory course in modern American history. If there is anyone here who has not yet taken that class, you should leave now. I'm sorry, but this is the policy of the History Department. Please do not come and ask me to make an exception. Without the background you get from the introductory course, it'll be very difficult for you to understand the material we'll cover in this class. Now, please take a look at the course syllabus I distributed earlier. As you can see, our class meets three times a week——on Monday, Wednesday, and Friday from 10:00 to 10:50. My office hour will be right after class on Friday, from eleven to noon. If that time is not convenient for you, you can make an appointment. Also, I'm often around on Tuesday morning, but not every week. There will be three exams during this semester, two mid-terms and a final exam. The first mid-term will be given at the end of the fifth week and the second mid-term at the end of the tenth week. The two mid-terms will be objective exams, with a combination of multiple-choice and short-answer questions. The final exam will consist entirely of essay questions. I haven't made up the test yet, but it will address all the material we cover during the whole term. Probably you will be required to respond to four or five essay questions. There will be no term paper for this class. In terms of grading, your attendance and participation will count for one-fifth of your grade, your mid-terms combined will count 35 percent, and the final will count for the rest. Thus, it is essential that you prepare well for this exam given at the end of the term during exam week.

> prerequisite 基礎必須科目　lower-division 下級の　introductory 入門の　make an exception 例外とする　syllabus （講義の）摘要　distribute ～ ～を配布する semester 学期　objective 客観的な　multiple-choice 選択 （式） の

39. 正解 (A)

Q: When is this talk most likely being given?

TYPE 7 When問題　最初に教授が「I'm Dr. Phillips」と自己紹介をし、「this is History 320」とコースの説明をしている。アメリカの大学の授業には、たいてい3桁の数字がついていて百の位の数が大きいほど難しくなる。「the history of African-Americans after the Second World War. （第二次世界大戦後のアフリカ系アメリカ人の歴史クラス）」の学期初めである。

40. 正解 (B)

Q: What should students who have not taken the prerequisite course do?

TYPE 9 What問題　教授は「If there is anyone here who has not yet taken that class, you should leave now. （そのクラスを未修の人は、今、退出してください）」と言っている。

41. 正解 (C)

Q: What types of questions will appear on the final exam?

TYPE 9 What問題　教授は「The final exam will consist entirely of essay questions. （期末テストは全て論述式問題から成る）」、「Probably you will be required to respond to four or five essay questions. （おそらく4～5つの論述式問題に答えてもらう）」と言っている。

Practice Test 1

42. **正解** (D)

Q: What will count the most in determining the course grade?

TYPE 9 What問題　アナウンスの最後のほう、「In terms of grading（成績に関しては）」で始まる文で、教授は①「your attendance and participation（クラスへの出席率と参加度）が5分の1」、②「your mid-terms combined（2回の中間テストの合計）で35パーセント」、③「the final（期末テスト）が残り全部」と言った後、最後に「Thus, it is essential that you prepare well for this exam given at the end of the term ...（よって、この学期末にある試験の準備が大切）」と強調している。

mp3 **049-052**

Questions 43-45

Listen to the following talk given by a city official.

Good morning. The mayor has asked me to speak to all city employees today about a new program she has initiated. This program is of direct relevance to you, since many of you deal directly with senior citizen issues in your jobs. Essentially, the program allows you to spend part of your work week doing volunteer work in one of the city's six nursing homes for the elderly. You will be assisting the medical staff and other personnel there by performing a variety of interesting tasks. Now, some of you may have volunteered for similar work during your university days. And what you'll be doing now will be similar to what you did as a student volunteer. However, the main purpose of this program is not simply to help alleviate the boredom and loneliness of the elderly. In fact, we're very proud of our city's well-staffed senior citizen's homes and the many organized activities they offer for the elderly to participate in. The main reason for this program is to give you a chance to better know the issues that are important to senior citizens, to really understand what's on the minds of the elderly. For more details about this program, please visit any one of the six senior citizen homes. The administrative officials there can give you all the information you need. I hope you decide to take advantage of this program. You'll have the satisfaction of knowing you're doing something good and, in addition, it will help you do your own job better.

initiate 〜 〜を始める　relevance 関連　alleviate 〜 〜を緩和する　boredom 退屈、退屈なこと　participate in 〜 〜に参加する　administrative 管理の　take advantage of 〜 〜を利用する

43. 正解 (B)

Q: For whom is this announcement primarily intended?

TYPE⑩ Who/Whom問題　文頭で、「The mayor has asked me to speak to all city employees ...（市長が全ての市職員に話すよう頼んだ）」と言っている。

44. 正解 (C)

Q: What is the main reason that this program has been created?

TYPE⑨ What問題　本文で「The main reason for this program is ...（このプログラムの主旨は）」と言った後、「to really understand what's on the minds of the elderly.（高齢者の心のうちを理解すること）」と言っている。

45. 正解 (A)

Q: Where should people who need more information go?

TYPE⑧ Where問題　「For more details about this program, please visit any one of the six senior citizen homes.（このプログラムのさらなる詳細については、6カ所の高齢者ホームのどれかを訪問するように）」と言っている。

mp3 053-058

Questions 46-50

Listen to a talk given in a university class.

Today, I'm going to talk about the early evolution of something I'm sure you're all interested in——food, and the relationship of food to culture. In the earliest and longest period of human development, the Paleolithic Period, people ate roots, berries, and shrubs. Less often they trapped fish and hunted small animals. The Paleolithic hunter-gatherers of this time spent most of their lives searching for food——namely, edible plants; there was no other way for them to survive. As a result, perhaps the most important step in human evolution came in the Mesolithic and Neolithic periods when humans made the transition from food gathering to food production. During this time, early cultures learned to cultivate crops and livestock. They learned to plant seeds and to raise large herds of animals. As a result, people no longer needed to spend their lives wandering but were able to settle in one area and create permanent cities. As the early agricultural methods became refined with the invention of the hoe, the scythe, and the plow, human history was altered forever, for food surpluses meant the beginning of commerce. Groups of people who would otherwise have had no contact began to communicate and to trade food for other types of products. And this interaction led to a sharing of ideas, a mixing of cultures, and the creation of new cultures entirely.

> Paleolithic 旧石器時代の　period 時代　shrub 灌木　edible 食べられる
> Mesolithic 中石器時代の　Neolithic 新石器時代の　transition 変化　cultivate ～
> ～を耕作する　herd（牛、豚などの）群れ　refine ～ ～を洗練する、改良する
> hoe くわ　scythe 草刈りがま　plow すき　interaction 相互作用

46. 正解 (C)

Q: What is the main subject of this talk?

TYPE 9 What問題　冒頭で「I'm going to talk about ... the relationship of food to culture.（食物と文化の関係について話す）」と言っている。

47. 正解 (B)

Q: What was the main diet of Paleolithic peoples?

TYPE 9 What問題　本文の2カ所にヒントがある。ひとつは「people ate roots, berries, and shrubs（植物の根や果実、灌木を食べていた）」という箇所、もうひとつは「The Paleolithic hunter-gatherers ... searching for food—namely, edible plants;（旧石器時代の狩猟民は……食糧、つまり食べられる植物を探していた）」という箇所。つまり「野生の植物」を食べていたのだ。

48. 正解 (D)

Q: According to the speaker, what important transition occurred in the Mesolithic and Neolithic periods?

TYPE⑨ What問題 「As a result, perhaps the most important step in human evolution came (その結果、おそらく人類の進化における最も重要な進歩が訪れた)」で始まる文のwhen以下に注目。「when humans made the transition from food gathering to food production. (人々が食物を採取する生活から食物を生産する生活に移った時)」とある。

49. 正解 (A)

Q: What important effect did the invention of agricultural tools have on human civilization?

TYPE⑨ What問題 「As the early agricultural methods became ... (初期の農耕手段がくわ、草刈りがま、すきの発明によって洗練され) ... food surpluses (余剰な食糧) により the beginning of commerce. (商業が始まった)」とある。この文の最後の部分の言い換えが(A)。

50. 正解 (D)

Q: What was one result of the increased contact between different groups of people?

TYPE⑨ What問題 最後の文に「And this interaction ... new cultures entirely. (交互作用が概念の共有や文化の融合、まったく新しい文化の創造へと繋がった)」とある。

Section 2
Structure and Written Expression

Structure

Questions 1-15

1. 正解 (C)

TYPE 14 語彙 空所の前に冠詞のthe、後に前置詞のofがある。よって名詞が入る。(C) treatment (治療) が正解。

2. 正解 (B)

TYPE 16 動詞の形 主語のThe physicist Richard Feynmanの後、カンマに挟まれた部分は挿入句。空所には動詞を入れる。後に続くthat節の中でcouldが使われていることから過去形の(B)を選ぶ。

conceive the notion：アイディアが浮かぶ

3. 正解 (C)

TYPE 13 文構造 カンマに挟まれた部分は挿入句。when以下は従属節になるので、その前には主節が必要。空所には主語と動詞のそろった完全な文が入る。

4. 正解 (B)

TYPE 13 文構造 カンマまでが主節。続く従属節では、関係代名詞whichを使いthe lost generationを説明する。the lost generationの動詞となるfocusedを含む(B)が正解だとわかる。(A)はfocusの後にwasが必要。

5. 正解 (C)

TYPE 14 語彙 空所の前後は、ともに主語と動詞のそろった完全な文。よって、空所には前置詞は入らない。コロンの後の「full or new (満月か新月)」はtwo phasesの単なる説明なのでwhetherも違う。よってwhenで前後2つの節をつなぐ。

6. 正解 (B)

TYPE 15 語順　「形容詞（大小→性質）＋名詞」の語順と決まっているので「enormous（絶大な）、critical（批評家の）、acclaim（絶賛）」という順番が正解。

7. 正解 (C)

TYPE 13 文構造　問題文を見ると、動詞が欠落していることがわかる。The cockroachが主語。空所に必要不可欠なのは動詞isのみ。

8. 正解 (A)

TYPE 16 動詞の形　問題文が「カエルの足の筋肉」という名詞を主語にして始まっているので、空欄に必要なのは動詞。enable ~ to ... は「~に……することを可能にする」という他動詞なので目的語が必要。ここは、「カエルの足の筋肉が、カエルのジャンプを可能にする」という意味なので、カエルを指すitが必要。

9. 正解 (B)

TYPE 15 語順　「the＋序数＋形容詞＋名詞」、という語順。「the second（2番目に）、brightest（明るい）、object（目標物）」が正解。

10. 正解 (A)

TYPE 14 語彙　「make＋目的語＋形容詞」の形を完成させる。make it possible for ~ to ... は「~に……することを可能にする」という意味。itはto以下を指す。

11. 正解 (B)

TYPE 14 語彙　まず選択肢を見ると「言葉の選択」の問題だとわかる。空所の後がlight goods, と複数形の名詞になっているので、この名詞を修飾できるのは(B)のみ。「other＋複数名詞」という組み合わせを覚えておこう。

12. 正解 (D)

TYPE 17 並列　空所の前にandがあり、その前に「its＋scenic＋beauty」とあるので、同じ組み合わせ（代名詞の所有格＋形容詞＋名詞）を選んで並列の形を作ればよい。

13. 正解 (A)

TYPE⑬文構造 The skinが主語で、カンマに挟まれた部分は挿入句。空所には動詞が必要。(B)、(D)は名詞句なので不適。(C)ではitが余分な主語になる。

14. 正解 (B)

TYPE⑬文構造 この文にはbelieveとincreasesという動詞が2つあるので、ひとつは節に入れなければならない。節を作るためには接続詞が必要 (that)。前置詞句betweenからfiveまでは挿入句なので抜いて考える。空所にはincreasesという動詞の主語が必要。よって動名詞listeningをこの従属節の主語にする。

15. 正解 (A)

TYPE⑭語彙 問題文をよく見るとthat以下は従属節で、その前にisという動詞を含んだ主節がすでにあり、このままでも文が成り立つ。(C)のThatを空所に入れると従属節が2つになってしまう。Despite、Unlikeは節でなく句を導く。よって文構造を変えない形容詞Oneを入れる。

Written Expression

Questions 16-40

16. 正解 (C) consisting and → 削除

TYPE㉔重複 consisting and made up ofは、同じ意味を表す言葉の重複になるので、consisting andを取ると正解。

17. 正解 (C) a → the

TYPE㉘冠詞 最上級mostには、theをつける。「the most powerful men (最も力のある人物)」とする。

18. 正解 (C) influence exerted → exerted influence

TYPE㉗語順 exertは「~を及ぼす」という意味の他動詞なので、influenceという目的語 (名詞)が直後に必要。よって語順を入れ替え、exerted influenceにする。

解答と解説

19. 正解 (D) differ → different
TYPE⑱品詞 differは動詞。「substances (物質)」という名詞を修飾するようにdifferentという形容詞に変える。

20. 正解 (D) feeling → feel
TYPE㉑並列 to dig, eat, and … とくれば、次も動詞の原形 (feel) にしなければならない。

21. 正解 (C) long human → long as human
TYPE㉖語の脱落 下線 (C) の前のasに注目。has existed as long ( ) human culture has＝「人類の文化と同じくらい長く存在した」という意味の同等比較にするには、( )にasが必要。

22. 正解 (D) sweetener → sweeteners
TYPE⑳単複 「one of the … (〜の中のひとつ)」という表現の後部には可算名詞の複数形が入る。よって、sweetenersとするのが正しい。

23. 正解 (D) it → its
TYPE㉒代名詞 it exhibitionでは、名詞が2つ続いてしまう。そこでitをitsという所有格にする。

24. 正解 (B) of → one of
TYPE㉖語の脱落 ofの前にoneが抜けているのでone of … animalsとする。これは22の設問と同じ構文。

25. 正解 (C) and → or
TYPE㉙接続詞 either … or … の構文。andをorに変える。

26. 正解 (B) arrive → arrived
TYPE㉕動詞の形 主節の動詞numberedが過去形になっていることに注目。従属節の動詞の時制を一致させてarrivedとする。

27. 正解 (A) retire → retirement

TYPE ⑱ 品詞 下線(A)の直前がafter hisと所有格になっているので、その後は名詞retirementになる。retireは動詞。

28. 正解 (B) but → that

TYPE ㉙ 接続詞 「Research has shown (研究結果が示したのは……)」の後に目的語、つまり「何を」を意味するものがない。そこでbutをthatに変えて名詞節にし、that以下を目的語とする。

29. 正解 (A) form → forms

TYPE ⑲ 数の一致 下線(A)の直前のA body (of air)が単数名詞なので、formという動詞に三人称単数現在形のsが必要。

30. 正解 (C) sustain → sustaining

TYPE ㉑ 並列 カンマやandなどを含む文ではその前後の品詞や語形を統一する。動名詞が連なっているので、organizing, directing, and sustainingにする。

31. 正解 (D) their → its

TYPE ⑲ 数の一致 Oklahomaという単数名詞を指すのは、theirでなくits。

32. 正解 (A) they → 削除

TYPE ㉔ 重複 Geysers theyと名詞が2つ続いていて主語が重複している。従ってtheyはいらない。

33. 正解 (C) large → largely

TYPE ⑱ 品詞 ignoredという動詞を修飾するには、largelyと副詞にする (動詞を修飾するのは副詞)。largeは形容詞 (形容詞は直後の名詞を修飾する)。

34. 正解 (D) becoming → became

TYPE ㉕ 動詞の形 「主語＋動詞and動詞」という構造 (soon afterは挿入)。従って、XX had become ..., and soon after became ... にする。

35. 正解 (B) place → places

TYPE 20 単複 下線 (B) の直前に注目。those の後には複数名詞がくるので、place を places に変える。

36. 正解 (B) mate → mates

TYPE 19 数の一致 カンマに挟まれた部分は挿入句なので主語は crow。三人称単数現在なので、動詞は s をつけて「mates (つがいになる)」にする。

37. 正解 (B) too → so

TYPE 29 接続詞 「非常に〜なので」という意味を表す組み合わせは、so … that … か too … to … の構文。ここでは、too を so に変える。

38. 正解 (C) they → them

TYPE 22 代名詞 他動詞 makes の後には目的語がこなければならないので、主格の代名詞 they を目的格 them にする。

39. 正解 (B) itself → themselves

TYPE 19 数の一致 主語が the defenders と複数形なので、目的語 itself を themselves にしなければならない。A find oneself B は、「A が B の状態になったのに気づく」という構文。

40. 正解 (C) sophisticate → sophisticated

TYPE 18 品詞 「most primitive (形容詞) and most ＋形容詞」の形。並列の問いにもなっている。よって sophisticate (動詞) を sophisticated と形容詞形にする。

Section 3
Reading Comprehension

Questions 1-9

1. 正解 (C)

TYPE 30 要旨　本文では、メディスン・ホイール（またの名をビッグホーン・ホイール）の場所と構造について第1パラグラフで、使用目的の考察を第2パラグラフで述べている。(A)の天体観測や(B)のクロー族の伝統、(D)のビッグホーン・ナショナル・フォレストについて触れてはいるが、これらは詳細の一部であり、主題ではない。

2. 正解 (D)

TYPE 34 語法　主格代名詞theyの前にある複数形の主語を探す。3行目のtheyも同じ人々を指すとわかれば、本文の主題となっているPlains Indiansを指すことがわかる。「彼らが天体の動きに関心を持っていたことを示す遺跡は〜」という文意。

3. 正解 (D)

TYPE 31 事実の確認　Medicine Wheelという語が最初に登場するのは5行目。which stands〜と続いているのでこの後を見てみると「on an exposed shoulder of the Bighorn Mountains (ビッグホーン山脈の剥き出しの尾根) に」あったと書かれている。従って(A)「Valley (谷)」、(B)「Plain (平原)」、(C)「Forest (森林)」は当てはまらない。

terrain 地形、地勢

4. 正解 (B)

TYPE 37 理由　全体を読んでみても(C)や(D)のような事柄は出てこない。(A)に関しては6行目から詳しく説明している。(B)の所在地に関連する描写としては、18行目に「uninhabitable (住むことができない)」とある。だから、それを強調するために5行目にan exposed shoulder (剥き出しの尾根) と述べた。

5. 正解 (D)

TYPE 33 語彙　pileもしくはheapの意味を知っていれば答えは簡単。pileは「積み重なったもの」という意味で(D)「heap (山、堆積)」と同じ。(A)「circle (円)」、

(B)「post (柱)」、(C)「structure (構造)」は意味が異なる。

6. 正解 **(D)**

TYPE 33 語彙 antiquity の意味を「アンティーク」という外来語から想像できた人もいるだろう。very old という意味なので (D)「age (老齢)」が答え。また「created before the light came (光がやってくる前に創造された)」という1文も決め手になる。(A)「strength (強さ)」は force と同義、(B)「ingenuity (賢さ)」は cleverness と同義。(C) fragility は「もろさ、はかなさ」を表す。

7. 正解 **(A)**

TYPE 33 語彙 superficially は「表面的に」という意味で、(A)「at first glance (一見したところ)」が正解。superficially の意味を知らなくても、前後の文脈から考えてみればわかるはず。13行目から、「クロー族の言語で Bighorn Wheel は Sun's House と呼ばれ、and superficially、儀式をする建物の見取り図に似ている」とある。前半で説明された Wheel の形状なども頭に入れて選択肢から選んでみよう。(B) in every respect は in every way「あらゆる面で」、(C) with great power は「強大な力で」という意味、(D) upon careful study は「注意深く研究したところ」という正解と反対の意味。

8. 正解 **(C)**

TYPE 32 推論 13行目から the Sun's House に関する説明が始まる。まず、「In Crow language (クロー族の言語で)」とあり、名付け親はクロー族であることがわかる。また、15行目最後からの文に「very likely originated from later visitors who had no part in the design of the original structure. (元来の構造の設計に何もかかわりのない、後の時代の訪問者が作り出したものである可能性がかなり高い)」とある。これらから正解は (C) だと判断できる。

9. 正解 **(D)**

TYPE 32 推論 本文4〜5行目にメディスン・ホイールは「the movement of the heavenly bodies (天体の動き) に対するインディアンの興味を表している」と記されているが、(A)「watch over the surrounding area (周辺地域を観察する)」については一切述べられていない。(C)「establish safe living quarters

Practice Test 1

（安全な生活圏を確立する）」は、最後の文にその場所は「uninhabitable（住めない）」とあるので間違い。(B)の「rituals（儀式）を執り行う」は、設計がceremonial lodgeに似ていたとしか書かれていないので不適切。

> **重要語句**
>
> astronomically 天文（学）の　sophisticated 洗練された　observation 観察
> site 遺跡　expose 風雨にさらされた　longitude 経度　latitude 緯度　altitude 高度
> diameter 直径　hub ハブ（車輪の中心）　cairn ケルン、石塚　rim 縁、（特に円形物
> の）端　antiquity 古代、大昔　Crow クロー族　superficially 一見したところ
> ceremonial 儀式上の　plan 平面図　teepee インディアンのテント状の小屋
> architectural 建築上の　monument 記念碑、記念建造物　uninhabitable 居住に適し
> ない　blizzard 暴風雪、ブリザード

Questions 10-19

10. 正解▶ (C)

TYPE30 要旨　本文中の2行目と第3パラグラフの頭に出ている、crocodilians（ワニ目）という上位の分類は、下位項目に第1パラグラフにあるCrocodylidae（クロコダイル科）そして、第2パラグラフにある Alligatoridae（アリゲーター科）を含んでいる。さらに下の分類項目の、crocodies（クロコダイル種）とalligaters（アリゲーター種）については特に区別せずにまとめて第4パラグラフで扱っている。よって4つのパラグラフ全てにあてはまる本文の目的は、(C)「ワニ目の特徴の全体像の提示」である。(A)「特定の種の描写」(B)「進化の過程」(D)「どこに生息するか」などは、内容の一部であり、全体像ではない。

11. 正解▶ (B)

TYPE34 語法　2行目のthemは直前の可算名詞の複数形を指す。つまり20species of living crocodiliansが答え。この生物の種を表す単語「species」は単数でも複数でも同形なので、注意が必要。

12. 正解▶ (A)

TYPE35 Not問題　第1パラグラフ、第2文に注目。There are about 20 speciesof ... among them alligators, caimans, and gavials ... と(A)以外の選択肢が全

部ある。つまりKomodo dragonsは述べられていない。15行目からコモドオオ
トカゲに触れた記述があるが「コモドオオトカゲは遠いいとこに当たる……、恐竜
に近い爬虫類との、最後の生ける繋がり」とあり、ワニ目の種類には含まれない。

13. 正解▶ (A)

TYPE(33) 語彙 この問題はswamps (沼地) の意味を知らなければ正解を確定で
きないだろう。ただし、swampsの後にlakes、riversと続くので水に関係する場所
だと推測はできる。さらに読み進むと5行目にLike the saltwater crocodile from
the coastal marshes of southern India and Malaysiaとあるので「クロコダイル
はmarshes (沼) にも住むようだ」などと、選択肢をしぼる手がかりはいくつかある。

14. 正解▶ (B)

TYPE(31) 事実の確認 4〜6行目に「The best known species is (最もよく知られ
ている種は) the Nile crocodile, found mainly on the African continent. (ナイル・
クロコダイルで、主にアフリカ大陸に生息する)」、「Like the saltwater crocodile ...,
(塩水に住むクロコダイルのように) it can be a man-eater. (人食いである場合が
ある)」とある。その他の選択肢についてはこの本文の情報だけでは特定できない。

15. 正解▶ (D)

TYPE(33) 語彙 localeは「場所、現場」という意味で、local (地元) と語源は一
緒。(D) areasが同意語である。

16. 正解▶ (C)

TYPE(31) 事実の確認 第2パラグラフの第1文に「Alligators, ... are found in two
freshwater locales. (アリゲーターは2つの淡水の場所で見られる)」とある。こ
れは選択肢の(C)と同じである。(A)については13〜14行目、(B)は17〜18行目、
(D)は11〜12行目にそれぞれ記載があり、本文と食い違っていることがわかる。

17. 正解▶ (B)

TYPE(31) 事実の確認 14行目に「... reach 6 meters, though 1.8 to 2.4 meters
is the average. (6メートルにもなるが、平均は1.8〜2.4メートル)」と記され
ている。

Practice Test 1

18. 正解 (C)

TYPE 33 語彙 awkwardlyとは「ぶざまに、ぎこちなく」という意味の副詞で、(C) clumsilyと同意語。

19. 正解 (D)

TYPE 31 事実の確認 第4パラグラフ1行目に「Crocodiles and alligators are by far most at home in the water (クロコダイルとアリゲーターが最も慣れているのは水中だ)」とある。この事実を踏まえている選択肢は(D)だ。他の選択肢も当てはまるかもしれないが、「According to the passage (この文章によれば)」と質問されているのだから、自分の知識ではなく問題文に書かれていることを根拠にすること。

重要語句

reptile 爬虫類　Crocodylidae クロコダイル科　crocodilians ワニ目　swamp 沼、沼地　coastal marsh 沿岸の沼地　Alligatoridae アリゲーター科　inhabit 居住する　lizard-like トカゲに似た　composed of ～ ～で成り立っている　close-set すき間なく並んだ　overlapping 重なり合う　constitute ～の構成要素となる　belly 腹、腹部　gallop ギャロップで、全速力で　awkwardly ぶざまに、ぎこちなく　muscular 筋肉の　oar-like オールに似た

Questions 20-30

20. 正解 (A)

TYPE 30 要旨 第1文よりLenny Bruceというコメディアンの名前が登場し、最後のパラグラフまで彼の名前がある。よって、(A)「重要なアメリカ人エンターテイナーの経歴」が正解。(C)にも彼の名前があるが、これは彼の経歴の一部であり主旨ではない。つまり引っかけの選択肢。

21. 正解 (D)

TYPE 31 事実の確認 第1パラグラフの最後に、「His irreverence ... after his death. (彼の無作法な言動は、彼の死後に登場したコメディアンのほとんどが用いる、冷笑的なお決まり芸を助長した)」とある。これを言い換えた(D)「現在のコメディアンたちは彼に多大な恩恵を受けている」が正解。

22. 正解 (B)

TYPE 33 語彙 despair（絶望）という意味を知らなければ正解するのは難しい。(B)「despondency（落胆）」が正解。(A)「cynicism（皮肉）」、(C)「violence（暴力）」、(D)「insolence（横柄）」はどれも意味が異なる。

23. 正解 (D)

TYPE 33 語彙 この種の問題は本来文脈に最もふさわしい意味を探すのだが、ここでは intend（意図する）の意味から比較的素直に (D)「designed（計画された）」を選べる。ちなみにその他の選択肢の意味は (A)「employed（用いられた）」、(B)「created（作られた）」、(C)「expected（予期された）」である。

24. 正解 (C)

TYPE 31 事実の確認 7～8行目に「intended to shock rather than amuse the audience.（聴衆を面白がらせるというより、むしろショックを与えようとするものであった）」とあり、この言い換えである (C)「彼は本来、聴衆を楽しませることに関心がなかった」が正解。

25. 正解 (B)

TYPE 32 推論 本文の8行目にある staccato がポイント。スタッカートは音楽用語で短く音を切ること。つまり His staccato delivery は「短く区切った話し方」。これを言い換えた「ダッダッダ」というマシンガンの破裂音 (B) が正解と推測できる。

26. 正解 (A)

TYPE 32 推論 11行目に「However, in his later years ...」とあるので、この後に注目する。このパラグラフの最後に「and audiences eventually lost interest.（そして、聴衆はやがて、興味を失った）」とあるので、これを言い換えた (A)「聴衆の興味あることから離れた」が正解。

27. 正解 (C)

TYPE 33 語彙 deteriorated とは「悪化した」という意味で、(C)「disintegrated（崩壊した）」と同意語。(A)「progressed（進歩した）」、(B)「shifted（移行した）」、(D)「digressed（脱線した）」。

Practice Test 1

28. 正解▶ (B)

TYPE ③②推論 本文で「皮肉な理由は〜だ」とは言い切っていないので、選択肢の中から推測する。第3パラグラフで彼がユダヤ人夫婦の間に生まれ、母親は自分がユダヤ人であることを隠していたという記述があった。そこで (B)「彼自身がユダヤ人として育てられた」を正解とする。その他の選択肢は本文に反するか、本文から特定できない。

29. 正解▶ (A)

TYPE ③②推論 19〜20行目に「The wit and cleverness (機智と賢さ) did not come through any formal schooling. (正規の学校教育で育まれたものではなかった)」、20行目に「After dropping out of high school (高校を中退して)」とあり、この部分を言い換えた (A) が正解。

30. 正解▶ (C)

TYPE ③⑤Not問題 (C) の「彼が擁護した革新的な政治変化」については一切触れられていない。他の選択肢は全て10行目の「his favored targets were ... (彼が好んだ対象は……)」以下に関連している。(B) の iconoclastic とは、「偶像破壊的」という意味。

重要語句

hipster 通、流行の先端を行く人　obscenity わいせつ　satirist 風刺家　Savonarola サヴォナローラ (15世紀の宗教改革者。火刑で殉教した)　despair 絶望　irreverence 不敬、不遜　foster 育成する　cynical 冷笑的な　routine (ここでは) お決まりの芸、ネタ　stand-up comic 漫談　controversial 物議をかもす　freewheeling 自由奔放に動き回る　improvisation 即興　staccato スタッカートの、断音の　lewd みだらな　vulgarity 下品な行為　apathetic 無感情な　indecent わいせつな　narcotic 麻薬　possession 所持　rambling とりとめない　monologue 独白、ひとり芝居　deteriorate 悪化する　diatribe 痛烈な非難の演説　heritage 先祖から受け継いだもの　cleverness 賢さ　enlist 兵籍に入る　discharge 除隊　mediocre 二流の　impressionist 物まねタレント　circuit 巡回　uninhibited 抑制されない　presumably 思うに　overdose (薬物の) 過量服用　obscurity 名もない人　premature 早すぎる　ultimately ついに、結局　declining (勢力などが) 衰える　reputation 名声、評判　posthumously 死後に　resuscitate 生き返らせる　contribution 貢献、業績

Questions 31-40

31. 正解 (D)

TYPE 30 要旨　第1文（トピックセンテンス）に「cursive script（筆記体）is gradually disappearing ...」とあり、これを言い換えた(D) The decline of cursive handwriting が正解。その他の選択肢は本文のごく一部分しか表していない。

decline 減退

32. 正解 (C)

TYPE 31 事実の確認　3行目に注目。「The main cause of its decline is the assault by technology ...（〈筆記体が〉減退した主な原因は、テクノロジーの来襲にある）」と書かれている。よって(C)「Technological innovation（技術革新）」が一番適切。

33. 正解 (B)

TYPE 31 事実の確認　5～6行目に「Americans now opt for（選ぶ）printing ... were taught at the start of elementary school（小学校）」とあり、この言い換えに当たる(B)「at the beginning of grade school（小学校の最初に）」が正解。

34. 正解 (A)

TYPE 31 事実の確認　8～9行目に、「... specialists ... believe that the shift ... suggests a transition from community to selfishness.（共同社会から利己主義への移行を示していると専門家は信じる）」とあり、この要点を短く言い表した(A)「アメリカ人がより自己中心的になった」が正解。その他の選択肢は本文の記述に反する。

35. 正解 (D)

TYPE 33 語彙　verticalは「upright（垂直の）」と同意。またvertical strokeを同じ文の後半で「stand on their own ...（自立して立ち……）」と言い換えているので、他の選択肢(A)「attractive（魅力的な）」、(B)「legible（判読できる）」、(C)「appealing（好ましい）」などではないことが推測できる。

36. 正解 (C)

TYPE(34) 語法　直前の可算名詞の複数形を探すと、handwritten addresses が
すぐに見つかる。「unreadable by machine (機械では読めない)」の意味がわか
ればすぐに正解できる問題だ。

37. 正解 (D)

TYPE(31) 事実の確認　22行目の「illegible addresses (判読不可能な住所)」や
24行目の「cannot be read」などから、(D)「アメリカ人の手書き文字の読み難
さ」とわかる。

38. 正解 (A)

TYPE(33) 語彙　「カムバック」は日本語でも外来語として使われている。「返り咲
く、カムバックする」という意味なので (A)「人気の復活」と同意。(B)「undergo
a transformation (変革を経る)」、(C)「serve a purpose (目的にかなう)」、(D)
「come to be abandoned (見捨てられる)」。

39. 正解 (B)

TYPE(36) 段落要旨　このパラグラフの構造を見極めよう。Now that ..., や Also,
since ..., は because ..., と同じ意味で「理由」を表し、これらのカンマの後には
「結果」が入る。つまり、26行目の「cursive script may make a comeback ...」
や、最終文「cursive writing could once again emerge (浮上する)」などから、
このパラグラフは (B)「手書きが再び prevalent (広まる) かも知れない理由」に
ついてだとわかる。

40. 正解 (D)

TYPE(32) 推論　本文の構造は原因と結果の関係で成り立っている。influence
(影響) と、その factor (要因) という言葉の入っている (D) が正解。(D) は本文全
体に当てはまるが、その他の選択肢は本文が述べていることの一部分にしか相当
しないので、論拠としては不十分。

【重要語句】

reflection 反映　cursive script 筆記体　decline 減退、衰退　assault 急襲　opt for 〜 〜を選ぶ　flowing 流れるような　interconnected（字と字の）間がつながった graphologist 筆跡学者　transition 移行、変遷　selfishness 利己主義、自己中心 consist of 〜 〜から成る　vertical 垂直の　stroke 字画、筆致　make time 時間をとる　repetition 繰り返し　crawl 這うように動くこと　ironically 皮肉にも　legibility （筆跡などの）読みやすさ　automated オートメーションで製造した　illegible 読解不可能　decode（暗号などを）解く　emerge 現われる　hallmark 品質優良の証明、太鼓判

Questions 41-50

41. 正解 (B)

TYPE 30 要旨　選択肢全てにantimatter（反物質）という言葉が入り、本文にも繰り返し登場しているので、これがトピックだとわかる。しかし、(A)「反物質の起源」、(C)「新たに可能な反物質の利用目的」、(D)「SFが反物質をどう描いているか」などは、本文の一部、枝葉である。本文の概要を最も的確に捉えている(B)「物理学における反物質」が正解。

42. 正解 (A)

TYPE 33 語彙　前後の文脈から学術的な理論の話だとわかるが、posit that以下に仮説が入っているのがポイント。positは「（理論に基づいて）仮定する」という意味。「（理論などを）提案する」という意味のproposeがここでは近い。(B)「assumed（推測した）」、(C)「investigated（調査した）」、(D)「disputed（議論した）」。

43. 正解 (A)

TYPE 40 視点　(C)や(D)は実際にありえることかもしれないが、"皮肉"な要素はない。また、反物質の概念について(B)の「複雑ではない」とは言えない。(A)の「non-scientists（非科学者たち）」は本文の「the general public（一般大衆）」に相当し、「little knowledge（ほとんど知識のない）大衆が理解したthe few concepts（数少ない概念）」と皮肉を示している。

44. 正解 (C)

TYPE 31 事実の確認 　本文の第1文に「particle has its "anti" counterpart : a reverse twin of the same mass but opposite characteristics. (素粒子には "逆" に相当するものが、つまり同じ質量でありながら、正反対の特徴を持つ相反する双子の片割れがある)」とある。これは選択肢の(C)とまったく同じである。

45. 正解 (D)

TYPE 34 語法 　10行目ではandで文と文をつなぎ、しかもitが主語に使われているのに注意。itは前文の主語と同一、つまり「the hopeful response (有望な答え)」である。

46. 正解 (A)

TYPE 33 語彙 　"far-reaching" は「遠大な」という意味。「実現するのにかなりの時間や困難が伴う」というニュアンス。選択肢の中でこれに近い意味となるのは(A)の「野心的な」だ。

47. 正解 (B)

TYPE 32 推論 　11〜13行目に、「only a few seconds after the Big Bang …, there were nearly identical amounts of matter and antimatter. (ビッグバンのほんの数秒後……、ほぼ同量の物質と反物質が存在した)」とあり、また15〜16行目に「and it is these remains of ordinary matter that make up the universe as we know it today. (現在私たちが知る宇宙を作っているのが、これらの通常の物質の残り物である)」とあるので、(B)「今よりビッグバンの直後のほうが多くの反物質が存在していた」が正解。

48. 正解 (B)

TYPE 33 語彙 　promptlyは「即座に」という意味。(B) quicklyが同意語。(A)「必然的に」、(C)「暴力的に」、(D)「驚異的に」。

49. 正解 (C)

TYPE(31) 事実の確認 第3パラグラフに「Of course, this creation and extinction of antimatter particles is a phenomenon that can be observed only in the most costly of labs; that is, particle accelerators ... (反物質素粒子の生成と消滅は、最も費用のかかる実験室、つまり素粒子加速器の中だけで観察される現象である……)」とある。よって(C)「素粒子加速器の中」が正解。

50. 正解 (C)

TYPE(32) 推論 本文の最後に「New theories and new technology now suggest that it may be possible to create "jars" of antimatter that can be studied for months or even years. (新しい理論と技術は、何カ月、何年でも観察することができる反物質の「つぼ」を作ることができる可能性を示している)」とある。つまり(C)の「反物質は、より注意深く、詳しく研究されるだろう」が正解。

[重要語句]

posit 仮定する counterpart 片割れ、(形や機能などが)よく似たもの substance 物質 annihilate ~ ~を絶滅させる cosmology 宇宙論 promptly 即座に obliterate ~ ~を痕跡も残さずに消す、抹消する preponderance 優勢 artificially 人工的に lab 研究室 duration 存続(期間) collides 衝突させる extinction 消滅 phenomenon 現象 particle accelerator (粒子)加速器 antiparticle 反粒子 collision 衝突 jar つぼ、びん

Practice Test 2
解　答　と　解　説

解答の冒頭にある「TYPE」アイコンは「出題傾向と対策」（pp.12〜35）で解説した問題タイプを示しています。

はその問題が「難問」であることを示しています。正解できたら自信を持ってください。

解答済みのマークシート（別冊巻末）と照らし合わせましょう。

正答一覧

Section 1

#	Ans	#	Ans	#	Ans	#	Ans	#	Ans
1	D	11	A	21	C	31	C	41	A
2	B	12	D	22	A	32	D	42	B
3	D	13	C	23	B	33	B	43	B
4	C	14	A	24	B	34	D	44	C
5	B	15	B	25	C	35	C	45	B
6	A	16	D	26	C	36	A	46	A
7	B	17	C	27	B	37	A	47	C
8	D	18	D	28	C	38	B	48	A
9	A	19	A	29	B	39	D	49	D
10	A	20	A	30	D	40	C	50	C

Section 2

#	Ans	#	Ans	#	Ans	#	Ans	#	Ans
1	D	9	A	17	D	25	B	33	C
2	C	10	A	18	B	26	B	34	B
3	C	11	B	19	A	27	A	35	B
4	D	12	D	20	B	28	A	36	B
5	B	13	A	21	C	29	A	37	D
6	C	14	D	22	C	30	D	38	B
7	A	15	C	23	D	31	D	39	D
8	B	16	B	24	A	32	C	40	C

Section 3

#	Ans	#	Ans	#	Ans	#	Ans	#	Ans
1	C	11	D	21	D	31	B	41	B
2	A	12	B	22	C	32	B	42	A
3	D	13	A	23	B	33	C	43	D
4	B	14	A	24	C	34	A	44	A
5	B	15	D	25	A	35	C	45	A
6	C	16	C	26	D	36	A	46	C
7	C	17	C	27	A	37	A	47	D
8	A	18	B	28	C	38	D	48	B
9	D	19	D	29	A	39	B	49	A
10	C	20	B	30	C	40	D	50	B

Practice Test 2　解答と解説

Section 1
Listening Comprehension

Part A

mp3 060-064

1. 正解 (D)

M: Professor Richardson, when do we have to hand in our lab reports?
W: Well, I've already given you a lot to do. How about the end of the month—at the latest?
Q: What does the woman mean?

TYPE 1 発言の意味　学生が「hand in our lab reports（実験レポートを提出する）」時期を聞くと、教授は「最も遅くて今月末まで」と答えている。

hand in ～　～を提出する　due 締め切り

2. 正解 (B)

W: Excuse me. Is this seat taken?
M: I'm sorry. I'm saving it for my wife.
Q: What does the man mean?

TYPE 1 発言の意味　女性が「Is this seat taken?（この席はふさがっていますか？）」と聞き、男性は「妻のために席を取っている」と答えている。(B)のoccupyは「〈場所を〉ふさぐ」という意味。

3. 正解 (D)

W: Professor Haze's test was impossible even if you really studied hard.
M: Well, what do you expect from the Dean of the Graduate School?
Q: What does the man imply?

TYPE 2 言外の意味　女性が「教授のテストはたとえがんばって勉強しても無理だった」と嘆くと、男性は「what do you expect ...（当然だろう）」と返した。つまり、易しい問題を出してくれるはずがない、教授のテストはいつも難しいと示唆している。

4. 正解▶ (C)

M: When I edited your paper I found a lot of typos, Nancy.

W: Oh, I know. I'm an awful proofreader.

Q: What does the woman mean?

TYPE①発言の意味 男性が「typos（タイプミス）がたくさんあったよ」と言うと、女性は「私はawful（ずさんな）proofreader（校正者）なんです」と言った。彼女は、間違いをチェックするのがあまり得意ではないのである。

5. 正解▶ (B)

W: I really need to find out what we're supposed to read this week.

M: Why don't you get a hold of somebody in the class?

Q: What does the man suggest?

TYPE④提案・示唆 男性のget a hold ofが聞き取りのポイント。女性が「今週何を読むことになっているのか、どうしても知る必要がある」と言うと、男性は「get a hold of somebody（誰かをつかまえ［て聞い］たら？）」と言った。よって、(B)の「別の学生にコンタクトを取る」が正解。

get a hold of ～ （人）をつかまえる　hold off ～ ～を先延ばしする

mp3 065-069

6. 正解▶ (A)

W: After not seeing you for so long, it's great to bump into you again, Patrick.

M: Same here, Ann.

Q: What does the man mean?

TYPE①発言の意味 女性が「あなたにばったり会えて最高だわ」と言うと、男性も「同感だ」と返している。(B)はbump（ドンとぶつかる）、(C)はsame（同じ）の意味にかけたひっかけの選択肢なので注意。

bump into ～ ～に偶然出会う　Same here. 同感だ。

7. 正解 (B)

M: We should have your reservations confirmed in just a second, Ms. Jones.

W: Unless the computers are down again.

Q: What can be inferred from this conversation?

TYPE (3) 推論　女性は「コンピューターがまたdownし（調子が悪く）ない限りは」と言っている。この会話から「ときどきコンピューターの調子が悪くなる」ことが推測できる。アメリカでの大学生活においてもコンピューターは必須アイテム。関連用語を覚えておこう。

down 故障して、壊れて　fail to work（機械の）調子が悪くなる

8. 正解 (D)

W: John, what are you going to do with your apartment when you're gone this summer?

M: My brother will look after it for me.

Q: What will happen to the apartment?

TYPE (5) 未来予測　「この夏、出かけている間、アパートはどうするの？」と女性が聞くと、男性が「弟がlook after（世話をする）」と答えたので、この言い換えにあたるtake care of（面倒を見る）を含む(D)が正解。

9. 正解 (A)

W: Guess what! I've decided to change my major.

M: Not again!

Q: What does the man imply?

TYPE (2) 言外の意味　男性が「Not again!（またか！）」と言っている。その意味するところは「この女性は前にも同じことをした」ということ。

Guess what! ちょっと聞いて。、ねえ、知ってる？

10. 正解 (A)

M: I can't believe the bookstore's closed today.

W: Yeah, the last two days of the term they always take inventory.

Q: What can be inferred from this conversation?

Practice Test 2

TYPE③ 推論 inventoryの意味がわからなくてもあわてないこと。その前が聞き取れれば本屋さんが閉まっているとわかるはず。男性が「今日、本屋さんが閉まっているなんて」と驚いていると、女性が「the last two days of the term（学期末の最後の2日間は）always take inventory.（いつも在庫チェックをする）」と述べている。

inventory 在庫チェック、棚卸し

mp3 070-074

11. 正解 (A)

M: My parents are complaining because tuition is so high.
W: I get the same thing from my folks.
Q: What does the woman mean?

TYPE① 発言の意味 男性が「tuition（=school fees：学費）がすごく高いと両親がこぼしている」と言うと、女性は「（私も）get the same thing（同じ小言）をfolks（両親）からもらっている」と同調している。

12. 正解 (D)

W: I think I'm going to look for a new apartment.
M: How come? I thought you liked your old place.
Q: What does the man want to know?

Rare⑧ Want問題 男性は「How come?（どうして？）」と不思議がり、「I thought you liked your old place.（今の場所を気に入っていると思ってた）」と言った。つまり、女性がなぜ引っ越したいのかを、男性は知りたがっているのだ。

How come? どうして？（＝Why?）

13. 正解 (C)

W: Haven't you ever gotten stopped for going too fast on this road?
M: At least three or four times!
Q: What does the man mean?

TYPE① 発言の意味 女性が「この道でスピードを出し過ぎて止められたことな

238

いの?」と聞くと、男性が「少なくとも3~4回あるよ!」と答えた。この会話から
わかるのは、(C)「彼は何枚かスピード違反の切符を受け取っている」ことだけ。

speeding tickets スピード違反の切符

14. 正解 (A)

M: Ann, did the library have that economics journal you were looking for?
W: No, I'm afraid they stopped getting it when the budget was cut.
Q: What does the woman imply about the magazine?

TYPE 2 言外の意味 男性が「図書館にeconomics journalはあった?」と尋ねると、女性が「budget was cut (予算が削られて)、stopped getting (取るのを止めてしまった)」と答えている。

no longer~ もはや~ない subscription 定期購読

15. 正解 (B)

M: Patty, I don't know if I'll ever learn how to use this software.
W: Well, Dave, to start with you might try looking at the user's guide.
Q: What does the woman suggest that Dave should do?

TYPE 4 提案・示唆 男性が「I don't know if I'll ever learn how to use this software. (いつになったら、このソフトの使い方がわかるのやら)」と嘆いていると、女性は「try looking at the user's guide (試しにユーザーズガイドを読んでみたら?)」とアドバイスした。user's guideの類義語manualを含む(B)が正解。

to start with 手始めに

mp3 **075-079**

16. 正解 (D)

W: Did you make those copies for me?
M: I got Brenda to do it.
Q: What does the man mean?

TYPE 1 発言の意味 男性は「I got Brenda to do it. (ブレンダにしてもらった)」

と言っている。使役動詞を使う「get＋人＋to do」「have＋人＋do」「make＋人＋do」「let＋人＋do」の形は、「人に〜してもらう、させる」という意味になる。

17. 正解 (C)

M: This is some of the best food I've ever had at the cafeteria.
W: Umm hmm. You can say that again!
Q: What does the woman mean?

TYPE ① 発言の意味　女性の言葉は「そのとおり！」という意味のイディオム。同意を表している。

18. 正解 (D)

M: I don't believe I've ever seen Tom so happy.
W: He's been like that ever since he won the speech contest.
Q: What can be inferred about Tom?

TYPE ③ 推論　男性が「トムがあれほど幸せそうなのは今まで見たことがない」と驚いていると、女性は「He's been like that (彼はずっとあの調子よ)、ever since he won the speech contest. (スピーチコンテストで優勝して以来)」と答えた。(D)「彼は勝ったことをとても喜んでいる」のだ。

19. 正解 (A)

M: Gosh. My back is so sore from sitting at a desk all day.
W: Well, that's what you get for taking such a heavy course load.
Q: What does the woman imply?

TYPE ② 言外の意味　「1日中机に向かっていたから、My back is so sore (背中がとても痛い)」と嘆く男性に、女性が「たくさんコースを取り過ぎ」と言っている。

20. 正解 (A)

W: I've just about had it with this research paper!
M: Don't quit now. You're more than half finished!
Q: What does the man suggest that the woman should do?

TYPE ④ 提案・示唆　女性が「I've just about had it with ... (もうたくさん)」と言った。had it の意味がつかめなかったかもしれないが、男性の「Don't quit now (今やめちゃダメだ)」の意味だけでもわかれば、正解を見つけられるはず。

just about ほとんど　have had it with ～ ～はもうたくさん、もうだめ　paper 論文、リポート　keep doing ～し続ける

21. 正解 (C)

M: Professor Holmes, can we get together tomorrow afternoon to talk about the topic for my term paper?

W: Tomorrow's not good for me. How about Friday?

Q: What does the professor mean?

TYPE 1 発言の意味　教授は「Tomorrow's not good for me. (明日は都合がよくない)」と言っている。

get together 会う、集まる

22. 正解 (A)

W: Can you believe Bill left his wallet in the taxi last night?

M: Again? He may be the most irresponsible person I know!

Q: What does the man imply about Bill?

TYPE 2 言外の意味　女性が「Bill left his wallet (ビルが財布を置き忘れた)」と言うと、男性は「Again? (また？) 彼は the most irresponsible person (最もいい加減な人間だ)」と言ったことから、(A)「彼はいつも物を紛失する」が正解。

23. 正解 (B)

M: I'm looking for a dress for my wife but these are all too large. Don't you carry petite sizes?

W: Why don't you try Erikson's on the other side of the mall? They carry only petite sizes.

Q: Where will the man probably go?

TYPE 5 未来予測　男性が妻のために「Don't you carry petite sizes? (小さいサイズの服はないのですか？)」と尋ねると、女性の店員が「ショッピングモールの反対側の Erikson へ行けば、They carry only petite sizes. (小さいサイズだけを取り扱っています)」と言った。つまりその店は小さいサイズの「専門店」だということ。従って (B) が正解。

24. 正解▶ (B)

M: I have no idea how to spell Professor Szpanski's name.
W: Who does?
Q: What does the woman mean?

TYPE 1 発言の意味 男性が「教授の名前をどうつづるかさっぱりわからない」と言うと、女性が「Who does?（誰がわかるの？）」と返した。つまり誰もわかる人がいないという意味。それほど、教授の名前のつづりは難しいということ。

I have no idea. わからない。(=I don't know.)

25. 正解▶ (C)

W: Has George been working hard on his dissertation?
M: I'll say. He scarcely does anything else.
Q: What does the man imply about George?

TYPE 2 言外の意味 女性が「Georgeは一生懸命 dissertation（学位論文）に取り組んでいる？」と聞くと、男性が「それ以外のことはほとんどやっていない」と答えている。

I'll say.（同意して）そうだね。、その通り。、確かに。、もちろん。

mp3 085-089

26. 正解▶ (C)

M: Did you hear that Marilyn got the highest grade on the chemistry exam?
W: No! She didn't!
Q: What does the woman mean?

TYPE 1 発言の意味 女性のアクセントに注意。「まさか！」という驚きを表しているのがわかる。

27. 正解▶ (B)

W: What did you think of the film festival? My roommate and I are planning on going tonight.
M: It's outstanding. Get there early like I did, though, or you'll have to stand up for the whole four hours.

Q: What does the man imply about the film festival?

TYPE 2 言外の意味 「フィルムフェスティバルどうだった?」という女性の質問に、男性が「It's outstanding. (素晴らしいよ)」と言い、「Get there early ... (早く着かないと) or you'll have to stand up for the whole four hours. (4時間ずっと立ち見になるよ)」と忠告している。ここから、そのフィルムフェスティバルはとても人気があることがわかる。

or (= otherwise) さもなくば

28. 正解 (C)

W: I'm going to pick up some potato salad and drinks on my way to the picnic.
M: So you are going after all.
Q: What had the man assumed?

Rare A 推量 質問文が過去完了形であることに注意。発言前の男性の考えを推測しなければならない。男性は、「So you *are* going after all. (それじゃあ行くんだ、結局)」と are にアクセントを置いて答えた。よって解答は現実の反対。つまり、この男性は女性がピクニックに行かないだろうと思い込んでいたのだ。

29. 正解 (B)

M: Haven't you gotten in touch with the dean yet about the scholarship fund?
W: Only two months ago.
Q: What does the woman imply?

TYPE 2 言外の意味 男性が「gotten in touch with the dean? (学部長と連絡を取っていなかった?)」と聞くと、女性が「Only two months ago. (ほんの2カ月前)」、つまり、「とっくに連絡を取った」と反語的に答えているので、「quite a while ago (かなり前)」を含む(B)が正解。

get in touch with ~ (人) と連絡を取る a while ago しばらく前

30. 正解 (D)

W: You still haven't found your keys, have you?

M: Would I be standing out here if I had?

Q: What can be inferred from the man's comment?

TYPE ③ 推論 男性は「見つかっていたらこんな外に立っていると思う？」と答えている。ということは、まだ鍵は見つかっていないのだ。

Part B

mp3 091-095

Questions 31-34

Listen to a conversation about handmade crafts.

W: This was really a great idea—coming to the Arts and Crafts exhibit.

M: Yeah, I read about it in the Friday newspaper. The article made it sound pretty interesting.

W: I've always liked handmade gifts, but I've never been much good at making them.

M: Me neither. When I was younger, though, I used to do a lot of woodworking. I made bookcases, tables, and stuff like that.

W: Really? What was the most difficult thing you ever made?

M: Hmm. A black walnut coffee table. I gave it to my parents for their 25th wedding anniversary.

W: What a present! Hey, look over here. Custom-made jewelry. These silver earrings are gorgeous.

M: I wonder how they are able to work such fine detail into the silver. Too bad they're not for sale. Tomorrow's my sister's birthday.

W: Do you think there are any ceramics here? I really love clay bowls and cups.

M: Yeah, I think I remember reading something about them. Should we ask the museum staff where they are?

W: Good idea. This place is huge.

M: After we look around a bit more, do you want to grab a bite to eat?

W: Sure, I'm starving.

exhibit 展覧会　clay 陶器　grab a bite（少し）食べる　starving 空腹だ、飢えている

31. 正解 (C)

Q: How did the man and woman find out about the exhibit?

TYPE⑫How問題　男性が最初に「I read about it in the Friday newspaper.（金曜日の新聞で読んだ）」と言い、また「The article … sound pretty interesting.（その記事によれば、けっこう面白そうだった）」と言っているので、(C)「新聞で触れられていた」が正解。

32. 正解 (D)

Q: In the past, what kinds of crafts did the man make?

TYPE⑨What問題　男性の2つ目の発言に注目。「When I was younger,（もっと若かった頃）I used to do a lot of woodworking.（よく木工をしたものだ）I made bookcases, tables, and stuff like that.」と言っているので、(D)「木製の家具」が正解。

33. 正解 (B)

Q: What do the speakers suggest is the best thing about handmade crafts?

TYPE⑨What問題　男性はかつて「黒クルミで作ったコーヒーテーブルを結婚25周年の記念に両親にあげた」と言い、それに対して女性が「What a present!（素敵なプレゼントね！）」と言っている。従って正解は(B)「素晴らしい贈り物になりえる」。それ以外は会話からは特定できない。

34. 正解 (D)

Q: What will the speakers probably do when they leave the exhibit?

TYPE⑨What問題　最後に男性が「After we look around a bit more,（もう少し見たら）do you want to grab a bite to eat?（何かちょっと食べに行かない？）」と誘い、女性が「Sure, I'm starving.（そうしましょう、おなかペコペコ）」と締めくくっている。よって(D)が正解。

Practice Test 2

mp3 096-100

Questions 35-38

Listen to the following conversation between two students at school.

W: Hi, John. Gee, you look really tired.

M: Oh, hi, Patty. Yeah, I was up all night finishing an essay for my applied psychology class.

W: That doesn't sound fun. What were you writing about?

M: Believe it or not, optimum study methods. How to absorb new material, how to take notes, how to memorize specialized vocabulary. Things like that.

W: Well, I suppose it's useful, but it doesn't sound very exciting.

M: Actually, it's really interesting. There's a lot of research, for example, on how many times you should review new words to learn them most efficiently.

W: You mean for, say, a biology course?

M: Sure. Or for anatomy, or chemistry, or any class in which there's a lot of specialized vocabulary.

W: Well, I suppose that's OK for pre-med students.

M: Yeah, but it's also good for other classes.

W: John, by the way, what is your major? I don't think you've ever mentioned it to me.

M: Oh, I'm a sociology major, but I need to take applied psych for a general education requirement.

W: So that's why you're taking the psychology course.

M: Yeah, and I've got three more classes left before I'm finished with them.

W: I'm heading over to the student union. How about a cup of coffee?

M: Thanks, Patty, but coffee is the last thing I need. I'm heading back to the dorm to take a nap.

Believe it or not 信じられないかもしれないけれど　optimum 最適な　absorb ～ ～を吸収する　review ～ ～を復習する　efficiently 能率的に　say 例えば、そうね、あのね　anatomy 解剖学　pre-med 医学部進学課程の　psych (＝psychology) 心理学の略　general education requirement 一般教養、必修 (科目)　head (～に向かって) 進む　take a nap ちょっと寝る

35. 正解▶ (C)

Q: Why is John tired?

TYPE 6 Why問題　最初にジョンが「I was up all night finishing an essay for my applied psychology class. (応用心理学のエッセーを仕上げるのに徹夜した)」と話している。よって(C)「彼は徹夜でリポートを書いていた」が正解。

36. 正解▶ (A)

Q: What did John write about?

TYPE 9 What問題　パティの質問に答えて、ジョンは「optimum study methods (最適な学習方法)」と答えている。optimumの意味を知らなくても、その後で「いかに新しい題材を吸収し、いかにノートを取り、いかに専門用語を覚えるか、などなど」と例を挙げているので、この言い換えにあたる(A)「効率的な学習方法」が正解とわかる。

37. 正解▶ (A)

Q: What field do the memorization techniques John referred to seem most suited for?

TYPE 9 What問題　パティが「say, a biology course? (例えば生物学のコースとか?)」と言うと、ジョンは「Or for anatomy, or chemistry, or any class in which there's a lot of specialized vocabulary. (解剖学とか化学とか専門用語をたくさん使うクラスなら何でも)」と述べ、さらにパティの「医学部進学課程の学生にはよさそうね」にも同意している。よって(A)「科学」が正解。

38. 正解▶ (B)

Q: Where did John go after he talked with Patty?

TYPE 8 Where問題　最後にジョンは「I'm heading back to the dorm (寮に戻って) to take a nap. (ちょっと寝る)」と言っている。従って(B)が正解。

Practice Test 2

Part C

mp3 102-106

Questions 39-42

Listen to the following talk about a "missing link."

Good morning students. In today's class I'd like to discuss the importance of a recent find that provides a "missing link" in human evolution. No, I don't mean the missing link between apes and humans, but rather the gap between the earliest primates such as lemurs and the later primates such as monkeys. For a long time, this portion of the chain of evolution has had a big gap in it. Now, thanks to a recently discovered mouse-like creature, we can more fully piece together our evolutionary transition from mice to men. At the moment, we have only the animal's fossilized jaw and teeth. The creature was a small one—it weighed only about 100 grams, but it had the deep chin and teeth of a monkey. Probably it lived on fruits and insects and inhabited forests and jungles.

> link リンク、鎖　evolution 進化　ape 類人猿　primate 霊長類　lemur キツネザル portion 部分、一部　gap ギャップ、すき間　piece together 継ぎ合わせる　transition 変遷、変化　fossilize 化石にする　jaw あご　live on ～　～を糧に生きる　inhabit 生息する、住む

39. 正解 (D)

Q: In what class is this lecture probably being given?

TYPE 9 What問題　選択肢を見ると、学問名について質問がくることが予測できるだろう。講義に出てきた human evolution（人類の進化）、apes and humans（類人猿と人間）、animal などの言葉から「Biology（生物学）」に関するクラスだとわかる。

40. 正解 (C)

Q: Which "missing link" does the newly discovered creature fill?

TYPE 11 Which問題　通常、生物学で missing link（失われた環）と言うと、猿か

248

ら人への進化の過程で化石の見つかってない時代を指す。しかし、この講義では最初に「I don't mean the missing link between apes and humans, (類人猿と人間の間のミッシング・リンクではなく) but rather the gap between the earliest primates and the later primates. (最初期の霊長類と後期の霊長類のギャップ)」と、一般の知識と異なることを断っている。

reptile 爬虫類

41. 正解 (A)

Q: Which of the following best describes the animal's physical characteristics?

TYPE 11 Which問題 中ほどに「mouse-like creature (ネズミのような生物)」、「from mice to men (ネズミから人間)」という説明があり、「The creature was a small one (小さい生き物だった)」と言っている。

42. 正解 (B)

Q: According to the speaker, what did the creature probably eat?

TYPE 9 What問題 講義の最後に「Probably it lived on fruits and insects (おそらく果実と昆虫を食べていた)」と言っている。

mp3 **107-111**

Questions 43-46

Listen to the following talk about healthy living.

　Good evening. I'd like to welcome all new Fitness Center club members to the first lecture in our "healthy living series." I'm one of the club's trainers who specializes in diet and exercise and that's exactly what I'd like to talk about. Recently there has been a tremendous boom in "fat-free products"—but did you ever wonder exactly what that means? Actually, all that the "low-fat" or "fat-free" label suggests is a reduction in the number of grams of fat in a product. It doesn't necessarily mean that a "low-fat" food is a low-calorie food. In fact, many companies have filled their products with high-calorie replacements such as sugar even while they've lowered the fat content. So just because you're eating a low-fat product doesn't mean you're not taking in a lot of calories. If you want to be careful about your diet and your weight, I strongly recommend that you pay more attention to calorie count than to fat ratio. I know that a lot of you want to reduce your weight; and of course, to lose weight, you need to burn more calories than you consume. One way to do this is to take in fewer calories; another way is to increase the calories you burn through exercise. If you're interested in weight control, here at the health club we especially recommend exercise because when you exercise you not only burn off more calories while you are working out but you increase your metabolism throughout the day and burn more calories even when you're reading or sleeping. Most people don't know about this special advantage to exercise. Now, please turn your attention to the screen. I'd like to show you a chart that illustrates exactly how exercise affects the body's use of calories.

> tremendous とても大変な -free（〜の）ない reduction 縮小、削減 replacement 代替品 ratio 比率、割合 metabolism 新陳代謝 illustrate 〜 〜を図解する

43. 正解 （B）

Q: Where is this talk being given?

TYPE⑧Where問題　音声を聞く前に選択肢をざっと見ておくと、場所に関する内容がこの講義の冒頭に来そうだと予測できる。講義の最初で「... welcome all new Fitness Center club members to the first lecture ...」と言っている。

44. 正解 （C）

Q: What does the speaker say about "fat-free" products?

TYPE⑨What問題　講義では、"fat-free" 製品について「It doesn't necessarily mean that a "low-fat" food is a low-calorie food. ("低脂肪" 食品は必ずしも低カロリーという意味ではない)」と述べ、「just because you're eating a low-fat product (低脂肪食品を食べているからと言って) doesn't mean you're not taking in a lot of calories. (たくさんのカロリーを取っていないわけではない)」と断っている。よって(C)が正解。

45. 正解 (B)

Q: According to the speaker, what is one of the little-known effects of exercise?

TYPE 9 What問題 講義の終盤に「... when you exercise（運動をすると）... you increase your metabolism throughout the day（1日を通じて新陳代謝が上がり）and burn more calories even when you're reading or sleeping. （読書したり、寝たりしている時でさえもより多くのカロリーを燃やす）」とあり、「Most people don't know about this special advantage to exercise. （ほとんどの人は運動することによるこの特別な利点を知らない）」とつなげている。下線部がポイント。

46. 正解 (A)

Q: What is the speaker going to do next?

TYPE 9 What問題 講義の最後でscreenという単語が出て、「I'd like to show you a chart that illustrates exactly how exercise affects ...（厳密に運動がどのように影響するのか図解する表を見せる）」と締めくくっているので、(A)「視覚的な図を用いる」つもりなのだ。

Practice Test 2

Section 1
Part A
Part B
Part C

mp3 **112-116**

Questions 47-50

Listen to a talk about meteorites given in an astronomy class.

This afternoon I'd like to begin by talking about meteorites, rocks of stone and metal which have fallen from space. In recent years, systematic and deliberate searches have turned up a great number of meteorites all over the world, from Japan to France to the Desert Southwest in the United States. But by far the largest finds have been near the South Pole where the ice of the Antarctic continent has preserved many meteorites almost in their original state.

The question of where meteorites originate is an interesting one. The majority seem to have been the remnants of asteroids that collided and knocked the smaller pieces out of their normal paths around the Sun.

Practice Test 2

Over the years some of these tiny asteroids eventually crossed the path of the Earth. While most disintegrated due to the friction of the Earth's atmosphere, a few managed to strike the surface of the planet before breaking up. But asteroids may not be the only source of meteorites. One controversial theory which has recently been gaining wider support is that some of the smaller meteorites are the remains of comets which have lost their volatile material and have coalesced into stone. Evidence for this theory is that many of these smaller bodies have strangely shaped orbits which resemble the orbits of comets more than asteroids. Furthermore, these unusual orbits lie outside the asteroid belt between Mars and Jupiter.

The most accurate way of determining the age of meteorites is by using the technique known as radioactive dating. Over time the chemical composition changes as the radioactive elements present in the meteor decay into atoms of other elements. This decay proceeds at a known rate, so this method is much more accurate than analyzing the surrounding rock or simply looking at the types of metals found in the meteorites themselves. OK. Now, if you'll take out the sheet I gave you to do as homework, we'll go over questions 12 through 20.

> meteorite 隕石　deliberate 計画的な　turn up 〜 〜を見つける　remnant 残存物
> asteroid 小惑星 collide 衝突する　knock ... out of 〜 ...を〜からたたき出す
> disintegrate 崩壊（分解）する　friction 摩擦　controversial 論争の的になる　volatile
> 揮発性の　coalesce 合体する　orbit 軌道　radioactive 放射性の　atom 原子

47. 正解▶ (C)

Q: Where are the greatest number of meteorites found?

TYPE(8)Where問題　選択肢全てが In で始まるので、場所に関する設問だと予想できる。講義の最初のほうで述べられる all over the world と、the South Pole は聞き取れただろうか。講義では世界中でたくさんの隕石が見つかったが、「... by far the largest finds have been near the South Pole（これまで最も多くの発見があったのは、南極点の近くだった）」と言っているので (C)「In Antarctica（南極大陸で）」が正解とわかる。

252

🔊 **48.** 正解 (A)

Q: Why do many scientists believe that some small meteorites may have originated from comets?

TYPE 6 Why問題 講義中盤で「隕石はcomet（彗星）の残存物である」という説を紹介した後、「Evidence for this theory is（この説の証拠は）that many of these smaller bodies have strangely shaped orbits（それらの小さめの物体は奇妙な形の周回軌道を有しており）which resemble the orbits of comets more than asteroids.（小惑星の軌道〈火星と木星の間〉よりも彗星の軌道に似ていることにある）」と説明しているので、(A)「それらはかなり特異な軌道を持つ」が正解。

49. 正解 (D)

Q: How can the age of a meteorite best be determined?

TYPE 12 How問題 選択肢にはBy … ingが並んでいる。手段・原因などが聞かれそうだと判断しよう。最終パラグラフの1文目「The most accurate way of determining」が聞き取れたらしめたもの。隕石の年齢を決定する最も有効な方法はradioactive datingと言っており、その原理が次のように説明されている。「Over time the chemical composition changes（時間を経ると化学成分は変化する）as the radioactive elements present in the meteor decay（なぜなら隕石に含まれる放射性元素が崩壊し）into atoms of other elements.（他の元素の原子になる）」。よって(D)が正解。

50. 正解 (C)

Q: What will the students do next?

TYPE 9 What問題 講義の最後で「OK. Now, if you'll take out the sheet I gave you to do as homework, we'll go over questions 12 through 20.（はい、では、宿題にしたプリントを出して、問12〜20を見ていきましょう）」と言っているので、これを言い換えた(C)が正解。

go over 〜 〜を見返す

Section 2
Structure and Written Expression

Structure

[Questions 1-15]

1. 正解 (D)

TYPE ⑬ 文構造 この文には動詞がない。understandとmanipulateはあるが、これはtoを前に伴う不定詞である。空所には、主語 Genetic engineering に対する動詞が必要。

2. 正解 (C)

TYPE ⑭ 語彙 空所の前に冠詞theがついて前置詞ofが後ろにあるので、空所には名詞が入る。(C)「development（発展）」を選ぶ。

3. 正解 (C)

TYPE ⑬ 文構造 existsが動詞なので、その前に入るのは節の主語。つまり名詞だが、itだとそれが何を指すのかわからない。そこでthereを入れれば、「場所を表す言葉＋動詞＋主語」という語順で、節の主語が動詞の後ろの a strong relationship となり、文が成立する。There is a car. ＝ A car is there. と言うときの表現と同様に、これは倒置表現。existsをisに置き換えるとわかりやすいだろう。

4. 正解 (D)

TYPE ⑮ 語順 文末のin North America「北アメリカの中で」に注目。「最も～なひとつで」という意味になる「one of the＋最上級」を選ぶ。largerは、比較級で2つのものを比べるときに使うので、(B)と(C)は誤り。(D)なら「～の中で最大級の」となる。

iron ore deposits 鉄鉱層

5. 正解 (B)

TYPE ⑯ 動詞の形 主語のthe Gulf Coastが自分で「prized（評価した）」だと意味が通らない。be動詞を入れて「評価された」という受け身にする。文末のuntil recentlyを見れば、過去形wasが入るとわかる。

6. 正解 (C)

TYPE 13 文構造　文中にbe動詞のis、しかも選択肢全てにdrawsという動詞がある。基本的に「ひとつの文に主語と動詞はひとつずつ」というルールがあるので、drawsは節に入れなければならない。関係代名詞のある(B)と(C)が残るが、(B) which it drawsだと、主格のwhichと主語のitが重複になってしまう。(C)を入れれば、関係代名詞thatが節の主語、そして先行詞が直前のThe powerになり、The power ... orbitまでが本文の主語になる。

7. 正解 (A)

TYPE 13 文構造　文中にwhich markedとあり、これで「節」と「節の動詞」が見つかった。あとは「文の主語と動詞」を入れる。(D) Was the electionだと疑問文となり、文末に "?" が必要。(C) The election it wasだと主語が重複、(A)のIt was the electionを入れれば、It is/was～that/whichの強調構文となる。完成した文からIt wasとwhichを抜いても文法的に正しい。

8. 正解 (B)

TYPE 14 語彙　カンマの前までにhave been performedという動詞表現が入っている。カンマの後にもhas yet to be identifiedという動詞表現がある。そこで、空所には接続詞を入れてカンマの前までを従属節にしなければならない。(A)と(D)は後ろに名詞を導くのでふさわしくない。後ろを節として導くのは(B) Even thoughのみ。

9. 正解 (A)

TYPE 13 文構造　従属節の主語が主節と同じなら、主語がわかったものとして、従属節の「主語＋be動詞」を省略できる（例：Though [he is] poor, he is satisfied with his life.)。この例と同じで、動詞のある(C)と(D)は誤り。略された「主語＋be動詞」を補うとThough (James Polk) himself (was) not an imaginative statesman, ... となる。

10. 正解 (A)

TYPE 15 語順　「make ＋ A（名詞）＋B（名詞）」で「AをBにする」という意味になる。ここでのBは「冠詞＋形容詞＋名詞」という語順。

11. 正解 (B)

TYPE 16 動詞の形 reduce to で「(〜に) 還元する」。that節の主語は thought (思考)。思考が「還元される」と考え、受け身を選ぶ。During the 1950s, とあるので過去時制の(B)が正解。

12. 正解 (D)

TYPE 13 文構造 that以後に would have という動詞があるのでこれは従属節。that の前に主節の主語と動詞が必要になる。It is/was ... that の構文で、It は that以下の内容を指す。

13. 正解 (A)

TYPE 14 語彙 空所の前の have から完了形だと推測できる。過去分詞が含まれる選択肢は(A)のみ。また、「measures of intelligence (知能測定) は reliable predictors (信頼できる予測値) にならない」という意味なので be動詞が必要。

14. 正解 (D)

TYPE 16 動詞の形 選択肢から空所には動詞が必要とわかる。一般的な事柄を述べているので、時制は現在形。extend という動詞には「言葉の意味範囲を拡大する」という意味がある。ここでは「porpoise という呼び名が広く適用される」という受け身の意味になるので、(D) is extended が正解。

15. 正解 (C)

TYPE 17 並列 カンマに注目。「viral, fungal, and ... (形容詞、形容詞、and空所)」とあるので同じ品詞を入れる。最後の名詞 infection を修飾する bacterial を含む(C)が正解。(D)の infectious も形容詞だが、fungal bacteria (菌性の細菌) では意味が通らない。

Written Expression

Questions 16-40

16. 正解 (B) economic → economically

TYPE(18)品詞 下線(B)の直後にfeasible（便利な＝suitable）という形容詞があるので、その前の形容詞economicをeconomically（経済的に）という副詞に変え、feasibleを修飾する。

17. 正解 (D) who → which

TYPE(22)代名詞 colonies（植民地）という「人」でない「もの」が先行詞の場合、whoでなくてwhichを使う。

18. 正解 (B) in which → by which

TYPE(23)前置詞 下線(B)の前のyardstick（尺度）が、関係代名詞(B) whichの先行詞になる点と、文末に be measured (by)（〜によって測られる）という受け身の動詞があるのがポイント。in whichでなくby whichとする。

19. 正解 (A) a → the

TYPE(28)冠詞 たったひとつしかないこと／ものにはtheを、たくさんあるもののひとつ (one of ...) を表すにはaを使う。mid-20th century（20世紀半ば）は限定された期間なので、冠詞はtheをつける。

20. 正解 (B) look → looks

TYPE(25)動詞の形 下線(B)の前にあるa fixed-end lensはaがついているのでlens（レンズ）は単数名詞、それを受けるlookを三人称単数現在の動詞looksにする。なお、lensの複数形はlenses。

21. 正解 (C) he was → 削除

TYPE(21)並列 複数の項目がカンマでつながっているときは、品詞が一致しているかどうかを見る。ここでは、「名詞句、名詞句、and文」になっているのでhe wasは不用。andの後も名詞句にする。

22. 正解 (C) administration → administrating
TYPE 18 品詞 下線(C)の名詞の直後にまたthe oath「the＋名詞」がある。これを目的語として取る動名詞administrating ～（～すること）に変える。the administration of the oathでもよい。

23. 正解 (D) said → is said
TYPE 25 動詞の形 「the company said（会社は言った）」は意味としておかしいので、isを入れて「～と言われる」という受け身にする。

24. 正解 (A) Much → Many
TYPE 20 単複 可算名詞の複数形lawmenを修飾するのはMuchでなくMany。

25. 正解 (B) retreat → retreated
TYPE 25 動詞の形 文中の完了形を見抜く。it hasの後ろが過去分詞。andで並列されたhas takenと動詞retreat（後退する）にもhasがかかっているので、retreatedとするのが正しい。

26. 正解 (B) deserts → desert
TYPE 19 数の一致 本文の動詞は has been、つまり単数の主語を受ける。よって主語をthe desertという単数名詞にする。of southwestern Arizonaは前置詞句なので、カッコでくくって抜いて考えると、主語が何かわかりやすいだろう。

27. 正解 (A) sick → sickness
TYPE 18 品詞 下線(A)の前の「contagious（伝染性の）」は語尾からも明らかなように、形容詞。形容詞は名詞を修飾し「a＋形容詞＋名詞」となるので、a contagious sicknessとする。He is sick. というように、sickは形容詞。

28. 正解 (A) that → which
TYPE 22 代名詞 カンマにはさまれた部分（that stands ... source,）は「A quasar（準星）」の追加説明にあたる非制限用法。説明の節を挿入するには「カンマ＋which」を使うので、, which ... に変える。誤った形「カンマ＋that」はTOEFLに頻出。

解答と解説

29. 正解 (A) powerful → power

TYPE 21 並列 Q21と同様に、複数の項目がカンマでつながっているときは、品詞が一致しているかどうかを見る。ここでは、「名詞、形容詞、and名詞」になっているので真ん中もpowerという名詞にする。

30. 正解 (D) gradually → gradual

TYPE 21 並列 2つの形容詞で文末にある名詞processを修飾。(D) graduallyは副詞。「a＋形容詞＋yet/but＋形容詞＋名詞」という順番にするためにgradualという形容詞に直す。形容詞を使うべき所に副詞を入れた間違いはTOEFLに非常によく出る。

31. 正解 (D) than → as

TYPE 23 前置詞 「as low a temperature as ～（～のように低い温度）」と同等比較になることを見抜く。下線(A)の直後にあるasは「～として」という意味なので、注意が必要。

32. 正解 (C) it drains → drains

TYPE 24 重複 主語はThe Colorado River。カンマにはさまれた部分は挿入句なのでカッコでくくって抜いて考えてみる。itは主語の重複だとわかる。

33. 正解 (C) and → but

TYPE 29 接続詞 下線(C)の前にあるnot onlyに注目。「～だけでなく～も」という意味を表す、not only ... but alsoの構文にする。

34. 正解 (B) refer → referred

TYPE 25 動詞の形 refer to A as Bは「AをBと呼ぶ」という動詞句。ここではWashington自身が「呼ぶ」のではないので、is referredと受け身にし、「Washingtonが子どもたちによって～と呼ばれる」とする。

35. 正解 (B) as such → such as

TYPE 27 語順 英語は日本語と違って語順を変えると意味が通じなくなる。such as ～で「～のような」という意味。

Practice Test 2

Section 2
Structure
Written
Expression

259

36. 正解 (B) a → an

TYPE 28 冠詞 下線(B)直後に注目。母音で始まるunusuallyには、anをつける。landscapeは可算名詞。

37. 正解 (D) it → them

TYPE 19 数の一致 主語は複数形のelectronsなので、それを指す代名詞はitでなくthemを使う。

38. 正解 (B) those → that

TYPE 19 数の一致 下線(B)の直前 in contrast to は「〜と対比して」という意味。ここでは「A of B, in contrast to A of C」という構造になっている。Aが主語で単数形のThe valueなので、それを指す代名詞は複数形のthoseでなく単数形のthat。

39. 正解 (D) planet → planets

TYPE 20 単複 基本的にthe otherの後には単数名詞も複数名詞も入るが、直前に「the orbits (軌道の数々)」と、sがついているので、planet「惑星」はひとつでなく複数とわかる。

40. 正解 (C) less denser → denser

TYPE 24 重複 比較級は語尾にerをつけるか、単語の前にmoreをつけるかのどちらか。両方つけると重複する。ここでは、lessを削る。

Section 3
Reading Comprehension

Questions 1-9

1. 正解 (C)

TYPE 30 要旨 (A)の「初期の移民がどのようにアメリカへ渡ってきたか」については本文で詳しく触れていない。(D)の「どのようにしてアメリカが少しずつ文明化されていったか」も適切ではない。なぜなら、文明化していく「段階」については全く述べられていないからだ。ここでは生活は困難で野蛮なものだと述べられている。(B)の「初期の移民たちの苦難」については述べられているものの、それは彼らがアメリカやネイティブ・アメリカンを、どう見なしたかということを説明するために触れているだけ。本文の主旨は、「初期の移民たちがどのようにアメリカと先住民たちを見なし、またなぜそう思ったか」ということなので、答えは(C)。

2. 正解 (A)

TYPE 35 Not問題 選択肢(B)(C)(D)は全て初期の移民たちの考え方に影響を与えた自然や環境の困難に関連している。しかし(A)の「インディアンの攻撃」については一切述べられていない。

3. 正解 (D)

TYPE 33 語彙 (D)「utopia(理想郷)」はParadise(楽園)とほぼ同義。その他は(A)「prison(刑務所)」、(B)「arena(闘技場、競技場)」、(C)「retreat(避難所)」という意味で、どれもあてはまらない。

4. 正解 (B)

TYPE 31 事実の確認 3〜4行目の「Unlike Native Americans who had essentially lived in harmony with nature, ...(元来自然と調和して生きていたネイティブ・アメリカンとは違い)」というところから(B)「彼らは自然環境によく適応していた」が答えだとわかる。

5. 正解 （B）

TYPE 31 事実の確認　7～8行目に「sugar and cotton cloth, were in short supply（砂糖と綿の布が不足していた）」とあるので、これを言い換えた(B)が正解。

basic goods 生活必需品　had to do without ～ ～なしで済ます

6. 正解 （C）

TYPE 31 事実の確認　6行目に「Their traditional crops often failed（彼らの伝統的な作物は実らないことが多々あり）」とある。従って正解は(C)。(A)や(D)のような記述はない。(B)については、「the long sea journey（長い航海）」とはあるが、「longer ... than they had imagined（想像以上に長かった）」とは言っていない。

7. 正解 （C）

TYPE 37 理由　なぜ筆者が"道徳的使命"について述べているのかが問われている。本文12行目以下に、その使命とは、「荒涼とした景色とそこに居住する人たちを手なずけ、文明化することだった」と書いてある。このことから(B)と(D)は除外できる。(A)については触れられていない。「mindset（心的態度、考え方）」がどのように形成されたかという意味になる(C)が正解。

8. 正解 （A）

TYPE 33 語彙　(A)「point of view（視点、ものの見方）」が正解。lookとviewはどちらも見ることに関係している。また、outlookの直後に「regard A as B（AをBと見なす）」という表現があるのもヒントになる。

9. 正解 （D）

TYPE 33 語彙　slaughterは「虐殺する、殺りくする」。同意語にはslay、massacre、murderなどがある。(C)のterrorizeは「～に恐怖を起こさせる、脅迫する」といった意味だが、必ずしも人の命を奪うということではないので(D)が最適。

重要語句

immigrant 移民　corruption 腐敗　uncharted 未知の　wilderness 荒れ地
essentially 本質的に　in harmony with ～ ～と調和して　settler 植民者、移住者
adjust to ～ ～に順応する　suffer from ～ ～に苦しむ　crops 作物　commodity (農)
産物　be in short supply 不足している　day-to-day 日々の　sheer まったくの
struggle 闘争　regard ... as ～ ...を～とみなす　hostile 敵意ある　force 力
conquer ～ ～を征服する　tame ～ ～を手なずける　inhabitant 居住者　physical 肉
体の　philosophical 哲学的な、理性的な　noble 高貴な　savage 野蛮人　subhuman
類人、人間以下の　convert to ～ ～に変える　slaughter ～ ～を殺りくする

Questions 10-19

10. 正解 (C)

　TYPE30 要旨　本文は、GNP (第1パラグラフ) とISEW (第2パラグラフ前半)
を直接比較し、それぞれの長所や短所を述べ、異なった経済活動の指針が示す違
い (第2パラグラフ後半) について論じている。GNPだけでなくISEWについて
も論じているので、(A)は誤り。(B)も抽象的で広範囲すぎる。また、(D)はISEW
とGNPの違いを説明するための例として触れているだけであり、主旨ではない。

11. 正解 (D)

　TYPE34 語法　itは先に出た名詞を指す。しかも「it measures (それは測る)」
とあることから、「Gross National Product (GNP)」だとわかる。

12. 正解 (B)

　TYPE32 推論　第1パラグラフ後半で、「環境問題への対策に当てられる費用を
差し引かない」という理由で、環境保護主義者たちはGNPに対して批判的であ
ると述べている。その例としてthe expense of cleaning up pollutionを挙げて
いるので(B)「危険廃棄物処理場の浄化」が正解。

13. 正解 (A)

TYPE 33 語彙 「be critical of ～（～に批判的で）＝ be skeptical of ～（～に懐疑的で）」。どちらも「信用してない」という意味で同じ。(B) curious about と (C) interested in は「be inquisitive of ～（～に興味がある）」という意味。(D) serious about は「～に対して真剣である」という意味。

14. 正解 (A)

TYPE 33 語彙 subtract と deduct は、どちらも「引く」という意味で同意語。(B) consider は「take into account（考慮に入れる）」、(C) mention は refer や bring up（言及する）という意味。(D) allocate は「designate（割り当てる、配分する）」といった意味。同じ文の後半で例として挙げられているものが「depletion（枯渇）、loss（損失）、expense（出費）」となっているところからも推測できるだろう。

15. 正解 (D)

TYPE 32 推論 最後の文に注目。「1951年から1986年の間、ISEWの数値は quality of life が20パーセントしか向上してないことを示している」。(D)の選択肢中「only somewhat better（いく分か良くなっただけ）」が本文の「only improved 20 percent（20パーセントしか向上していない）」に相当している。

16. 正解 (C)

TYPE 31 事実の確認 第1パラグラフの最終文に示されているように、環境保護主義者から見て主な欠点となるのは、「GNP が資源の損失や環境破壊などを差し引かないこと」。よって(C)が正解。

17. 正解 (C)

TYPE 37 理由 13行目に「the goods and services that genuinely contribute to a better quality of life（より良い生活の質に真に貢献する商品やサービス）」とあり、それに含まれるものとして「unpaid household labor（無報酬の家事労働）」が挙げられている。従って正解は(C)。(A)や(B)のようなことは言っていない。また税金の話はしていないので(D)も不適切。

18. 正解 (B)

TYPE③ 語彙 (B)「nonessential（必須でない）」と同じ意味。文中で、superfluous itemsについてthat以降で「慣例として経済的価値を付加されてきたものが、実際には生活の質の向上に寄与していないもの」と説明しているところから推測できる。superfluousは「extra（余分の）、dispensable（なくても済む）、unnecessary（不必要な）」と同意。反意語は(A)のvaluable。(C)「traditional（伝統的な）」、(D)「useless（役に立たない）」。

19. 正解 (D)

TYPE㉟ Not問題 15行目でhighways、health、educationの費用は、ISEWに含まれると述べている。また、Advertisingは17行目にISEWから差し引かれるsuperfluous itemの例として挙げられている。

重要語句

commonly 一般的に severe 厳密な limitation 制限 output 産出 take into account 〜 〜を考慮に入れる burn to the ground 焼け落ちる net gain 純益 net loss 正味の損失 genuinely 本当に expend 〜 〜を費やす environmentalist 環境主義者 in particular 特に fail to 〜 〜し損なう deduct 控除する non-renewable 再生・更新できない expense 経費 pollution 汚染 measurement ものさし propose 〜 〜を提案する substitute for 〜 〜の代用として sustainable 持続できる add up 〜 〜を合計する contribute to 〜 〜に貢献する subtract 〜 〜を引き算する superfluous なくてもよい conventionally 慣習として、伝統的に insight 洞察 comparison 比較

Questions 20-29

20. 正解 (B)

TYPE㉜ 推論 第1パラグラフの最後の文に「potential for increased meat production, milk yield,（肉や牛乳の産出量を増加させる潜在力）」とある。この内容を言い換えた(B)「水牛はpromising（有望な）タンパク質源」が正解。

21. 正解 (D)

TYPE㉛ 事実の確認 3行目に「They are noted for their rather unusual horns（かなり風変わりな角が特徴）」とある。つまり、(D)「非常に特徴的な角を持っている」のである。

22. 正解 (C)

TYPE 33 語彙 roughlyという副詞は連結詞 (主語と述語をつなぐ語、例えばbe動詞) と共に用いられると「おおよそ、ざっと (＝ approximately ＝ about)」という意味になる。ちなみに、動作を表す動詞を修飾するときは「乱暴に、粗く」といった意味。

23. 正解 (B)

TYPE 34 語法 代名詞が指すものは、前の文に入っていることが多い。文脈を読み取ると、「これまで無視されてきたが、they have recently begun to receive recognition (最近 [世界で] 認知され始めている)」ということで、theyとはこのパラグラフの主題であるwater buffaloだとわかる。このパラグラフには何度もtheyが出てくるが、それらは全てwater buffaloを指している。

24. 正解 (C)

TYPE 31 事実の確認 「水牛の身体的特徴」が正解。最初のパラグラフの前半は全て水牛の「見た目」を描写している。(A)「水牛に関する迷信」(B)「水牛が好む気候」(D)「水牛を繁殖させる可能性」などは、全て次のパラグラフで詳しく扱っている。

25. 正解 (A)

TYPE 33 語彙 genialは性質・態度などが「温和な、優しい」という意味。(C)「genuine (本物の)」のように、音やスペリングが似た紛らわしい選択肢はひっかけなので、意味をはっきり知っているとき以外は選ばないこと。

26. 正解 (D)

TYPE 31 事実の確認 設問中のthriveは「よく育つ、成長する」ということ。13～14行目に「they in fact grow and reproduce normally without it, as long as adequate shade is available. (実際、水がなくても適切な [木陰さえあれば] 普通に育ち、繁殖する)」とある。よって(D)「太陽光からの保護」が正解。

解答と解説

27. 正解 (A)

TYPE 33 語彙 tolerance の意味を知っていれば「the breed's tolerance for heat and humidity（その種の熱や湿気に対する耐性）」、言い換えれば「暑さや湿気に adjust（適応）できること」という意味で (A) が正解だとわかるだろう。知らなかったとしても、「水草を好み、熱と湿気に XXX という長所」という文脈から (B)「〜への依存」、(D)「〜に対する無関心」を消去できる。さらに Q26 の説明でも触れた adequate shade is available という1文を思い出せば、(C)「preference for（〜への好み）」よりは (A)「adaptability to（〜へ適応能力）」のほうがふさわしいとわかる。

28. 正解 (C)

TYPE 35 Not問題 (C) の「人を be averse to（嫌う）傾向がある」が本文の内容に反している。第2パラグラフの初めのほうに、「they are probably the gentlest farm animals in the world: sociable, genial, and fond of humans.（おそらく世界で最も穏和な家畜であろう。社交的で、おおらか、人なつっこい）」とあり、この部分が選択肢 (A) と (D) の「a mild temperament（穏やかな性格）」の言い換え、つまり (C) の反対になる。(B) は 15〜16行目の「their adaptability has allowed them to be raised in a number of climates.（その適応力により、水牛はさまざまな気候で成長することができる）」という部分と同意。

29. 正解 (A)

TYPE 31 事実の確認 (A) の「水牛の元々の生息地に似た気候条件がある」が正解。まず、設問に Florida と出てくるので、本文中で University of Florida とある文を探す。次にこの文の先頭に「For this reason（この理由で）」という接続語がついているので、その直前の文を読む。「in a climate similar to the water buffalo's original native environment（水牛が元々生息していた環境に似た気候）」とあり、選択肢 (A) は「akin to 〜（=similar to 〜：〜に似て）」を使い言い換えている。

Practice Test 2

Section 3

267

Practice Test 2

重要語句

unrelated 関係がない　bison バイソン、野牛　refer to ... as ～ …を～と呼ぶ
roughly 大体、おおよそ　be noted for ～ ～でよく知られている　horn 角
sweptback 後ろに伸びた　rancher 牧場（農園）主　recognition 認められること
domestic 国内の　unexplored 未知の　potential 可能性　work output 労働力
abound 多分に　vicious 癖の悪い、狂暴な　breed 種　whereas ところが（事実は）
sociable 社交的な　genial 明るくて優しい　wallow 転げ回る　reproduce 繁殖する
adequate 十分な　misconception 思い違い　exclusively 限定して　adaptability
適応能力　raise ～ ～を育てる、飼育する　despite ～ ～にも関わらず　commercial
商業的な　herd 群れ　subsequent その後の　definite 明確な　under conditions
of ～ ～の状況下で　competitive advantage 競争になっても負けない優利性
　calf 子牛　tolerance 耐久（力）　humidity 湿度　considerable かなりの
corresponding 対応する、類似の

Questions 30-39

30. 正解 (C)

TYPE30 要旨　本文の主なテーマはジョン・アダムズの財源について。副大統領
時代、大統領時代の給与、そして退職後、資産をくずしながら生活したこと、そ
して彼の遺産などについて触れている。(A)の「Major events（主な出来事）」に
ついては扱っていない。(B)の「Early presidents of the United States（アメリ
カ初期の大統領）」についても多くは語られていない。(D)初期の大統領や副大統
領たちの給与については述べられているが、これは主旨を説明するための詳細の
一部に過ぎない。(C)が正解。

31. 正解 (B)

TYPE33 語彙　「A short, XXX man ... enjoyed a robust life（背が低く、XXX
な男は活発な生活を楽しんだ）」とあるので、答えは見た目についてだとわかる。
よって(A)「健康な」や(D)「感じのよい」などが消える。ではsturdyはというと、
これは「（体が）たくましい、頑健な」という意味。(B) chubby（ふっくらした）
が正解である。

32. 正解▶ (B)
TYPE 32 推論 出だしの1文、「... John Adams enjoyed a robust life (活発な生活を楽しんだ), in contrast to (〜に対比して) his predecessor, George Washington.」に注目。文中の「robust (活発な、丈夫な)」から、アダムズはワシントンよりも健康であったことがわかる。他の選択肢は、本文から読み取れるほどはっきりとは書かれていない。

33. 正解▶ (C)
TYPE 32 推論 6〜7行目にアダムズの副大統領時代の給料は「too little to live on (生活するには少なすぎた)」、7〜8行目に大統領時代の給料は「still too little to cover his official expenses (公務上の費用を賄うには少なすぎた)」とある。よって、(C)「稼いだ額よりも多くを使った」が正解。(A)は反対の意味で、(B)「lived in relative poverty (比較的貧しく暮らした)」というのは大統領や副大統領、土地所有者として生きた彼には当てはまらない。(D)の his wife については、少し触れているだけで、彼女の収入が多かったとも「裕福であった」とも記されていない。

34. 正解▶ (A)
TYPE 31 事実の確認 6行目に「... as vice president when his salary was a pitiful $5,000, ...」とある。アダムズが副大統領だったときの給料の額がはっきり述べられている。

pitiful 乏しい、みじめな、不十分な

35. 正解▶ (C)
TYPE 34 語法 it は前の文の単数名詞 his salary、つまりアダムズの給与を指す。それより前の単数名詞、(A)「a single term in office (在職中の1期)」や(B)「financial difficulty (経済的困難)」などは示さない。(D)の「Adams' fortune (アダムズの財産)」については後の文で述べられている。

36. 正解▶ (A)
TYPE 31 事実の確認 8行目に「大統領を serving a single term (1期務めた)」後、退職したとある。

37. 正解▶ (A)

TYPE 33 語彙 seclusionは「隔離、隠遁」、つまり(A)「relative isolation (比較的孤独な状態)」と同じこと。in solitude (ひとりで、寂しく) とも同義。一方(B) active retirementは「活発な退職者生活」を示唆し、(C)「periodic consultation (定期的な相談)」については触れられていない。(D)「intermittent depression (断続的なうつ状態)」をアダムズが経験したとは本文にない。

38. 正解▶ (D)

TYPE 33 語彙 直前に「Adams had lived so long off his fortune that ... (アダムズは自分の財産を使ってとても長生きした)」とある。そこでdwindledが「減少した」という意味だと推測できる。(A)「doubled (2倍になった)」、(B)「increased (増加した)」、(C)「equaled (等しくなった)」はいずれも不適切。

39. 正解▶ (B)

TYPE 31 事実の確認 まず、(C)のようなことは書かれていない。また、年上の息子が大統領になったとは書いてあるが(A)のようにアダムズが息子を「groom (仕込む)」したとは述べていない。(D)の「presidential library (大統領の蔵書)」があったのは確かだが、それが「first (初の)」図書館だったか、またそのための「materials (資料)」を「compile (集めた)」のかどうかの記述はない。libraryには蔵書という意味もあるので注意。9行目に「in seclusion at his Quincy estate (クインシーにある自邸でひっそり過ごし)」とあることからも(B)が正解だとわかる。

重要語句

plump 肉付きのよい　robust 活発な、丈夫な　in contrast to ~ ~と対照的に　predecessor 前任者　vice 副~　dip into ~ (金) に手をつける　expense 費用　in seclusion 隠遁生活をする　beneficiary (保険金などの) 受取人　surviving 生き残っている　dwindle 次第に減少する　inherit ~ ~を相続する　portion 分与産、相続分　asset 遺産　be confused with ~ ~と混同する　foreshadow ~ ~の前兆となる、~を予示する　footstep 足跡、歩み

解答と解説

Practice Test 2

Section 3

Questions 40-50

40. 正解 (D)

TYPE 30 要旨　本文の最初で、「A fiber may be defined as ... its width. (繊維とは、長さが幅の200倍大きい物質のまとまりと定義できる)」とfiberの定義がなされ、第2文で「Natural fibers comprise three categories: ... (天然繊維は3つのカテゴリーから成る)」と繊維を種類ごとに分けてそれぞれの利用法について述べている。(D)「天然繊維：その分類と利用」が答え。

41. 正解 (B)

TYPE 31 事実の確認　3～4行目に「Although more than 2,000 types of fibrous plants have been identified (2,000種以上の繊維植物が見つかったが)」とある。

42. 正解 (A)

TYPE 34 語法　代名詞の問題が出たら、直前にある名詞を見ればいい。この場合はtheseなので、複数形のものを探す。前文の複数名詞「fibrous plants (繊維植物)」で商用に向くものを指している。

43. 正解 (D)

TYPE 33 語彙　cultivatingは「栽培すること」。(D)の「growing (育てること)」が近い。(A)「producing (製造すること)」は直前の説明に出てきているので除外する。(B)「exporting (輸出すること)」、(C)「marketing (販売すること)」は、それぞれ本文には関係ない。

44. 正解 (A)

TYPE 31 事実の確認　3行目に「The first, cellulose base,... (ひとつ目のセルロース質のものは……)」とあるので、以降の文に説明があるとわかる。直後の文Although more than 2,000 types ...50 have commercial uses.を見れば、2,000のうちの50だけなので(A)「比較的小さな割合の繊維植物が元になっている」が正解。

271

45. 正解 (A)

TYPE 33 語彙 retainは(A)「hold（保つ、維持する［＝keep、control]）」と同義。(B) claimは「主張する、要求する（＝assert、demand)」、(C) transferは「移す（＝change、move、shift)」、(D) resistは「反対する、抵抗する（＝oppose、contest)」。

46. 正解 (C)

TYPE 31 事実の確認 第3パラグラフで、「asbestos（石綿、アスベスト）」について言及されている。設問のbeen replaced by other materialsは第3パラグラフの最終文のasbestos has given way to other materials.を言い換えたもの。直前の「with the revelation that continued exposure to it can cause cancer, （継続的にさらされていると、ガンを発症する可能性が明らかとなり)」がその原因。(C)の「健康に危害を及ぼすものが含まれている」が正解。

47. 正解 (D)

TYPE 35 Not問題 最初のパラグラフの最後から2番目の文に、「the cost of cultivating jute is much lower（ジュートの栽培費は〈綿に比べて〉かなり低い)」とある。つまり(D)「製造がより安価」が正解。第1パラグラフの最後の文では、ジュートは「coarse（きめが粗い)、difficult to dye（染めにくい)、lacking in tensile strength（伸長性に欠ける)」と述べられている。言い換えると、綿はジュートより(A)「肌触りの滑らかさ」(B)「生地の強さ」(C)「染めやすさ」などの点で優れているということ。

48. 正解 (B)

TYPE 34 語法 代名詞itの問題は、直前の名詞に注目すればいいのだが、この設問のポイントは、直前の17行目に2つある代名詞itsも同じものを指し、しかも答えとなるasbestosがsで終わる不可算名詞であること。

49. 正解 (A)

TYPE 33 語彙　capacity は (A)「ability（能力 [＝capability、adequacy]）」のこと。(B) volume は「量（＝amount、quantity）」、(C) tendency は「傾向、趣向（＝inclination、predilection）」、(D) characteristic は「特徴、資質、特性（＝attribute、quality、feature）」という意味。

50. 正解 (B)

TYPE 31 事実の確認　第4パラグラフの最初の文で「except asbestos（石綿以外）」と断った上で、「The capacity of these natural fibers to absorb moisture makes them suitable for use in clothing ...（天然繊維の湿気を吸収する能力は……、衣服への使用に適している）」と述べている。従って、(B)「湿気を吸収できない」が正解。

【重要語句】

fiber 繊維　comprise ～ ～から成る　cellulose セルロース　identify 確認する　commercial uses 商業利用　by far はるかに　in terms of ～ ～の点から　consumption 消費　application 応用　range 種類　textile 織物　stalk 茎　be second to ～ ～に次いで　be inferior to ～ ～に劣った　coarse 粗い　tensile 伸張の　pelt 生皮　extrude ～ ～を（押し）出す　filament 細糸　silkworm カイコ　asbestos 石綿　brittle もろい　subsequent その次の　fire-resistance 耐火　revelation （～だと）明らかにされた事実　exposure to 触れさせること　hydrophilic 親水性の　affinity for ～ ～との相性　vapor 蒸気　absorb 吸収する　artificial 人工の　inability できないこと

Practice Test 3
解 答 と 解 説

解答の冒頭にある「TYPE」アイコンは「出題傾向と対策」(pp.12〜35) で解説
した問題タイプを示しています。

 はその問題が「難問」であることを示しています。正解できたら自信を持って
ください。

解答済みのマークシート（別冊巻末）と照らし合わせましょう。

正答一覧

Section 1

#	Ans	#	Ans	#	Ans	#	Ans	#	Ans
1	A	11	B	21	D	31	C	41	D
2	C	12	C	22	C	32	B	42	A
3	B	13	B	23	B	33	D	43	C
4	B	14	A	24	A	34	B	44	A
5	D	15	A	25	C	35	B	45	A
6	C	16	B	26	D	36	C	46	C
7	A	17	D	27	C	37	C	47	B
8	B	18	C	28	A	38	D	48	D
9	C	19	A	29	B	39	A	49	B
10	D	20	D	30	C	40	B	50	D

Section 2

#	Ans	#	Ans	#	Ans	#	Ans	#	Ans
1	B	9	A	17	D	25	C	33	C
2	A	10	B	18	D	26	B	34	D
3	C	11	C	19	A	27	A	35	C
4	B	12	A	20	A	28	A	36	B
5	D	13	C	21	D	29	A	37	B
6	C	14	B	22	C	30	D	38	C
7	C	15	B	23	D	31	D	39	C
8	B	16	D	24	A	32	A	40	A

Section 3

#	Ans	#	Ans	#	Ans	#	Ans	#	Ans
1	B	11	C	21	A	31	B	41	C
2	B	12	A	22	C	32	C	42	D
3	D	13	B	23	B	33	C	43	C
4	A	14	D	24	B	34	A	44	B
5	A	15	B	25	D	35	D	45	A
6	C	16	D	26	C	36	B	46	C
7	C	17	C	27	B	37	B	47	C
8	B	18	C	28	C	38	A	48	A
9	C	19	B	29	B	39	B	49	C
10	D	20	C	30	A	40	C	50	D

Section 1
Listening Comprehension

Part A

mp3 **118-122**

1. 正解 (A)

W: Fred! How's your science project coming along?
M: It couldn't be better. I'll have the final results in a couple of days.
Q: What does the man imply about his science project?

TYPE 2 言外の意味　「It couldn't be better.」が聞き取りのポイント。「これ以上良くなりようがない、最高だ」という意味。科学のプロジェクトは順調に進んでいるのだ。

come along (仕事などが) うまく進む　final result 最終結果　in a couple of days 2〜3日中に　proceed 進む

2. 正解 (C)

M: How come you're writing an essay about the Depression?
W: It's an assignment for my history class.
Q: What does the woman mean?

TYPE 1 発言の意味　ポイントは、「assignment」。女性が「It's an assignment (それは課題なの)」と言っているので、そのエッセーは授業で課されている (required) ということ。

How come? =Why?　the Depression 世界大恐慌　assignment 課題、宿題　be required for 〜 〜(のコースのため) に課されている

3. 正解 (B)

W: How often does the shuttle bus leave for the airport?
M: Every half hour.
Q: What does the man say about the bus?

Rare C Say about問題　バスの頻度は30分毎なので、1時間には2本出る。よって、(B)が正解。

Practice Test 3

4. 正解 (B)

M: I can't believe I've got final papers and final exams in every class.
W: Wow, you've really got your work cut out for you at the end of this term.
Q: What does the woman mean?

TYPE 1 発言の意味 「全部のクラスに期末リポートと期末試験がある」と嘆く男性に、「大変な仕事をかかえている」と言っている。つまり、(B)「男性はたくさん勉強しなくてはならない」という意味。

5. 正解 (D)

M: Why don't you come over and watch a movie this afternoon?
W: Picked up a couple DVDs from the rental shop, did you?
Q: What is the woman assuming?

Rare A 推量 口語によくある省略、「(You) Picked up a couple (of) DVDs」は、「(あなたは) DVDを2〜3本手に入れたのね」という意味。つまり「has rented some DVDs (何枚かDVDを借りたんだろう)」と考えている。

come over 立ち寄る　a couple (of) 〜s　ofを略すのは (米) 口語

mp3 **123-127**

6. 正解 (C)

W: Tom, you haven't been in art history class all week!
M: Yeah, that's right. And as a matter of fact, I was wondering if you might let me copy your notes.
Q: What does the man mean?

TYPE 1 発言の意味 男性が「if you might let me copy your notes (ノートをコピーさせてもらえないかな)」と言っているので(C)「ノートを借りたい」が正解。

as a matter of fact 本当のところ、実際　borrow 〜 〜を借りる

7. 正解 (A)

W: I've decided to go ahead and take that extra job on weekends.
M: Gee, Carol, are you sure you can handle that on top of everything else you have to do?
Q: What does the man mean?

278

TYPE①発言の意味　on top of ~は「~に加えて」という意味のイディオム。男性は、女性が「trying to do too much（多くをやり過ぎ）」だと言っているのだ。

🔊 **8. 正解** (B)

M: I heard you and Jane ate at that new German restaurant last night. What'd you think?
W: I've definitely had better.
Q: What does the woman mean?

TYPE①発言の意味　女性の発言は、「I've definitely had better food at other places.」の略で、「他のところでもっとおいしいものを食べたことがあった」という意味。つまり(B)「そこの食事はあまりおいしくなかった」のだ。

definitely 絶対に

9. 正解 (C)

W: Did you finish writing your essay yet? It's due tomorrow, you know.
M: Finish it? I haven't even decided on my topic yet.
Q: What does the man imply about the essay?

TYPE②言外の意味　「Finish it?」のように相手の言葉を繰り返すパターンは会話でよくある。「終わったかって？　まさか」と反対の事実を強調したいときに用いる表現だ。それを補足するように、男性が「題材すらまだ決めていない」と言っている。よって(C)「書き始めてすらいない」が正解。

be due 期限である　topic 題材

10. 正解 (D)

W: Have you had a chance to look over the Wilson contract we signed last week?
M: I haven't gotten around to it yet.
Q: What can be inferred about the man from this conversation?

TYPE③推論　「I haven't gotten around to it yet.」が聞き取りのポイント。「not get around to」は「忙しくて手が回らない」という意味。(D)「他の仕事でずっと忙しい」のだ。(A)と(B)に登場するcontractという単語にまどわされないこと。

contract 契約書　get around to ~ ~に取りかかる、~のための時間を見つける

Practice Test 3

Section 1
Part A
Part B
Part C

279

Practice Test 3

11. 正解 (B)

M: There's no way I can get all the anthropology reading done before the mid-term.

W: You're not alone. Everyone in the class is in exactly the same boat as you.

Q: What does the woman imply about the members of the anthropology class?

TYPE ② 言外の意味 女性の発言にある「in the same boat」は「同じボートに乗っている＝同じ境遇（苦境・立場・運命）にある」という意味のイディオム。男性が「どうしても人類学のリーディングが終わらない」と言ったのに対して、女性が「みんなが同じ状況よ」と答えている。よって正解は(B)。

> There's no way どうしても〜ない　anthropology 人類学　in the same boat 同じ境遇にある　be behind in 〜 〜が遅れている

12. 正解 (C)

W: Here's my credit card to pay the bill.

M: I'm sorry, Ma'am, we only accept cash.

Q: What will the woman probably do?

TYPE ⑤ 未来予測 「we only accept cash（現金しか受け付けない）」という部分が聞き取れれば、おのずと正解は出る。女性は、(C)「現金で支払う」はずだ。

> accept 〜 〜を受け取る

13. 正解 (B)

M: Oh, no! I forgot to make the plane reservations for my trip to San Antonio.

W: Well, you'd better get on it right away if you still want to go.

Q: What does the woman suggest the man should do?

TYPE ④ 提案・示唆 男性が忘れたのは、「make the plane reservations（飛行機の予約を取る）」こと。そして女性の発言「you'd better get on it right away」が聞き取れれば正解は(B)とわかる。bookは「〜を予約する」という意味の動詞。

> get on it 取りかかる　at once (=right away) すぐに

14. 正解 (A)

M: What a beautiful bird! Have you ever seen one like it?

W: Not in these parts. I think they're almost always found further south.

Q: What does the woman imply about the bird?

TYPE 2 言外の意味 男性の「なんてきれいな鳥だ！ こんなの見たことある？」という質問に対する女性の答え、「Not in these parts.（この辺りでは見ない）」が聞き取りのポイント。これは「I don't see it in these parts.」ということなので、正解は(A)「この辺ではめったに見られない」だ。

further south もっと南のほう　rarely めったに〜ない

15. 正解 (A)

W: I've been standing in line here for 15 minutes.

M: I'm sorry, Ma'am. When we have a lot of customers, our principle is first come first served.

Q: What does the man imply?

TYPE 2 言外の意味 男性の発言中の「first come first served」は、「早く来た人から順番に応対する」という意味。つまり、「全員に即座に対応するのは困難」ということなので、(A)の「女性はもっと辛抱強くあるべき」が正解。

in line 並んで　patient 忍耐強い

mp3 133-137

16. 正解 (B)

M: It's 5 o'clock. Where is Murray?

W: You didn't know? He's been under the weather the last few days.

Q: What does the woman say about Murray?

Rare C Say about問題 女性の言った「He's been under the weather the last few days.」という一文が、マレーの状況を表わしている。「under the weather」とは「体調が優れない、悪い（＝not feeling well）」という意味のイディオム。

Practice Test 3

17. 正解 (D)

M: The cold spell they forecast for the weekend turned out to be nothing.

W: Didn't it, though?

Q: What does the woman imply?

TYPE 2 言外の意味 女性の発言が聞き取りのポイント。この「Didn't it, though?」(否定＋代名詞, thoughの形で使う) は「そうね」という意味。

turn out to be 〜 〜だとわかる

18. 正解 (C)

W: The cross-town expressway looks pretty crowded this morning.

M: We might be better off taking another route.

Q: What does the man imply?

TYPE 2 言外の意味 女性の「高速道路が混んでいる」という発言に対して、男性が「another route (他の道) で行ったほうが better off (まし) かも」と答えている。よって (C)「別の道のほうが速いかもしれない」が正解。(B) のように、発音の似た単語 (clouds ← crowded) を含む選択肢は避けること。

the cross-town expressway 都市部を横断する高速道路　be better off 状況がよくなる　route 道

19. 正解 (A)

W: I don't know why I'm always so tired lately.

M: Think it could have something to do with all of those late-night study sessions you and your friends have been having?

Q: What does the man imply the woman should do?

TYPE 2 言外の意味 女性が「なぜか最近疲れる」と言うと、男性は「have something to do with (関係しているのは) late-night study session (深夜の勉強会じゃないか)」と言った。つまり、暗に「stop studying so hard (勉強をしすぎないように)」と言っているのだ。

have something to do with 〜 〜と関係がある

解答と解説

20. 正解 (D)

M: How about this weather we're having?
W: You couldn't ask for anything nicer.
Q: What can be inferred about the weather?

TYPE 3 推論 couldn't ask for anything nicer は「これ以上良いのは（求められ）ない」、つまり (D) の「almost perfect（ほぼ完璧）」という意味。

ask for 〜 〜を求める

---

mp3 138-142

21. 正解 (D)

M: Have you learned how you did on your comprehensive exam?
W: As a matter of fact I have. My professor told me this morning that I had one of the top scores in the entire class.
Q: What does the woman suggest about her performance on the exam?

TYPE 4 提案・示唆 女性の発言にある、「one of the top scores」が聞き取りのポイント。「最高点のひとつ」という意味なので (D)「彼女は（総合試験で）立派な成績を収めた」（＝ performed very well）が正解。

comprehensive exam 総合試験　as a matter of fact 実を言うと　perform（任務などを）果たす、やり遂げる

22. 正解 (C)

M: What do you say to a cup of coffee after our biology class?
W: Why not? My Canadian history class was cancelled today, so I don't have another class until 1:00.
Q: What does the woman mean?

TYPE 1 発言の意味 女性が言った「Why not?」は「もちろん」という意味。ここが聞き取れれば答えは簡単。「授業の後、コーヒーでもどう？」という男性の誘いに女性は同意しているのだ。「What do you say to 〜（〜をどう思う？）」は、よく使われる勧誘表現。

class was cancelled 授業が休講になった

Practice Test 3

Section 1
Part A
Part B
Part C

283

23. 正解 (B)

M: Patricia, there's a call on line 3 for you.

W: For me? Who would be phoning me at the office?

Q: What can be inferred from the woman's question?

TYPE③ 推論 電話がかかっていると伝えられた女性が「For me?（私に？）Who would be phoning me（誰が電話してきているのかしら）at the office?（会社にまで？）」と言っている。ここから(B)「彼女は仕事場でめったに電話を受けない」と推論できる。

seldom めったに～ない

24. 正解 (A)

W: When do you think we could get together to talk about next year's budget?

M: What's wrong with right now?

Q: What does the man mean?

TYPE① 発言の意味 女性の「When ～」という時間を問う質問に対して、男性が「What's wrong with right now?（今じゃだめですか？）」と答えている。つまり(A)「すぐに（＝immediately）会うべきだ」と言っている。

get together 集まる、寄り合う　budget 予算　What's wrong with ～? ～ではいけませんか？

25. 正解 (C)

M: Class starts in just 15 minutes and Mark forgot to bring all the photographs we need to make our group presentation. What'll we do now?

W: Didn't I tell you something like this would happen?

Q: What does the woman imply?

TYPE② 言外の意味 男性が「マークがグループ発表に必要な写真を全て忘れた」と言うと、女性が「Didn't I tell you（言ったでしょ）something like this would happen?（こんなことが起こりそうだって）」と答えている。つまり、(C)「彼女はマークがlet them down（彼らをがっかりさせる）のではないか」と疑っていたのだ。

mp3 **143-147**

26. 正解 (D)

W: My mother sent me a box of chocolates. You want some?

M: If I hadn't stepped on the scales this morning, I might have taken you up on your offer.

Q: What does the man imply?

TYPE 2 言外の意味 「the scales」は「体重計」。男性が「今朝、体重計に乗っていなければ」と言っているところから、体重(weight)を気にしていることがわかる。男性の発言は、「もしも〜だったなら、〜だっただろう」という事実に反する仮定法過去完了。

step on 〜 〜に乗る　take one up on 〜（人の意向に）応じる　offer 申し出

27. 正解 (C)

M: Something's wrong with this printer.

W: What?

Q: What does the woman want to know?

Rare B Want問題 男性がプリンターの調子が悪いと言うと、女性が下げるイントネーションで「What?」と聞いている。つまり「何が？」と、プリンターの問題そのものを具体的に尋ねているのだ。もしもこれが上がるイントネーションであったならば、ただの聞き返しで(A)が正解になり得る。

something is wrong with〜 〜の調子が悪い

28. 正解 (A)

W: You actually think you're going to get that teaching job you applied for?

M: Absolutely. It's already in the bank. I heard from them yesterday.

Q: What does the man mean?

TYPE 1 発言の意味 「be in the bank」とは、「安全である」という意味のイディオム。「応募した仕事、本当に受かると思う？」と言われて、男性は「（もう銀行に預けたように）安心している」と言っているのだ。よって解答は銀行そのものには関係ない。正解は(A)の「彼は本当に望んでいた仕事を得た」。

apply for 〜 〜に申し込む

29. 正解 (B)

M: Pick you up to go to the football game around seven?
W: You're going to a football game?
Q: What does the woman imply about the man?

TYPE 2 言外の意味　女性が驚いた様子で「あなたがフットボールの試合に行くの？」と反応しているので、(B)「彼は頻繁にはフットボールを見ない」と推測できる。

pick one up（車で）（人を）迎えに行く

30. 正解 (C)

M: Too bad about today's picnic, huh?
W: Yeah, I'm really surprised we got rained out. Maybe we can reschedule it for next week.
Q: What can be inferred about the man and woman from the conversation?

TYPE 3 推論　男性の「今日のピクニックは残念だね」という発言に対する女性の返事から、雨にたたられたことがわかる。その後に女性が「来週に計画を変更（reschedule）できる」と言っているので、2人はピクニックを延期する（postpone）はずである。

Part B

mp3 149-153

Questions 31-34

Listen to the following conversation about a debate tournament.

W: Ed! What are you doing here on a Sunday?
M: I'm meeting the other members of my debate team.
W: On Sunday? I thought you lived more than an hour from campus.
M: I do, but the regional debate tournament our university sponsors begins the first thing tomorrow and we need all the practice we can get.
W: Oh, that's right. I've seen posters up all around school. Students

from all the local universities will participate, right?

M: That's right. And this year our team is going to win it all!

W: You're pretty confident, aren't you? By the way, who'll make the decision about who wins?

M: Would you believe that there are people who make a living from judging debate contests?

W: You mean professionals? Isn't it expensive to pay people like that?

M: It sure is. In the past we've just asked members of the local community or professors from other schools. But with the reputation our tournament has achieved the past couple of years we decided we need judges with formal training and experience.

W: What do they base their decision on? The creativity of your arguments and stuff like that?

M: Actually, making an original argument is not nearly as important as how the argument is presented.

W: What do you mean?

M: Well, for example, you get points for your team's delivery style and for how favorably the audience responds to your argument. And you need to organize the argument clearly so that each point follows logically from the next. That's really tough to do, because we don't learn what the topic is until a few minutes before the debate actually begins.

W: Sounds like you do need to practice even on the weekend! Good luck, Ed! I hope your team wins.

M: Thanks. We'll do our best.

> debate ディベート、討論   regional 地域の、地方の   participate 参加する
> confident 自信がある   make the decision 決定する   make a living from ~ ～で
> 生計を立てる   reputation 評判   and stuff like that そんなようなもの   favorably
> 好意を持って   logically 論理的に   tough 難しい

31. 正解▶ (C)

Q: When is the tournament going to take place?

TYPE 7 When問題   男性が2つ目の発言で「the regional debate tournament ... begins the first thing tomorrow(ディベートの地区大会は明日の朝一番に始まる)」と言っている。

32. 正解 (B)

Q: Who will judge the debate contest?

TYPE 10 Who/Whom問題　中盤で、男性が「In the past we've just asked ...」と、(今は違うが)過去のこととして(C)のMembers of the local communityや(D)のProfessors from area colleges (= other schools) に審査員を依頼していたとある。その後で、「やはり正式な訓練を受けた審査員が必要だ」と言っているので、正解は(B)の「プロのディベートの審査員」。

33. 正解 (D)

Q: How will the debaters know which topic to debate?

TYPE 12 How問題　男性の最後から2番目の発言に「That's really tough to do, (それはとても大変なことで) because we don't learn what the topic is until a few minutes before the debate actually begins. (ディベートが実際始まる数分前までトピックが何なのかわからない)」と言っている。よって(D)の「それは、ディベートの直前に発表される」が正解。

34. 正解 (B)

Q: According to the man, what will NOT be one of the major criteria used in deciding the winner?

TYPE 9 What問題　女性が「What do they base their decision on? (何を基準に判定するの?)」と尋ねると、男性が「Actually, making an original argument is not nearly as important as how the argument is presented. (実は独創的な主張を述べることは、主張のプレゼンの仕方ほど重要じゃないんだ)」と明かしている。

mp3 **154-158**

Questions 35-38

Listen to a conversation between two students.

M: You look really tired, Theresa. Have you been sleeping OK?
W: Well, actually, it's been a while since I got a full night's sleep.

You see, the art department is putting on the senior exhibit next week, and we have to mount and frame all of the photographs and paintings.

M: Wow. That sounds like a big job.

W: It is. All of the seniors have been working every night until about 3 a.m. We're almost done with the mounting and framing. Next, though, we're going to have to actually hang the exhibit.

M: I'm shocked. I thought all you did as an art major was paint and take pictures! By the way, where's the exhibition going to be?

W: Like every year, it's in the fine art gallery in the performing arts center. In fact, that's one of the problems. There's already an exhibition in the gallery. As a result, there's only two days between the time that that exhibition will be taken down and the time that we have to put ours up.

M: It looks like you'll have some more sleepless nights next week.

W: Yes. I can't believe that the exhibition hasn't even started and already I can't wait until it's finished.

> it's been a while since ... しばらく〜していない put on 〜 〜を催す mount 〜 〜を台紙に貼る、パネルにする hang 〜 〜を掛ける

35. 正解 (B)

Q: Why is the woman so tired?

TYPE 6 Why問題 男性が「疲れているようだけど、眠れてる？」と尋ねると、女性が「来週senior exhibit（4年生の展覧会）があるからぐっすり眠れていない」と答えている。また、「All of the seniors have been working every night until about 3 a.m.（4年生全員、毎晩午前3時まで働いている）」とも言っているので(B)が正解。

36. 正解 (C)

Q: Why does the man say he is surprised?

TYPE 6 Why問題 女性が「We're almost done with the mounting and framing（台紙貼りとフレーム入れはほとんど終わった）」と言い、次は「hang the exhibit（展示物をかけなければならない）」と言うのを聞いて、男性が「I'm

Practice Test 3

Section 1
Part A
Part B
Part C

289

shocked.」と驚いている。つまり、(C)「彼は美術の学生たちが展示用に自身の作品を準備すると思っていなかった」というのがその理由だ。

37. 正解 (C)

Q: Where will the exhibit be held?

TYPE 8 Where問題　男性が3つ目の発言で「where's the exhibition going to be?」と尋ねると、女性が「Like every year, it's in the fine art gallery in the performing arts center.」と答えている。

38. 正解 (D)

Q: What is the woman looking forward to?

TYPE 9 What問題　女性が最後に「I can't believe that the exhibition hasn't even started and already I can't wait until it's finished. (展覧会がまだ始まってもいないのに、もうそれが終わるのが待ちきれないなんて信じられないわ)」と言っているので、(D)「展覧会の閉会」が正解。

Part C

mp3 160-164

Questions 39-42

Listen to a talk given by a medical doctor.

　　Good afternoon. I'm Dr. Thompson and my pre-natal talk today is going to be about post-birth depression. OK, I know it might not be exactly a topic that you want to hear about right now, but as expecting mothers it's also important to prepare yourself for what is going to happen to you after the birth of your child, not just to think about the big day when your pregnancy comes to an end. To begin, did you know that about 80 percent of all mothers report that they are physically and emotionally exhausted during the first weeks of caring for their new child? Most feel better quickly, but about 10 percent——that's right, one out of ten——continues to feel depressed for months. Recently, however, research may have given us some insight into the cause of this depression. It appears as if the depression is brought on by a lack of estrogen in the woman's body. As you know, estrogen is the hormone closely related with a woman's reproductive cycle. After birth, estrogen levels in a woman's body drop dramatically. New clinical studies have shown that women who receive additional estrogen after delivery recover more quickly from post-child birth depression than those who do not. Now, I'm going to pass around an experimental skin patch that clinical subjects wore on their arms like a bandage. This patch slowly introduces estrogen into the body and decreases the chance of long-term depression.

> pre-natal 出産前　post-birth depression 産後憂うつ症　pregnancy 妊娠　come to an end 終わる　exhausted 疲れきる　insight 洞察　give an insight into the cause 原因がわかる　estrogen エストロゲン（卵胞ホルモン）　reproductive 生殖の　clinical 臨床の　delivery 分娩、出産　pass around 〜 〜を配る　patch シール　bandage 包帯　introduce ... into 〜 …を〜に（導き）入れる　decrease 〜 〜を減らす

39. 正解 (A)

Q: For whom is this talk intended?

TYPE 10 Who/Whom問題　ドクターが「as expecting mothers（妊婦として）it's also important to prepare yourself（自分の心の準備をしておくことも大切）」と言っている。よって(A)が正解。

40. 正解 (B)

Q: According to the speaker, what percentage of women experience long-term depression after giving birth?

TYPE 9 What問題　トークで「Most feel better quickly, but about 10 percent——that's right, one out of ten——continues to feel depressed for months.（ほとんどの人はすぐ改善するが、約10パーセント、まさしく、10人にひとりは数カ月にわたって落ち込む）」と述べられている。

Practice Test 3

Section 1
Part A
Part B
Part C

Practice Test 3

41. 正解 (D)

Q: What happens to estrogen in a woman's body after a baby is born?

TYPE 9 What問題　トーク後半に「After birth, estrogen levels in a woman's body drop dramatically. (出産後、女性の体内のエストロゲンのレベルが急激に落ちる)」とある。つまり (D)「It significantly decreases. (大幅に減る)」ということ。

42. 正解 (A)

Q: What is the speaker going to do next?

TYPE 9 What問題　最後から2文目で、「Now, I'm going to pass around an experimental skin patch (では、実験用スキンパッチを配ります)」と言っている。よって (A)「Distribute a new medical device (新しい医療器具を配る)」が正解。

mp3 **165-169**

Questions 43-46

Listen to the following talk about a cave man.

Welcome to the Nevada State Museum. I hope you've had an enjoyable time wandering around and looking at our various artifacts. What I'd like to briefly talk to you about now is our most important holding: the "Spirit Cave Man." This mummy was found in 1940 in a cave. At that time, it was thought to be about 2,000 years old. However, advances in our dating techniques—specifically, radio-carbon dating— have completely changed our original estimate of the age of these human remains. It is now clear that the Spirit Cave Man lived not 2,000 years ago but about 9,400 years ago. The mummy's great age and excellent preservation are giving us completely different ideas about what life was like for our human ancestors in North America at the end of the last ice age. Here's a little bit of the picture that we have so far. The Spirit Cave Man was wearing moccasins when he died—so we know that his people had the ability to tan animal skin and use it for footwear. Also, the cloth that he was wrapped in, made from the fibers of marsh plants, is so finely woven that it's clear his tribe was using looms to weave cloth. This suggests that weaving appeared on this continent far earlier than anyone suspected. Finally, fish bones and vegetables were discovered in the mummy's stomach. So while we can't draw definite conclusions about the Cave Man's diet, it appears as if he did not eat meat so much as vegetables and fish.

> artifact 人工遺物　cave 洞窟　mummy ミイラ　advance（科学などの）進歩　radio-carbon 放射性炭素　preservation 保存　tan ~（獣皮）をなめす　fiber 繊維　marsh 沼地　weave ~ ~を織る　loom はた織り機　definite 確かな　diet 日常の飲食物

43. 正解 (C)

Q: Who is probably giving this talk?

TYPE 10 Who/Whom問題 講義の最初に「Welcome to the Nevada State Museum.」と言っているので、ここで働いている人、つまり(C)「博物館の従業員」と推測がつく。

44. 正解 (A)

Q: What important recent discovery was made about the Spirit Cave Man?

TYPE 9 What問題 「Spirit Cave Man」を紹介した後、「At that time, it was thought to be about 2,000 years old. However ...（当時は、約2000年前のものだと思われていたが）advances in our dating techniques ...（年代測定の技術が進み）changed our original estimate（元々の私たちの推定を翻した）」と述べている。よって(A)が正解。

45. 正解 (A)

Q: According to the speaker, what does the cloth found with the mummy suggest about early North American peoples?

TYPE 9 What問題 ミイラが包まれていた布について説明する後半で、「it's clear his tribe was using looms to weave cloth.（彼の部族がはた織り機を使って布を織っていたのは明らかである）」と述べている。つまり、(A)「彼らは編む技術に長けていた」ということ。

Practice Test 3

Section 1
Part A
Part B
Part C

293

46. 正解 (C)

Q: What was found in the Cave Man's stomach?

TYPE(9)What問題 最後から2文目で「Finally, fish bones and vegetables were discovered in the mummy's stomach.」と述べているので、(C)「魚の骨」が正解。

mp3 **170-174**

Questions 47-50

Listen to the following talk about dictionaries.

To begin our senior seminar today I'd like to spend a few minutes talking about the bibles of language: that is, of course, dictionaries. Few people know that the American revolution, and its aftermath, was not only a matter of taxes and democratic government, but also involved language. Especially in the early days of the Republic, language and its use were matters of real public controversy. This is mostly because the United States was a land of immigrants — and so the country was linguistically insecure, so to speak. Americans, through their dictionaries, sought a guide to good usage and correctness. By contrast, in England, the making of dictionaries was always considered an elitist activity. People studied dictionaries as an adjunct to language rather than as authoritative guides. Americans therefore think of *the* dictionary, the English of *a* dictionary. The American approach is prescriptive, emphasizing how words should be used; the British approach has always tended to be descriptive, emphasizing how words are used.

In recent years, the differences between these approaches have begun to fade. The main reason is the sheer number of words in the English language: approximately 4,000,000. The largest dictionary, however, contains only 500,000. As a result, makers and publishers of dictionaries have more and more given up the idea of prescriptive and authoritative dictionaries.

aftermath 直後の時期 controversy 物議 linguistically 言語的に insecure 不安定な so to speak いわば by contrast 反対に elitist エリート主義者の an adjunct to ~ ~の付属物 authoritative 権威のある prescriptive 模範主義的な emphasize ~ ~を強調する descriptive 記述的な fade 消える approximately およそ

47. 正解 (B)

Q: Who is the likely audience for this talk?

TYPE 10 Who/Whom問題 講義の最初で「To begin our senior seminar today（本日の４年生向けセミナーを始めるにあたり）」と言っているので、聴衆は学生だと推測できる。

48. 正解 (D)

Q: What does the speaker compare dictionaries to?

TYPE 9 What問題 講義の最初に「talking about the bibles of language: that is, of course, dictionaries. （言語の聖書、つまり、もちろん辞書）」と述べている。

49. 正解 (B)

Q: What is the reason Americans were concerned with English usage and correctness?

TYPE 9 What問題 講義の中ほどで「the United States was a land of immigrants——and so the country was linguistically insecure（アメリカは移民の土地で、だから国は言語的に不安定だった）」とアメリカの歴史に触れ、その後に By contrast（反対に）と、イギリスの社会的背景を述べている。そして「The American approach is ...」と両国を比較している。よってアメリカ人が言葉の用法や正しさにこだわった理由は、(B)の「多くは言葉に不安のある移民だった」が正解。

50. 正解 (D)

Q: How does the traditional American approach to dictionaries differ from the British?

TYPE 12 How問題 講義の中で、「The American approach is prescriptive, ... how words should be used. （アメリカの扱い方は規範主義的……、言葉がどう使われるべきかを強調している）」とある。

Practice Test 3

Section 1
Part A
Part B
Part C

Section 2
Structure and Written Expression

Structure

Questions 1-15

1. 正解▶ (B)

TYPE ⑯ 動詞の形 「(人) regard A as B」で、「人がAをBと見なす」という熟語。Aの部分に当たる関係詞whatは、address(取り組む、扱う)の目的語となっている。

2. 正解▶ (A)

TYPE ⑬ 文構造 文頭の名詞Plasticsが主語になるので、空所には動詞が必要。主語が無生物で自分では動作を起こせないので、受け身にする。「A is made from B」で、「AはBから作られる」という熟語。

3. 正解▶ (C)

TYPE ⑮ 語順 カンマに挟まれた空所部分は挿入の役割を果たす。「一緒に食されたとき」という意味の文が入る。when (they are) eaten togetherが分詞構文になり、(主語＋be動詞)が省略されてwhen eaten togetherとなる。

4. 正解▶ (B)

TYPE ⑬ 文構造 前置詞(through)の後には、目的語となる名詞が必要。よってthe establishmentが入る。

5. 正解▶ (D)

TYPE ⑭ 語彙 「By means of ～」は「～によって、～を使って」という意味のイディオムで、カンマまでが前置詞句になる。主語はowlsで動詞はhunt。

6. 正解▶ (C)

TYPE ⑯ 動詞の形 節の中の主語は三人称単数のbad weatherなので(A)は真っ先に除外できる。文末にsoonがあるので、未来を表す時制がくる。

解答と解説

7. 正解 (C)

Rare F 前置詞 期間を表す表現（thousands of years）の前なので、forを用いる。

8. 正解 (B)

TYPE⑬ 文構造 空所の前までにhave developedという動詞がすでにあり、S＋V＋Oが完成しているので、空所以後には、従属節がくる。もうひとつの動詞increaseを入れる節が必要。関係詞thatを使って直前のthe exact level of exertionを説明している。

9. 正解 (A)

TYPE⑭ 語彙 カンマに挟まれた部分は挿入。「惑星と同様に」という意味を表すlike＋名詞を使う。asの後には節がこなければならないので、(B)と(D)は誤り。(C)は語順が違う。

10. 正解 (B)

TYPE⑮ 語順 カンマに挟まれた部分は挿入なので抜いて考えてみると、初めのカンマの前までが主語になるとわかり、2つ目のカンマの後には、本動詞が必要。(A) whose ....、(C) that ... では、従属節になってしまう。(D)は動詞がない。[S, which ...,V＋C] という構造。

11. 正解 (C)

TYPE⑭ 語彙 本文には動詞areが2つあるので、ひとつを節に入れる。「トマトは野菜と思われがちだが、植物学的には果物である」という意味にするには、カンマの前までを従属節にする。そこで空所に(C) Even thoughを入れて、Even though S＋V, S＋Vという形にすればよい。

12. 正解 (A)

TYPE⑬ 文構造 「be subjected to ～（～にさらされる）」という熟語を含む関係詞節。the heatを修飾する形容詞節にはtoが必要。(A) to which it wasのitはsteelを指す。

13. 正解▶ (C)

TYPE⑯ 動詞の形 requireという動詞に続くthat節の中の動詞は原形になる（仮定法現在）。よって(C) be printedが正解。ほかにも要求・提案・主張・当然・決定などを表わす動詞は、同じ構文になる。例えば、「order/suggest/demand/insist＋that 〜 動詞原形」となる。

14. 正解▶ (B)

TYPE⑬ 文構造 isという動詞が文中にあるので、(C)や(D)では動詞が2つになってしまう。one of the 〜（〜の内のひとつ）という表現があるので、不特定でひとつのものを表す不定冠詞aを使う。

15. 正解▶ (B)

TYPE⑮ 語順 「it takes A＋B（時間表現）to 〜（Aにとって〜するのにBほど時間がかかる）」という構文。つまり「クマにとって、完全に目覚めるのに何日もかかる」という意味。fullyは副詞で動詞wakeを修飾する。

Written Expression

Questions 16-40

16. 正解▶ (D) their → its

TYPE⑲ 数の一致 the mountain cougarが単数名詞なので、代名詞はtheirでなくitsで受ける。

17. 正解▶ (D) dusty → dust

TYPE㉑ 並列 「名詞, 名詞, 名詞, and名詞」という組み合わせ。よってdustyという形容詞をdustという名詞にする。このように、カンマやandなどを含む文では品詞を統一する。

18. 正解▶ (D) great → greatly

TYPE⑱ 品詞 greatは形容詞。直前にある動詞「vary（変わる）」を修飾するには、greatlyという副詞に変える。

19. 正解 (A) Despite of → Despite

TYPE 23 前置詞 「~にもかかわらず」という意味の表現はDespite ~でofはいらない。同じ意味のIn spite ofと混同しないこと。

20. 正解 (A) can produced → can be produced

TYPE 25 動詞の形 助動詞canの後は動詞の原形。「by separating ~ (~を離すことにより)」という句があるのでcan be producedという受け身にする。

21. 正解 (D) other → another

TYPE 22 代名詞 otherは通常the other/othersの形を取る。ここは、one species (ある種) と比較するので、「もうひとつ別の」という意味を表わすanotherにする。(A)のbutはonlyという意味。

22. 正解 (C) renew → renewal

TYPE 18 品詞 urban (都会の) は形容詞なので直後に名詞を取る。「renew (新しくする)」という動詞をrenewalという名詞にすればよい。

23. 正解 (D) and also → but also

TYPE 29 接続詞 not only A but also B (AだけでなくB) の構文。andをbutに変える。

24. 正解 (B) close → close to

TYPE 26 語の脱落 closeは形容詞。後ろにtoをつけて「be close to ~ (~に近い)」とする。

25. 正解 (C) maintain → maintains

TYPE 19 数の一致 主語An objectと動詞maintainの形が一致していない。また後に出てくる代名詞がitsとなっているので、動詞maintainに三人称単数のsがいるとわかる。

26. 正解 (B) he → 削除

TYPE 24 重複 カンマに挟まれた部分は挿入なのでカッコでくくって抜いてみよう。主語は文頭のPete Seegerなので、下線(B)のheは余分になる。

Practice Test 3

Section 2

Structure
Written
Expression

299

Practice Test 3

27. **正解** (A) areas urban → urban areas

TYPE㉗ 語順 urban は形容詞なので、名詞の areas を修飾するためには語順を変えて urban areas にする。

28. **正解** (A) A → The

TYPE㉘ 冠詞 A two …s では数が合わない。The two principal forms にする。

29. **正解** (A) others → other

TYPE⑱ 品詞 others は「他のもの」という意味の代名詞。others metals だと、s のついた名詞が2つ繋がってしまう。other の s を取って、名詞を修飾する形容詞にする。

30. **正解** (D) made → making

TYPE⑱ 品詞 下線(D)の made は動詞である。前に冠詞 the があることから後ろには名詞が入る。よって、made を making にすればよい。

31. **正解** (D) of sizable → of a sizable

TYPE㉘ 冠詞 文末にある middle class (中産階級) は、集合体として考えるときは単数扱いなので sizable (かなり多くの) という形容詞の前に a が必要。このように冠詞に関する問題は、冠詞が抜けた形で出題されることが多いので注意。

32. **正解** (A) form → formed

TYPE㉕ 動詞の形 下線(A)の直前に be 動詞 was があるので、動詞 form を受身形の formed にする。

33. **正解** (C) most → more

TYPE㉑ 並列 than があるので、最上級 most ではなく、比較級 more にして並列の形 (比較級、比較級 and 比較級) にする。下線(B)の that are は省略が可能だが、あっても間違いではない。

34. 正解 （D）　there → 削除

TYPE 24 重複　場所の名前 Connecticut の後に、場所を表す there があるが、単に「, there」では意味が通じない。

35. 正解 （C）　herself → her

TYPE 19 数の一致　herself を her にして「her courage（彼女の勇気）」とすると意味が通る。

36. 正解 （B）　than → as

TYPE 23 前置詞　than を as にして、「the same 〜 as ...（……と同様の〜）」という構文にする。

37. 正解 （B）　excessively → excessive

TYPE 18 品詞　that 以下の節に動詞 may cause があるので、下線 (B) の直後の control は実は名詞であることに気づいただろうか。よって excessively という副詞を、名詞を修飾する形容詞 excessive に変える。

Practice Test 3

38. 正解 （C）　are found → is found

TYPE 19 数の一致　カンマに挟まれた部分は挿入なので抜いて考えてみる。主語の「The loon（アビ［鳥の名］）」は単数名詞なので、動詞は is found になる。

Section 2

Structure
Written
Expression

39. 正解 （C）　or → but also

TYPE 29 接続詞　「not only A but also B（A だけでなく B も）」の構文。or を but also に変える。

 40. 正解 （A）　whom → whose

TYPE 22 代名詞　主語「Transcendental meditation（瞑想）」は人ではないので whom は使えない。また whom は目的格だがここでは所有格が適切。そこで所有格を示す関係代名詞 whose にする。whose は物を先行詞に取れる。例：The computer whose keyboard has excellent touch is Macintosh.（キーボードの感触が素晴らしいコンピューターは、マッキントッシュだ。）

Practice Test 3

Section 3
Reading Comprehension

Questions 1-10

1. 正解 (B)

TYPE 32 推論 第1パラグラフ第1文に、「Bacteria are among the smallest of living creatures and their identification is often difficult. (バクテリアは生物の中で最小のものに数えられ、その正体を特定するのは往々にして困難である)」とある。つまりstudy (研究) は難しいということ。(B)のtinyはsmallと同意語。

2. 正解 (B)

TYPE 36 段落要旨 第1パラグラフの最後に「hundreds of other kinds wait to be discovered. (他の数百種が発見されるのを待っている)」とある。この言い換えが選択肢(B)。他の選択肢の内容は第1パラグラフでは述べられていない。

3. 正解 (D)

TYPE 35 Not問題 第1パラグラフ第2文に、「Among the kinds of information used for their classification are (分類のために使われる情報の種類には)」とあり、「their size, shape ... the structure of their bacterial "colonies," ... the chemical changes ...」などの語が挙げられている。よって(A)と(B)は除外できる。2つ目の下線にある「the structure of their bacterial "colonies" (バクテリア集団の構造)」と(C)「the organization of their groups (集団の構造)」が同意であるとわかれば、残るは(D)「生息地」。

4. 正解 (A)

TYPE 33 語彙 undergoは「〜を受ける、体験する」という意味で、(A)のexperienceと同意。

5. 正解 (A)

TYPE 31 事実の確認 vitaminという単語が出てくる11行目以下に注目。「For instance, the amount of vitamin in a given solution can be measured, (例えば、ある溶液内のビタミンの量が量られる)」とあり、「by observing the multiplication of a particular kind of bacterium.（特定の種のバクテリアの増殖を観察することにより）」と言っている。この部分が(A)「バクテリアの増殖率」の言い換えになっている。

6. 正解 (C)

TYPE(33) 語彙 givenは「ある特定の」という意味。(C)のparticularと同意。

7. 正解 (C)

TYPE(36) 段落要旨 第2段落の第1文で、「they are in reality essential to life on earth.（バクテリアは実際のところ地球上の生命にとって必要不可欠なものである）」と述べられている。(C)「バクテリアが人間にとって重要な理由」がこの段落の主題になると推測できるだろう。

8. 正解 (B)

TYPE(37) 理由 第2パラグラフの9～10行目に、「because bacteria often use the same vitamins as human beings or animals they are valuable aids in the laboratory.（バクテリアはしばしば人間や動物と同じビタミンを使うため、実験室において貴重な助けとなっている）」とある。この言い換えが、設問文と答えとなる(B)だ。

9. 正解 (C)

TYPE(34) 語法 直後に「This is a food prepared usually in liquid form.（通常、液状で用意された食べ物）」と定義が述べてある。これは、(C)の「particularly defined term（特別に定義づけられた語）」である。

10. 正解 (D)

TYPE(31) 事実の確認 第3パラグラフ冒頭で「culture medium（培養基）」がバクテリアの食べ物であることが説明されている。そして17～18行目に「The foods provided for bacterial colonies vary depending on the species.（バクテリア群体に供給される食べ物はその種類によってさまざまだ）」とある。よって正解は(D)。

Practice Test 3

Questions 11-21

11. 正解 (C)

TYPE 30 要旨　本文の主題は、第1文に述べてある。「the creation of debt was a practice of government even in colonial times. (国債の発行は、植民地時代すでに実施されていた)」が該当部分。つまり(C)の「colonies (植民地)における debt (負債、国債)」についてである。

12. 正解 (A)

TYPE 36 段落要旨　6～7行目にpaper money based on tobaccoという表現がある。この文の比較級に注目。8行目thanの後に... basing the dollar on gold bullionとあるので、(A)「one based on gold (金に基づく貨幣)」が比較の対象になっているとわかる。

13. 正解 (B)

TYPE 31 事実の確認　南部の植民地とは、Maryland、Virginia、Carolina を指す。設問中のat timesは「ときどき」という意味。5～6行目「On occasion, (時折) they even outlawed the use of precious metals as a means of currency exchange. (貴金属を換金の手段として使うことを禁じた)」の部分が、(B)の「banned (禁止した) the use of silver and gold for currency (銀や金を貨幣として使用すること)」と一致する。

14. 正解 (D)

TYPE 33 語彙　動詞deploreは「強い不賛成の意を示す」という意味なので、discourage ([不賛成であることを示して] 思いとどまらせる・やめさせる) が最も近い。

15. 正解 (B)

TYPE 34 語法 代名詞theirは、直前の可算名詞を指す。ここでは特に、パラグラフの最初なので、同じ文中の主語「precious metals (貴金属)」を指すことが明らかである。カンマに挟まれた「, silver and gold chief among them,」は挿入句で貴金属の例。

16. 正解 (D)

TYPE 31 事実の確認 第2パラグラフは、時間の流れに従って、お札を発行するまでの経緯を説明している。まとめると、「部隊は北上し、敵から金を取り上げて、その金を部隊の経費にあてようともくろんでいたが、予想がはずれて敗戦した。その結果、いずれは金と交換することを約束した紙切れ "お札" を植民地政府は発行した」という話である。これを一言で言い換えたのが(D)だ。

17. 正解 (C)

TYPE 33 語彙 ここでのeventualは「結果として起きる、いつかは生じる、来るべき」という意味。(C)「later (後ほどの、後々の)」が最も近い。

18. 正解 (C)

TYPE 32 推論 筆者は第3パラグラフの最後で「debt always carries with it the risk of loss and default. (国債は常に損失や債務不履行のリスクを伴う)」と述べている。(C)「be potentially risky (潜在的にリスクがある)」に該当する。

19. 正解 (B)

TYPE 33 語彙 with abandonは「奔放に、思うままに」という意味で、この文脈では否定的な意味合いで使われている。よって(B)「recklessly (無節操に)」が最も近い。

20. 正解 (C)

TYPE 32 推論 最終パラグラフ2文目に「on the eventual day ... the notes would one day become worthless. (最終的に ... お札はいつの日か価値がなくなってしまう)」とあるので、(C)が正解。

Practice Test 3

Section 3

21. 正解 (A)

TYPE ㉜ 推論 本文の最後に「debt always carries with it the risk of loss and default. (国債は常に損失や債務不履行のリスクを伴う)」とある。これと同様の主旨の(A)が正解。形容詞のhazardousは、名詞riskの形容詞形riskyの同意語。

重要語句

concern 懸念　debt 国債、負債　currency 通貨　outlaw ～ ～を法律の保護の外に置く　precious metals 貴金属　considerable かなりの、相当な　gold bullion 金塊　lure 魅力　expedition 遠征 (隊)　fortress 要塞　intend to ～ ～する傾向がある　capture 捕獲物　troop 隊　colonial treasury 植民地政府の金庫　circulate ～ ～を流通させる　solid assets 硬貨　in abundance 豊富に　with abandon 気ままに、無節操に　unbacked currency 不良通貨　condemn ～ ～を不適当だとする　default 不履行、怠慢

Questions 22-30

22. 正解 (C)

TYPE ㉚ 要旨 3つのパラグラフのトピックセンテンスの内容を確認する。第1パラグラフは赤ん坊の時のカーヴァーについて、第2パラグラフは若年のジョージ・ワシントン・カーヴァーについて、第3パラグラフは彼の業績について述べられている。その内容を包括しているのは(C)の「ジョージ・ワシントン・カーヴァーの生涯」である。

23. 正解 (B)

TYPE ㉛ 事実の確認 2～3行目にある「Moses Carver ... $300 racehorse, (300ドルの競争馬と引き換えに、赤ん坊を取り返すことができた)」の意味を正確に捉えられれば、正解は容易に得られる。早とちりをして(A)を選ばないこと。

24. 正解 (B)

TYPE ㉝ 語彙 「seize (強奪する)」の意味がわからなければ、正解は得にくい。(A) rescuedは「救助した」、(C) purchasedは「購入した」、(D) assaultedは「襲撃した」という意味。

25. 正解 (D)

TYPE 33 語彙 robustは「強健な、たくましい」という意味。「strong or robust enough to labor（重労働ができるほど強くor XXX）」という文脈の流れから、strongと同義である(D) healthyと推測できる。

26. 正解 (C)

TYPE 31 事実の確認 9～10行目の「worked his way ... and doing odd jobs.（雑多な仕事をしながら）」がポイント。この内容を一言で言い換えている(C)「彼はちょっとした仕事をいろいろやった」が正解。

work one's way through (college) 働きながら（大学を）出る

27. 正解 (B)

TYPE 31 事実の確認 カーヴァーが卒業した学校は、第2パラグラフの最後に「Iowa State College of Agriculture and Mechanic Arts」であると明記されている。

28. 正解 (C)

TYPE 34 語法 there は場所を指す言葉。直前に出た場所名は「タスキーギーの農学部」なので(C)が正解。

29. 正解 (B)

TYPE 33 語彙 notable（注目に値する）はnote（注目する）の派生語で、(B)「重要な」が最も近い意味になる。

30. 正解 (A)

TYPE 32 推論 第2文に「カーヴァーは、300ドルの競走馬と引き替えに、赤ん坊を取り戻すことができた。しかし、その子の母親は決して戻らなかった」とあり、次の文には「the motherless child（母のない子）」と記されているので、(A)「自分の母親を知らなかった」が正解。

Practice Test 3

Section 3

Practice Test 3

重要語句

raider 侵略者　seize 〜 〜をつかむ　in exchange for 〜 〜と引き換えに　robust
強健な、たくましい　chore 退屈な仕事　have a gift for doing 〜の才能がある
odd 臨時の、雑多な　bachelor's degree 学士号　master's degree 修士号
achievement 成績　bring one to the attention of 〜 （人が）〜の目に留まる

Questions 31-40

31. 正解 (B)

TYPE30 要旨　3つのパラグラフのトピックセンテンスの内容を確認しよう。第
1、2パラグラフは主に「おとぎ話の起源」について、第3パラグラフは「おとぎ
話の起源やその発展と役目」について述べられている。(B)「おとぎ話の起源と目
的」が主題である。

32. 正解 (C)

TYPE31 事実の確認　第1パラグラフに「子ども向けに作られ子どもの領域のも
のと思われがちだが、これほど事実とかけ離れたことはない」と記してある。

33. 正解 (C)

TYPE35 Not問題　(A)は16〜17行目「The fairly tale ... through the use of
metaphors.」、(B)は3〜4行目「when tales ... communal bonds」、(D)は25
〜26行目「They instructed, amused, ...」のそれぞれの言い換えになっている。

34. 正解 (A)

TYPE33 語彙　communalは「共同体の」という意味なので、(A)「social（社会
の）」が正解。com(m)- という接頭辞は「共に」という意味。例えばcommunity
（共同体）、committee（委員会）、common（共通の）などがある。

35. 正解 (D)

TYPE33 語彙　catastropheは「大惨事、破局」の意味。これに最も意味が近い
のは(D)「disaster（大惨事）」だ。

308

36. 正解▶ (B)

TYPE③②推論　キーワードは「Bible（聖書）」という言葉。21～23行目に「（大人が大人に向けて語ってきた）モチーフが記憶され、言い伝えられ、聖書や西洋の古典に入り込んだ」とあるので、(B)「初期のおとぎ話のいくつかは、聖書の中に見出せるかもしれない」が正解。

37. 正解▶ (B)

TYPE③⑦理由　16～17行目に「The fairy tale thus sets out to conquer this concrete terror mainly through the use of metaphors.（おとぎ話は、それゆえ、この具体的な恐れを、主に隠喩の使用を通じて克服しようとしている）」とある。これを言い換えているのは(B)「overcome fear（恐れを克服する）」だ。conquerは「克服する、征服する」という意味で、同義語。

38. 正解▶ (A)

TYPE③③語彙　conceiveは「考え付く」という意味。(A)「invented（考案された）」が最も近い。

39. 正解▶ (B)

TYPE③④語法　「Motifs from these（それらからのモチーフ）」の代名詞「these（それら）」は先にある複数名詞や、先にある関係代名詞whichと同じ物を指す。つまり(B)「oral folk tales（口承民話）」が正解。

🔊 40. 正解▶ (C)

TYPE③②推論　12行目のbothから14行目までにヒントがある。特に「おとぎ話はemerge from specific struggles ...（固有の苦闘から生じている）」という表現に注目。この言い換えに近いのが(C)の「おとぎ話は固有の人間の事情から生まれた」だ。

Practice Test 3

Section 3

Practice Test 3

重要語句

fairy tale おとぎ話　the domain of ～ ～の分野、領域　communal 共同体の
bonds 結束　in the face of ～ ～に直面して　on the brink of ～ ～にひんして
catastrophe 大惨事　mature 大人の　nurture 育てる　genre ジャンル　cut across
～ ～を渡る　numerous 多数の　shaman シャーマン、まじない師　mystify 惑わす
misinterpret 誤解する　quest 探究　archetype 原型　oral 口述の　be grounded
in ～ ～に基づく　emerge from ～ ～から脱する　struggle 苦闘　humanize ～ ～を
人間化する　bestial 獣性の　barbaric 野蛮な　terrorize ～ ～に恐怖を起こさせる
concrete 具体的な　threaten 脅す　compassion 同情　set out to ～ ～し始める
conquer ～ ～を克服する　metaphor 暗喩　wondrous 驚くべき　marvelous 不思
議な　pass on 伝える　make one's way into ～ ～に盛り込む　ritual 儀式　tribe
種族　foster 育成する　initiate 起こす　enlighten 啓発する　modify 緩和する

Questions 41-50

41. 正解 ▶ (C)

TYPE 30 要旨 (A)「統合失調症の症状」、(B)「統合失調症の治療法」、(D)「統
合失調症の発見」。これらは全て、本文で触れられてはいるが、主題を支える
詳細でしかない。本文は「A dramatic change is underway in the scientific
understanding of schizophrenia（統合失調症の科学的理解に大きな変化が起
こっている）」という一文で始まり、全文を通して(C)「統合失調症の新理論」が
解説されている。

42. 正解 ▶ (D)

TYPE 31 事実の確認 3行目に「The first sign ... late 20s（病の最初の兆候は、
通常20代後半に現れる）」とある。late 20sを言い換えている(D)「成人期の初
め」が正解。

43. 正解 ▶ (C)

TYPE 36 段落要旨 難しい言葉が続くが、一字一句、理解する必要はない。ここ
は脳細胞について述べられており、それも統合失調症にかかった脳についての話
だとわかればよい。つまり、ただの脳ではなく(C)「統合失調症の脳の発達」につ
いてである。

44. 正解 (B)
TYPE 33 語彙 speculationは「推論」という意味なので、(B)「hypothesis (仮説)」が最も近い意味になる。

45. 正解 (A)
TYPE 34 語法 theseは、前に出た可算名詞複数形を指す。(B)「delusions (妄想)」、(C)「voices (声)」などを一言でまとめた(A)「symptoms (症状)」が正解。

46. 正解 (C)
TYPE 35 Not問題 第3パラグラフの第1文に、(B)「apathy (無関心)」、「a blunting of emotions (感情の鈍化)」、(D)「delusions (妄想)」、(A)「hearing of internal voices (幻聴)」とあり、(C)「violent impulses (暴力的な衝動)」は含まれない。

47. 正解 (C)
TYPE 36 段落要旨 キーワード「laboratory (実験室)」という言葉が登場する直前の文 (19～20行目) に、「かつては家庭内でのコミュニケーションの欠落が原因だとされていたが、現在は脳の病気だと認識されている」とある。つまり、(C)の「統合失調症は身体的な病気」であることを説明するためだ。

48. 正解 (A)
TYPE 33 語彙 wax and waneは、元来「月が満ち欠けする」という意味。そこから(A)「増減する」という意味になった。

49. 正解 (C)
TYPE 33 語彙 proは「賛成」を表し、proponentは「支持者」、そして(A)は「opponent (反対者)」。よって「advocate (援護者)」が同意語となる。

50. 正解 (D)

TYPE32 推論 第2パラグラフの最後の文に「One speculation, however, is that brain misconnections may occur when the mother catches a virus early in pregnancy.（脳の接続ミスは、母親が妊娠初期にウイルスに感染した時に起こるのかもしれない）」とある。これにより (D)「母親たちは、いつか統合失調症の原因となる病気を持っているかどうか調べられるかもしれない」が導き出せる。(B)の「true cause（本当の原因）」はひっかけ。あくまで仮説である。

重要語句

underway 進行中　schizophrenia 統合失調症　devastating ひどい、強烈な　neuroscientist 神経科学（者）　disorder 障害　fetal 胎児の　nerve cell 神経細胞　divide 分裂する　flaw 欠陥　migrate 移動する　out of place 場違いの、位置のずれた　mis-wired 配線が誤った　subplate サブプレート　neuron ニューロン（神経細胞単位）　pregnancy 妊娠期　speculation 推論　misconnection 混線　virus ウイルス　symptom 兆候　apathy 無気力　blunting 鈍化　delusion 幻覚　wax and wane 増減する　attribute to ～ ～に帰する、～のせいだとする　tissue 組織　dissection 切開、解体、解剖　prefrontal 前頭葉前部の　bothersome やっかいな　proponent 支持者　conception 概念、考え　abnormality 異常、奇形　overlooked 見過ごされた

Practice Test 4
解 答 と 解 説

解答の冒頭にある「TYPE」アイコンは「出題傾向と対策」（pp.12〜35）で解説
した問題タイプを示しています。

　はその問題が「難問」であることを示しています。正解できたら自信を持って
ください。

Practice Test 4

解答済みのマークシート（別冊巻末）と照らし合わせましょう。

正答一覧

Section 1

#	Ans	#	Ans	#	Ans	#	Ans	#	Ans
1	C	11	A	21	B	31	C	41	D
2	A	12	D	22	D	32	C	42	C
3	D	13	A	23	A	33	D	43	B
4	B	14	B	24	C	34	B	44	A
5	B	15	A	25	A	35	D	45	B
6	A	16	C	26	C	36	C	46	D
7	C	17	B	27	A	37	A	47	C
8	B	18	C	28	D	38	B	48	A
9	C	19	D	29	B	39	D	49	A
10	C	20	C	30	D	40	A	50	B

Section 2

#	Ans	#	Ans	#	Ans	#	Ans	#	Ans
1	B	9	C	17	C	25	D	33	D
2	A	10	B	18	C	26	C	34	D
3	A	11	B	19	D	27	B	35	A
4	B	12	D	20	D	28	B	36	C
5	D	13	D	21	D	29	B	37	B
6	C	14	B	22	A	30	C	38	D
7	C	15	C	23	C	31	D	39	D
8	B	16	C	24	B	32	D	40	D

Section 3

#	Ans	#	Ans	#	Ans	#	Ans	#	Ans
1	D	11	D	21	B	31	A	41	C
2	A	12	B	22	D	32	D	42	C
3	C	13	A	23	B	33	B	43	B
4	B	14	D	24	A	34	B	44	D
5	A	15	B	25	C	35	C	45	C
6	C	16	D	26	B	36	B	46	B
7	C	17	D	27	A	37	C	47	A
8	D	18	B	28	B	38	B	48	D
9	C	19	C	29	C	39	D	49	A
10	B	20	A	30	A	40	A	50	D

Practice Test 4　解答と解説

Section 1
Listening Comprehension

Part A

mp3 **176-180**

1. 正解 (C)

W: Is Kathy majoring in both psychology and business administration?
M: She was. But I heard she's given up on psychology.
Q: What does the man imply about Kathy?

TYPE 2 言外の意味　「Kathyは心理学と経営学の両方を専攻してるの？」と聞かれた男性が、「以前はそうだったけど」と言い、「I heard she's given up on psychology. (心理学はあきらめたと聞いた)」とつけ加えている。

> major in ～　～を専攻する　give up on ～　～をあきらめる　no longer ～　もはや～していない

2. 正解 (A)

M: Do you think you could lend me a few dollars?
W: Where's the money you borrowed last week?
Q: What can be inferred from this conversation?

TYPE 3 推論　「少しお金を貸してくれないか？」と言われた女性が「Where's the money you borrowed last week? (先週借りたお金はどうしたの？)」と答えている。(A)「女性はすでに男性にお金を貸していた」ということ。

3. 正解 (D)

W: I just found out I got the job I applied for.
M: You don't say! That's terrific.
Q: What does the man mean?

TYPE 1 発言の意味　女性が「申し込んだ仕事に受かったことが、ちょうどわかったわ」と言うと、男性は「You don't say! (ほんと！)」と言った。You don't say! は、Really? などと同様、驚きを表わすときに使われる表現。文脈と男性のアクセントから(D)「be pleased about ～ (～について喜んでいる)」が正解だとわかる。

Practice Test 4

Section 1
Part A
Part B
Part C

315

4. 正解 (B)

W: Hi, Dr. Peterson. Is it true that you were looking for me?
M: Yes. I just want to have a word with you about your paper.
Q: What does the man want?

Rare (B) Want問題 「have a word with (ちょっと話をする)」が聞き取れれば正解できる。「私を探していましたか?」と聞いた女性に、博士は「I just want to have a word with you. (ちょっと話したいことがある)」と言っているので正解は(B)。

5. 正解 (B)

W: Did you hear that Susan lost her scholarship?
M: Well, that would account for her getting another part-time job.
Q: What does the man imply about Susan?

TYPE 2 言外の意味 女性が「Susanがscholarship (奨学金)を失ったって聞いた?」と言うと、男性が、「that would account for (それで、説明がつく) her getting another part-time job (彼女がもうひとつアルバイトを得たのが)」と答えている。つまり、(B)「彼女は、以前よりも働いている」ということ。

account for ～ ～の説明となる

mp3 181-185

6. 正解 (A)

M: What's the status of the new renovation to the men's dorm?
W: Nothing to report. It hasn't even gotten off the ground.
Q: What does the woman mean?

TYPE 1 発言の意味 男性が「男子のdorm (寮)のnew renovation (改築工事)はどうなっているか」と聞くと、女性が「It hasn't even gotten off the ground. (離陸してもいないのよ)」と言っている。つまり改築工事は(A)「has not started (まだ始まっていない)」ということ。

What's the status of ～? ～(の現状)はどうなっている? get off the ground 離陸する、順調にスタートする

7. 正解 (C)

W: Do you know what time the student recreation center opens on Sundays?

M: One, isn't it?

Q: What does the man mean?

TYPE ① 発言の意味　男性の One, isn't it? は付加疑問の形。「~でしょ?」という意味になる。この One は時刻を指している。レクリエーションセンターはおそらく1時に開く。

8. 正解 (B)

W: Are you happy that you went ahead and changed your major?

M: Happy? I'm ecstatic!

Q: What does the man mean?

TYPE ① 発言の意味　女性の質問に対し、男性が「Happy? (幸せかって?)」と聞き返し、「I'm ecstatic! (有頂天さ!)」と喜びを強調して答えている。従って (be) pleased with (~に喜んでいる) を含む (B) が正解。

go ahead (計画などを) 進める

9. 正解 (C)

W: Could you give me a hand carrying this refrigerator up to my room?

M: Mary, you know it's against the rules to have a personal refrigerator in the dorm.

Q: What does the man imply?

TYPE ② 言外の意味　「Could you give me a hand (手伝ってくれる?) carrying this refrigerator ...?」と言われて、男性は「you know it's against the rules to ... (……がルール違反だって知ってるだろ)」と答えている。(C)「女性は the housing policies (居住規則) に従うべき」が正解。

10. 正解 (C)

M: I've looked everywhere in my pockets and in my apartment for my car keys but can't find them.

W: Are you sure you didn't leave them in the car?

Practice Test 4

Section 1

Part A
Part B
Part C

Practice Test 4

Q: What does the woman imply?

TYPE ② 言外の意味　「車の鍵が見つからない」と言っている男性に対し、女性が「Are you sure you didn't leave them in the car?（車の中に置いていないのは確かなの？）」と聞いている。ここから、この女性が「鍵は車の中にあるのではないか」と思っていることがわかる。よって(C)「男性は車内に鍵を忘れた」が正解。

mp3 186-190

11. 正解 (A)

W: How about a picnic this Sunday, Ralph?
M: Thanks. I'm afraid I won't be able to fit it in this weekend.
Q: What does the man imply?

TYPE ② 言外の意味　ピクニックに誘われて、男性が「残念だけど、それはこの週末には入れられないよ」と答えている。つまり(A)「ちょっと忙しい」という意味。fit in は「ぴったりと合う、うまくはまる」。ここでは、スケジュールが合わないということになる。

12. 正解 (D)

M: It sounds like you have a lot of labs for your chemistry class.
W: I'll say. Would you believe three a week?
Q: What does the woman imply?

TYPE ② 言外の意味　「君の化学の授業には実験実習がたくさんあるね」と言われて女性は、「I'll say.（まったくよ）」と同意して、「週に3回って信じられる？」とも言った。(D)「彼女の授業には多くの実験が求められている」のだ。

13. 正解 (A)

M: We're really late——can't you drive a little faster?
W: Not in this fog. Better late than never.
Q: What does the woman mean?

TYPE ① 発言の意味　男性が「もうちょっと速く運転できない？」と頼むと、女性が「Not in this fog.（この霧じゃあ無理）Better late than never.（遅くとも着かないよりはまし＝急がば回れ）」と答えた。つまり、霧で危険なので、(A)「引き続き注意深く運転する」という意味。

14. **正解** (B)

M: Is it true Jack isn't feeling better yet?
W: Yeah. He still has a fever.
Q: What can be inferred about Jack?

TYPE 3 推論 男性がJackの具合を尋ねると、女性が「He still has a fever. (まだ熱がある)」と答えているので、(B)「彼は running a temperature (熱を出している)」が正解。

15. **正解** (A)

W: Listen, would you mind doing the vacuuming today so that I can study?
M: Honestly, Debbie, you'll use any excuse you can to get out of doing housework, won't you?
Q: What does the man imply about the woman?

TYPE 2 言外の意味 女性が「今日は、あなたが掃除機をかけてくれない？ そうすれば私は勉強できるから」と言うと、男性が「you'll use any excuse you can to get out of doing housework (君はどんな言い訳を使ってでも家事をさぼりたいんだね)」と皮肉を言っている。(A)「あまり家の手伝いをしない」が正解。

get out of ~ ~を避ける、のがれる　help out 手伝う、手助けする

mp3 **191-195**

16. **正解** (C)

M: That was probably the worst meal I've ever had here.
W: I'm with you. Either they changed cooks or the regular chef had a really bad day!
Q: What does the woman mean?

TYPE 1 発言の意味 男性は「the worst meal (最悪の食事だ)」と言っている。それに対して女性が「I'm with you. (私も同感)」と言っているので、(C)「彼女は男性と同じ意見」が正解。Either they changed cooks or the regular chef had a really bad day!は、「料理人を替えたか、いつものシェフの調子が本当に悪い日かどちらかね」という意味。

I'm with you. 同感だ (=I agree with you.)

Practice Test 4

Section 1
Part A
Part B
Part C

17. 正解 (B)

W: Did you like the CD I loaned you?

M: Like it? I went out and bought all the albums that artist has ever released.

Q: What does the man mean?

TYPE ① 発言の意味　「この前貸したCD気に入った？」と聞かれた男性は、「Like it?（好きかって？）出かけて、あのアーティストが今まで出した全てのアルバムを買ったよ」と強調して答えている。つまり(B)「彼は、そのアーティストのファンになった」ということ。

18. 正解 (C)

M: Can you believe the heat wave we're having?

W: Yeah, the temperature is so high you could fry an egg on the sidewalk.

Q: What does the woman imply?

TYPE ② 言外の意味　男性が「この熱波、信じられる？」と尋ねると、女性は「you could fry an egg（目玉焼きができそうね）on the sidewalk（歩道で）」と述べた。つまり、(C)「very hot outside（外は非常に暑い）」という意味。

19. 正解 (D)

W: Would it be OK if I took a look at your lecture notes?

M: It would be if I had them. I let Tim borrow them.

Q: What can be inferred about the man's lecture notes?

TYPE ③ 推論　女性が「lecture notes（講義ノート）を見てもいい？」と言うと、男性が「It would be if I had them.（持っていればね）I let Tim borrow them.（ティムに貸しちゃった）」と答えた。つまり、(D)「他の人が使っている」ということ。

20. 正解 (C)

W: Guess what! I was able to take Dr. Richardson's Psychology 339 class after all.

M: Good luck! Guess you won't be having much of a social life this term.

Q: What does the man imply about the woman?

解答と解説

TYPE ② 言外の意味 女性が「心理学339のクラスが取れることになった」と言うと、男性が皮肉を込めたアクセントで「Good luck!」と言い、続けて、「Guess you won't be having much of a social life (今学期は、あまり人と付き合えなくなるね)」と言った。つまり、(C)「彼女は並外れて難しいコースに入った」という意味。social lifeは「社交生活、交流」を表す。

Guess what! ちょっと聞いてよ

mp3 **196-200**

21. 正解 (B)

M: What do you feel like for dinner? My treat.
W: Your treat? I can't believe it. Did you win the lottery or something?
Q: What does the woman imply about the man?

TYPE ② 言外の意味 男性が「My treat. (僕のおごりだ)」と言うと、女性が「Your treat? (あなたのおごり？)」と驚いた調子で答え、さらに「Did you win the lottery or something? (宝くじか何か当たったの？)」と返した。つまり男性の申し出が意外なものだったのだ。よって(B)が正解。

22. 正解 (D)

W: Listen, I'm not your mother, but you really ought to see someone about that cough.
M: Yeah, I suppose you're right.
Q: What will the man probably do?

TYPE ⑤ 未来予測 see someone (about that cough)という表現は、see a doctorを便宜的に言い換えたもの。「その咳、誰かに診てもらったほうがいいわ」と言われて、男性が「Yeah, I suppose you're right. (ああ、君の言う通りかも)」と同意している。(D)「doctor's office (病院) に行く」。

23. 正解 (A)

W: Professor Bailey said she's going to fail me in English just because I turned in my essay two minutes after the deadline.
M: She shouldn't be allowed to get away with that!
Q: What does the man imply?

Section 1
Part A
Part B
Part C

TYPE②言外の意味　女性が「教授が私を落とすと言ったのよ。ただ、締め切りの２分後にエッセーを提出しただけで」と苦情を言っていると、男性が「She shouldn't be allowed to get away with that! (そんなことをして許されるべきではない！)」と言って、教授が道理にかなっていないことを表している。よって(A)「教授は不合理極まりないことをしている」が正解。is being と進行形にすることで一時的な行為という面を強調している。

> get away with ～（軽い罪）で済む（否定と共に用いられることが多い）
> 例：You're not going to get away with it.（ただじゃ済まないからな）

24. 正解▶ (C)

M: What's wrong, Alice? You look like you just lost your best friend.
W: I was using my computer to write my research paper and I accidentally erased everything I'd already written.
Q: What is the woman's problem?

Rare Ⓔ Problem問題　「What is the woman's problem?」という質問形式はたまに出題される。男性が「親友を失ったような顔をしてどうしたの」（日本語でいう「この世の終わりみたいな顔をして」というような一種の慣用句）と言うと、女性が「論文を書くのにコンピューターを使っていて、書いたもの全てを、誤って消してしまったのよ」と答えている。つまり、(C)「彼女は file（書類）を失った」が正解。

25. 正解▶ (A)

W: I'm absolutely wilting in this car. Would you mind turning on the air?
M: At your service. A touch warm for you, is it?
Q: What will the man probably do?

TYPE⑤未来予測　女性の「I'm absolutely wilting（すごく暑い）...Would you mind turning on the air?（エアコンつけてくれる？）」という言葉に、男性が「At your service.（いいとも）」と答えている。文脈によっては air conditioner は単に the air でも通じる。

> a touch (=a little bit) 少し

解答と解説

26. 正解 (C)

M: Bye, Jane. I'm off to that job interview I told you about.

W: Not wearing that tie, you're not.

Q: What does the woman imply?

TYPE ② 言外の意味 男性が「I'm off to that job interview (仕事の面接に行ってくる)」と言うと、女性が「Not wearing that tie, you're not. (そのネクタイでは、行かないわよね)」と注意している。女性は別のネクタイをするよう勧めているのだ。

be off 去る

27. 正解 (A)

W: I really enjoyed the theater department's fall production.

M: So you did go to see it after all.

Q: What had the man assumed?

Rare Ⓐ 推量 女性が「I really enjoyed the theater department's fall production. (演劇部の秋の公演は本当に楽しかった)」と言うと、男性はdidを強調して「So you did go to see it after all. (じゃあ見に行ったんだ、結局)」と返している。つまり、(A)「彼女は劇を見に行かなかった」と思っていたのだ。設問の時制に注意。

28. 正解 (D)

W: I'm crazy about Mexican food.

M: I know. That's why I brought you to this place.

Q: What can be inferred from this conversation about the man and woman?

TYPE ③ 推論 女性が「メキシコ料理には目がないの」と言うと、男性は、「I know. That's why I brought you to this place. (知ってるよ。だから君をここへ連れてきたんだ)」と答えている。よって、彼らが、レストランにいるのがわかる。

be crazy about ～ ～に夢中である

Practice Test 4

Section 1
Part A
Part B
Part C

323

29. 正解 ▶ (B)

M: How was your camping trip to the mountains at the end of the summer?

W: Would you believe it snowed every day we were there?

Q: What does the woman imply?

TYPE ② 言外の意味 「山でのキャンプはどうだった？」と聞かれて、女性が「Would you believe（信じられる？）私たちがいた間、毎日雪が降ったのよ」と言っている。従って(B)「彼女が予期していたより寒かった」が正解。

30. 正解 ▶ (D)

W: That was one of the best talks I've ever attended.

M: I couldn't agree with you more.

Q: What does the man mean?

TYPE ① 発言の意味 女性が「あれは、今までで最高の講演会だわ」と言うと、男性が「I couldn't agree with you more.（君にこれ以上は同意できない＝まったく同感だ）」と非常に強く同意している。こういった逆説的な表現はTOEFLによく登場するので注意が必要。「Who could ask for anything more?（誰がこれ以上望めますか？）」などとも言える。

Part B

mp3 **207-211**

Questions 31-34

Listen to the following conversation about a student election.

W: I'm really excited about running for student council president.

M: I can tell. But there's a lot of work to be done, Sally. The campaign's going to take a lot of time and effort. And we'll need a campaign plan.

W: What do you think is the best way to advertise and to get my views across?

M: Well, I figure those are two separate things. We can take out some ads in the campus newspaper, but there's not a lot of space in those for ideas, so we'll have to think of some way for you to get in touch with the voters.

W: Maybe I could give a short talk on the college radio station. The station managers are always looking for programs.

M: Good idea. And we could set up a booth outside of the cafeteria the week before the election. Everyone would have to walk past it.

W: That's right. After dinner is a good time to talk with people because they're not in too much of a hurry. So we've got ads in the campus newspaper, a talk on the radio, and a booth outside the cafeteria. Any other ways to get publicity?

M: Umm … we'll also need to put up some posters. Probably the best place for those is in the dormitories and student union. We could even get started on those tonight.

W: All right, I'll get some paper and let's sketch out some rough drafts.

run for ～ ～に立候補する　student council 学生自治会　I can tell. わかるよ。
get ～ across (考えなど) を広める　take out some ads in ～ ～に広告を載せる
get in touch with ～ ～と連絡を取る　get publicity 注目を浴びる

31. 正解 (C)

Q: What position is the woman running for?

TYPE (9) What問題　会話の冒頭に注意。女性が会話の一番初めに「I'm really excited about running for student council president. (学生会長に立候補するのでワクワクしている)」と言っている。

32. 正解 (C)

Q: Where do the man and woman plan to take out advertisements?

TYPE (8) Where問題　会話は選挙広報活動についての打ち合わせ。女性が「What do you think is the best way to advertise and to get my views across? (宣伝をして私の意見を広く知らしめる一番いい方法は？)」と聞くと、男性が「We can take out some ads in the campus newspaper (学校新聞に広告を載せられる)」と言っている。

Practice Test 4

Section 1
Part A
Part B
Part C

33. 正解▶ (D)

Q: When will the woman speak to students outside the cafeteria?

TYPE ⑦ When問題 男性が「Good idea. And we could set up a booth outside of the cafeteria (カフェテリアの前にブースを置こう) the week before the election.」と言うと、女性が「After dinner is a good time to talk with people (人と話すなら、夕食後がいいわね)」と言っている。

34. 正解▶ (B)

Q: What will the man and woman do next?

TYPE ⑨ What問題 男性が「we'll also need to put up some posters. (いくつかポスターを揚げる必要もあるね)」と言うと、会話の最後で女性が「All right, I'll get some paper and let's sketch out some rough drafts. (わかったわ。私が紙を取ってくるから、大まかな下書きを描きましょう)」と言っている。

mp3 212-216

Questions 35-38

Listen to the following conversation about student housing.

M: I'd like to speak with the director of Student Housing.

W: I am the director of Student Housing. My name is Ms. Stanton. How can I help you?

M: My name is Edward Jones. I'll be a freshman student here in the fall, and I'd like to get some information about the college dormitories.

W: All right. We have four dormitories at the college. One for female students: that's Franklin Hall. One is for male students: Morris Hall. One of the dormitories——Fennel Hall——is reserved for international students. And one of our dormitories is co-ed: that's Cooper Hall.

M: I see. Could you tell me about Cooper Hall?

W: I'm afraid that dormitory is only for upperclassmen. You must be at least a sophomore in order to live there.

M: Could you tell me about Morris Hall then?

W: There are some special regulations for Morris Hall. All freshmen are put in 3-person rooms. Upper-class students live in 2-person rooms.

M: Is there a curfew?

W: No, there is no curfew. But there is a quiet time from midnight to eight a.m.. During those hours students should play their stereos quietly so others are not disturbed.

M: How do I apply?

W: Just send in your housing application form. You should do it very soon though. The dormitories are almost full for the fall term. If your application is too late, you'll have to search for off-campus housing.

> student housing 学生寮、学生の住居　freshman 大学1年生　dormitory 寮
> international student 外国人学生　co-ed 男女共学の　upperclassman 上級生
> sophomore 大学2年生　regulation 規則　curfew 門限　be disturbed 邪魔される
> application form 申込書用紙　off-campus 大学敷地外の

35. 正解 (D)

Q: Who may live in Cooper Hall?

TYPE 10 Who/Whom問題　男性に「Could you tell me about Cooper Hall?（クーパーホールについて教えてくださいますか）」と尋ねられた直後の女性の答えに注目。「I'm afraid that dormitory is only for upperclassmen.（残念ですが、あの寮は上級生専用です）」と告げ、続けて「You must be at least a sophomore in order to live there.（あそこに住むには、少なくとも2年生でなければなりません）」と言っている。この「2年生以上」という条件を言い換えているのが(D)だ。

36. 正解 (C)

Q: What special regulations are in effect for Morris Hall?

TYPE 9 What問題　男性に「Is there a curfew?（門限はありますか？）」と尋ねられた女性の返答がポイント。「No, there is no curfew.（いいえ、門限はありません）But there is a quiet time from midnight to eight a.m..（でも、深夜0時から午前8時までは静かにしておく時間です）」と言っている。

Practice Test 4

Section 1
Part A
Part B
Part C

Practice Test 4

37. 正解 (A)

Q: What advice does the director of Student Housing give to the man?

TYPE 9 What問題 最後の女性の発言がポイント。「Just send in your housing application form. (住居申込用紙を送るだけです) You should do it very soon though. (ただし、あなたはすぐにそうすべきですが)」と言っていて、最終的に「If your application is too late, (もし、申し込みが遅すぎたら) you'll have to search for off-campus housing. (大学敷地外の住居を探さないといけませんよ)」と念を押している。従って(A)「できるだけ早く申込みをすべき」が正解。

38. 正解 (B)

Q: Which dormitory is the student eligible to live in?

TYPE 11 Which問題 男性が、まず自己紹介で「I'll be a freshman student (大学の1年生になります)」と、言っている。(A) Franklin Hallは「for female students (女子学生専用)」、(C) Fennel Hallは「for international students (留学生専用)」、(D) Cooper Hallは「for upperclassmen (上級生専用)」なので、この学生が住めるのは唯一、(B)「Morris Hall (男子学生専用)」だけになる。

Part C

mp3 218-222

Questions 39-42

Listen to the following talk about railway stations.

Last week we looked at the role played by railroads in the development of the American economy in the late 19th century. Today I'd like to examine the evolution of railroads during the 20th century. In order to do so, let's focus on New York's Grand Central Station as a prime example of the trend I'd like to point out. When it first opened in 1913, Grand Central Station was a temple to both railroading, which had provided the arteries for America's growth as an industrial power, and also to the vigor of New York City itself. It boasted vast kitchens to prepare meals for passengers departing on long transcontinental journeys, as well as Turkish baths, private changing rooms, and showers. Without question, that was the heyday of railroading in this country. Today, the farthest destination from Grand Central is New Haven, Connecticut, just 90 minutes away.

For most of the 20th century, Grand Central Station and all of the once great railroad stations of the eastern United States were allowed to slide into a neglect that reflected the slow displacement of the passenger train, first by the automobile and then by the airplane. Because of this shift, very little money was put into maintaining the stations. They were still used for commuter traffic, but they were no longer the comfortable, cheery places they had been early in the century.

Several decades ago city planners realized that they needed to do something to lure people back into the inner city. As a result, a great deal of money was put into restoring the former glory of the old downtown railway stations. Now these stations are like modern shopping malls, with something for everyone. And they have succeeded to a certain degree in getting people to ride trains again, even if only to venture into the city on the weekend. Grand Central Station will likely never again be what it once was, but the signs of a revival in rail travel are starting to appear.

> focus on ～ ～に焦点をあてる　point out ～ ～を指摘する　artery 動脈　vigor 活気　boast ～ ～を誇る　transcontinental 大陸横断の　heyday 全盛期　destination 目的地、行く先　slide into ～ （罪悪癖など）に陥る　neglect 無視、注目されないこと　displacement 置き換え　put A into B A を B につぎ込む　cheery 陽気な　lure ～ ～を呼び戻す、誘い込む　restore ～ ～を取り戻す　to a certain degree ある程度は　venture into ～ 思い切って～に出かける　revival 再生

39. 正解 (D)

Q: What was the subject of last week's lecture?

TYPE 9 What問題　出だしを注意して聞くこと。最初にズバリ「Last week we looked at the role played by railroads（先週、私たちは鉄道が果たした役割に目を向けました）in the development of the American economy...（アメリカ経済の発展における）」と言っているので、(D)「鉄道と経済の発展」が正解。

40. 正解 ▶ (A)

Q: What period of history does the speaker point to as being the high point in American railroading?

TYPE ⑨ What問題 講義で「ニューヨークのグランドセントラル駅を例にとる」と断った上で、「When it first opened in 1913, Grand Central Station was a temple（神殿であった）to both railroading ... and also to the vigor（活気）of New York City itself.」と述べている。さらに、「Without question,（疑いなく）that was the heyday of railroading（この頃は鉄道の全盛の頃）in this country.」と言っている。1913年は「20世紀の初頭」に該当するので正解は(A)。

41. 正解 ▶ (D)

Q: According to the speaker, why did railroads slide into neglect?

TYPE ⑥ Why問題 第2パラグラフで「... that reflected the slow displacement（それは緩やかな排除を反映していた）of the passenger train, first by the automobile and then by the airplane.（まずは自動車、そして飛行機によって）」とある。つまり(D)「他の交通手段のほうが魅力的だった」ということ。

42. 正解 ▶ (C)

Q: How does the speaker view the future of rail travel in the United States?

TYPE ⑫ How問題 最終パラグラフで、街づくりに絡ませて鉄道の再生を語り、最後に「Grand Central Station will likely never again be what it once was,（かつてのようにはなることは決してないだろう）but the signs of a revival in rail travel are（しかし鉄道旅行復活の徴候は）starting to appear.（現れ始めている）」と言っている。つまり(C)「Cautiously optimistic（注意深くも楽観視）」していると言える。

mp3 223-227

Questions 43-46

Listen to the following announcement made by a university student.

Good morning, everyone. Welcome to Brixton College. I'm Brenda Barkley and I'm a sophomore here. As part of your orientation week here you will hear many presentations from various clubs to help you decide which activities you'd like to participate in during your next four years of school. I'd like to encourage you to think about joining the college orchestra. Many of you, I know, have musical backgrounds. But you also may have heard the rumors about how hard you'll need to study in your first year. These rumors are true! But don't let this frighten you away from participating in our orchestra. We students are totally responsible for the orchestra, from purchasing equipment to setting the times for rehearsals — which by the way are held only on Saturdays and Sundays so they don't conflict with your busy class schedule. And we are very serious about our music. You may know the name of Mark Steinburn, the world-famous conductor. Well, Mark was part of our orchestra during his student days here at Brixton and still stops by to visit whenever he's in town. We give concerts several times a year in the local community. Mainly we play traditional classical music, of course, but we actually have a rather broad repertoire and in fact will devote much of our next concert to a program of Native American folk music which has been specially arranged for the orchestra by Gerald Hugging Bear, one of our college's alumni. If you're interested in finding out more about the orchestra, and I hope you are, please come up and talk to me anytime during orientation.

rumor うわさ responsible 責任のある conflict with ～（ここでは）～に支障が生じる stop by 立ち寄る、訪れる repertoire レパートリー devote ～ to ... ……に～を捧げる、時間を割く alumni 同窓会

43. 正解 （B）

Q: For whom is this announcement primarily intended?

TYPE 10 Who/Whom問題 最初に「Welcome to Brixton College（ようこそブリクストン大学へ）... As part of your orientation week（オリエンテーションの週の一部として）」と言っている。ここから (B)「University freshmen（大学の1年生）」向けだとわかる。

Practice Test 4

Section 1

Part A
Part B
Part C

🔊 **44.** 正解 (A)

Q: What is special about the Brixton College orchestra?

TYPE 9 What問題　アナウンス半ばで「We students are totally responsible for the orchestra, (私たち学生がオーケストラ全ての責任を持ちます) from purchasing equipment to setting the times for rehearsals (器材の購入から、リハーサルの時間を決めることまで)」と言っている。つまり、(A)「全て学生によって運営されている」ということ。

45. 正解 (B)

Q: How often does the orchestra meet to rehearse?

TYPE 12 How問題　アナウンス中盤にこの設問に関係する一節がある。「... the times for rehearsals——which by the way are held only on Saturdays and Sundays ...」と言っているので、(B)「週末だけ」が正解。

46. 正解 (D)

Q: What type of music will the orchestra mainly play at its next concert?

TYPE 9 What問題　後半で「... but we actually have a rather broad repertoire (かなり幅広いレパートリーがあり) and in fact will devote much of our next concert to a program of Native American folk music (実は、次のコンサートの大部分を、アメリカ先住民の民族音楽に捧げる)」と述べている。(D)の「民族音楽」が正解。

mp3 **228-232**

Questions 47-50

Listen to the following talk about bees.

I'd like to make my oral presentation today on honeybees. Specifically, I'm going to discuss the influence the queen bee has on her hive. Before I begin, though, I'd like to thank Professor Miller for introducing me to several professional beekeepers who gave me a wealth of information. Prior to beginning this project I had seen an exhibit of bees in a museum, but all I really knew was that bees make honey. The queen bee doesn't rule her subjects in the same way as a human queen does, but she does have a profound influence on the lives of all the bees in the hive. Her most important duty is to lay eggs and she lays between 1500 and 2000 every day during the summer. In addition, she continually secretes a glandular material called pheromone, a substance known as the "social hormone" because it is passed by the worker bees from mouth to mouth so that all workers receive an oral sample. This hormone controls almost every facet of the bees' lives, particularly in the area of reproduction, because it blocks normal reproductive activity to ensure that other queens do not develop. However, when the queen becomes old or dies, her pheromone secretions slow down or stop, and this lack of queen substance allows some workers to begin to lay eggs on their own. But since these workers have not mated, all the eggs develop into male drones. The queen's importance in the hive is shown by the fact that if she is killed or removed, all activity is disturbed and the bees will not work properly. They quickly become aware of the loss of their queen because the normal supply of pheromone has been disrupted.

> hive ミツバチの巣　a wealth of information 豊富な情報　prior to ~ ~より前に
> lay egg 卵を産む　continually 継続的に、頻繁に　secrete 分泌する　glandular 腺
> の　substance 物質　facet 面　reproductive 繁殖の　secretion 分泌物　mate 交
> 尾する　drone（ミツバチの）雄バチ　be disturbed 乱される　become (be) aware
> of ~ ~に気づく　be disrupted 中断する、途絶する

47. 正解▶（C）

Q: Who is giving this talk?

TYPE⑩ Who/Whom問題　トークの最初に「my oral presentation（私の口頭発表）」と言っているので、単なる講義ではなさそうだ。続けて聞いていると「I'd like to thank Professor Miller（ミラー教授に感謝します）」と述べている。そこで、学生であることがわかる。

Practice Test 4

Section 1
Part A
Part B
Part C

333

48. 正解▶ (A)

Q: According to the speaker, what is the most important function of the queen bee?

TYPE 9 What問題 9行目で「Her most important duty is to lay eggs (最も重要な務めは卵を産むこと)」と言っている。よって正解は(A)。

49. 正解▶ (A)

Q: What is pheromone?

TYPE 9 What問題 選択肢にざっと目を通してみると、A hormone..., A substance... という語が並んでいる。トークの中で、「... pheromone, a substance known as the "social hormone"... (フェロモン、"社会性ホルモン"として知られている物質)」が聞こえてきたら注意。その後に「This hormone controls almost every facet of the bees' lives, (ハチのほとんど全ての生活面を制御する) ... it blocks normal reproductive activity (それは通常の繁殖行為を封じる)」と続く。よって(A)「A substance which inhibits reproduction (繁殖を抑制する物質)」が正解。

50. 正解▶ (B)

Q: What happens to worker bees who have not mated?

TYPE 9 What問題 「But since these workers have not mated, (それらの働きバチは交尾してないので) all the eggs develop into male drones. (全ての卵はオスのハチになる)」と言っている。(B)「They are unable to produce female offspring (彼らは雌の子孫を作れない)」が正解。

Section 2
Structure and Written Expression

Structure

Questions 1-15

1. 正解 (B)

TYPE (13) 文構造 カンマまではThomas Edisonを説明する句。過去分詞のbeenがあるので、現在完了を表すhasが必要。

2. 正解 (A)

TYPE (13) 文構造 主語になる名詞が必要。「the＋名詞＋of＋名詞」という構造。

3. 正解 (A)

TYPE (16) 動詞の形 文中のthe以下は従属節になる。つまり主語と動詞が必要。節の主語はEuropeansという複数名詞、しかも内容は過去の出来事を表すので(A)が正解。(B)の過去完了形は、過去時制のさらに前の時制を表すので、通常、周りに過去形の動詞（文）がないときは使わない。

4. 正解 (B)

TYPE (15) 語順 「動詞（を得る）＋形容詞（国際的な）＋名詞（賞賛）」という語順になる。

5. 正解 (D)

TYPE (13) 文構造 カンマの後が完全な文になっていて、しかも接続詞がないので、空所には主語も動詞も入らない。「Of＋複数名詞」を入れて、「～の内で」という意味の前置詞句を完成させればよい。

6. 正解 (C)

TYPE (14) 語彙 2つの完全な文がカンマで区切られている。文頭には前文を従属節にする接続詞が必要。Despite（前置詞）は後に名詞句が、Nonetheless（副詞）は後に主節がくる。「トラは一般的にジャングルのネコ科動物と見なされて

いるが、北はシベリアまで住んでいた」という逆説の意味にするには、(C) Even thoughが適切。

7. 正解 (C)
TYPE 16 動詞の形 that節内の主語が the next dayという「単純な未来」を表す単語なので、(C)のwillが必要。would be fair（晴れたかもしれない）では仮の話になってしまい、この文脈と合わない。

8. 正解 (B)
TYPE 13 文構造 文中のbutが何と何を接続しているかに注目。「主語Uranium＋動詞＋but＋空所」なので、空所には動詞が必要。「ウランを多く含む鉱石から抽出されなければならない」という受け身にするには、be動詞が必要。

9. 正解 (C)
TYPE 15 語順 「The＋比較級、the＋比較級」の構文を完成させる。「The heavier ..., the more ...」となる。

10. 正解 (B)
TYPE 13 文構造 ここでのwhichは目的格の関係代名詞。その場合、which以降に主語と動詞が必要。agreementは不可算名詞なので、fewではなくlittleを使う。

11. 正解 (B)
TYPE 13 文構造 空所の前のカンマから、banks,までは挿入句。これは直前のthe prime interest rate（貸し付けレート）と同格になる。「(銀行が) お金を貸し付けるレート」いう名詞句を作るには、the rate at which it loans moneyとすればよい。

12. 正解 (D)
TYPE 13 文構造 複数形の主語Large primatesを修飾する形容詞節を作るには、「that/which＋動詞の原形」の形が必要。

13. 正解 (D)

TYPE⑭ 語彙　moreという副詞の後には形容詞が続く。persuasiveは「説得力がある」という意味。

14. 正解 (B)

TYPE⑯ 動詞の形　demand（要求する）という動詞に続くthat節の中の動詞は原形になる（仮定法現在）。他にも要求・提案・主張・当然・決定などを表わす動詞は、同じ構文になる。（例: desire/propose/suggest/insist/require/order + that + 動詞の原形）

15. 正解 (C)

TYPE⑭ 語彙　「ability + to不定詞」で「〜する能力」という意味になる。「adapt oneself to 〜」は「〜に慣れる、順応する」という意味。

Written Expression

Questions 16-40

16. 正解 (C)　relative → relatively

TYPE⑱ 品詞　下線(C)直後のconstantが「一定の」という意味の形容詞なので、直前のrelativeにlyをつけて、副詞にする。

17. 正解 (C)　did → do

TYPE㉕ 動詞の形　この文は現在時制isを使い、一般的な事実を述べている。そこで接続詞asが導く節の時制も現在になり、動詞は過去形didでなく、現在形doになる。

18. 正解 (C)　if as → as if

TYPE㉗ 語順　「まるで〜のように」という表現はas ifを用いる。語順が逆。

Practice Test 4

Section 2
Structure
Written
Expression

337

19. 正解▶ (D)　adopt → adopting

TYPE㉑ 並列　orの前後にある動詞の形はそろえること。つまりchoosing ... or adopting ... にする。

20. 正解▶ (B)　flames → flame

TYPE⑳ 単複　flamesはしばしば複数形で「炎」という意味だが、前に不定冠詞単数形のaがあるので、この文ではsを取ってflameにする。

21. 正解▶ (D)　judged → is judged

TYPE㉖ 語の脱落　by which (それによって) があるのでjudgedの前にbe動詞isを入れて、受け身にする。「fine porcelain (磁器) はjudged (判断した)」では意味も通じない。

22. 正解▶ (A)　, they → 削除

TYPE㉔ 重複　文頭の名詞Indian arrowheadsが主語、その後に主格代名詞theyがあると主語の重複になるので、取り除く。

23. 正解▶ (C)　ourselves → themselves

TYPE⑲ 数の一致　「Hispanics (ヒスパニック系の住民)」は三人称。そこで、代名詞ourselvesをthemselvesにする。

24. 正解▶ (B)　until → up

TYPE㉓ 前置詞　untilをupに変え、「up to (～まで)」にする。survive up to three months (3カ月まで生きる) という意味。

25. 正解▶ (D)　strength → strengthens

TYPE㉑ 並列　increases ..., raises ..., and ... と動詞が2つつながり、さらにandがある。よって、名詞strengthを動詞strengthens (～を強くする) にする。

26. 正解▶ (C)　was → is

TYPE㉕ 動詞の形　下線(B)の直後に現在形canがあり、本文は一般的な事柄を述べている。時制の一致の法則で、下線(C) wasを過去形でなく現在形isにする。

解答と解説

27. 正解 (B) a → 削除

TYPE 28 冠詞 information は不加算名詞。a を取り除く。

28. 正解 (B) attract → attracts

TYPE 19 数の一致 主語が Museum で単数形、カンマに挟まれた部分は挿入句。三人称単数現在なので動詞 attract を attracts にする。下線(C)も単数形。

29. 正解 (B) him → his

TYPE 22 代名詞 目的格の him を、下線(B)直後の generation という名詞を修飾する所有格 his にする。

30. 正解 (C) before → 削除

TYPE 24 重複 before と ago が重複している。before を取って「2億年以上前」という意味にする。過去のある時点から見て「〜日／年前」と言う時は、ago ではなく before を使う。

31. 正解 (D) expression → express

TYPE 18 品詞 the best ways to 〜は「〜する最善の方法」という意味で、to の後には原形不定詞 express がくる。

32. 正解 (D) breakthrough → breakthroughs

TYPE 20 単複 「one of 〜 (〜の中のひとつ)」という、数を示す表現の最後は s のつく複数名詞。つまり one of the ... breakthroughs となる。

33. 正解 (D) there are also → 削除

TYPE 21 並列 下線(D)の前の接続詞 and が何をつないでいるかに注目。lava, gases and solid rock fragments (溶岩、ガス、硬い岩の破片) は「名詞、名詞 and 名詞」という構造。There are also を取り除く。

34. 正解 (D) it → its

TYPE 22 代名詞 カンマに挟まれた部分は挿入句。下線(D) it origin では、名詞が2つ続いてしまう。its origin は、「cowboy ballad の起源」という意味。

Practice Test 4

Section 2

Structure
Written
Expression

Practice Test 4

35. 正解 （A） respect → respected

TYPE 18 品詞 文頭の The widely ... Marshall までが主語。respect は動詞なので respected として形容詞にし、名詞 jurist（裁判官）を修飾する形にするのが正しい。widely respected jurist（副詞→形容詞→名詞）という修飾の関係。

36. 正解 （C） are → is

TYPE 19 数の一致 主語となる名詞は Clothing で、made ... wool は Clothing の説明。Clothing の後に関係代名詞 that + is を入れると文の構造がわかりやすい。Clothing は三人称単数名詞なので動詞は単数形 is になる。

37. 正解 （B） of → by

TYPE 23 前置詞 下線(B)の前に先行詞 means（手段）とあり、また文末は is now conducted と受動態になっている。そこで of を by（～によって）に変える。

38. 正解 （D） as well as → and

TYPE 29 接続詞 both A and B という相関関係を完成させる。as well as を and に変える。

39. 正解 （D） healthy → health

TYPE 18 品詞 in skin healthy では、前置詞＋形容詞＋形容詞になってしまう。前置詞の後ろには目的語になる名詞がくる。また、形容詞が修飾するのは名詞。そこで、healthy を名詞の health にする。

40. 正解 （D） object → objectivity

TYPE 21 並列 接続詞 and が何を並べているかに注意。「detachment（公平性）、objectivity（客観性）and abstraction（抽象性）」のように、カンマの前後を全て不可算の抽象名詞に統一する。なお、可算名詞 an object は「物体、対象、目的」といった意味になるので文脈に合わない。これは倒置の形になっており、「Among ... discourse」は副詞の働きをする前置詞句で、are 以下が主語。

Section 3
Reading Comprehension

Questions 1-8

1. 正解 (D)

TYPE 30 要旨 英語の文章は第1パラグラフが、文全体のイントロダクションになっていることが多い。さらにそのパラグラフの最初の部分で「一般的な話」について触れ、パラグラフの終わりで「この文では〜について書きます」と、要点を述べることが多い。ここでは、「In reality ... statistics show.（犯罪率に見られる実際の男女差は、公的な統計が示す値より小さいかもしれない）」を言い換えた(D)が正解。

2. 正解 (A)

TYPE 33 語彙 imbalanceはdisparityと同意語で「不等、不同」という意味。(B) unfairnessは「不公平」、(C) improbabilityは「起こりそうにないこと」、(D) inconsistencyは「矛盾」の意。

3. 正解 (C)

TYPE 37 理由 ここでは、パラグラフを一読しておおよその要旨をつかみ、次に選択肢に目を通してその内容が本文の内容と合致しているものを選べばよい。第1パラグラフ1行目のgender mythは「性別に関する根拠のない作り話」、debunkは「うそを暴く、事実誤認を証明する」という意味。つまり1〜2行目では、「性別によって痛みに耐える能力に違いがあるという説は事実誤認だ」という内容を述べている。これと同内容なのは(C)だ。

4. 正解 (B)

TYPE 31 事実の確認 lost lettersについての記述は第2パラグラフにある。14〜16行目に、「These studies showed ... was an affluent man（これらの研究によると、被害者が裕福でそれが現金の場合、最もお金が盗まれやすい）」とあるので、(B)の「被害者の経済状態が重要な役割を果たしている」が正解。

5. 正解▶ (A)

TYPE㉝ 語彙　alteredは「変えられた」という意味。これに一番近い意味は(A)である。

6. 正解▶ (C)

TYPE㉞ 語法　13行目からの文章構成と主語を見る。「... the letters were observed and ... they were posted or kept.」とある。つまり代名詞theyは、直前の文の主語the lettersを指している。

7. 正解▶ (C)

TYPE㉝ 語彙　rarelyは、「まれに、めったに～しない」という意味で(C) seldomが最も近い。(A)「hardly (ほとんど～ない)」はほぼゼロという意味で強すぎる。(B) plausiblyは「まことしやかに」、(D) unlikelyは「ありそうもない」の意。

8. 正解▶ (D)

TYPE㉜ 推論　最後の一文に、「警察やその他の役人はおそらくは女性は男性よりも危険ではないと見なし、そして結果的に男性ならば逮捕されていたかもしれないような (女性の) 行為を見逃しているのかもしれない」とある。これと同内容なのが(D)だ。(A)と(C)の内容は本文と逆。(B)については述べられていない。

重要語句

tolerate ～ ～を我慢する　gender 性別　myth 作り話、神話　cursory 大まかな utilized 利用された　reveal ～ ～を明らかにする　enormous 巨大な、莫大な imbalance 不均衡　dictum 意見　commit ～ ～を犯す　money order 郵便為替 affluent 富裕な　sum 総額　conviction 有罪判決　shoplift 万引き　domestic 家庭の　dispute ～ ～を論じる　arrest ～ ～を逮捕する

Questions 9-19

9. 正解▶ (C)

TYPE㉚ 要旨　経済と芸術との関連は第1パラグラフでしか触れられていないので(A)は消去。ジャクソン・ポロックは、abstract expressionismの代表とし

て挙げられているだけなので、(B)と(D)も消去できる。著者が最も言いたいことは(C)「抽象表現主義は重要な芸術ムーブメントであった」ということ。

10. 正解 (B)

TYPE 31 事実の確認 文頭に「第二次大戦中、多くのヨーロッパの芸術家がアメリカに移民した」とあり、続けて「そうした芸術家の集団がムーブメントを起こした」とある。よって(B)「immigrant painters（移民の画家たち）」が正解。

11. 正解 (D)

TYPE 31 事実の確認 6〜7行目に「The movement especially flourished in the 1950s（このムーブメントは1950年代に特に盛んだった）」とある。

12. 正解 (B)

TYPE 33 語彙 profoundは「深遠な」という意味。deep（深い）が同意語。

13. 正解 (A)

TYPE 33 語彙 uniformityはuni=one、form=型で「画一性」という意味。ここでは(A) sameness（同一性：same＋ness）が最も近い。(B)「表現」、(C)「服従」、(D)「進展」という意味。

14. 正解 (D)

TYPE 32 推論 第1パラグラフのサポート情報に注目。6〜8行目「The movement ... political expansion.（その動きは、アメリカの経済と政治の大きな発展期である1950年代に特に隆盛を極めた）」とあることから、(D)の「経済と芸術は関連している」と推論できる。

15. 正解 (B)

TYPE 31 事実の確認 第1パラグラフの最後に「the United States ... the Western art world.（歴史上初めてアメリカは西洋芸術界の中心となった）」とあるので、(B)「芸術の世界でアメリカを傑出した存在にした」が正解。

Practice Test 4

Section 3

Practice Test 4

16. 正解 (D)

TYPE 37 理由 本文15行目に「"Blue Poles" is an example of his mature work.("ブルー・ポールズ"[青い柱]は彼の円熟した作品の一例である)」とある。his mature(彼の円熟した)が鍵だ。これに気付けば(A)は除外できる。(B)は的外れ。ポロック個人の話をしているのだから(C)も除外できる。従って正解は(D)。

17. 正解 (D)

TYPE 33 語彙 verticalは「垂直の」という意味。(D)「upright(縦長の)」が同意語。(A)は「輝いた」、(B)は「目立つ」、(C)は「あいまいな」の意。

18. 正解 (B)

TYPE 31 事実の確認 18〜19行目「The picture ... unlike most traditional paintings(ほとんどの伝統的な絵画と違って……その絵には関心の中心になるものがない)」を言い換えた(B)「視点の中心になるものがない」が正解。

19. 正解 (C)

TYPE 38 構成 2つのパラグラフのつながりを見る。本文は、最初の段落でアメリカにおけるabstract expressionismの一般的な概念を説明し、次の段落で具体的に例証している。すなわち(C)が正解。第2パラグラフはポロックの例が挙げられているだけなので(A)「一連の例示によって支持された主張」と(D)「解説してから要約する」は消去。伝統的な絵画と抽象表現主義について言及されているだけなので(B)「いくつかのタイプの分類」も消去できる。

重要語句

profound 深遠な　large in scale 大規模　energetic 精力的な　individualistic 個人主義の　flourish 栄える　expansion 拡大、発展　convey 〜 〜を伝える　nonetheless それでもなお　proclaim 宣言する　uniformity 画一性　depersonalization 非人格化　advent 出現　prominence 傑出　mature 円熟した　punctuate 〜 〜を強調する　vertical 垂直の　tangle もつれ　jagged ギザギザの　extend 広がる　undiminished 衰えない　pigment 顔料　spontaneity 自発性　scorn 軽蔑

Questions 20-31

20. 正解 (A)

TYPE(36) 段落要旨　第1パラグラフのトピックセンテンス「Boontling is the name ... California. (ブーントリングは、その話者が人為的に作った方言に与えた名前で、カリフォルニア州メンドシーノ群のアンダーソン・バレーで1880年から1920年にかけて広く話された)」に注目。ブーントリングの定義、つまり(A)「ブーントリングという名前の起源」を示している。

21. 正解 (B)

TYPE(31) 事実の確認　設問文の最後がBoontling is NOTと否定形であるのに要注意。(A)の「理解が難しい」、(C)の「地域色が濃い」、(D)の「一般的な英語と違う」は全てlocal language (現地語・地域言語) の特徴で、ブーントリングに当てはまる。よって、(B)「(ブーントリングは) 一般的な意味での言語だ」が正解。

22. 正解 (D)

TYPE(33) 語彙　lexiconは「語彙」という意味。その後に続くunique words and phrasesからも推測できるだろう。(D) vocabularyが同意語。(A)「語法」、(B)「配列」、(C)「補語」という意味。

23. 正解 (B)

TYPE(32) 推論　1行目に「Boontling is ... contrived jargon (ブーントリングとは、その話者が人為的に作った方言に与えた名前)」とある。(B)「(ブーントリングは) 地域住民によって特別かつ意図的に作られた」が正解。

24. 正解 (A)

TYPE(33) 語彙　virtuallyは「事実上、実質的には」という意味。ここでは(A) practicallyと同意。(B)「いく分」、(C)「部分的に」、(D)「確かに」という意味。

25. 正解 (C)

TYPE(32) 推論　7～8行目「during the first decade of the 20th century (20世紀初頭の10年の間に)」とあるので、1900～1910年を指していることがわかる。

Practice Test 4

Section 3

26. 正解▶ (B)

TYPE 34 語法　前にある複数名詞を探す。しかし outsiders は unable to understand の主語なので、目的語 them と同じであるはずはない。もうひとつ前の複数名詞「local residents（地元の居住者）」が正解。

27. 正解▶ (A)

TYPE 32 推論　15〜16行目「those few outsiders who ventured into the Anderson Valley（あえてアンダーソン・バレーに入ってきた数少ない部外者）」、また27〜28行目「The role that ... cannot be denied.（谷の独特の地形が地域社会を形成するのに果たした役割は否めない）」とあるので、(A)「アンダーソン・バレーそれ自体が行き難い場所だった」のである。

28. 正解▶ (B)

TYPE 31 事実の確認　13〜14行目に、「the extensive use of obscure words ... virtually incomprehensible（世に知られない単語が多用されるので、ブーントリングは理解不能であった）」とある。つまり、(B)の「unfamiliar words（なじみのない、見慣れない単語）を多く用いている」ことが原因。

29. 正解▶ (C)

TYPE 33 語彙　intimately は「密接に」という意味の副詞。(C) closely（密接に）が同意語。(A)は「誤って」、(B)は「感情的に」、(D)は「外見上」という意味。

30. 正解▶ (A)

TYPE 31 事実の確認　個々の選択肢の正誤を確認するには本文全体から情報を拾う必要がある。ただし選択肢(A)に関しては、第3パラグラフの最初に「for Boontling "context is everything." Certainly ...（ブーントリングでは"文脈が全て"である。確かに……）」とあることから、正しいとわかる。(B)や(C)のようなことは述べられていない。(D)については明言されていないが、この文章自体がブーントリングの細かな分析であることを踏まえれば誤りだとわかる。

31. 正解 (A)

TYPE 32 推論 推論問題の場合、本文の内容を基に論理的に選択肢の正誤を考える必要がある。まず(A)については、本文11行目に「isolated rural valley(孤立した地方の谷)」とあることから、外部の影響を受けにくかったことが考えられる。よって正しい。(B)の「infertile soil(痩せた土地)」は本文で触れられていない。(C)の「steep-sloped hills(急斜面の丘)」は最終文で出てくるが、それにより「人々が近くで生活するようになった」とは述べられていない。(D)の内容自体は正しいかもしれないが、外部からの物資を得ることが困難であることと独自の言語が発達したことの間にどんな関連があるのかが不明だ。

重要語句

deliberately 故意に contrive ~ ~を考案する extensively 広範囲に abbreviate ~ ~を略して書く zenith 頂点 lexicon 語彙 prominent 顕著 rural 田舎の the focal point 焦点 identical 同一の obscure あいまいな virtually 事実上 incomprehensible 理解できない glee 歓喜 badge 象徴 close-knit しっかりと結束した forebear 先祖 be tempted to do ~する気になる dialect 方言 intimately 密接に context 文脈 topography 地形

Questions 32-41

32. 正解 (D)

TYPE 30 要旨 本文全体にgoldという単語が散りばめられているので、goldが主題だということはわかるだろう。選択肢を見ると、(A)の「金特有の性質」、(B)の「さまざまな種類の通貨の定義」、(C)の「通貨の発展の概略」は、全て本文で取り上げられている要素だ。しかし、それらがいったい何のために本文で触れられたかというと、(D)「金に価値がある理由を説明する」ためである。

33. 正解 (B)

TYPE 31 事実の確認 2行目「stones, salt, cattle, and seashells ...」に注目。(A)「貝殻」と(C)「塩」があるので消去できる。(D) livestockはlive(生きた)+ stock(蓄え)で「家畜」という意味。つまり、cattleが言い換えられている。よって述べられていないのは(B)「ビーズ」。

Practice Test 4

Section 3

34. 正解 (B)

TYPE 31 事実の確認 (A)は2行目から不正解だとわかる。(C)は述べられていない。(D)「金は常に宝飾品を作るのに必要だった」は25～26行目「make gold very useful, entirely apart from its value as jewelry ...（宝飾品としての価値とは全く別に、金は有益）」と矛盾する。よって(B)「人々は金そのものが貴重であることに同意している」が正解。

35. 正解 (C)

TYPE 33 語彙 surpassは「sur=super＋pass（超える）」という意味。(C) exceedと同意。(A)は「置き換える」、(B)は「価値を下げる」、(D)は「スピードを上げる」という意味。

36. 正解 (B)

TYPE 34 語法 第3パラグラフの構造を見ると、First, ... Second, ...と続いている。「First, money must be durable.（まず、通貨には耐久性がなければならない）」をヒントに、moneyがitで置き換えられていることがわかるだろう。

37. 正解 (C)

TYPE 31 事実の確認 10～11行目「This is why ... for money.（こういうわけで食べ物、石油、手工芸品は通貨として使われない）」に注目。直前の文「It must not ... inert.（蒸発したり、かびたり、さびたり、砕けたり、壊れたり、腐ったりしてはいけない。金は化学的に不活性である）」より、(C)「長持ちしない」ためだとわかる。

38. 正解 (B)

TYPE 36 段落要旨 13行目に、「In contrast, when a diamond is split, its value is destroyed, ...（[金とは]対照的に、ダイヤモンドが分割されると、その価値は崩れてしまう）」とある。つまり、(B)「金は少量に分割できる」が正解。

39. 正解 (D)

TYPE 33 語彙 gemsは「宝石」という意味。(D)「precious stones（貴石）」が最も近い。(A) jewelryだとイヤリング、ネックレスなどを含む宝飾品という意味になる。(B)は「珍しい鉱石」の意。

40. **正解** (A)

TYPE 33 語彙 intrinsic は「本来備わった、本質的な、固有の」という意味。(A)「inherent（固有の、本来の、生来の）」が最も近い。(B)「異常な」、(C)「明白な」、(D)「実用的な」という意味。

41. **正解** (C)

TYPE 32 推論 第1パラグラフでは、なぜ金が通貨として適しているかを歴史を絡めて紹介し、第3パラグラフでは、通貨として必要な資質を「First, 〜. Second, 〜. Third, 〜. Fourth, 〜. Fifth, 〜.」と5つ挙げ、第4パラグラフでそれらの話をまとめている。よって(C)「金は信頼の置ける通貨としての役割を現在でも果たし得る」が正解。

重要語句

transaction 取り引き、売買　commodity 商品　surpass 〜 〜にまさる　consent 同意　property 財産　durable 耐久性のある　evaporate 蒸発する　mildew かびがはえる　rust さびる　crumble 砕ける　rot 腐る　inert 化学作用をおこさない　divisible 分けることができる　ounce オンス（重量の単位）　bullion 金塊　split 分割する　equivalent 同等の　copper 銅　lead 鉛　zinc 亜鉛　consistent 不変で、一貫した　gem 宝石　intrinsic 本来備わった、本質的な　malleable 打ち延ばしのできる　reactive 化学反応しやすい　withstand 〜 〜に耐える　obviously 明らかに

Questions 42-50

42. **正解** (C)

TYPE 30 要旨 全てのパラグラフにcavity in a tooth、decay（虫歯）という単語が出てきており、またこれは子どもの話だともわかるはず。そこで「Dental decay in children is（子どもの虫歯は）a serious and overlooked problem（深刻かつ見落された問題である）」という文(C)が導き出せる。(A)、(D)はともに詳細の一部分、(B)に関する記述は本文にない。

Practice Test 4

Section 3

43. 正解▶ (B)

TYPE 31 事実の確認 2〜3行目に「... half of the school children in the United States have never had a cavity in a tooth.」とある。よって(B)「50 パーセント」が正解。

44. 正解▶ (D)

TYPE 31 事実の確認 9行目からの記述に注目。「... that the agency's 50 percent cavity-free claim is a myth derived by ignoring decay in "primary teeth" ... by averaging the decay in permanent teeth among children from 5 to 17 years old. (その研究所の50パーセントは虫歯がまったくないという主張は根拠のない説であり、乳歯にあった虫歯を無視して、5〜17歳の子どもの永久歯の虫歯の数を平均化したことから生じている)」とある。つまり(D)「乳歯、第一生歯の虫歯を含めなかった」のだ。(A)と(B)はともに本文の記述に反する。(C)は本文から特定できない。

45. 正解▶ (C)

TYPE 33 語彙 extensiveは「広い、広範囲な」という意味。ここでは(C) large が最も近い意味。(A) criticalは「重要な」、(B) preliminaryは「予備的な」、(D) ongoingは「進行中の」という意味。

46. 正解▶ (B)

TYPE 33 語彙 inspectは「in (中を) ＋spect (見る) =look into (調査する)」という意味で、ここでは(B) checkedが最も近い。

47. 正解▶ (A)

TYPE 32 推論 第2パラグラフで著者が述べているのは、統計処理の仕方の間違いであり、また本文の最後では「Recognition of this fact (この事実の認識が) points to the need for particular public health policies (具体的な公衆衛生政策の必要性を指摘している)」と言っている。ここから著者が同意すると思われるのは、(A)「More accurate research (より正確な調査が) would be helpful (役立つだろう) in establishing the extent of dental diseases. (歯の疾患の程度を立証するのに)」だとわかる。

解答と解説

48. 正解 (D)

TYPE 33 語彙 track は「(証拠などの跡を追い) 何かを突き止める」という意味。つまり (D) の「analyzed (分析した)」が最も近い。(A) は「抑制された」、(B) は「増加した」、(C) は「孤立した」という意味。

49. 正解 (A)

TYPE 34 語法 この文で they の前に登場している複数形の名詞は results と data だが、前置詞句の of the data は付け足しの要素に過ぎない。従って they = results だとわかる。つまり (A) the results が that 節の中の主語になる。

50. 正解 (D)

TYPE 37 理由 理由を問う問題では消去法が有効。選択肢を見ると (A) から (C) までは本文で述べられていないことがわかる (最後の問題なので本文の内容はほぼ頭に入っているはず)。(D) については、17行目に「Only one in six 17-year-olds can legitimately be said to have had no cavities. (正当に虫歯がないと言えるのは、17歳人口の6人に一人だけである)」とあることから正しいとわかる。

重要語句

federal 連邦の　devote to ~ ~に専心する　oral 口内の　cavity 虫歯　alleged 主張された　prompt 促して~させる　derived by ~ ~によって生じている　decay 虫歯、腐食する、虫歯になる　kindergartner 幼稚園児　legitimately 正当に　widespread 広く行きわたっている　recognition 認識 (すること)　preventable 予防可能な

Practice Test 4

Section 3

学習の記録

模試をやり終えたら正解数と予想スコアを記録し、学習の目安にしましょう。

		Section 1	Section 2	Section 3	予想スコア
第1回 20　年 月　日	Practice Test [　]				～
第2回 20　年 月　日	Practice Test [　]				～
第3回 20　年 月　日	Practice Test [　]				～
第4回 20　年 月　日	Practice Test [　]				～
第5回 20　年 月　日	Practice Test [　]				～
第6回 20　年 月　日	Practice Test [　]				～
第7回 20　年 月　日	Practice Test [　]				～
第8回 20　年 月　日	Practice Test [　]				～

※スコア換算表は p.37 にあります。

memo

著者紹介

Paul Wadden, Ph.D.　ポール・ワーデン

順天堂大学国際教養学部教授。ヴァーモント大学大学院修了（修辞学博士）。イリノイ州立大学大学院修了（英米文学博士）。著述家・文学者。ニューヨーク・タイムズ、ウォールストリート・ジャーナル、ワシントン・ポストなど、多数の新聞および雑誌に執筆。著書に Teaching English at Japanese Universities: A New Handbook (Routledge)、A Handbook for Teaching English at Japanese Colleges and Universities (Oxford University Press)、TESOL Quarterly、College Composition、College Literature に掲載の言語教育に関する論文、50冊を超える TOEIC TEST、TOEFL TEST 対策教材など多数。

Robert A. Hilke　ロバート・ヒルキ

企業研修トレーナー。元国際基督教大学専任講師。カリフォルニア大学大学院修士課程修了（言語学）。異文化研修および TOEIC、TOEFL、GRE など、テスト対策のエキスパートで、年間約250日、国際的な大企業向けに講座を行っている。共著に『聞いて覚える英単語 キクタン TOEFL® TEST [イディオム編]』（アルク）、『TOEFL®テスト ライティング問題100 改訂版』（旺文社）など。

藤井哲郎

東京慈恵会医科大学教授。セントマイケルズ大学大学院修士課程修了（英語教育学）。東京 YMCA 英語専門学校や国際基督教大学の英語教育プログラムのカリキュラム改革に携わり、英語教育教材の研究と開発を専門にしている。監修に『英語で味わう聖書のことば』『聖書で英語を習得する』（いのちのことば社フォレストブックス）、共著に『一流の朗読で聴く名文-「智」を求める』（マクミランランゲージハウス）、『TOEIC® L&Rテスト究極単語 Basic 2200』『TOEIC® L&Rテスト究極単語 Advanced 2700』（語研）など。

改訂版　完全攻略！ TOEFL ITP® テスト 模試4回分

発行日　2022年11月 4日（初版）
　　　　2024年 4月19日（第3刷）

著者	ポール・ワーデン、ロバート・ヒルキ、藤井哲郎
編集	株式会社アルク 文教編集部
編集協力・翻訳	五十嵐 哲
英文校正	Peter Branscombe、Margaret Stalker
カバーデザイン	早坂美香（SHURIKEN Graphic）
本文デザイン・DTP	新井田晃彦（有限会社共同制作社）、鳴島亮介
ナレーション	Greg Dale、Carolyn Miller
録音・編集	株式会社ジェイルハウス・ミュージック
印刷・製本	シナノ印刷株式会社

発行者	天野智之
発行所	株式会社アルク
	〒141-0001 東京都品川区北品川6-7-29 ガーデンシティ品川御殿山
	Website：https://www.alc.co.jp/

地球人ネットワークを創る

アルクのシンボル
「地球人マーク」です。

完全攻略！
TOEFL ITP® テスト
模試4回分【別冊】

>>> REVISED EDITION:

PERFECT MASTER!
FOUR COMPLETE PRACTICE TESTS
FOR THE TOEFL ITP® TEST

問 題 の 対 訳

※解答用マークシートは巻末にあります。

Directions 対訳

　各セクションとパートの冒頭には、問題形式と解答の要領についての指示文（Directions）がある。指示文は問題冊子に掲載されており、リスニング・セクションではその音声も流れる。以下の各セクションとパートの指示文をよく読んで頭に入れ、本番で戸惑うことのないようにしておこう。

Section 1
Listening Comprehension

このセクションでは、英語による会話やトークを理解する能力を示してもらいます。このセクションは3つのパートに分かれており、それぞれのパートに個別の指示文があります。テストでは、話者が述べたことやほのめかしたことを基準に、すべての質問に解答してください。指示があるまで、ページをめくってはいけません。

Part A

指示文：パートAでは、2人の話者の短い会話を聞きます。それぞれの会話の後で、会話に関連した設問が流れます。会話と設問は繰り返されません。設問を聞いた後に問題用紙に書かれた4つの選択肢を読み、最適なものを選びなさい。その後、解答用紙で問題番号を見つけ、選んだ解答に該当する箇所を塗りつぶしなさい。

Part B

指示文：このパートでは、いくつかの長めの会話を聞きます。それぞれの会話の後に、いくつかの設問が流れます。会話と設問は繰り返されません。設問を聞いた後に問題用紙に書かれた4つの選択肢を読み、最適なものを選びなさい。その後、解答用紙で問題番号を見つけ、選んだ解答に該当する箇所を塗りつぶしなさい。

Part C

指示文：このパートでは、いくつかの短いトークを聞きます。トークの後にいくつかの設問が流れます。トークと設問は繰り返されません。設問を聞いた後に、問題用紙に書かれた4つの選択肢を読み、最適なものを選びなさい。その後、解答用紙で問題番号を見つけ、選んだ解答に該当する箇所を塗りつぶしなさい。

━━━ Section 2 ━━━

Structure and Written Expression

制限時間：25分

このセクションは、標準的な英語の書き言葉として適切な言葉づかいを認識する能力を測ることが目的です。このセクションには2つのタイプの設問があり、それぞれに個別の指示文があります。

Structure

指示文：設問1から15は、不完全な文です。それぞれの文の下には(A)、(B)、(C)、(D)と印字された語や句が4カ所あります。文を完成させるのに最もふさわしい語または句を選びなさい。その後、解答用紙で問題番号を見つけ、選んだ解答に該当する箇所を塗りつぶしなさい。

Written Expression

指示文：設問16から40では、それぞれの文に下線が引かれた語や句が4つあります。文中の4つの下線部にはそれぞれ、(A)、(B)、(C)、(D)と印字されています。英文が正しい意味になるように、訂正すべき下線の語句を選びなさい。その後、解答用紙で問題番号を見つけ、選んだ解答に該当する箇所を塗りつぶしなさい。

━━━ Section 3 ━━━

Reading Comprehension

制限時間：55分

指示文：このセクションでは、いくつかの文章を読みます。それぞれの文章の後には、それに関する設問が続きます。1から50までの各設問に対し、選択肢(A)、(B)、(C)、(D)の中から、最もふさわしい解答を選びなさい。次に、解答用紙で問題番号を見つけ、選んだ解答に該当する箇所を塗りつぶしなさい。文章中で述べられたりほのめかされたりしたことを基に、文章に続く全ての設問に答えなさい。

Section 1 Listening Comprehension 対訳
■ Part A

1. **女性**：バリー、カナダへの旅はどうだった？
   男性：素晴らしかったよ。ブリティッシュ・コロンビアはみんなが言っていた通りとてもよかった。
   質問：男性の発言はどういう意味か？
   (A) 彼は旅行中、何人か興味深い人々に会った。
   (B) 彼は代わりにイギリスへ行っていればよかったと思っている。
   (C) 彼はなぜもっと大勢の人たちが行かなかったのだろうと思っている。
   (D) 彼はカナダで美しい風景を見た。

2. **男性**：望んでいた水曜午後の化学実験のクラスには登録できた？
   女性：いいえ、小クラス全部が埋まっていたの。とりあえず金曜日にするしかなかったわ。
   質問：女性は何をほのめかしているか？
   (A) 彼女は水曜日に化学（の授業）を取るだろう。
   (B) 彼女は化学（の授業）に登録できなかった。
   (C) 彼女の第一希望はかなわなかった。
   (D) 金曜日の化学の演習はすでにいっぱいだった。

3. **男性**：君が聞いているの、ガース・ブルックスじゃない？ 君がカントリー・ミュージックが好きだなんて、知らなかったな。
   女性：好きですって？ 実際のところ、最近これしか聞いていないわ。
   質問：女性はカントリー・ミュージックについて何をほのめかしているか？
   (A) 彼女にはそれを聞く時間がない。
   (B) それがとても実践的だと彼女は思う。
   (C) 彼女はそれを大いに楽しんでいる。
   (D) かつて彼女は今よりもそれを好んでいた。

4. **女性**：もう一杯、コーヒーはいかが？
   男性：けっこうです、ありがとう。
   質問：男性の発言はどういう意味か？
   (A) 彼は気分がだいぶよくなっている。
   (B) 彼はもっと飲み物が欲しい。
   (C) 彼はそれを自分で注ぐことができる。
   (D) 彼はすでに十分にコーヒーを飲んだ。

5. **男性**：いくらか晴れてきているようだね。公園に散歩に行かない？
   女性：もちろん。でも、念のために傘を持っていったほうがいいでしょうね。
   質問：女性は何をほのめかしているか？
   (A) また雨が降り始めるかもしれない。
   (B) 彼女はそんなに遠くまでの散歩には行きたくない。
   (C) 彼らはそこに車を停めるべきではなかった。
   (D) その男性はしばしば傘を忘れる。

6. **男性**：君の庭は本当にきれいだね！
   女性：きれいでなくちゃ。午後中ずっと、草むしりをしていたの。くたくたに疲れたわ。
   質問：女性の発言はどういう意味か？
   (A) 彼女は庭の雑草を全て抜いた。
   (B) 彼女は懸命に働いたのでとても疲れている。
   (C) 彼女はもっとよい庭を造らなければならない。

（D）彼女は毎日午後に庭で働いている。

7. **女性**：パトリシアの最近の紀要についてどう思った？

   男性：彼女のいつもの高い基準に達していると思ったよ。

   質問：男性はパトリシアの紀要について何をほのめかしているか？

   （A）それは彼の基準を満たさなかった。

   （B）彼はその語彙が難しすぎると思った。

   （C）彼はそれを図書館で見つけられなかった。

   （D）それはとてもよく書けていた。

8. **男性**：リンダが授業に来るようにならない場合、彼女、今期は卒業できなくなるね。

   女性：わかってる。彼女に話してみたんだけど、何をやってもうまくいかないの。

   質問：女性の発言はどういう意味か？

   （A）リンダは彼女が言うことに耳を貸さない。

   （B）リンダは自分の仕事が好きではないようだ。

   （C）リンダは職探しで忙しい。

   （D）リンダはそれでも予定通り卒業するだろう。

9. **男性**：今日はどうしてバスがこんなに遅いんだろう。もうここにほぼ15分も立っているのに。

   女性：バスの運転手が今朝早くストに入ったのを聞いてないようね。仕事へはタクシーを拾ったほうがいいわよ。

   質問：女性は何をほのめかしているか？

   （A）バスは約15分遅れている。

（B）その男性は歩き始めなければいけない。

（C）その男性はタクシーから降りるべきだ。

（D）バスが走っていない。

10. **女性**：本部ビルの前にあるあの新しい彫刻はひどいわね。

    男性：そんなにけなすべきじゃないと思うな。たくさんの人が、あれを真の芸術作品と見なしているんだ。

    質問：男性の発言はどういう意味か？

    （A）その女性は批判しすぎている。

    （B）その彫刻は醜悪だと彼は同意している。

    （C）彼はまだその彫刻の制作を終えていない。

    （D）その女性は美術の授業を取るべきだ。

11. **女性**：あのテーブルがうるさくて、頭痛がする。ここに来たのは静かに夕食を楽しむためと思ったけど。

    男性：そのためさ。接客係に話してみる。

    質問：この会話から何が推測できるか？

    （A）この男女は注文する用意ができている。

    （B）女性は料理が提供されるのをまだ待っている。

    （C）大声で話している客が何人かいる。

    （D）接客係はただ今、とても忙しい。

12. **男性**：ベロニカを見かけた？ 彼女がこれらの箱を梱包するのを手伝ってくれると思ってたんだけど。

    女性：彼女はインフルエンザにかかっていると聞いたわ。

5

質問：女性はベロニカについて何と言っているか？
(A) 彼女はまだ（複数の）箱を下の階に持ってきていない。
(B) 彼女はどうも今日は調子があまりよくなさそうだ。
(C) 彼女はまだ旅行の荷物の梱包を終えていない。
(D) 彼女は明日の遅くまで飛行機で着かない。

13. 女性：ゲイリー、今朝あなたにあげたファイル、まだ持っている？ファイルキャビネットの中になかったけど。
男性：昼食の直後、君の机の上に戻したよ。
質問：男性の発言はどういう意味か？
(A) 彼はファイルキャビネットを移動させるのを手伝ってくれる。
(B) 彼は昼食の後に戻る。
(C) 彼もそのファイルのありかを知らない。
(D) 彼はもはやそのファイルを持っていない。

14. 男性：もうレイチェルをほとんど見かけないな。音楽専攻になってから、彼女はいつも練習ルームでクラリネットを演奏しているね。
女性：いいことよ。習うより慣れろよね。
質問：女性はレイチェルについて何をほのめかしているか？
(A) 彼女は完璧なパフォーマンスを行った。
(B) 彼女はよりよい演奏家になるだろう。
(C) 彼女はとても思いやりのある人物だ。
(D) 彼女はもっと頻繁に練習する必要がある。

15. 男性：デビー！　小さい子たちと一緒にこの動物園で何をやっているんだい？
女性：地元の小学校でボランティアをやっていて、今日は遠足なの。
質問：女性の発言はどういう意味か？
(A) 彼女は小学校の先生だ。
(B) 彼女は動物園でアルバイトをしている。
(C) 彼女は子どものグループの面倒を見ている。
(D) 彼女はめったに地元の動物園を訪れない。

16. 女性：私たちのグループは今週末スキーに行くの。私たちに加わらない？
男性：ありがとう、マーシー、でも、スキーは好きなスポーツではないんだ。
質問：男性の発言はどういう意味か？
(A) 彼は今週別の予定がある。
(B) 彼はその女性の招待を断っている。
(C) 彼はスキークラブに加入しない。
(D) スキーは彼が大好きなスポーツだ。

17. 男性：キャロル、君は昨晩、夜ふかししたんじゃないかな？
女性：何が言いたいの、クラレンス？
質問：女性は何を知りたいか？
(A) 男性のコメントが意味すること。
(B) 男性が彼女にあげるもの。
(C) 男性が次にすること。
(D) 男性が昨夜やったこと。

18. 女性：おめでとう。応募していた学生ローンを受け取ったと聞いたわ。
男性：ああ、でも新しい学費を考えると、大海の一滴だね。
質問：男性は何をほのめかしている

か？
(A) 学費が値下がりすると予想されている。
(B) 学生ローンでは足りない。
(C) 彼は新しい仕事に応募する。
(D) 彼はバケツをその女性に貸した。

19. 男性：僕達が後でバスケットボールの試合をしに、体育館に入れる確率はどのくらいあるかな？
女性：まずないわね。バレーボールチームが練習の予定を入れてるから。
質問：女性の発言はどういう意味か？
(A) 彼女はバスケットボールの練習をしたくない。
(B) 彼らはこの後にバスケットボールはできない。
(C) 彼女はむしろ代わりにバレーボールをやりたい。
(D) その男性はバレーボールの練習に行くべきだ。

20. 男性：ボブが締切前夜に期末の論文全部を書いたって聞いた？
女性：彼がそんなことをしたのは、これが初めてじゃないのよ。
質問：女性はボブについて何をほのめかしているか？
(A) 彼はしばしばぎりぎりのタイミングで物事にかかる。
(B) 彼はタイピングが得意ではない。
(C) 彼は課題を最初に提出した人ではなかった。
(D) 彼が期限通りに課題を提出することはめったにない。

21. 女性：マーガレットという名の女性が電話してきて、あなたからすぐに連絡がほしいって。
男性：マーガレット？ 本当に？ その名前にはピンとこないな。

質問：男性の発言はどういう意味か？
(A) 彼はとにかくマーガレットに会いたい。
(B) なぜマーガレットは呼び鈴を鳴らさなかったのかと彼は思っている。
(C) マーガレットがすぐに電話をかけてくることを願っている。
(D) 彼はマーガレットという名前の人はひとりも知らない。

22. 男性：オードリー、週末に何か予定ある？
女性：まだないわね。何が起こるか次第で、成り行きにまかせるわ。
質問：女性の発言はどういう意味か？
(A) 彼女は講堂で行われる演劇を見にいく。
(B) 彼女は週末に練習する予定だ。
(C) 彼女は耳の検査を受ける必要がある。
(D) 彼女は何が起こるのかを待ってみるつもりだ。

23. 女性：聞いて！ デービッドがガールフレンドと婚約したわ！
男性：世に驚きの種は尽きないね。彼は結婚などしないと思っていたよ。
質問：男性は何を思い込んでいたか？
(A) 彼女はデービッドがどこに行ったのかと思っている。
(B) デービッドはすでに結婚していた。
(C) デービッドが結婚することはないだろう。
(D) 彼女とデービッドは一度も会ったことがない。

24. 男性：パターソン博士が物理学でつけた成績は本当に腹立たしいよ。これについて彼女に何か言うべ

きだと思う？

女性：私だったらやめにしておくわ。私
が聞いたところによると、彼女が
一度決めたらとにかくそれは変え
られないそうよ。

質問：女性は男性にどうすべきだと提案
しているか。

(A) 教授のオフィスを訪ねる。

(B) 彼の教授に一筆書く。

(C) 成績を上げるため懸命にがんばる。

(D) 起きたことを受け入れる。

25. 女性：ジャンが退職を発表したって聞い
た？

男性：へえ。それは痛手だ。より優れた
マネージャーを得るのは確かに難
しいだろうな。

質問：男性はジャンについて何をほのめ
かしているか？

(A) 彼女に仕えるのは大変だ。

(B) 彼女は間違いなく復帰しない。

(C) 彼女はいい管理職だ。

(D) 彼女は新しいマネージャーを雇っ
た。

26. 女性：先月引っ越して来た時、大家は家
賃の値上げはないと確約したのに、
今になってさらに50ドル、アパー
トに払わなければならないと言う
のよ。

男性：それは不愉快な不意打ちだね！そ
れじゃあまるで君を欺いたみたい
じゃないか。

質問：男性の発言はどういう意味か？

(A) 大家の行動は予想外だった。

(B) その女性のアパートは手ごろな価
格がつけられている。

(C) その女性はもっと静かなアパート
を見つけるべきだ。

(D) 町の至る所でたくさんの大家が家
賃を上げている。

27. 男性：テリーは彼の姉（妹）と同じくら
い数学が得意だね。

女性：それはあまり褒めたことになって
いないわね。

質問：女性は何をほのめかしているか？

(A) テリーの姉（妹）は数学が得意で
はない。

(B) テリーの姉（妹）は彼の宿題を手
伝う。

(C) テリーとその姉（妹）はどちらも
恥ずかしがりやだ。

(D) テリーは姉（妹）に話しかけない。

28. 女性：アドバイザーに会ったんだけれど、
彼は私の専攻の計画に賛成してく
れたわ。

男性：じゃあうまくいったんだ。まさに
僕が言った通りにね。

質問：男性は何を思っていたか？

(A) その女性の計画は承認されないだ
ろう。

(B) アドバイザーとの面談はうまく
いくだろう。

(C) アドバイザーは女性に会うことが
できないだろう。

(D) その女性はアドバイザーのオフィ
スを訪ねる必要があるだろう。

29. 男性：新しいルームメートは耐え難い。
彼女はいつも自分の思い通りにや
ろうとするんだ。

女性：で、あなたは譲ることが好きなわ
けね、トム？

質問：女性はトムについて何をほのめか
しているか？

(A) 彼はルームメートを批判すべきで
はない。

(B) 彼はルームメートと妥協するよう
試みるべきだ。

(C) 彼は別のルームメートを見つける
べきだ。

(D) 彼はとても思いやりのある人物だ。

30. 女性：このフルーツポンチはおいしいわ。
　　　男性：まったく同感だね。
　　　質問：男性の発言はどういう意味か？
　　　(A) 彼はフルーツポンチをもう一杯欲
　　　　　しい。
　　　(B) 彼は女性の意見に反対している。
　　　(C) 彼はフルーツポンチの味が気に入
　　　　　らない。
　　　(D) 彼はそのフルーツポンチがおいし
　　　　　いと思っている。

■ Part B

Questions 31-34

特待プログラムに関する次の会話を聞きなさい。

女性：ねえ、リチャード、大学が特待プログラムを始めるって聞いた？

男性：本当に？ それって新しい学長のアイデアのひとつなのかな？

女性：その通り。学校のステータスを上げて、よりよい学生を引きつける方法は、最上位の学生向けに特別プログラムを作ることだと彼女は信じているみたいね。

男性：それで、この新プログラムにはどうやって入るんだ？

女性：まだ計画は発表されていないわ。でも、聞いたところによると、高校のクラスの上位10パーセントに入る必要があるみたい。入ってくる新入生はこのプログラムに応募できるけど、転入生には許可されていない。そして受け入れられた場合、彼らは大学で一番の教授陣が教える特別小規模クラスを取ることになるの。それから、卒業時に彼らは"優等"で卒業したと言うことができるの。

男性：へえ。それはかなり素晴らしいね。でもこのプログラムをやるには、学校に多大な経費がかかるんじゃないの？

女性：そうは思わないわ。少なくとも当初はね。というのも新しい教員を雇う計画はないから。

男性：全体的に見て、この提案は素晴らしい感じだな。僕に言える限りでは、これに関して間違っているのはひとつだけだ。

女性：何？

男性：僕らはもう3年生だから、そのプログラムには入れない。

31. 誰が特待プログラムを提案したのか？
- (A) 学長
- (B) 学部長
- (C) 入学してくる1年生
- (D) 最も優秀な教授陣

32. この特待プログラムを大学が設立する主な理由は何か？
- (A) 入学者数を増やすため
- (B) より良い学生を呼び込むため
- (C) より良い授業を促すため
- (D) より多くの奨学金を授与するため

33. 学生はどうすればそのプログラムに入る資格を得られるか？
- (A) テストで高得点を取らなければならない。
- (B) 素晴らしい推薦状を得るべき。
- (C) 高校で良い成績を収める必要がある。
- (D) 賞を取らなければならない。

34. この会話をしている2人は誰か？
- (A) 教授陣
- (B) 大学生
- (C) 高校生の応募者
- (D) 大学の理事

Questions 35-38

大学にいる二人の会話を聞きなさい。

男性：すみません、定期刊行物についていくつか質問があるのですが。

女性：はい、どうしましたか？

男性：ええと、政治学の授業のリポートに取り組んでいるのですが、必要なジャーナルの大半がこの図書館にないんです。

女性：ええ、最近、それがここで大きな問題になっています。以前はもっとたくさんジャーナルがあったのですが、予算削減のためいくつかの購読契約を打ち切ったのです。ですが、もしも記事の完全な参照データがあれば、つまり、著者、題名、その記事が掲載されたジャーナルの号数がわかれば、注文することは可能です。

男性：本当ですか？　つまり、たとえそのジャーナルがここになくとも、その号を注文できるんですか？

女性：そうです。図書館相互間の貸出しカードに記入する必要があるだけです。参照デスクの横のカウンターにその束があります。

男性：あまりに良い話すぎて本当のように思えません。お金はかかるんでしょうか？

女性：一銭もかかりません。それは私たちのサービス予算の一部です。

男性：それは素晴らしい。最後の質問です。それらの記事を手にするまでどのくらいかかりますか？

女性：そこが欠点になります。少なくとも約２週間見ておくべきです。ですので、特定の記事が必要だと思うなら、できるだけ早く要望を出すことです。

35. この会話はどこで行われているか？
    - (A) 政治学部
    - (B) 学生自治会
    - (C) 大学図書館
    - (D) 大学の書店

36. 女性によれば、男性が欲しがっているジャーナルがないのはなぜか？
    - (A) 貸し出されている。
    - (B) もう発行されていない。
    - (C) めったに必要とされない。
    - (D) 予算から削減された。

37. 記事を注文するのに手数料はいくらかかるか？
    - (A) まったくなし
    - (B) ほんの少額
    - (C) １ページにつき10セント
    - (D) ２ドル

38. 女性によれば、記事は注文してからどのくらいで受け取れるか？
    - (A) 約２日
    - (B) 約１週間
    - (C) まったく時間はかからない
    - (D) 約２週間

■ Part C

Questions 39-42

史学教授による次の話を聞きなさい。

　おはようございます。私はフィリップス博士で、これは歴史320、第二次世界大戦後のアフリカ系アメリカ人の歴史（のクラス）です。このクラスのための基礎必修科目は歴史101、現代アメリカ史入門コース下級クラスです。そのクラスを未修の者は、今、退出してください。すみませんが、これは史学部の方針です。どうか例外とするよう、私に頼みに来ないでください。入門コースで得る背景知識なしでは、このクラスで扱う素材を理解するのは非常に難しいでしょう。では、先ほど私が配布したこのコースシラバスを見てください。ご覧の通り、私たちのクラスは週に3回、月曜、水曜、金曜の10時から10時50分までです。私のオフィスの時間は、金曜日のクラスの直後、11時から正午までです。もしその時間が都合が悪い場合、予約を取ることができます。また、よく火曜日午前中にもいますが、ただし、毎週ではありません。今学期中、試験が3回あります。中間試験が2回、期末試験が1回です。最初の中間試験は5週目の終わりに、2回目の中間試験は10週目の終わりにあります。2回の中間試験は客観的な試験で、選択式問題と短文応答問題の組み合わせです。期末試験は完全に論述形式の問題です。まだテストは作っていませんが、しかし、これは学期全体を通じて取り上げた教材全てを対象とします。おそらくは、4〜5つの論述形式の質問に答えてもらうことになるでしょう。このクラスでは期末論文はありません。成績は出席と参加点が5分の1を占め、2回の中間試験は合わせて35パーセント、そして期末試験が残りとなります。従って、期末の試験週間に行われるこの試験にしっかり備えることが必須です。

39. この話はおそらくいつ行われているか？
    (A) 学期の最初に
    (B) 第5週中に
    (C) 試験の週の直前
    (D) 学期末の近く

40. 基礎必修科目を取っていない人はどうすべきか？
    (A) この教授に話す
    (B) 教室から去る
    (C) 別の歴史の授業を取る
    (D) 友人に助けを求める

41. 期末試験にはどんなタイプの問題が出題されるか？
    (A) 主に選択式問題
    (B) 客観的問題と主観的問題の両方
    (C) 論述式問題のみ
    (D) 一連の短文応答式の問題

42. 授業の成績の決定に一番関わるのは何か？
    (A) 研究リポート
    (B) 学生の出席率
    (C) 中間試験
    (D) 期末テスト

Questions 43-45

市の職員による次のアナウンスを聞きなさい。

　おはようございます。市長より、市長が開始した新プログラムについて本日、市職員全員に話をするよう依頼されました。このプログラムは皆さんに直接関係があります。というのも、皆さんの多くは職務において直接高齢者問題を扱っているからです。基本的に当プログラムは、皆さんの1週間の労働時間の一部を、市の6つの高齢者介護施設のボランティアに当てることを許すものです。皆さんはその施設の医療スタッフとその他職員を、さまざまな興味深い業務をすることで助けることになります。さて、皆さんの何人かは、大学時代に類似のボランティアをしたことがあるかもしれません。そして今回していただくことは、学生ボランティアとしてやったことと似ています。しかしながら、このプログラムの主旨は、高齢者の退屈や孤独を緩和する手助けだけではありません。実際、私たちは当市のスタッフがよくそろった高齢者ホームと、そこで提供される高齢者参加の多くの組織的活動をとても誇りにしています。このプログラムの最大の理由は、高齢の市民にとって重要な課題をよりよく知り、高齢者の心のうちを実際に理解する機会を皆さんに与えることです。このプログラムに関するさらなる詳細については、6カ所の高齢者ホームのどれかを訪問してください。そこにいる管理役員が、必要な情報を全て提供できます。皆さんがこのプログラムの利用を決心することを期待しています。自分が何か良い行いをしているという実感から満足を得られるでしょうし、それに加えて、これは皆さん自身の仕事をより良く実行する手助けをしてくれるでしょう。

43. このアナウンスは誰に向けられているか？
    (A) 高齢者
    (B) 市職員
    (C) 医療専門家
    (D) 学生ボランティア

44. このプログラムが作られた主な理由は何か？
    (A) 医療スタッフ不足に対処するため
    (B) 高齢者の孤独感と退屈を緩和するため
    (C) 人々が高齢者の不安をよりよく理解できるよう手助けするため
    (D) 未来の看護士に有益な経験を提供するため

45. もっと情報が欲しい人はどこに行くべきか？
    (A) 地元の高齢者ホームのどれか
    (B) 公営の健康クリニック
    (C) 大学の医療センター
    (D) 市の管理事務所

Questions 46-50

大学の授業で行われている講義を聞きなさい。

　今日は、きっと皆さんが関心あるであろうものの初期進化—食べ物、そして食べ物と文化の関係について話します。人類の進化のうち最も初期、かつ最も長い期間である旧石器時代に、人々は根っこや果実、灌木を食べました。まれに彼らは魚を捕まえ、小動物を狩りました。旧石器時代の狩猟民は人生の大半を食糧、つまり食べられる植物を探すことに費やしました。彼らが生きのびるにはそれ以外の方法などなかったのです。その結果、おそらくは人類の進化において最も重要な進歩が、中石器時代と新石器時代に訪れます。この時、人類は食糧収集から食糧生産への移行を成し遂げたのです。この時期、初期の文明が穀物を耕作し、家畜を飼う術を身に付けました。彼らは種をまくこと、そして動物を大きな群れで飼うことを学んだのです。その結果、人々はもはや放浪しながら生活する必要がなくなり、ある地域に腰を落ち着け、永続的な都市を造ることができました。くわ、草刈りがま、すきの発明により初期の農耕手段が改良されると、人類の歴史が永遠に変わりました。余剰な食糧により商業が誕生したのです。何も接触がなかったであろう人々の集団が、交流を始め、そして食糧を別の種類の物資と交換するようになったのです。そしてこの交互作用が概念の共有、文化の融合、そして新しい文化の創造へと全体的に繋がったのです。

46. この講義の主題は何か？
(A) 最初の人類の食べ物
(B) 初期の農業のタイプ
(C) 文化と食物の関係
(D) 交易路の発展

47. 旧石器時代の人々の主な食物は何だったか？
(A) 魚と小動物
(B) 野生の植物
(C) 家畜
(D) 耕作された作物

48. 中石器時代と新石器時代では、どんな重要な変化が起こったか？
(A) 人々は直立歩行を身に付けた。
(B) 人々の大集団が移住し始めた。
(C) より多くの人々が幼少期を生きのびるようになった。
(D) 人々は食べ物の採取から生産へと移行した。

49. 農機具の発明が文明に及ぼした重要な影響は何か？
(A) 食物の余剰、従って商業を生み出した。
(B) 工業化の過程を開始した。
(C) 動物の大群の保有を可能にした。
(D) 境界線を作り、よって土地所有に至った。

50. 異なるグループ間での人々の接触が増えて、どんな結果が生じたか？
(A) さらに大量の肉の消費
(B) 農業社会の絶滅
(C) 狩猟のより良い手法
(D) 新しい文化の出現

Section 2 Structure and Written Expression 対訳
■ Structure

1. 特定の種類のチーズから得られるかびは、細菌性感染の治療に不可欠な複合物を生み出す。

2. 物理学者のリチャード・ファインマンは、数学の代わりに時空図を使い、亜原子粒子が時間を逆方向に移動できるという概念を思いついた。

3. 株式市場がその価値の10パーセント以上を失った時、下げ相場として知られる一定の期間があった。

4. ガートルード・スタインは"失われた世代"の作家と見なされており、これはアイデンティティーや疎外といったテーマに焦点を当てた。

5. 大潮は、月が満月か新月の2つの段階のどちらかにあるときにのみ発生する。

6. ノーマン・メイラーの『裸者と死者』は、ほぼ発刊直後から批評家の大絶賛を浴びた。

7. ゴキブリはおそらく世界で最も嫌われている、都市に住む虫だろう。

8. カエルの足の筋肉により、カエルは自分の背丈の何倍もジャンプすることができる。

9. 新月の際の典型的な冬の夜には、犬の星であるシリウスが金星に次いで2番目に明るい目標物である。

10. 電力網を連結させることにより、各都市は需要最盛期にお互いに電力を貸すことが可能になる。

11. 南北戦争以前の南部の州の経済は、ある程度繊維と軽量品の生産に依存していたが、しかし主として農業から生じた所得に頼っていた。

12. 眺望の美しさとサンフランシスコに近い距離のため、マリンカウンティにはカリフォルニア全体で最も価値の高い不動産のいくつかがある。

13. 一般に信じられているのとは逆に、皮膚は人体の最大の器官である。

14. 児童心理学者は、1歳から5歳の間に音楽を聞くことが、子どもの空間認識能力を高めると信じている。

15. ある主要な宇宙理論によれば、宇宙は"ビッグバン"と呼ばれる巨大な爆発を起源としている。

■ Written Expression

16. 地球から10〜50キロの空間に大量に存在するオゾンは、酸素の３つの原子から成る分子のガスである。

17. 1950年には、長きにわたる連邦捜査局長官、J・エドガー・フーバーがワシントンで最も力のある人物の一人となっていた。

18. 写象主義は20世紀初頭から中期にかけて影響を及ぼしたアメリカの詩におけるムーブメントである。

19. 塗料は当初野菜と鉱物源から作られたが、現在は多様な物質から製造されている。

20. 釣りをする人の主要な餌の元となるミミズは、穴を掘ったり食べたり感じたりするために□を使う。

21. 考古学者は、芸術はおそらく人類の文化と同じくらい長く存在してきたと立証している。

22. サトウカエデからしみ出るメイプルシロップは、人に知られている天然の甘味料の中で最も甘いもののひとつだ。

23. 現代美術館は伝統的に、展覧会で展示し得る現代アートのうち最善のものを紹介してきた。

24. その評価にもかかわらず、豚はあらゆる家畜の中で最も知的な動物のひとつである。

25. 浸食は、風または水によって生じ得る。

26. 北アメリカに最初の居住者が到着した時、野生のバッファローの数は6000万頭近かった。

27. プロテニス選手生活から引退した後、アーサー・アッシュは多くの慈善団体のための有名なスポークスマンとなった。

28. 研究は、風邪のばい菌の大半は鼻と目の粘膜に手を触れることにより感染していくことを示している。

29. 空気の固まりは、温度が露点以下になると雲を形成する。

30. 経営科学とは、組織化と指揮、さらには社会的・経済的組織の維持の研究を指す。

31. オクラホマの最も重要な天然資源のひとつが、石油だ。

32. 間欠泉は、一定の間隔を置いて蒸気と水を空中に放出する温泉の一種である。

33. おそらくは19世紀の最上の小説である『白鯨』は、発刊から50年以上にもわたりほとんど無視されていた。

34. リョコウバトは19世紀末には希少になっており、そのすぐ後に絶滅した。

35. 火力発電所は、地表近くで地熱により熱せられた水が見つかるような場所にある温泉や間欠泉の熱を利用する。

36. カラスは、ハトやその他多くの鳥と同じように、生涯を通じてつがいになる。

37. 30ヤードの間のジャガー（ヒョウ）の加速は非常に大きいため、うまく忍び寄った獲物ならほぼどんなものでも捕まえることができる。

38. 精米していない玄米の殻は繊維状の物質でできており、そのため部分的にしか消化されない。

39. アラモにおいて、砦の守備隊はより優れた武器を持つメキシコ人兵士の優秀な軍隊に数で負けていることに気づいた。

40. ワシントンD.C.にある航空宇宙博物館は、人類の飛行機の歴史に関する最も原始的で洗練された機体のいくつかを展示している。

Section 3 Reading Comprehension 対訳
■ Questions 1-9

　北アメリカのプレインズ・インディアンは、中南米の先住民ほど天文学的に進んでいなかったかもしれないが、彼らもまた天空を研究し、天体観測を行っていた。彼らが天体の動きに関心を持っていたことを示す遺跡のひとつがメディスン・ホイールで、これはワイオミング州にあるビッグホーン山脈の剥き出しの尾根に位置している。西経107度55分、北緯44度50分、海抜9,640フィートに位置するこの構造物は、車輪のスポークのように並べられた石でできた28本の線から成る。中心にある直径約4メートルの石の山がハブを形成している。（線の）端を直径25メートルの大きな円が取り囲んでいる。さらにリムのすぐ外側には6つの石塚がある。

　これを作ったクロー族の祖先の口頭伝承によれば、ビッグホーン・ホイールは「光がやってくる前に創造された」と言われているが、これは（構造物が）非常に古いことを示唆している。クロー族の言語では、この構造物は"太陽の家"と呼ばれ、また見かけの上では、このホイールは確かに円形の儀式小屋の見取り図に似てはいる。太陽とメディスン・ホイールのこの言葉の上での関連は、しかし、元来の構造の設計に何もかかわりのない、後の時代の訪問者が作り出したものである可能性がかなり高い。この遺構がティピー（テント小屋）あるいは記念建造物として実用的な場所でないことは確かだ。ここは住むには不可能な場所で、ビッグホーン・ナショナル・フォレストの森林臨界よりかなり上にあり、6月中旬ですら暴風雪に見舞われることがあるのだ。

1. **この文章の主題は**
   (A) 原始の部族の天体観測
   (B) クロー族の伝統
   (C) いわゆるメディスン・ホイール
   (D) ビッグホーン・ナショナル・フォレスト

2. **4行目"they"が指しているのは**
   (A) 中南米の先住民
   (B) 天体
   (C) 天体観測
   (D) プレインズ・インディアン

3. **メディスン・ホイールは以下のうちのどんなタイプの地形にあったか？**
   (A) 谷
   (B) 平原
   (C) 森林
   (D) 山

4. **筆者が5行目でメディスン・ホイールはビッグホーン山脈の"an exposed shoulder"に位置していると述べたのはなぜか？**
   (A) この構造物の形状を描写するため
   (B) この遺構に住めないことを強調するため
   (C) この遺構から眺められる光景を示すため
   (D) この構造物を建てるための石が入手できることを強調するため

5. **8行目"pile"に最も意味が近いのは**
   (A) 円
   (B) 柱
   (C) 構造
   (D) 堆積

6. **13行目"antiquity"に最も意味が近いのは**
   (A) 強さ
   (B) 賢さ
   (C) もろさ
   (D) 老齢

7. **14行目"superficially"に最も意味が近いのは**

(A) 一見したところ
(B) あらゆる面で
(C) 強大な力で
(D) 注意深く研究したところ

(D) この遺構を発見したアメリカ人文
化人類学者たち

8. "太陽の家"という名称を最初に使った
のはおそらく誰か？
(A) クロー族の遠い祖先
(B) この構造物の最初の建築者たち
(C) 完成した後に構造物を訪問したク
ロー・インディアンたち

9. この文章によると、ビッグホーン・ホ
イールは主にどういった目的の場所と
して機能を果たしていたか？
(A) 周辺地域を観察する
(B) 伝統儀式を執り行う
(C) 安全な生活圏を確立する
(D) 天体観測を実施する

■ Questions 10-19

　クロコダイルは熱帯の爬虫類で、クロコダイル科に属している。既存のワニ目は約20種あり、これにはアリゲーター、ケイマン、ガビアル、そして真性のクロコダイルが含まれる。これらは通常アジア、オーストラリア、アフリカ、マダガスカル、南北アメリカの沼地、湖、川で見られる。最もよく知られている種はナイル・クロコダイルで、主にアフリカ大陸に生息する。南インドとマレーシアの沿岸の沼地にいる塩水クロコダイルのように、人食いである場合がある。

　アリゲーター科に属するアリゲーターは、2カ所の淡水で見られる。アメリカ・アリゲーターはノース・カロライナからフロリダにかけて、そして西方のリオグランデ南部のアメリカ南東部に生息する。中国アリゲーターは中国の長江の谷間に見られる。

　アリゲーターを含む全てのワニ目の特徴は、トカゲのような形状と隙間なく重なった骨板からできた分厚い皮膚だ。これらはかなり大きなサイズまで成長することがある。成長したクロコダイルの全長は2〜9メートルで、アリゲーターは6メートルに達することが知られている。ただし、その平均は1.8〜2.4メートルだ。クロコダイルは現代の爬虫類の中では最大で、遠いいとこがコモドオオトカゲだ。クロコダイルは、先史時代の恐竜のような爬虫類との、最後の生ける繋がりと言える。

　クロコダイルとアリゲーターが最も慣れているのは断然水中だが、腹ばいで滑りながら、足を伸ばして歩いたり、ぎこちなく速く進んだりして、地上を移動することもできる。巨大な大人ならば、息継ぎなしで1時間以上水中にとどまることができる。特に食べ物を捕獲する時、彼らは蛇のように体を動かし、筋肉質で舟のオールのような尾を力強く振り、泳ぐ。また、その尾は効果的な武器でもある。

10. この文章の主な目的は？
(A) クロコダイルとアリゲーターの
特定の種を細かく描写すること
(B) クロコダイルの進化をたどるこ
と
(C) ワニ目の特徴の全体像を提示す
ること
(D) 世界のどこにクロコダイルが生
息するかを示すこと

11. 2行目"them"が指しているのは
    - (A) 熱帯の爬虫類
    - (B) 既存のワニ目20種
    - (C) クロコダイル
    - (D) アリゲーター

12. ワニ目の種類として触れられていないのは？
    - (A) コモドオオトカゲ
    - (B) ケイマン
    - (C) ガビアル
    - (D) アリゲーター

13. 3行目"swamps"に最も意味が近いのは
    - (A) 沼
    - (B) ジャングル
    - (C) 湾
    - (D) 小川

14. この文章によれば、ナイルのクロコダイルに当てはまるのは？
    - (A) アフリカにしか生息していない。
    - (B) 時折、人間を食べる。
    - (C) 最大のクロコダイルである。
    - (D) 主に塩水に生息する。

15. 8行目"locales"に最も意味が近いのは
    - (A) 湖
    - (B) 資源
    - (C) 川
    - (D) 地域

16. 筆者がほのめかすクロコダイルとアリゲーターのひとつの違いは何か？
    - (A) アリゲーターのほうがクロコダイルより大きい
    - (B) クロコダイルだけが地上と水中の両方に住む
    - (C) アリゲーターは淡水に住む傾向がある
    - (D) クロコダイルの皮膚は骨板から成る

17. この文章によれば、アリゲーターの平均サイズは
    - (A) 1.8メートル未満
    - (B) 約2メートル
    - (C) 6メートル前後
    - (D) 最長で9メートル

18. 19行目"awkwardly"に最も意味が近いのは
    - (A) 鋭く
    - (B) 素早く
    - (C) 不器用に
    - (D) 攻撃的に

19. この文章によれば、クロコダイルとアリゲーターに共通するひとつの特徴は何か？
    - (A) どちらも解剖学的に、恐竜によく似ている。
    - (B) どちらも蛇と同じように子どもを産む。
    - (C) どちらも走ることができない。
    - (D) どちらも水がある環境を強く好む。

■ Questions 20-30

1964年にニューヨークで先進的なコメディアン、レニー・ブルースがわいせつ行為で逮捕された時、彼は世論により"スウィフト、ラブレー、トウェーンの伝統に則した"社会風刺家として、そしてブラックユーモアのサヴォナローラとして擁護された。ブルース自身、「私のユーモアは破壊と絶望に基づいている」と言及。彼の無作法な言動は、彼の死後に登場したほぼ全てのコメディアンが用いた冷笑的なお決まり芸を助長した。

大変な議論を巻き起こしたこのエンターテイナーは、ショービジネスの世界に革命を起こした。というのも、彼の自由気ままな即興は聴衆を面白がらせるのではなく、むしろショックを与えようとするものであったからだ。彼のスタッカートを効かせた話し方は、内容と概念の両方において、わいせつで悪趣味な味付けがされていた。政治に関して彼が無関心でなかったのは明らかだったが、それは彼の最大の関心事ではなかった。代わりに彼が好んだ対象は、ユダヤ人、黒人、宗教、ドラッグ、そしてセックスだった。しかし、晩年、不敬なパフォーマンスや非合法の薬物所持で繰り返し逮捕された後には、彼のとりとめもない独白はたいてい自分の裁判に関する痛烈な非難へと変わっていき、やがて聴衆も興味を失ったのだった。

レニー・ブルースは1925年10月13日にレナード・アルフレッド・シュナイダーとして生まれる。ユダヤ人で靴屋の店員のマイロン・シュナイダーとセイディ・キッチンバーグのひとり息子だった。両親は彼が5歳の頃に離婚し、彼は親戚と暮らすようになる。同時に母はサリー・マンあるいはブーツ・マロイといった舞台名でダンサーの仕事を探し、自分のユダヤ人としての出自を隠そうとした。

ブルースの独白劇の機知や賢さは正規の学校教育によって育まれたものではなかった。1942年に高校を中退するとレニーは海軍に入隊する。1946年の除隊後、彼は復員兵援護法の支援を受けハリウッドにある演劇学校に通う。彼は凡庸なものまねタレントとしてキャリアを始めた。ナイトクラブの巡業で働くうちに——彼はこれを束縛のないエンターテインメントの"最後の砦"と見なしていた——彼は1951年にストリッパーのハリエット・ロイドと結婚する。ブルースはハリウッドの自宅にて1966年8月3日に死去。誤ってヘロインを過剰摂取したのが原因と推測されている。皮肉なことに、もしも彼が死んでいなかったなら、彼は次第に無名の存在となり消え去っていた可能性が高い。若くして死んだことが、結局低下しつつあった彼の評判を死後に甦らせ、彼の偉大な貢献を未来の世代の人々が認識できることとなったのだ。

20. この文章は主に何について論じているか？
- (A) 重要なアメリカ人エンターテイナーの経歴
- (B) アメリカの漫談の歴史
- (C) レニー・ブルースの影響の最終的な低下
- (D) 1960年代のショービジネスにおける革命

21. 筆者は、レニー・ブルースについて以下のどれが真実だと示唆しているか？
- (A) 彼はわいせつを理由に全面的に非難された。
- (B) 彼はネタの大半をマーク・トウェーンから拝借した。
- (C) 周到な準備が彼の成功の鍵だった。
- (D) 現在のコメディアンは彼に多大な恩恵を受けている。

22. 4行目"despair"に最も意味が近いの
は
(A) 皮肉
(B) 落胆
(C) 暴力
(D) 横柄

23. 7行目"intended"に最も意味が近い
のは
(A) 用いられた
(B) 作られた
(C) 予期された
(D) 計画された

24. この文章によれば、レニー・ブルース
はどのようにショービジネスを変革し
たのか？
(A) 彼はそれまでタブーとされていた
話題を扱った。
(B) 彼は漫談をやった最初の人物だっ
た。
(C) 彼は基本的に聴衆を楽しませるこ
とに関心がなかった。
(D) 彼は自分の薬物の長期使用を隠そ
うとしなかった。

25. 筆者はおそらくレニー・ブルースの話
し方を何に例えるだろうか？
(A) オペラのスターが歌う詩的なメロ
ディー
(B) マシンガンの短い破裂音
(C) 津波の圧倒的な力
(D) とても塩辛い魚の味

26. 筆者によると、レニー・ブルースの
キャリアの終わり頃はどうだったか？
(A) 聴衆の興味あることから離れた
(B) 史上、最も有名なコメディアンに
なった
(C) それまでよりも、皮肉が大幅に
減った
(D) 漫談を完全にやめた

27. 13行目 "deteriorated" に最も意味
が近いのは
(A) 進歩した
(B) 移行した
(C) 崩壊した
(D) 脱線した

28. レニー・ブルースのユダヤ人に関する
漫談はどのような面で皮肉に思われた
のか？
(A) 彼はユダヤ人の女性と結婚した。
(B) 彼自身がユダヤ人として育てられ
た。
(C) 多くの著名なエンターテイナーが
ユダヤ人である。
(D) あるユダヤ人が彼が初仕事を得る
手助けをした。

29. 筆者が示唆するところによれば、レ
ニー・ブルースの芸に表れた知性は、
なぜ驚きなのか？
(A) 中等教育を終えていなかった
(B) 自分の両親を知らなかった
(C) 貧困にあえぐ中で育った
(D) 凡庸な演劇技量しか持っていな
かった

30. レニー・ブルースをとりまいた物議の
原因として述べられていないのは？
(A) お決まり芸の際に彼が使ったわい
せつな言葉
(B) 彼が示した偶像破壊的な態度
(C) 彼が擁護した革新的な政治変化
(D) 教会を非難した彼のやり方

■ Questions 31-40

　かつて人々の手書き文字はその人の性格や人格を真に反映していると見なされていたが、筆記体の文字はアメリカ全土で次第に姿を消しつつある。この減退の主な理由はテクノロジーの来襲にある。まずタイプライター、続いてコンピューターによる襲撃だ。その結果、何かのメッセージやエッセー、あるいは申込書を手書きで書かなければならない時、今やますます多くのアメリカ人が活字体を、つまり、小学校の初め頃に教わった書体を使っていて、その後に学んだもっと流れるようなお互いが連結した文字は使っていない。ある筆跡学者たち——つまり手書き文字の専門家らは——手書きから活字体の文字への移行は、共同社会から利己主義への移行を示していると考えている。筆記体のお互いが連結した文字とは異なり、ばらばらの活字体の文字は垂直の筆致から成る。ある筆跡学者はこれを「自分ひとりで立ち、ひとりだけの自己を反映している」と表現している。活字体への回帰はまた、おそらくはアメリカの学校の教室における時間不足を示している。学校では相変わらず筆記体の手書き文字を教えているかもしれないが、しかし、練習帳を使って何度も繰り返すような昔のようなやり方でそれを練習する時間はほとんど取れない。現在のカリキュラムは過密すぎて、教師への要求があまりに差し迫ったものになっている。

　実に多くの大人が小学生のように活字体で書くため、国の手書き速度は這うようなレベルまで低下しつつある。皮肉にも、手書き速度の低下は読みやすさの度数向上には繋がっていない。この全国規模の手書き文字の傾向に関し、アメリカ郵便局が的確な例証をひとつ提供している。郵便局の自動住所読み取りシステムは大きく向上しているにもかかわらず、郵便局員は相変わらず全ての手書きによる住所の60％をひとつひとつ直接処理しなければならない。なぜなら、それらは機械では判読できないからだ。いくつかの大きめの郵便局は判読不可能な住所の郵便物を解読の専門家に送っている。それでもなお、毎年1000万通の郵便物の住所が読めないために未配達に終っている。

　しかしながら、手書き文字を見限るのはたぶん早すぎるだろう。現在、大学入試の標準テストではエッセーが求められており、読みやすい筆記体の文字が再評価されるかもしれないのだ。というのも、エッセー試験の全部を活字体で書いて時間を無駄にし、大学からはじかれる危険は誰も冒したくないからだ。また、自分の手で流麗に書ける人が少なくなりつつあるため、筆記体の文字が教養とエリートとしての目印として再浮上する可能もあるかもしれない。

31. この文章の主題は何か？
- (A) 手書きに対する印刷の優位性
- (B) 手書き文字教育の学校の失敗
- (C) アメリカ郵便局が抱える住所判読の困難
- (D) 筆記体の衰退

32. この文章によれば、筆記体が減少した主要な理由は次のどれか？
- (A) 活字体のより素晴らしい明快さ
- (B) 筆記体の文字を書く速度の遅さ
- (C) 技術革新
- (D) 過密なカリキュラム

33. 筆者によれば、アメリカ人が活字体を学ぶのは？
- (A) コンピューター・プログラムを通じて
- (B) 小学校の最初に
- (C) 習字手本帳から
- (D) 初めてタイプライターを使う時

34. 第1段落で筆者は専門家が考える筆記体から活字体への変化について何と述べているか？
- (A) アメリカ人がより自己中心的になった。
- (B) 学校に筆記体の文字を教える十分な時間がない。
- (C) 教師はもはや書き方を教える訓練を受けていない。
- (D) 活字体は書くことよりも魅力的だ。

35. 10行目"vertical"に最も意味が近いのは
- (A) 魅力的な
- (B) 判読できる
- (C) 好ましい
- (D) 垂直の

36. 22行目"they"が指しているのは
- (A) 大幅な向上
- (B) 郵便局員
- (C) 手書きの住所
- (D) 自動住所読み取りシステム

37. 筆者はアメリカ郵便局を何の例とするために取り上げたのか？
- (A) 住所読み取り機の能力不足
- (B) 手書き速度の低下
- (C) 粗雑な活字体を解読するための専門家の必要性
- (D) アメリカ人の手書き文字の読み難さ

38. 26行目"make a comeback"を置き換えるのに、最もふさわしいのは
- (A) 人気の復活
- (B) 変革を経る
- (C) 目的にかなう
- (D) 見捨てられる

39. 第3段落は主に何について書かれているか？
- (A) 現在大学入学試験の一部となっているライティングテスト
- (B) 手書きが再び広まるかもしれない
- (C) 上流階級で使われる洗練された手書き文字
- (D) 次の十年における手書き文字の目的

40. 次の一般論のうち、この文章によって一番強く支持されるものは？
- (A) コンピューターがますます手書き文字に取って代わる。
- (B) 学校は子どもたちに活字体で書くことを教えるためにもっと時間を費やすべきだ。
- (C) ある人物の性格はその人の筆記体の文字に明確に反映される。
- (D) 手書き文字の使用は、幅広い要素に影響されている。

■ Questions 41-50

　1928年の時点で物理学の理論では各種の素粒子にはそれぞれ"逆"に相当するものが、つまり同じ質量ながら正反対の特徴を持つ相反する双子の片割れがあると仮定していた。"反物質"と呼ばれるようになったこの物質は、科学者だけではなくSF作家の想像力をも刺激した。小説や映画の中では間もなく反物質エンジンが宇宙船を推進し、反物質兵器が彼らの目標物を壊滅させることになった。その結果、物質と反物質の概念は皮肉にも、素粒子物理学において一般大衆に広く理解された数少ない概念のひとつとなった。

　一方で、本当の科学において反物質理論の中心的問いのひとつは、自然界が普通の物質と反物質を同じように扱っているのか否かである。50年にわたりその問いへの有望な答えは「イエス」であり、そしてこれが現在の標準的な宇宙論の見方を形成している。現在の考えによると、約120億年前、宇宙を作ったビッグバンのわずか数秒後にはほぼ同量の物質と反物質があった。それらはすぐさまお互いを破壊した。しかし何らかの理由から、この破壊は通常の物質をわずかに残した（約１億分の１）。そして現在私たちが知る宇宙を作っているのが、これらの通常の物質の残り物である。宇宙創世の直後の初期段階以降、ほぼすべての存在する反物質が、研究室で人工的に作られてきた。

　残念なことに、研究室で作られる反物質の寿命は非常に短期であり、これは反物質の素粒子は生成されるといつもすぐに物質と衝突し、破壊されるからだ。もちろん、この反物質素粒子の生成と消滅は、最も費用のかかる実験室でしか観察できない現象である——すなわち、（複数の）素粒子の速度を超高速まで上げ、それらを一挙に粉砕する素粒子加速器が必要なのだ。そのような衝突で作られる反物質は、通常100億〜400億分の１秒しか存在しない。物理学における最も遠大な計画のひとつが、反物質を作り、それをより長い間捕えておくこと、そして反物質の素粒子をひとつにまとめ、反物質による原子の固まりを作ることだ。現在の新理論と新技術は、もしかしたら何カ月も、あるいは何年もの間研究できる反物質の入った「つぼ」を作ることも可能であることを示唆している。

41. この文章の主題は何か？
- (A) 反物質の起源
- (B) 物理学の分野における反物質
- (C) 新たに可能な反物質の利用目的
- (D) SFが反物質をどう描いているか

42. １行目"posited"に最も意味が近いのは
- (A) 提案した
- (B) 推測した
- (C) 調査した
- (D) 議論した

43. 筆者が６行目で"ironically"という語を使っているのは、次の何をほのめかすためか？
- (A) 科学者でない人たちは物理学の知識がほとんどない
- (B) 反物質の概念はそう複雑ではない
- (C) SFで描かれているアイディアはしばしば広く受け入れられる
- (D) 一般大衆は実際の科学に基づくSFを好む

44. 第1段落によれば素粒子に対する反物質の片割れの特質はどういうものか？
- (A) 同一の特徴ながら、質量が異なる
- (B) 速度がもっと速いが、質量が少なめ
- (C) 同じ質量だが、特徴が逆
- (D) 寿命が長いが、安定性に劣る

45. 10行目"it"が指しているのは
    (A) １世紀の半分（50年）
    (B) 自然
    (C) 中心的命題のひとつ
    (D) 有望な答え

46. 25行目"far-reaching"に最も意味が
    近いのは
    (A) 野心的な
    (B) 永続する
    (C) 革新的な
    (D) まれな

47. 第２段落から導き出せるのは？
    (A) 大量の反物質が研究室内で作ら
        れている
    (B) 現在よりもビッグバン直後のほ
        うがより多くの反物質が存在し
        ていた
    (C) 反物質はやがて現在の宇宙の大
        半を破壊するかもしれない
    (D) 宇宙理論の標準的な見解は間違っ
        ているかもしれない。

48. 20行目"promptly"に最も意味が近い
    のは
    (A) 必然的に
    (B) 素早く
    (C) 暴力的に
    (D) 驚異的に

49. 第3段落によれば、通常、反物質の素
    粒子は、どこで最もよく観察される
    か？
    (A) 特製の"つぼ"の中
    (B) 宇宙の遠方
    (C) 素粒子加速器の中
    (D) 化学実験室の中

50. この文章から導き出せるのはどの文
    か？
    (A) いつの日か、反物質が宇宙船の動
        力に使われるだろう。
    (B) 反物質の存在はあらゆる物理学者
        から認められているわけではない。
    (C) 反物質はまもなく、より注意深く、
        より綿密に研究されるだろう。
    (D) 反物質に関する調査には主に政府
        が資金を提供している。

Section 1 Listening Comprehension 対訳
■ Part A

1. **男性**：リチャードソン教授、私たちの実験レポートはいつ提出しなければなりませんか？
   女性：そうね、すでにやるべきことを多く与えているから……。最も遅くて——今月末でどうかしら。
   質問：女性の発言はどういう意味か？
   (A) 授業はこの月の最後の日に終わる。
   (B) 締め切り後のレポートは受け付けられない。
   (C) 彼女はたくさんの宿題を課そうと計画している。
   (D) 実験の課題は月末が締切だ。

2. **女性**：すみません。この席はふさがっていますか？
   男性：ごめんなさい。妻のために席を取っているんです。
   質問：男性の発言はどういう意味か？
   (A) 彼は自分の妻が来られないことを申し訳なく思っている。
   (B) その席はすでにふさがっている。
   (C) その女性は座るのを歓迎されている。
   (D) その座席は高額ではない。

3. **女性**：ヘイズ教授のテストは、たとえがんばって勉強しても無理だったわ。
   男性：いや、大学院の学部長なんだから、当然だろう。
   質問：男性は何をほのめかしているか？
   (A) その女性はもっと懸命に勉強すべきだ。
   (B) そのコースを再び取ることは可能だ。
   (C) 大学院に行くことが必要だ。
   (D) その教授の試験はたいてい難しい。

4. **男性**：君の論文を編集した際、タイプミスがたくさんあったよ、ナンシー。
   女性：ああ、わかっています。私はずさんな校正者なんです。
   質問：女性の発言はどういう意味か？
   (A) 彼女は論文はかなり良かったと感じている。
   (B) 彼女はタイプの仕方を知らない。
   (C) 彼女誤りを見つけるのが得意ではない。
   (D) 彼女はその男性の褒め言葉をありがたく思っている。

5. **女性**：今週、私たちは何を読むべきなのか、どうしても知る必要があるの。
   男性：そのクラスの誰かをつかまえたら？
   質問：男性は何を提案しているか？
   (A) 課題を先延ばしする
   (B) 別の学生にコンタクトを取る
   (C) 後でその授業に登録する
   (D) 間違いなくその読み物に目を通しておく

6. **女性**：本当に長らくあなたに会っていなかったけれど、ばったり会えて最高だわ、パトリック。
   男性：同感だよ、アン。
   質問：男性の発言はどういう意味か？
   (A) 彼はその女性に会えてうれしい。
   (B) その女性は自分が歩く場所に気を付けるべきだ。
   (C) その女性は全く変わっていない。
   (D) 彼はその女性にあまり長く話せない。

7. **男性**：私たちはすぐにあなたの予約を確認できるはずです、ジョーンズさん。
   女性：コンピューターがまたダウンし

ない限りは、ですね。
質問：この会話から何が推測できる
　　　か？
　(A) その女性は予約を間違えた。
　(B) コンピューターも時にはうまく
　　　動かない。
　(C) ジョーンズさんは予約に関して
　　　気持ちが変わった。
　(D) ジョーンズさんはありえそうな
　　　目的地についてアドバイスがほ
　　　しい。

8. **女性**：ジョン、この夏、出かけている
　　　　間、アパートはどうするの？
　男性：弟が家の番をするんだ。
　質問：アパートに何が起こるか？
　(A) ジョンのガールフレンドが引っ
　　　越してくる。
　(B) ジョンはそこに住む誰かを探す
　　　つもりだ。
　(C) ジョンはほんの短期間だけ留守
　　　にする予定だ。
　(D) ジョンの弟が家の番をする。

9. **女性**：ちょっと聞いて！　私、専攻を
　　　　変えることにしたの。
　男性：またか！
　質問：男性は何をほのめかしている
　　　　か？
　(A) その女性は以前それをやったこ
　　　とがある。
　(B) 彼はその女性が言ったことを信
　　　じていない。
　(C) 彼は何も得ていない。
　(D) その女性は間違いを犯した。

10. **男性**：今日本屋が閉まっているなんて
　　　　信じられないよ。
　女性：ええ、学期末の最後の2日間は、
　　　　いつも在庫チェックをするのよ。
　質問：この会話から何が推測できる
　　　　か？

　(A) この時期、その本屋はたいてい
　　　閉まっている。
　(B) その女性はなぜその本屋が開い
　　　ていないのか理解していない。
　(C) その本屋の本の品揃えはあまり
　　　にも限られている。
　(D) その女性は学期末の前にその本
　　　屋で買い物をしなければならな
　　　い。

11. **男性**：学費がすごく高いと両親がこぼ
　　　　しているんだ。
　女性：私も家族から同じ小言をもらっ
　　　　ているわ。
　質問：女性の発言はどういう意味か？
　(A) 彼女の両親は学費が高いと思っ
　　　ている。
　(B) 彼女は状況を理解していない。
　(C) 彼女の両親が彼女に新しい贈り
　　　物をした。
　(D) 学費は間もなく上がる。

12. **女性**：新しいアパートを探そうと思うの。
　男性：どうして？　今の場所を気に
　　　　入っていると思ってたけど。
　質問：男性は何を知りたいのか？
　(A) その女性がいつ到着するか
　(B) 彼が手助けできるのかどうか
　(C) その女性がアパートを好きかど
　　　うか
　(D) その女性がなぜ引っ越したいの
　　　か

13. **女性**：今までにこの道でスピードを出
　　　　し過ぎて止められたことない
　　　　の？
　男性：少なくとも3〜4回あるよ！
　質問：男性の発言はどういう意味か？
　(A) 彼はとても注意深い運転手だ。
　(B) その道はけっこう危険だ。
　(C) 彼は何枚かスピード違反の切符
　　　を受け取っている。

(D) その道は家に一番早く着ける道だ。

14. 男性：アン、図書館に君が探していた経済誌はあった？
女性：いいえ、残念ながら予算が削られた際に取るのを止めてしまったのよ。
質問：女性は雑誌について何をほのめかしているか？
(A) 図書館はもはやそれを受け取らない。
(B) 経済学のコースにはもはやそれは必要とされていない。
(C) それは定期購読でしか入手できない。
(D) それは読む価値がない。

15. 男性：パティ、一体いつになったら僕はこのソフトの使い方がわかるのやら。
女性：そうね、デイブ、手始めにユーザーズガイドを読んでみたら？
質問：女性はデイブは何をすべきだと提案しているか？
(A) 彼の友人のコンピューターを使う
(B) マニュアルを見る
(C) コンピューターのクラスを取る
(D) 違うソフトウエアを使う

16. 女性：私のためにあなたがこれをコピーしたの？
男性：ブレンダにしてもらったんだ。
質問：男性の発言はどういう意味か？
(A) 彼は彼女が頼んだことをやるのを忘れた。
(B) 彼はそのブレンドのコーヒーが好きだ。
(C) 彼は友人に会う予定だ。
(D) 彼にはそれを自分のためにやってくれる人がいた。

17. 男性：これはこのカフェテリアで今まで食べた中で最高のものだ。
女性：ああ、ええ。そのとおりね！
質問：女性の発言はどういう意味か？
(A) 彼女はその男性に言ったことを繰り返してもらいたい。
(B) 彼女は通常カフェテリアでは食事しない。
(C) 彼女はその男性の意見に同意している。
(D) 彼女はむしろ後でまた戻ってきたい。

18. 男性：トムがあれほど幸せそうなのは今まで見たことがないと思う。
女性：彼はスピーチコンテストで優勝して以来、ずっとあの調子よ。
質問：トムについて何が推測できるか？
(A) その女性は彼を元気づけたい。
(B) その女性も彼に会っていない。
(C) 彼はたいていあまりに話し過ぎる。
(D) 彼は勝利にとても喜んでいる。

19. 男性：まいったな。一日中机に向かっていたから背中がとても痛い。
女性：うーん、そんなにたくさんコースを取るから、そうなるのよ。
質問：女性の発言はどういう意味か？
(A) その男性は授業を多く取り過ぎている。
(B) その男性はそんなにたくさんのものを持ち上げるべきではない。
(C) その男性はできるだけ早く帰宅すべきだ。
(D) その男性はいく分運動が必要だ。

20. 女性：この調査リポートはもうたくさんよ！
男性：今やめちゃダメだ。半分以上終えているんだから！

質問：男性は、女性はどうすべきだと
　　　提案しているか？
(A) そのリポートに取り組み続ける
(B) 最後の部分を終えるために誰か
　　 別の人に頼む
(C) 終えていない部分を無視する
(D) しばらく休憩する

21. 男性：ホームズ教授、私の期末論文に
　　　　関するトピックについて話すた
　　　　めに、明日の午後会えるでしょ
　　　　うか。
　　女性：明日は都合がよくないわね。金
　　　　曜日はどうかしら？
　　質問：教授の発言はどういう意味か？
(A) 彼女はその男性の話題は適切だ
　　 と思わない。
(B) その男性は金曜日までに論文を
　　 提出しなければならない。
(C) 彼女は明日その男性に会えない。
(D) その男性は午後に彼女のオフィ
　　 スに来るべきだ。

22. 女性：昨晩、ビルが財布をタクシーに
　　　　置き忘れたって信じられる？
　　男性：また？　私が知る中で彼はたぶ
　　　　ん最もいい加減な人間だ！
　　質問：男性はビルについて何をほのめ
　　　　かしているか？
(A) 彼はよく物を紛失する。
(B) 彼はタクシーに乗るべきだった。
(C) 彼はとても信頼できる人物だ。
(D) 彼はタクシーへの支払いを忘れ
　　 た。

23. 男性：妻のためにドレスを探している
　　　　のですが、これらはどれも大き
　　　　過ぎます。小さいサイズの服は
　　　　ないのですか？
　　女性：ショッピングモールの反対側の
　　　　エリクソンを見てみてはどうで
　　　　すか？　あそこは小さいサイズ

だけを取り扱っています。
質問：男性はおそらくどこに行くか？
(A) 百貨店へ
(B) 専門店へ
(C) 別のショッピングモールへ
(D)（洋服の）仕立て業者へ

24. 男性：スズパンスキー教授の名前をど
　　　　うつづるかさっぱりわからない。
　　女性：誰がわかるの？
　　質問：女性の発言はどういう意味か？
(A) 誰か他の人がスペルを知ってい
　　 るに違いない。
(B) その教授の名前をつづるのは難
　　 しい。
(C) 彼女は教授の名前がよくわかっ
　　 ていない。
(D) 彼女の名前もまたつづるのが難
　　 しい。

25. 女性：ジョージは一生懸命に学位論文
　　　　に取り組んでいる？
　　男性：そうだね。彼はそれ以外のこと
　　　　はほとんどしていないよ。
　　質問：男性はジョージについて何をほ
　　　　のめかしているか？
(A) 彼は多くのいろんなことをする
　　 のに忙しい。
(B) 彼は何か他のやることを探して
　　 いる。
(C) 彼は一生懸命に取り組んでいる。
(D) 彼とその男性は間もなく会うだ
　　 ろう。

26. 男性：化学の試験でマリリンが最高点
　　　　を取ったって聞いた？
　　女性：いいえ！　まさか彼女が！
　　質問：女性の発言はどういう意味か？
(A) 彼女はその男性は間違われたと
　　 思っている。
(B) 彼女はマリリンがその試験を受
　　 けたことを知らなかった。

(C) 彼女はマリリンの成績に驚いて
いる。
(D) 彼女はマリリンは素晴らしい生
徒だと思っている。

27. **女性**：フィルムフェスティバルどう
だった？　ルームメートと一緒
に今晩行こうと思っているんだ
けど。
男性：素晴らしいよ。でも僕がやった
みたいに早く着かないと。そう
しないと4時間ずっと立ち見に
なるよ。
質問：男性はフィルムフェスティバル
に関して何をほのめかしている
か？
(A) 彼はそれを見るために立ち上が
らなければならなかった。
(B) それはずば抜けて人気がある。
(C) もう入手できるチケットはない。
(D) 彼はそれは長過ぎたと思ってい
る。

28. **女性**：ピクニックに行く途中にポテト
サラダと飲み物を手に入れる予
定なの。
男性：それじゃあ行くんだ、結局。
質問：男性は何を推測していたか？
(A) その女性は彼を迎えに行くつも
りだった。
(B) ピクニックは取りやめになった。
(C) その女性は行くつもりはなかっ
た。
(D) 彼は何か食べ物を用意すること
になっていた。

29. **男性**：奨学金に関して、学長と連絡を
取っていなかったっけ？
女性：ほんの2カ月前にね。
質問：女性は何をほのめかしている
か？
(A) 彼女は自分の授業料を払わなけ
ればならない。
(B) 彼女はかなり前に学部長に連絡
した。
(C) 彼女は学校を退学しなければな
らない。
(D) 彼女はまだ学部長に話をしてい
ない。

30. **女性**：まだ鍵が見つかっていないの
ね？
男性：見つかっていたらこんな外に
立っていると思う？
質問：男性の発言から何が推測できる
か？
(A) 彼はバスを待っている。
(B) 住居管理室はまだ彼の鍵を戻し
ていない。
(C) 彼はドアを開けっ放しにした。
(D) 彼の鍵はまだ見つかっていない。

■ Part B

Questions 31-34

手工芸品に関する会話を聞きなさい。

女性：これは本当に素晴らしいアイデアだったわね。芸術と工芸品の展覧会に来たのは。

男性：ああ、金曜日の新聞で読んだんだ。その記事によればけっこう面白そうだった。

女性：手作りの贈り物はずっと好きだったの。でも自分で作るのはあまり得意じゃなかったわ。

男性：僕もそうさ。でももっと若かった頃はよく木工をしたものだよ。本棚やテーブルなんかを作ったんだ。

女性：本当に？　今まで作った中で何が一番難しかった？

男性：黒クルミで作ったコーヒーテーブル。それを結婚25周年記念として両親にあげたんだ。

女性：素敵なプレゼントね！　ねえ、こっちを見て。手作りの宝飾品よ。銀のイヤリングが豪勢ね。

男性：銀にこんな細かい作業をどうやったらできるんだろうね。売り物じゃないのが残念だ。明日は僕の姉（妹）の誕生日なんだ。

女性：ここに何か陶器のものはあるかしら？　陶器の椀とカップが大好きなの。

男性：ああ、それらについては読んだ記憶があるな。どこにあるか、美術館スタッフに聞いてみようか。

女性：いい考えね。ここはとても広いし。

男性：もう少し見た後、何かちょっと食べに行かない？

女性：そうしましょう、おなかペコペコなの。

31. 男性と女性はその展覧会をどうやって知ったか？
   (A) それはテレビのニュース番組に登場した。
   (B) 彼らはそれをラジオで聞いた。
   (C) それは新聞で触れられていた。
   (D) 彼らは広告を見た。

32. 男性は以前、どんな工芸品を作ったか？
   (A) 銀製の宝飾品
   (B) 陶製のカップと鉢
   (C) 手透きの紙
   (D) 木製の家具

33. 話者が示唆している手工芸品の最もいいところは何か？
   (A) それらは作るのが楽しい。
   (B) それらは素晴らしい贈り物になりえる。
   (C) それらは広く販売されることができる。
   (D) それらは並外れて高価だ。

34. 展覧会を出たら、2人は何をするか？
   (A) 家に戻る
   (B) 公園へ行く
   (C) 買い物をする
   (D) レストランで食事する

学校にいる二人の学生の次の会話を聞きなさい。

女性：ハーイ、ジョン。どうしたの、かなり疲れているみたいね。

男性：ああ、ハーイ、パティ。うん、応用心理学のクラスのエッセーを仕上げるのに徹夜したんだ。

女性：楽しそうには聞こえないわね。何について書いたの？

男性：信じられないかもしれないけれど、最適な学習方法についてさ。いかに新しい題材を吸収し、いかにノートを取り、いかに専門用語を覚えるか。そういったことさ。

女性：ううん、それは有益だと思うわ。でもあまりワクワクする感じじゃないわね。

男性：実際には、とても興味深いよ。たくさんの研究があって、例えば、最も効率よく新語を習得するには何回復習すべきか、とかね。

女性：つまり、例えば、生物学のコースとか？

男性：もちろん。あるいは解剖学であれ化学であれ専門用語をたくさん使うクラスなら何でも。

女性：まあ、医学部進学課程の学生にはよさそうね。

男性：ああ、でも、他のクラスにも言えるよ。

女性：ジョン、ところであなたの専攻は何？　今まで私に言ったことなかったわよね？

男性：ああ、僕は社会学専攻だよ。でも一般教養科目のために応用心理学を取る必要があるんだ。

女性：それで心理学のクラスを取っているのね。

男性：そう、終えるまであと３回あるんだ。

女性：学生ユニオンに行くところなんだけれど、コーヒーでもどう？

男性：ありがとう、パティ。でも、今一番いらないのがコーヒーなんだ。寮に戻って、ちょっと寝るから。

35. ジョンはなぜ疲れているのか？
    - (A) 彼は昨夜パーティーに行った。
    - (B) 彼は夜遅くの授業があった。
    - (C) 彼は徹夜でリポートを書いていた。
    - (D) 彼は仕事をするため早く起きた。

36. ジョンは何について書いたか？
    - (A) 効率的な学習方法
    - (B) 高校の教育
    - (C) 研究技術
    - (D) 彼の専門分野

37. ジョンの述べた記憶法はどんな分野に最も適していると思われるか？
    - (A) 科学
    - (B) 人文学
    - (C) 社会学
    - (D) 教育

38. パティとの話が終わり、ジョンはどこへ行ったか？
    - (A) コーヒーショップへ
    - (B) ベッドへ
    - (C) 授業へ
    - (D) 食事へ

■ Part C

"ミッシング・リンク" に関する次の講義を聞きなさい。

　学生の皆さん、おはよう。今日のクラスでは、人類の進化における "ミッシング・リンク" を提供する最近の発見の重要性について議論したいと思います。いいえ、類人猿と人間の間のミッシング・リンクのことではありません。そうではなく、キツネザルのような最初期の霊長類と、猿のような後期の霊長類の間のギャップについてです。長い間、進化の鎖のこの部分には大きなギャップがありました。さて、最近発見されたネズミのような生物のおかげで、私たちはネズミから人間への進化の変遷をより完全に継ぎ合わせることができるのです。現在、私たちにはその動物の化石化したあごと歯しかありません。その動物は小型で、約100グラムしかありません。しかし、猿のような深いあごと歯を持っています。おそらくこれは果実と昆虫を糧に生き、そして森林やジャングルに生息していたのでしょう。

39. 何のクラスでこの講義は行われるか？
- (A) 哲学
- (B) 地質学
- (C) 地理学
- (D) 生物学

40. 最近発見された生物が埋める「ミッシング・リンク」とは？
- (A) 類人猿と人間の中間の存在
- (B) 恐竜とほ乳類の中間の存在
- (C) 初期の霊長類と後期の霊長類の中間の存在
- (D) 魚類と爬虫類の中間の存在

41. その動物の特徴を示すのに最適なものは、次のうちどれか？
- (A) それは小さかった。
- (B) それは強かった。
- (C) それは速かった。
- (D) それはおとなしかった。

42. 話者によれば、その生物はおそらく何を食べていたか？
- (A) 植物だけ
- (B) 果物と昆虫
- (C) 他の動物
- (D) ナッツ類とベリー類

Practice Test 2

Questions 43-46

健康な生活に関する次の講義を聞きなさい。

　こんばんは。"健康な生活シリーズ" の最初の講義に、フィットネス・センタークラブの新会員全員をお迎えします。私はこのクラブの食事と運動の専門家であるトレーナーの一人で、それがまさに私がお話したいことなのです。昨今、"脂肪分なしの製品" が大変なブームになっています。しかし、正確にはそれがどういう意味なのか、考えたことはあるでしょうか。実際のところ、"低脂肪" や "脂肪分なし" というラベルが意味しているのは、その製品中の脂肪分の何グラムが減っているかということなのです。必ずしも "低脂肪" 食品は低カロリー食品だという意味ではありません。実際にも、多くの会社が、脂肪分を減らして、砂糖のような高カロリーの代替品を自社製品に使用しています。つまり、低脂肪食品を食べているから、カロリーを多量に摂取していないとはなりません。自分の食事と体重に注意したいのならば、私は脂肪分比率よりもカロリーの数値にもっと注意を払うことを強く推奨します。皆さんの多くが体重を減らしたいと思っていることを私は知っています。そして言うまでもなく、体重を減らすには、消費するよりも多くのカロリーを燃さなければなりません。これを行うひとつのやり方は、より少量のカロリーを摂取することです。また別のやり方としては、運動を通じて燃やすカロリーを増やすことです。体重管理に関心があるのであれば、このスポーツジムでは、特に運動を推奨しています。なぜなら、運動した場合、運動している間により多くのカロリーを燃やすだけでなく、一日を通じて新陳代謝が上がり、読書している時や寝ている時でさえもより多くのカロリーを燃焼するからです。ほとんどの人は、運動することによるこの特別な利点について知りません。では、スクリーンにご注目ください。厳密に運動がどのように身体のカロリー消費に影響するのかを図解する表をお見せしたいと思います。

43. この講義が行われている場所は？
    (A) 大学
    (B) スポーツジム
    (C) 病院
    (D) 食事療法センター

44. "脂肪分なしの製品" について話者は何と言っているか？
    (A) それらは優れた健康食品だ。
    (B) それらは実はたくさんの脂肪分を含んでいる。
    (C) それらは高カロリーかもしれない。
    (D) それらは常に避けるべきものである。

45. 運動の影響について、ほとんど知られていないものは何か？
    (A) けがの確率が増す
    (B) 一日中、カロリーの燃焼を増やす
    (C) より身体が健康になる
    (D) 夜、より深く良く眠れる

46. 話者は次に何をするか？
    (A) 視覚的な図を用いる
    (B) トレーニング技術をやって見せる
    (C) 食事療法を推奨する
    (D) 健康な食品の例をいくつか示す

Questions 47-50

天文学のクラスで行われている隕石に関する講義を聞きなさい。

　今日の午後は、宇宙から落ちてくる隕石、石と金属の固まりについて話すことから始めたいと思います。近年、組織的かつ計画的な調査により、数多くの隕石が発見されています。日本、フランス、そしてアメリカ南西部の砂漠に至るまで、世界中でです。しかし、圧倒的に多くの発見があったのは、南極点の近く、南極大陸の氷が数多くの隕石をほぼ原形のまま保存していた場所においてです。

　隕石が元々どこで生じたのかという質問は興味深いものです。大半は、衝突し、太陽の周囲の通常の軌道からたたき出された小惑星の残存物のように見えます。長い歳月のうちに、やがてそのうちのいくつかが地球の軌道を横切ったのです。ほとんどは地球の大気の摩擦のせいでばらばらになりますが、いくつかは壊れる前に地表に激突します。しかし、小惑星が隕石の唯一の源というわけではないかもしれません。ある論争の的になっている最近多くの支持を集めている理論では小さめの隕石のいくつかは、揮発性物質を失って石に合体した彗星の残存物である、としています。この理論の証拠は、そうした小さめの物体の多くは奇妙な形の周回軌道を有しており、それは小惑星よりも彗星の軌道に似ているということです。しかも、そうした特異な軌道は火星と木星の間にある小惑星帯の外側に位置しているのです。

　隕石の年齢を決定する最も正確な方法は、放射能年代測定法として知られる技術を利用することです。時間を経ると、隕石内部に存在する放射性元素が崩壊し他の元素の原子になるため、化学成分が変化するのです。この崩壊は既知の割合で進行するため、従ってこの方法は取り囲んでいる岩を分析したり、あるいは単純に隕石そのものの内部で見つかる金属の種類に目を向けるよりも、はるかに正確なのです。はい、では、宿題にしたプリントを出し、問12〜20を見ていきましょう。

47. 最も多くの隕石が発見された場所はどこか？
 - (A) ヨーロッパで
 - (B) アメリカ南西部で
 - (C) 南極大陸で
 - (D) 日本で

48. なぜ多くの科学者が、いくつかの隕石はもともと彗星を起源とすると信じているのか？
 - (A) それらはかなり特異な軌道を持つ。
 - (B) それらは小惑星帯に位置している。
 - (C) それらはすぐに崩壊する。
 - (D) それらは極めて揮発しやすい。

49. どうすれば隕石の年齢を最適に測定できるのか？
 - (A) 周囲の岩石とそれを比較することによって
 - (B) その金属成分を分析することによって
 - (C) その形状と大きさを見ることによって
 - (D) 放射性物質の崩壊を測定することによって

50. 学生たちはこの後、何をするか？
 - (A) 彼らの宿題を終える
 - (B) 教授に質問する
 - (C) 課題を見返す
 - (D) 講義のノートを取る

Section 2 Structure and Written Expression 対訳
■ Structure

1. 遺伝子工学はまず遺伝子コーディングの過程を理解することを、次にそれを操作することを目的にする。

2. 詩人、小説家、評論家のロバート・ペン・ウォレンは20世紀のアメリカ文学の発展にかなりの影響を及ぼした。

3. 金利とインフレの間に強い関係が存在するということは、経済学者たちに一般に受け入れられている。

4. ミネソタ州北部のアイアン・レンジは北アメリカで見つかっている最大の鉄鉱層の一部である。

5. 最近まで、ガルフ・コーストはその数多くのビーチと湿地と入り江と共に環境保護区として高く評価されていた。

6. 周回軌道の外側へ天体を引っ張る力は遠心力である。

7. 政治における女性の新時代の始まりを告げたのは、ひとつの州、カリフォルニアから立候補した二人の女性上院議員の選挙だった。

8. 数多くの実験が実施されたにもかかわらず、禿げることの正確な原因はまだ特定されていない。

9. 想像力に富んだ政治家ではないものの、ジェームズ・ポークは任期中の目標実現に並外れて成功した。

10. スパイスのブレンドはスパイス製造会社が、調味料の使いこなしを手早くかつ簡易にするため、スパイス製造会社により作られた。

11. 1950年代、言語相対性の擁護者は思考が言語または再現描写機能へと還元されうると信じていた。

12. 2000年代の最初の数年で、ほぼ全ての家庭が広帯域のインターネットを持つようになると予想された。

13. 一般の考えとは逆に、知性の測定数値が将来の成功の信頼できる予測値になったことは一度もない。

14. "porpoise"という名前は時に、イルカの仲間のある種を指すことがある。

15. 年をとると、免疫システムはウイルスや菌や感染性の細菌に対し、耐性が弱まってくる。

■ Written Expression

16. 広範囲に散らばりつつも多数の顧客に仕えるには、メールでの注文が経済的に適している。

17. マサチューセッツ州は1776年にアメリカを形作った最初の13の植民地のひとつだ。

18. ボストンマラソンは長距離走者の能力を測定できる尺度の役目を果たしている。

19. 20世紀中盤までに、ヘミングウェイ、スタインベック、フォークナーといったアメリカ人作家たちはようやくずっと以前から値していた批評家の称賛を受けた。

20. 天頂儀は、天頂の方角に向けて直接頭上を見る固定された対物レンズを含む。

21. ジョージ・メイソンは貴族の農民、成功したビジネスマン、独創的な思想家としての才能を示した。

22. 最高裁判所の裁判長は、新たに選ばれた大統領に就任の宣誓をすることに責任を持つ。

23. 企業が損失を減らしたり、競争力を上げたりするために戦略的なレイオフを利用する場合、その企業は"規模縮小している"と称される。

24. 初期のアメリカの法務執行官は彼ら自身が違法行為をしていた。

25. さまざまな形式や場合によっては後退があったものの、政治制度としての民主主義の広がりはずっと一定で漸進的で驚異的だった。

26. その不毛さにもかかわらず、アリゾナ南西部の砂漠地帯は多種多様な動物たちの生息地であり続けている。

27. コクシジウム症は馬以外のあらゆる家畜の仔を襲う感染病である。

28. 準恒星状電波源を意味するクエーサー（準星）は今、ブラックホールの反対側にあると考えられている。

29. 雌のライオンを驚異的な捕獲者にしている資質は、速さ、力強さ、どう猛さだ。

30. ダーウィンが提唱した進化論は、人間の進化を徐々にではあるが、しかし常に進む過程だと考察している。

31. セラミックスはしばしば超伝導体として利用されているが、これは他の軸受電流混合物のように低い温度に冷却する必要がないからである。

32. 北アメリカ最大の川のひとつ、コロラド川は63万7140平方キロメートルの地域の排水をしている。

33. ソーシャルメディアの広範な利用は近いうちに航空郵便だけではなくあるいは電子メールまでも、前時代のものにしてしまうかもしれない。

34. ジョージ・ワシントンはたいてい学校の子どもたちから"この国の父"と呼ばれている。

35. アメーバのような低次元の生物は、細胞分裂によって自分自身を複製することができる。

36. テネシー州には起伏の多い山脈から低い平地に至るまで、並外れて多様な風景がある。

37. 電子が動いている時、その周囲に磁場が形成される。

38. 製造された商品とは違い、企業の株式の価値はほぼ全て購入者の認識に依存している。

39. 準惑星である冥王星の軌道面は太陽系の他の惑星の軌道と比べて、大きく傾いている。

40. その分子構造がゆえに、水は液体の時よりも凍結した時のほうが密度が濃くなる。

Section 3 Reading Comprehension 対訳
■ Questions 1-9

　アメリカ大陸への初期の移民は新世界を、文明化したヨーロッパにある腐敗のない楽園としてばかりではなく、恐怖と危険に満ちた未開の大自然と見なしていた。元来自然と調和して生きていたネイティブ・アメリカンとは違い、初期の開拓移民は新しい環境に適応することを困難に感じていた。長い航海を生き抜いた人たちは、到着と同時に自分たちが寒さと飢えと病気に苦しむ運命にあることに気付いた。彼らの伝統的な作物は実らないことが多々あり、また、砂糖や綿の布など、手にすることに慣れ親しんでいた物も、たとえ手に入ったとしても、不足していた。往々にして開拓移民の新世界における日々の経験は、真に生き残るための格闘であった。その結果、多くの人々が自然を天然の楽園ではなく征服すべき敵と見なしたわけだが、その理由も容易に理解できよう。さらに、彼らが自然を恐れていたのはそれが"文明"の正反対だったからでもある。彼らはやがて荒涼とした景色とそこに居住する人たちを、文明の"光"を、未開の大陸の"闇"に持ち込み手なずけ、文明化することが、彼らの道徳的使命だと感じるようになった。それゆえ、彼らの物理的な在り方と哲学的な展望により、開拓移民はネイティブ・アメリカンを高潔な未開人としてではなく、白人の生活様式へと転換すべき、あるいは殺りくされるべき人間以下の存在だと見なすようになった。

1. **この文章の主題は何か?**
   - (A) 初期の移民がどのようにしてアメリカに来たか
   - (B) 初期の開拓移民の苦難
   - (C) 初期の開拓移民がどのようにアメリカとその居住民を見なしたか
   - (D) どのようにしてアメリカが少しずつ文明化されていったか

2. **初期の開拓移民が、克服する必要がある敵として自然を見なすようになった理由として、本文で述べられていないのはどれか?**
   - (A) インディアンの攻撃
   - (B) 食糧不足
   - (C) 産物の不足
   - (D) 厳しい気候

3. **1行目"paradise"に最も意味が近いのは**
   - (A) 刑務所
   - (B) 闘技場
   - (C) 避難所
   - (D) 理想郷

4. **この文章によると、ネイティブ・アメリカンに当てはまる記述は次のうちどれか?**
   - (A) 彼らは時折、開拓移民に食糧を供給した。
   - (B) 彼らは自然環境によく適応していた。
   - (C) 彼らはヨーロッパ人の移民の文明の影響を恐れていた。
   - (D) 彼らはしばしば寒さと飢えと病気に苦しんだ

5. **なぜ筆者は砂糖と綿について触れているのか?**
   - (A) それらは開拓移民が手にできるだろうと予想していた贅沢品だった。
   - (B) それらは開拓移民がしばしばそれなしで済ませなければならない基本的な品目だった。
   - (C) それらは開拓移民に金銭の一種として使用された。
   - (D) それらは頻繁にネイティブ・アメリカンと交換された。

6. ヨーロッパからの開拓移民たちは北アメリカについて、すぐに何を発見したか？

(A) 最初に思っていたほど、美しくなかった。
(B) 想像していたよりも、到達するのに時間が長くかかった。
(C) 栽培法を知っていた穀物を育てるのが簡単ではなかった。
(D) 予想していたよりも人口密度が高かった。

7. 筆者が12行目で"moral mission"に触れたのは何を示すためか？

(A) 多くの初期の開拓移民たちの行為が、どれほど道徳に反していたか
(B) 多くの初期の開拓移民たちが、どれほど強く自然の神聖さに敬意を払っていたか
(C) 多くの初期の開拓移民たちの考え方が、どのように形成されたか
(D) どれだけ多くの初期の開拓移民たちが、先住民を助けることを義務だと感じていたか

8. 15行目"outlook"に最も意味が近いのは

(A) 視点
(B) 疑い
(C) 生活様式
(D) 横柄さ

9. 17行目"slaughtered"に最も意味が近いのは

(A) 説得された
(B) 捕獲された
(C) 脅迫された
(D) 殺された

■ Questions 10-19

　経済活動の指標に使われている最も一般的なもののひとつではあるが、国民総生産（GNP）にはいくつか深刻な限界がある。これは経済的な生産量しか測定しないため、多様な経済的損失を完全には考慮に入れていないのだ。例えば、仮に10万ドルの家が全焼し、その所有者が同じ金額で再建した場合、富の純利益はないにもかかわらず、GNPは10万ドル増加する。実際には純損失が生じたのではないかと論じることすら可能だ。というのも、家主が真に生産的な目的で使えたかもしれない資金が消費されているからだ。特に環境保護主義者たちはGNPに批判的だが、これはGNPが再生不可能な天然資源の枯渇や農地の損失や汚染を取り除く費用などの経費を差し引いていないからだ。

　GNPの代わりとして1980年の終わりに提案されたひとつの指標がISEW（持続可能経済福祉指標）だ。この指標は、給料が支払われない家事労働や高速道路、健康、教育への公的支出などを含む数字を導き出すため、より良い生活の質に真に貢献する商品やサービスを全て加算している。この指標はそれから、これまで慣例として経済的価値を付加されてきたが、実際にはより良い生活の質に貢献していない、不必要な要素を差し引く。広告がその一例だ。GNPとISEWの比較はどんな見識をもたらすだろう。GNPの数値はアメリカ経済が1951年から1986年の間にほぼ2倍になったことを示しているが、ISEWの数値はその間の生活の質はわずか20パーセントしか向上していないことを示している。

10. この文章が主に論じていることは何か？
    (A) 国民総生産の概念
    (B) 新たな経済学の必要性
    (C) GNP対ISEW
    (D) アメリカの生活の質の向上

11. 2行目"it"が指しているのは
    (A) 経済活動
    (B) 10万ドルの家
    (C) 経済的な生産量
    (D) 国民総生産

12. 次のうちどのコストがISEWには含まれずGNPに含まれると本文から推測できるか？
    (A) 新しい公共スポーツセンターの建設
    (B) 危険廃棄物処理場の浄化
    (C) 企業の従業員への支払い
    (D) 地方の学校への交付金の拠出

13. 8行目"critical"に最も意味が近いのは
    (A) 懐疑的な
    (B) 関心を持つ
    (C) 興味を持つ
    (D) 本気の

14. 9行目"deduct"に最も意味が近いのは
    (A) 引く
    (B) 考慮する
    (C) 述べる
    (D) 割り当てる

15. GNPではなくISEWを用いて1986年の生活水準を測定すると、どのような結果が引き出されうるか？
    (A) 生活の質は1951年の2倍良くなった。
    (B) 生活の質は1951年以降、改善していない。

(C) 生活の質は1951年以降、経済的利得を反映している。
(D) 生活の質は1951年よりもいく分か良くなったに過ぎない。

16. 環境保護主義者の意見の中でGNPに関して主な欠点となるのは？
    (A) 破損あるいは破壊されたものを置き換える経費を含んでいる
    (B) 物々交換の形の経済活動を考慮していない
    (C) 汚染された土地や水などの資源の損失を差し引いていない
    (D) 個人消費よりも公的支出により焦点を当てている

17. 筆者が14行目で"unpaid household labor"と述べたのはなぜか？
    (A) 性別による不平等が相変わらず存在することを示すため
    (B) 家事労働のより公平な分配を奨励するため
    (C) 生活の質に貢献するものを説明するため
    (D) この労働の価値には税金をかけるべきだと勧めるため

18. 15行目"superfluous"に最も意味が近いのは
    (A) 価値のある
    (B) 必須でない
    (C) 伝統的な
    (D) 役に立たない

19. この文章によると、持続可能経済福祉指標に含まれないものは次のうちどれか？
    (A) 高速道路の建設
    (B) 健康医療支出
    (C) 教育費
    (D) 広告予算

■ Questions 20-29

　水牛はバイソン——しばしば誤って水牛とみなされる——とは無関係だ。水牛は畜牛とだいたい同じ形状で、ほとんどの場合灰色がかった黒色である。かなり風変わりな角が特徴で、それは後ろに向いているかまたは丸まっている。水牛の多くはかなり大きくなり1トン以上の体重になる。水牛はアメリカの牧場経営者からも、そして動物学者からも同様に、ほとんど無視されてきたが、最近は世界各地で認知され始めている。あらゆる家畜の中で水牛には、肉や牛乳の産出量あるいは仕事量の増加に関し、最大規模のポテンシャルがあるかもしれない。

　ほとんどの西洋人にとって水牛は馴染みがない動物であり、水牛に関する根拠のない話もたくさんある。例えば、特に別の動物が周りにいる時は凶暴な種であると言われているが、実際にはおそらく水牛は世界で最も穏やかな家畜だろう。社交性があり、おおらかで人間が好きなのだ。また、水牛は水浴びするための水を必要とすると広く伝わっているが、実際の水牛は水がなくとも適切な木陰があれば普通に成長し繁殖する。さらに、水牛は熱帯にしか生息しない動物だという誤った認識が共有されているが、現実には、その適応力のお陰で水牛はさまざまな気候で成長することができる。しかし、この適応力にもかかわらず、アメリカでの水牛の商業的なポテンシャルを突き止める実験は、まずは水牛が元々生息していた環境に似た気候で行われるべきだと見なされた。このため1978年にフロリダ大学がアメリカ初の水牛の群れを受け取ることとなった。その後の実験で、同大学の国際農業プログラムの動物学者たちは、水牛にはアメリカにおける商業的なポテンシャルが間違いなくあると結論を下した。実際のところ、餌が十分ではない条件下においては、他の牛よりも水牛に競争上の優位性があるようだ。そして水牛はより短期間で成長し、より多くの子牛を産む。科学者たちが観察した他の優位性としては、熱や湿気に対する耐性、それにフロリダの水路の多くを覆う水生植物を好むことなどがある。さらに彼らは水牛の肉はかなりの市場にポテンシャルがあることも見出した。実際、ブラインドテストで味見をした被験者の多くは、ビーフの一切れよりも水牛の肉を好んだのだ。

20. 水牛について本文から推測できることは何か？
- (A) 水牛の肉は牛肉よりもおいしくない。
- (B) 水牛はかなり有望なタンパク質源だ。
- (C) 水牛の食物は水生植物に限られている。
- (D) 水牛は本来の居住地の外では容易に繁殖させられない。

21. 次の特性のうち水牛の特徴はどれか？
- (A) 牛とは異なる形状である。
- (B) バイソンと同じ種族から派生している。
- (C) 体の色にはいろいろな種類がある。
- (D) 非常に特徴的な角を持っている。

22. 2行目"roughly"に最も意味が近いのは
- (A) 不意に
- (B) 正確に
- (C) おおよそ
- (D) ますます

23. 6行目"they"が指しているのは
- (A) 牛
- (B) 水牛
- (C) 牧場経営者
- (D) 動物学者

24. この文章の第1段落では次のうちどのトピックが主に述べられているか？
- (A) 水牛に関する迷信
- (B) 水牛が好む気候
- (C) 水牛の身体的特徴
- (D) 水牛を繁殖させる可能性

25. 12行目"genial"に最も意味が近いのは
- (A) 友好的な
- (B) 活発な
- (C) 本物の
- (D) 知的な

26. 水牛の成長に必要なのは何か？
- (A) ぬかるんだ野原
- (B) 水の大量供給
- (C) 高湿度
- (D) 太陽光からの保護

27. 25行目"tolerance"に最も意味が近いのは
- (A) ～への適応能力
- (B) ～への依存
- (C) ～への好み
- (D) ～に対する無関心

28. 水牛の習性について当てはまらないのは次のどれか？
- (A) 他の家畜と仲良くする。
- (B) 多くの異なる気候に適応できる。
- (C) 人間を嫌う傾向がある。
- (D) 穏やかな性格である。

29. フロリダが最初に水牛を輸入した州だったのはなぜか？
- (A) 水牛の元々の生息地に似た気候条件があるから。
- (B) アメリカ最大の農業大学があるから。
- (C) 水が大量にあるから。
- (D) 競合する畜牛産業が小規模だから。

■ Questions 30-39

　背が低く肉付きのよい男、ジョン・アダムズは前任者のジョージ・ワシントンとは対照的に、老齢になっても活発な生活を送った。しかし、ワシントンと異なり——彼の下でアダムズは副大統領として2期務めた——アダムズはアメリカの最も裕福な大統領のひとりではなかった。任期中の彼は、公務上の費用を賄うために繰り返し自分のそれほど多くはない貯金に手をつけた。おそらくアダムズの副大統領としての経済的困難は、給料がわずか5000ドルだった時に始まったのだろう。生活するにも少なすぎると彼は不平を口にした。大統領になり給料は2万5000ドルに上がったものの、それでも自分の公務上の費用を賄うには少なすぎた。1期務めた後、アダムズは早期退職し、人生最後の25年を（マサチューセッツ州の）クインシーにある屋敷でひっそり過ごし、84歳で遺言をしたためた。その頃には彼が優先権を与えた相続人——妻、2人の娘、息子の1人——は死去していた。生き残っていた2人の息子が彼の財産を分かち合った。しかし、アダムズは自分の財産を使ってとても長生きしたため、その価値は3万ドルに激減していた。年少の息子、トーマス・ボイルストン・アダムズは不動産の一部と遺産の金融資産の一部を相続した。年長の息子、ジョン・クインシー・アダムズ（父親と混同しないこと）は、遺産の一部のみならず大統領の蔵書も受け取ったが、これはおそらく彼自身の——父の政治的道程を追随し、アメリカの第6代大統領になるという——運命を予兆していたのだろう。

30. この文章が主に論じているのは？
    (A) ジョン・クインシー・アダムズの
        生涯の主な出来事
    (B) アメリカ初期の大統領
    (C) 第2代大統領、ジョン・アダムズ
        の金銭事情
    (D) 初期の大統領と副大統領の給料

31. 1行目"plump"に最も意味が近いのは
    (A) 健康な
    (B) ふっくらした
    (C) たくましい
    (D) 感じのよい

32. この文章からジョージ・ワシントンが
    どうだったと推測できるか？
    (A) 植民地の偉大な統率者
    (B) アダムズほど健康ではなかった
    (C) アダムズとほぼ同年齢
    (D) アダムズの親しい友人

33. この文章からアダムズはどんな人生を
    送ったと推測できるか？
    (A) あり金の大半を息子たちに与えた
    (B) 比較的貧しく暮らした
    (C) 稼いだ額よりも多くを使った
    (D) 妻の稼ぎをあてにして暮らした

34. アダムズが副大統領時代、彼の年収は
    (A) 5000ドル
    (B) 1万5000ドル
    (C) 2万5000ドル
    (D) 3万ドル

35. 7行目"it"が指しているのは
    (A) 大統領府の一任期
    (B) 経済的困難
    (C) 大統領の給料
    (D) アダムズの財産

36. ジョン・アダムズが大統領を務めた期
    間は？
    (A) 1期のみ
    (B) 3期
    (C) 2期
    (D) 半期

37. 9行目"seclusion"に最も意味が近い
    のは
    (A) 比較的孤独な状態
    (B) 活発な退職者生活
    (C) 定期的な相談
    (D) 断続的なうつ状態

38. 12行目"dwindled"に最も意味が近い
    のは
    (A) 2倍になった
    (B) 増加した
    (C) 等しくなった
    (D) 減少した

39. 大統領の任期を勤め上げた後、アダム
    ズは人生の大半をどのように過ごした
    か？
    (A) 一番年上の息子を大統領になるよ
        う仕込んだ
    (B) 自邸で一人で暮らした
    (C) いくつかの重要な慈善事業団体を
        設立した
    (D) 初の大統領図書館のための素材を
        収集した

■ Questions 40-50

　繊維とは、その長さが幅よりも少なくとも200倍大きい物質のまとまりと定義できるだろう。天然繊維は３つのカテゴリーから成る。セルロース質のもの、タンパク質のもの、ミネラル質のものだ。ひとつ目のセルロース質のものは植物が源である。2,000種以上の繊維質の植物が見つかっているものの、約50種類しか商業的に利用されていない。綿は、その中でも群を抜いて重要で、消費量でもその適用範囲の多様性の点でも、そうである。これから広範囲な種類の布地とその他の製品が製造されている。南アジアの植物の茎から製造されるジュートは生産量に関して綿の次にくる。しかし、ジュート栽培の費用はかなり低いのだが、さまざまな面でジュートは綿に劣る。ジュートはきめが粗く、漂白したり染めたりするのが難しく、また伸長性に欠ける。

　タンパク質の繊維は基本的に動物の体毛に由来する。羊のウール、ビーバーの毛皮、ウサギの毛は全てこの分類の例だ。唯一、自然の動物の繊維でありながら表皮を保護するために皮膚に生えていない絹は、長く繋がった繊維としてカイコが産出したものだ。

　唯一天然のミネラル質繊維はアスベストだ。これは非常にもろく、その長い繊維を押しつぶさないよう掘削の際とその後の加工の際にかなりの配慮が求められるが、最近までアスベストは広く使われていた。その理由はその耐火性と保熱能力ゆえだった。しかし、継続的にこれにさらされているとガンを発症する可能性が明らかとなり、アスベストは他の素材にその座を明け渡した。

　アスベストを除く全ての天然繊維は親水性である。すなわち、液体と気体の両方の状態の水との親和性が高い。天然繊維の湿気を吸収する能力は、これらの素材を衣類に使用するのにふさわしいものとしている。湿気を吸収し、それを周辺の空気に移すことで、そうした素材は服を着ている人をより快適にする。人工繊維はこういったことを同じようにはできないが、それは湿気を吸収する能力を持たないからだ。

40. この文章のタイトルにふさわしいのはどれか？
- (A) 綿とジュートの商業利用
- (B) 天然繊維と人工繊維の比較
- (C) 繊維：簡潔な定義
- (D) 天然繊維：その分類と利用

41. この文章によれば、何種類の繊維植物が確認されているか？
- (A) 少なくとも200種類
- (B) 2000種類以上
- (C) おおよそ50種類
- (D) ちょうど３種類

42. 5行目"these"が指しているのは
- (A) 商業利用される繊維植物
- (B) 繊維植物一般
- (C) 自然に生じる繊維
- (D) 天然繊維の種別

43. 9行目"cultivating"に最も意味が近いのは
- (A) 製造すること
- (B) 輸出すること
- (C) 販売すること
- (D) 育てること

44. この文章によれば、本文のひとつ目のカテゴリーの商業用の天然繊維について正しい記述はどれか？
- (A) 比較的小さな割合の繊維植物が元になっている。
- (B) まだ発見も分類もされていないものが多くある。
- (C) 主に動物の体毛から由来している。
- (D) それらの長さは非常に短いものから極度に長いものまである。

45. 18行目"retain"に最も意味が近いのは
    (A) 保つ
    (B) 主張する
    (C) 移す
    (D) 抵抗する

46. アスベストが他の素材に取って代わられた理由は？
    (A) 加工が難しい。
    (B) あまりにも壊れやすい。
    (C) 健康に危害を及ぼすものが含まれている。
    (D) 十分な量が採掘できない。

47. 綿がジュートより優れていないのはどんな点か？
    (A) 肌触りがより滑らか。
    (B) より強い生地を作る。
    (C) 染色が容易。
    (D) 製造がより安価。

48. 18行目"it"が指しているのは
    (A) 暴露
    (B) アスベスト
    (C) 熱
    (D) ガン

49. 21行目"capacity"に最も意味が近いのは
    (A) 能力
    (B) 量
    (C) 傾向
    (D) 特徴

50. この文章からアスベストが衣服に使えない理由は何だと推測できるか？
    (A) 人工繊維である
    (B) 湿気を吸収できない
    (C) ミネラル質の繊維である
    (D) 肌を刺激する

Section 1 Listening Comprehension 対訳
■ Part A

1. **女性**：フレッド！　あなたの科学プロ
　　ジェクトの進み具合はどう？
　　男性：これ以上良くなりようがないよ。
　　2～3日中に最終結果が得られ
　　る予定だ。
　　質問：科学プロジェクトについて男性
　　は何と言っているか？
　　(A) 順調に進んでいる。
　　(B) 提出が遅くなる。
　　(C) 彼はすぐにそれに取り掛かる。
　　(D) 彼はそれがもっと良かったなら
　　と望んでいる。

2. **男性**：どうして世界大恐慌に関する
　　エッセーを書いているんだい？
　　女性：歴史のクラスの課題なの。
　　質問：女性の発言はどういう意味か？
　　(A) 彼女は歴史について書くのが楽
　　しい。
　　(B) 彼女のエッセーはあまりうまく
　　いっていない。
　　(C) 彼女が取っているコースのため
　　にその論文が求められている。
　　(D) 彼女は最近、いく分落ち込んで
　　いる。

3. **女性**：空港行きのシャトルバスはどの
　　くらいの頻度で出るの？
　　男性：30分毎です。
　　質問：バスについて男性は何と言って
　　いるか？
　　(A) 30分後に出発する。
　　(B) 1時間に2本ある。
　　(C) 空港に着くのに1時間かかる。
　　(D) バスはすでに出発している。

4. **男性**：全部のクラスに期末試験と期末
　　レポートがあるなんて信じられ
　　ない。
　　女性：うわ、今学期の終わりには大変
　　な仕事があるわね。
　　質問：女性の発言はどういう意味か？

(A) その男性は少し仕事を休むべき
　　だ。
(B) その男性はたくさん勉強しなけ
　　ればならない。
(C) まもなく学期が終わる。
(D) その男性はそれほど頻繁に仕事
　　を休むべきではない。

5. **男性**：今日の午後、うちに来て、映画
　　を見ない？
　　女性：レンタル店から2～3本DVDを
　　借りたんでしょう？
　　質問：女性は何を推測しているか？
　　(A) その男性はテレビをずっと見て
　　いた。
　　(B) レンタル店は閉じている。
　　(C) そのカップルは買い物に行った。
　　(D) その男性は何本かDVDを借りた。

6. **女性**：トム、今週ずっと美術史のクラ
　　スにいなかったわよね。
　　男性：その通り。実のところ、君の
　　ノートをコピーさせてもらえな
　　いかなと思ってるんだ。
　　質問：男性の発言はどういう意味か？
　　(A) 彼はその女性がコピー機を使っ
　　たかどうかを知りたい。
　　(B) 彼はその女性にメモを書くつも
　　りだ。
　　(C) 彼はその女性の授業ノートを借
　　りたい。
　　(D) 彼はその女性の答えが正しいと
　　同意している。

7. **女性**：思い切って例の週末の追加仕事
　　を請け負うことに決めたわ。
　　男性：うーん、キャロル、本気でそれ
　　に対処できると思ってるの？
　　他にもやるべきことがある、そ
　　の上にだよ。
　　質問：男性の発言はどういう意味か？
　　(A) その女性はあまりに多くのこと

をやろうとしているのかもしれない。
(B) 成功のためには懸命に働くことが必要だ。
(C) ときおり休憩を取ることが重要だ。
(D) その女性は彼に助けを求めるべきだ。

8. **男性**：昨晩、君とジェーンが新しいドイツレストランで食事したって聞いたよ。どうだった？
女性：間違いなく、他でもっとおいしいものを食べたことがあるわ。
質問：女性の発言はどういう意味か？
(A) 早めに予約を取ったほうがよい。
(B) そこの食べ物はあまりよくなかった。
(C) サービスは次第に改善してきている。
(D) レストランは普段より早めに閉店した。

9. **女性**：もうエッセーは書き終わった？ 明日が締切って知ってるよね。
男性：終わったかって？ まだ題材すら決めていないよ。
質問：エッセーについて、男性は何をほのめかしているか？
(A) 彼はほぼそれを書き終えた。
(B) 彼は題材を変えたい。
(C) 彼はそれを書き始めてすらいない。
(D) 彼はそれが明日締切だと知らなかった。

10. **女性**：先週私たちが署名したウィルソンの契約書に目を通す機会はあったかしら？
男性：忙しくてまだです。
質問：この会話から男性について何が推測できるか？

(A) 彼は契約書を見つけられないようだ。
(B) 彼は来週契約書に署名する予定だ。
(C) 彼はすぐにウィルソン氏に連絡する必要がある。
(D) 彼は他の仕事でずっと忙しい。

11. **男性**：中間試験までに人類学のリーディングを全部終えるのはどうしても無理だ。
女性：あなただけじゃないわ。クラスのほぼ全員が全くあなたと同じ状況よ。
質問：人類学のクラスのメンバーについて、女性は何をほのめかしているか？
(A) 彼らはクラスのプロジェクトに一緒に取り組んでいる。
(B) 彼らは全員、読むのが遅れている。
(C) 彼らは中間試験で良い成績を取るだろう。
(D) 彼らは一緒にボートで実地見学旅行に行く。

12. **女性**：お支払いするためのクレジットカードです。
男性：すみませんが、現金しか受け付けてないんです。
質問：女性はおそらく何をするか？
(A) クレジットカードを申し込む
(B) 彼女の身分証明書を見せる
(C) 現金で支払う
(D) レシートを求める

13. **男性**：ああ、なんてことだ！ サンアントニオ行きの飛行機を予約するのを忘れていた。
女性：そうね、もしまだ行きたいなら、すぐに取りかかったほうがいいわね。

質問：女性は、男性がどうするべきだと提案しているか？

(A) ただちに飛行機に乗る

(B) すぐに飛行機を予約する

(C) サンアントニオへの旅をキャンセルする

(D) もっと安い便を探す

14. **男性**：なんてきれいな鳥だ！　こんなの今までに見たことある？

女性：この辺りでは見ないわ。たいてい、いつももっと南のほうで見つかるわね。

質問：この鳥について、女性は何と言っているか？

(A) それはこの地域ではめったに見られない。

(B) その色がそれを見えにくくしている。

(C) それは冬に向けて南に飛ぶ。

(D) 彼女はそのようなものを一度も見たことがない。

15. **女性**：この列に15分も並んでいます。

男性：すみません。たくさんお客様がいらっしゃるときのポリシーは早く来た方から順番に対応しております。

質問：男性は何をほのめかしているか？

(A) その女性はもっと辛抱強くあるべきだ。

(B) その女性は対応される列での順番が次である。

(C) その女性は予約すべきだった。

(D) その女性は今なら注文できる。

16. **男性**：5時だね。マレーはどこにいるんだ？

女性：知らなかったの？　彼はこの数日間、体調が悪いのよ。

質問：女性はマレーについて何と言っ

ているか？

(A) 悪天候のため彼は遅れた。

(B) 彼はあまり気分が良くない。

(C) 彼はこの数日間、休暇を取っていた。

(D) 彼はどこに行くべきか知らない。

17. **男性**：週末に向けて予報されていた寒い期間はなんでもなかったね。

女性：そうね。

質問：女性は何をほのめかしているか？

(A) 彼女はとても寒いと思った。

(B) 彼女はそれのつづり方を知らない。

(C) 彼女もまた、週末にやることが何もない。

(D) 彼女はその男性の意見に同意している。

18. **女性**：今朝は、市内横断高速道路がかなり混んでいるみたい。

男性：他の道で行ったほうがいいかもね。

質問：男性は女性に何をほのめかししているか？

(A) 彼らは地下鉄を使うべきだ。

(B) その雲はすぐに消えるだろう。

(C) 別の道のほうが速いかもしれない。

(D) 渋滞はいずれは緩和するだろう。

19. **男性**：最近どうしてこんなにいつも疲れているのか、わからないわ。

女性：君と君の友達でずっとやっている深夜の勉強会が関係しているんじゃない？

質問：女性はどうするべきだと男性はほのめかしているか？

(A) そんなに必死に勉強するのをやめる

(B) 別の友人を作る

(C) 深夜のパーティーは避ける
(D) 勉強グループに参加する

20. **男性**：今のこの天候はどう？
    女性：これ以上望めないわね。
    質問：天候について、何が推測されるか？
    (A) 最近はずっとよくない。
    (B) すぐには変わりそうにない。
    (C) 予測することは不可能だ。
    (D) ここ最近はずっとほぼ完璧だ。

21. **男性**：総合試験の出来がどうだったかわかった？
    女性：実を言うと、わかったわ。私の教授が今朝、私がクラスで最高点のひとつを取ったと言ったの。
    質問：試験での成績について、女性は何と言っているか？
    (A) 彼女は望んでいた程の高得点を取れなかった。
    (B) 事実に関する設問では彼女が最高点を取った。
    (C) 級友と比べると彼女は並みの結果だった。
    (D) 彼女は立派な成績を収めた。

22. **男性**：生物のクラスの後、コーヒーでもどう？
    女性：もちろん。今日はカナダの歴史のクラスが休講になったから、１時まで授業がないの。
    質問：女性の発言はどういう意味か？
    (A) 今日、彼女は授業がひとつしかない。
    (B) 彼女はこれ以上コーヒーを欲しくない。
    (C) 彼女はその男性に加わることができそうだ。
    (D) 彼女はカナダの歴史に興味がない。

23. **男性**：パトリシア、３番に君宛てで電話がかかってきているよ。
    女性：私に？　会社にまで、誰が電話してきているのかしら？
    質問：女性の疑問から何が推測できるか？
    (A) 彼女は電話で話すのに忙しい。
    (B) 彼女は仕事場でめったに電話を受けない。
    (C) 彼女はちょうど仕事場を出るところだ。
    (D) 彼女は伝言を受け取りたいと思っている。

24. **女性**：来年の予算について、いつ頃一緒に話ができそうかしら？
    男性：今じゃだめですか？
    質問：男性の発言はどういう意味か？
    (A) 彼らはすぐに会うべきだ。
    (B) 予算にいくつか問題がある。
    (C) 今は集まるのに良い時期ではない。
    (D) 予算は彼の責任ではない。

25. **男性**：授業があと15分で始まるのに、マークが私たちのグループ発表に必要な写真を全部、忘れてきたんだ。
    女性：こんなことが起こりそうだって、言ったでしょ？
    質問：女性は何をほのめかしているか？
    (A) 彼女はマークに写真を持って来てくれるよう頼むのを忘れた。
    (B) どのみち彼女はそれらの写真が気に入らなかった。
    (C) 彼女はマークが彼らをがっかりさせるのではないかと疑っていた。
    (D) 彼女は贈り物をサプライズにしたいと思っていた。

Practice Test 3

53

26. **女性**：母がチョコレートを一箱送って来たの。少しどう？
    男性：今朝、体重計に乗っていなかったなら、君の申し出に応じたかもね。
    質問：男性は何をほのめかしているか？
    (A) 彼は甘いものが好きではない。
    (B) 彼はその女性を車で送ることができない。
    (C) 彼にはチョコレート・アレルギーがある。
    (D) 彼は自分の体重に注意する必要がある。

27. **男性**：このプリンター、調子が悪いな。
    女性：何が？
    質問：女性は何を知りたいのか？
    (A) その男性が言ったこと
    (B) その男性に起こったこと
    (C) プリンターの何が問題か
    (D) その男性が書いていること

28. **女性**：応募した教師の職、本当に受かると思っているの？
    男性：絶対にね。もう、安心しているよ。昨日、先方から連絡があったんだ。
    質問：男性の発言はどういう意味か？
    (A) 彼は本当に望んでいた職を得た。
    (B) 彼は絶対にその職に応募する必要がある。
    (C) 彼は銀行で働くことに決めていた。
    (D) 彼はすでに昨日、銀行に行った。

29. **男性**：7時頃、フットボールの試合に行くために、君を迎えに行くよ。
    女性：あなたがフットボールの試合に行くの？
    質問：女性は男性について何をほのめかしているか？

    (A) 彼はもっと早めに彼女を迎えに行くべきだった。
    (B) 彼は頻繁にはフットボールを見ない。
    (C) 彼は試合でプレーすることになっている。
    (D) 彼はほぼ常に時間を守らない。

30. **男性**：今日のピクニックは残念だね？
    女性：ええ、雨に降られるなんて本当にびっくりだわ。たぶん来週に計画し直せるかも。
    質問：この会話から男性と女性について何が推測できるか？
    (A) 彼らは雨が降ると予想していた。
    (B) 彼らは多忙過ぎてピクニックに行けない。
    (C) 彼らはピクニックを延期しなければならないだろう。
    (D) 彼らは天気に恵まれて運が良い。

■ Part B

Questions 31-34

ディベート勝ち抜き戦に関する以下の会話を聞きなさい。
女性：エド！　日曜日にここで何をしているの？
男性：ディベートチームの他のメンバーと会うんだ。
女性：日曜日に？　あなたはキャンパスから１時間以上のところに住んでいると思ったけど。
男性：うん、でもうちの大学後援の地区ディベート大会が明日朝一番に始まるんだ。できる限りの準備をしておかないとね。
女性：ああ、そうね。学校中に張られているポスターを見たわ。地元の全大学の学生が参加するんでしょ？
男性：その通り。そして今年は僕らのチームが優勝するんだ！
女性：自信たっぷりじゃない？　ところで、誰が勝つかの判断は誰がするの？
男性：ディベートコンテストの審査員をやることで生計を立てている人がいるなんて信じられる？
女性：つまり、プロっていうこと？　そういった人たちへの支払いは高いんじゃないの？
男性：もちろんそうだね。以前は、地元のコミュニティーの人や他の学校の教授に頼んだんだ。でも、この２～３年で僕らのトーナメントが得た評判を踏まえて、正式な訓練と経験を持つ審査員が必要だと決めたんだ。
女性：彼らは何を判断基準にするの？　議論の創造性とかそういうこと？
男性：実際のところ、独創的な主張を述べることは、主張のプレゼンの仕方ほど重要じゃないんだ。
女性：どういう意味？
男性：例えば、チームの発言のスタイルや自分たちの意見に聴衆がどれくらい好意的に反応したかでポイントをもらえるんだ。それから、意見は明確に整理しておく必要がある。それぞれの主旨が次へと論理的に続くようにね。これを実行するのは本当に難しいことなんだ。ディベートが実際に始まる数分前にならないと、トピックが何なのかわからないからね。
女性：どうやら週末ですら練習しなければならないみたいね！　がんばってね、エド！　あなたのチームが勝つことを願っているわ。
男性：ありがとう。最善を尽くすよ。

31. 大会はいつ開催されるか？
   (A) 日曜日に
   (B) 今日この後に
   (C) 明日の朝に
   (D) 来週早々に

32. ディベート大会の審査員は誰か？
   (A) 他の大学の学生たち
   (B) プロのディベートの審査員
   (C) 地元のコミュニティーの一員
   (D) 地域の大学の教授

33. 討論者はどのようにしてディベートのトピックを知るか？
   (A) 自分たちでそれを選ぶかどうかは彼ら次第。
   (B) 対戦相手のメンバーが選ぶ。
   (C) 討論の前日に彼らに与えられる。
   (D) それは討論の直前に発表される。

34. この男性によると、勝利者を選ぶ際に特に考慮されない基準は何か？
   (A) 構成
   (B) 独創性
   (C) 意見を述べるスタイル
   (D) 聴衆への訴求力

Questions 35-38

2人の生徒の会話を聞きなさい。

男性：とても疲れているみたいだね、テレサ。しっかり眠れてる？

女性：ううん、実はしばらくの間ぐっすり眠れていないの。というのも、美術部が来週4年生の展覧会を開催するから、展示する写真と絵画全部を台紙に貼って、フレームに入れなくちゃならないのよ。

男性：うわ。大変な仕事みたいだね。

女性：そうよ。4年生は全員毎晩午前3時まで働いているわ。台紙貼りとフレーム入れはほぼ終わった。でも次は実際にその展示物を壁にかけないといけないわ。

男性：驚いたね。芸術学部の君は、絵を描いて、写真を撮ればいいだけだと思っていたよ！ところで展覧会はどこでやるの？

女性：例年通り、パフォーミング・アート・センター内の美術ギャラリーでよ。実はそれが問題のひとつなの。すでにそのギャラリーで展覧会が開催されているのよ。その結果、その展覧会を片付けて私たちが自分たちのを展示するまでたった2日間しかないのよ。

男性：どうやら来週はさらに何度か眠れない夜になりそうだね。

女性：ええ。展覧会がまだ始まってもいないのに、もうそれが終るのが待ちきれないなんて信じられないわ。

35. 女性はなぜ疲れているのか？
    (A) 彼女は夜遅くまで描いていた。
    (B) 彼女は展覧会（の準備）に取り組んでいる。
    (C) 彼女は美術の授業の課題を完成させようとしている。
    (D) 彼女は今朝早起きした。

36. 男性はなぜ驚いたと言っているか？
    (A) 彼は展覧会が来週あることを知らなかった。
    (B) 彼はその女性はすでにコースの必修科目を終えたと思っていた。
    (C) 彼は美術の学生たちが展示用に自身の作品を準備すると思っていなかった。
    (D) 彼はその女性は次の年に卒業すると思っていた。

37. 展覧会はどこで催されるか？
    (A) 芸術学部で
    (B) 市立美術館で
    (C) パフォーミング・アート・センターで
    (D) 個人のギャラリーで

38. 女性は何を楽しみにしているか？
    (A) 展覧会の開会
    (B) 彼女の作品を吊るすこと
    (C) 学期末
    (D) 展覧会の閉会

■ Part C

医者によるトークを聞きなさい。

こんにちは。私はトンプソン医師です。今日の妊婦さん向けのトークは、産後うつについてです。ええ、これが今皆さんが聞きたいと思っている話題でないことは私もわかっていますが、しかし、妊婦として、妊娠が終わりを迎える重要な日について考えるだけではなく、子どもを出産した後に起こることに対し、準備しておくこともまた重要です。はじめに、皆さんは母親全員の8割が、新生児の面倒を見る最初の週の間に身体的かつ感情的な疲労を報告していることをご存知でしたでしょうか？ ほとんどの人はすぐに改善しますが、しかし、約10パーセントが――そうです、10人に1人です――何カ月も落ち込んだ気分のままになります。しかしながら、最近、ある研究がこのうつの原因にある洞察をもたらしています。どうやら、このうつは女性の体内でエストロゲンが不足するために生じるようなのです。ご存知の通り、エストロゲンは女性の生殖サイクルと密接な関係を持つホルモンです。産後、女性の体内のエストロゲンのレベルは劇的に低下します。新しい臨床研究は、出産後に追加のエストロゲンを受けた女性は、そうでない女性よりも短期間で産後のうつから回復することを示しています。では、臨床実験被験者が腕に包帯のように着ける実験用スキンパッチを配ります。このシールはゆっくりとエストロゲンを体内に導き入れ、長期のうつの確率を減らします。

39. このトークは誰に向けられているか？
- (A) 妊婦
- (B) 看護婦
- (C) 医学生
- (D) 小さな子どもと一緒の親

40. 話者によると、女性の何パーセントが産後、長期のうつ状態に陥るか？
- (A) 1パーセント
- (B) 10パーセント
- (C) 20パーセント
- (D) 80パーセント

41. 出産後、女性の体内のエストロゲンはどうなるか？
- (A) 劇的に増加する。
- (B) 出産以前よりも高く留まる。
- (C) 完全に消える。
- (D) 大幅に減る。

42. 話者は次に何をするか？
- (A) 新しい医療器具を配る
- (B) エストロゲンを説明する図を表示する
- (C) 産後うつの原因を分析する
- (D) 実験のためにボランティアを募る

Practice Test 3

Questions 43-46

穴居人に関する次の講義を聞きなさい。

　ネバダ州立博物館へようこそ。あれこれ見て回ったり、さまざまな遺物を見たりして楽しい時を過ごされたことでしょう。今から皆さんに簡潔にお話ししたいのは、私たちの最も重要な収蔵品、"スピリット穴居人"についてです。このミイラは1940年にある洞窟内で発見されました。当時、これは約2000年前のものと思われました。しかし、年代特定技術の進化が――特に放射性炭素による年代測定技術が――これら人工遺物の元々の年代推定を完全に翻しました。現在は、スピリット穴居人が2000年前ではなく約9400年前に生きていたことが明らかとなっています。このミイラの古さと見事な保存状態が、最後の氷河期が終わる頃に北米にいた人類の祖先にとって生活がどのようなものであったか、私たちに完全に異なる概念を与えてくれています。こちらはこれまで私たちにわかってきた絵のほんの一部です。スピリット穴居人は、死んだ際にモカシンを履いていました――つまり、当時の人々に動物の皮をなめし、それを履物に利用する能力があったことがわかります。また、彼が包まれていた布は、沼地の植物の繊維から作られたもので、とても見事に織られていることから、彼の部族が布を織るのにはた織り機を使っていたことは明らかです。このことは、誰もが考えていたよりもずっと早く、この大陸にはた織り技術が登場していたことを示しています。最後に、このミイラの胃から魚の骨と野菜が発見されています。つまり、穴居人の日常の飲食物に関して確固たる結論を導くことはできないものの、どうやら彼は野菜と魚ほどは肉を食べなかったように見えます。

43. この講義をしているのは誰と思われるか？
(A) 教授
(B) 文化人類学の学生
(C) 博物館の従業員
(D) 地質学者

44. スピリット穴居人について最近どんな重要な発見がなされたか？
(A) 彼は以前に考えられていたよりもはるかに古い。
(B) 彼はおそらく熟達した漁師だ。
(C) 彼は大きなコミュニティーに住んでいた。
(D) 彼はやりを使って動物を狩った。

45. ミイラと一緒に発見された布は、北米人の祖先について何を示唆しているか？
(A) 彼らは編む技術に長けていた。
(B) 彼らは布を作るために植物を育てた。
(C) 彼らは温かくしておくために動物の毛皮を着ていた。
(D) 彼らは色染めに関心があった。

46. 穴居人の胃の中から何が見つかったか？
(A) 動物の皮
(B) 野生の液果
(C) 魚の骨
(D) 薬用植物

辞書に関する次の講義を聞きなさい。

　今日の４年生向けセミナーを始めるにあたり、数分間かけて言語の聖書について話したいと思います。つまり、もちろん、辞書のことです。アメリカ革命とその直後の時期は、税金と民主政治にとってだけ重要なのではなく、言語にとっても重要だったと知る人はほとんどいません。特に共和国の初期、言葉とその使用はまさに民衆の議論の的でした。理由は主に、アメリカが移民の国だったこと、従っていわば国が言語的に不安定だったことです。辞書を通じて、アメリカ人は適切な使用法と正しさの指針を求めました。反対に、イングランドでは、辞書の制作は常にエリート主義者の活動だと見なされていました。人々は権威ある指針としてではなく、言語の付属物として辞書を研究しました。従ってアメリカ人は唯一の辞書を、イギリス人は数ある辞書の内の一冊を考えているのです。アメリカの扱い方は規範主義的で、どのように言葉が使われるべきかを強調しています。イギリスの扱い方は常に記述的な傾向があり、どのように言葉が使われているかを強調しています。

　近年、そうした扱い方の違いは消えつつあります。その主な理由は、英語に含まれる言葉の純然たる数です。約400万語あるのです。しかし、最大の辞書にもわずか50万語しか含まれていません。その結果、辞書の制作者と出版社はますます規範主義的かつ権威ある辞書という概念をあきらめるようになっているのです。

47. この講義の聞き手としてあり得るのは？
(A) 出版社
(B) 学生
(C) 英語の教師
(D) 本を売る人

48. 話者は辞書を何にたとえているか？
(A) 百科事典
(B) アメリカ合衆国憲法
(C) 歴史書
(D) 聖書

49. アメリカ人が英語の用法や正しさにこだわった理由は何か？
(A) 彼らはイギリス人とは違うアイデンティティーを形成したかった。
(B) 多くは言語に関し不安のある移民だった。
(C) 彼らは言語とその用法に関しエリート的な見方をしていた。
(D) 大半の人たちは基礎教育を身に付けたいと思っていた。

50. アメリカ式の伝統的な辞書の使い方はイギリス式とどう違うか？
(A) より洗練されている。
(B) より説明的だ。
(C) より学問的だ。
(D) より規範的だ。

Practice Test 3

Section 2 Structure and Written Expression 対訳
■ Structure

1. 自身の詩の中で、ロバート・ハスは彼がアメリカの生活の精神的堕落と見なしているものに取り組んでいる。

2. プラスチックはさまざまな種類の石油から作ることができる。

3. 豆と米は、（人が）一緒に食べた場合、1日のタンパク質の最低摂取量の大半を満たす。

4. 内戦の後、連邦政府は公有地を供与した大学の設立を通じて、高等教育の発展を奨励した。

5. 優れた暗視能力を使い、フクロウは夕暮れから夜明けまでの夜の時間帯に獲物を狩る。

6. 気圧計の低下は一般的に間もなく悪天候になることを示している。

7. ミシシッピー渓谷における考古学的発掘物が、その地域に数千年にわたりネイティブ・アメリカンが居住していた証拠を提供した。

8. スポーツトレーナーは、心臓血管の状態を向上させる正確な活動レベルを推測するための、高度に科学的な基礎を開発した。

9. 多くの彗星は、惑星のように太陽の周囲を楕円軌道で周回する。

10. アーネスト・ヘミングウェイの『老人と海』は、最初に雑誌の『ライフ』に掲載され、大きな商業的成功を収めた。

11. しばしば野菜と思われているものの、トマトは植物学的に果物と見なされる。

12. 鋼の弾性は、その金属構成と鍛造されたときにさらされた熱に左右される。

13. 銀行小切手には、その金銭的価値が文字と数字の両方で記されていなければならない。

14. 正確さを重視する姿勢は、競争力が高い機械エンジニアに求められる基本的資質のひとつだ。

15. 冬眠の後、クマが完全に目覚めるには数日かかる。

■ Written Expression

16. アメリカ南西部に多数存在するマウンテン・クーガーは、獲物を襲うために速さと見つかりにくさを利用する。

17. 一般的なアレルギーの根本原因として、花粉、塵、煙、汚染がある。

18. 土の酸性度は植生と降雨に影響され、地域によって大きな違いがあり得る。

19. 選挙では僅差だったにもかかわらず、ジョン・F・ケネディは最も敬服されたアメリカ大統領のひとりとなった。

20. 水素は、水の分子を構成する2つの水素原子からひとつの酸素原子を分離することによって、簡単に生成できる。

21. 大きさと解剖学的構造は、ある種を別の種と比較する際に用いられる2つの基準である。

22. 1960年代のグレート・ソサエティ・プログラムは、アメリカ全土の主要都市の都市再開発のための資金を提供した。

23. 男性と女性の社会における行動の違いは、文化だけではなく生態にも依存している。

24. 最大の厚みの北極の氷は北極点に近く、そこでは年間を通じて気温が低いままである。

25. 無重力の真空で動く物体は、最初の加速度を永遠に維持する。

26. アメリカ人のフォーク歌手、ピート・シーガーは50年を超える間、ポップスの書き手であり、また社会活動家だった。

27. アメリカの都市部の大半には、元々製造業や農業の基盤があった。

28. 形式推論の2つの基本形式は、演繹的論理学と帰納的論理学である。

29. 他の金属よりも軽いアルミニウムは、住宅の羽目板と屋根ふき材料に広く使われている。

30. シリコン製ウェハースは、コンピューターの集積回路製作に使われているハイテク合成物である。

31. 休暇という概念そのものは、かなり多くの裕福な中産階級の登場の後に生じた。

32. 連邦捜査局は、深刻な連邦犯罪を捜査し、また地域の警察官たちを援助するために組織された。

33. 現在のプラスチックを使えば、金属製のものよりも軽く、強固に、かつ耐久性のある車体が作られる。

34. 原子力潜水艦製造のための最も重要な場所は、コネチカット州グロトンにある造船所だ。

35. 不公平なビジネス手法への手強い反対者、イーダ・ターベルは、スタンダード・オイル社の批判記事を書き、その勇気を示した。

36. アリゲーターはクロコダイルと体の構造が同じだが、ただし、頭部がより幅広く、鼻がより丸まっている。

37. 多くの心理学者が、子どもたちの食事に対する過度のコントロールは彼らが後に摂食障害に苦しむ原因になると論じている。

38. ネイティブ・アメリカンの間でその耳に残る鳴き声が伝説になった鳥、ルーン（アビ）は、北アメリカ北部各地にある湖で見られる。

39. パイプのU字型の部分は、物が詰まるのを防ぐだけではなく、配管の修理をより簡単にしている。

40. 超越瞑想法は――そのリラックスの技術はストレスを大きく減らすことがわかっている――1960年代に初めて脚光を浴びた。

Section 3 Reading Comprehension 対訳
■ Questions 1-10

　バクテリアは生物の中で最小のものに数えられ、それらを特定するのは往々にして困難である。分類に用いられる情報の種類には、大きさ、形状、外見、バクテリア集団の構造、増殖する際に起こる化学変化がある。特定されたバクテリアの多くの種はほとんど研究されてなく、しかも数百もの別の種が発見されるのを待っているのだ。

　一般的にバクテリアは病気の原因と思われているが、実際のところ、それらは地球上の生命にとって不可欠なものだ。土、空気、それに水までもが、ある程度はバクテリアによって「生成」されている。実際ある、バクテリアは多くの場合、人間や動物と同じビタミンを使うため、実験室において貴重な助けとなっている。例えば、ある溶液内のビタミンの量は、注意深く統制された条件の下、ある種のバクテリアの増殖量を観察して測定することが可能だ。多くの例では、数週間と数百の動物を要することが、成長していくバクテリアを入れたほんの数十本の試験管で数日のうちに測定できる。

　バクテリアを育てるには"培養基"を使わなければならない。これは通常、液状で用意された食べ物だ。バクテリアは培養基の表面で育ち、やがて顕微鏡でも容易に観察できるバクテリア群体へと広がっていく。バクテリア群体に供給される食べ物はその種類によってさまざまだ。あるバクテリアは粉状の硫黄やその他の無機物の上で最もよく育つ。別の種は砂糖、アミノ酸、あるいはビタミンで繁殖する。バクテリアを培養する食べ物の種類には実質、際限がない。

1. この文章からバクテリアの研究が困難な理由は次のどれだと推測できるか？
   - (A) ゆっくり成長する
   - (B) 小さい
   - (C) 危険だ
   - (D) 簡単に死ぬ

2. 第1段落によれば、バクテリアについて正しいのは何か？
   - (A) 人間の病気の主原因である。
   - (B) 未発見の数多くのタイプがある。
   - (C) 繁殖しないいくつかのタイプがある。
   - (D) 土の主たる構成物質である。

3. 筆者が、バクテリアを分類する方法として述べていないのは
   - (A) その大きさと形状
   - (B) その化学構成
   - (C) その集団の構造
   - (D) 生息している場所

4. 4行目"undergo"に最も意味が近いのは
   - (A) ～を体験する
   - (B) ～に抵抗する
   - (C) ～を引き起こす
   - (D) ～を必要とする

5. 科学者はビタミンのような化学物質の分析にバクテリアを使うことがあるが、その際、何を観察するか？
   - (A) バクテリアの増殖率
   - (B) 出現するバクテリアの種類
   - (C) バクテリアが作る群体の形状
   - (D) バクテリアが生き残る時間の長さ

6. 11行目"given"に最も意味が近いのは
   - (A) 受け取った
   - (B) 測定された
   - (C) ある特定の
   - (D) 甘い

7. 第2段落で筆者が主に議論しているの
は次のどれか？
    (A) どのようにしてバクテリアが病気
を引き起こすか
    (B) バクテリアが最もよく繁殖する場
所
    (C) バクテリアが人間にとって重要な
理由
    (D) バクテリアが実験室でどのように
利用されるか

8. なぜバクテリアは実験室の科学者たち
にとって大きな関心の対象なのか？
    (A) バクテリアは、しばしば、増殖す
る際に突然変異する。
    (B) バクテリアはよく人間が使うもの
に似たビタミンを使う。
    (C) バクテリアは後の研究のために容
易に保存できる。
    (D) バクテリアは研究室の環境にすぐ
に適応する。

9. 15行目"culture medium"が引用符に
入れられた理由は
    (A) 直接引用されている
    (B) 特別に強調されている
    (C) 特別に定義されている
    (D) 反語的に使われている

10. バクテリアが消費する食べ物について
正しいのは次のどれか？
    (A) ほぼあらゆる種類の食べ物が、バ
クテリアの繁殖を可能にする。
    (B) ほとんどのバクテリアは無機物を
好む。
    (C) 培養基は液体でなければならな
い。
    (D) バクテリアは種類が異なれば、異
なる培養基が必要になる。

■ Questions 11-21

　債務に関する懸念は今日でも存在しているのだが（賢明なことだ）、国債の発行は植民地時
代ですら政府の慣行となっていた。南部の植民地——メリーランド州、バージニア州、当時"
カロライナ"と呼ばれていた場所——は、タバコの価値を自分たちの貨幣の基準にしており、
支払い手段として金または銀を要求することを大いに非難していた。場合によっては、彼らは
貨幣交換の手段として貴金属を使うことを禁じたりもした。メリーランド州では、タバコを基
準にした紙幣がほぼ2世紀にわたり通貨の役目を担った。これは金塊をドルの基準として実施
していた期間をはるかに上回る長さだ。
　それでもなお、銀と金を筆頭とする貴金属には魅力があった。1690年、サー・ウイリア
ム・フィップスは非正規軍の遠征隊を、マサチューセッツ・ベイ・コロニーから現在のカナダ
にあるケベック砦まで率いた。その遠征の費用の支払いには、砦からぶん取る金を使うつもり
だった。だが彼らが落胆し驚いたことに、砦は陥落せず、また隊が戻った時には植民地の金庫
にはそれらを支払うための——金貨も銀貨も——硬貨がまったくなかった。その後、最終的に
金または銀の支払いを約束する紙の手形を発行することは、当時の植民地政府にとって小さな
一歩のように思えた。それから20年後、その紙幣は約束の根拠である金属と並んで流通して
いた。この場合、マサチューセッツ州の紙手形での債務額は、仮に一度に全ての紙幣が換金さ
れた場合に手に入る量よりも少ない固形資産（つまり硬貨）の下支えしかなかった。
　紙幣の不思議はすぐに他の植民地に広まり、紙幣は大量に——実際は気ままに——発行され

た。例えばロードアイランド州は裏付けのない貨幣を大量に発行した。そこでも、他の場所と同様に、いずれやって来る清算日には、紙幣はある日、無価値になることとなる。この歴史から得られる教訓は、国債は常に使用禁止にされるべきだということではない——結局のところ、独立戦争時のワシントン軍には紙幣で払われた——そうではなく、国債は常に損失や債務不履行のリスクを伴うということなのだ。

11. この文章の主題は何か？
- (A) 現金に使用されたタバコ
- (B) 金と銀の価値
- (C) 植民地における国債の利用
- (D) お金の起源

12. 第1段落で筆者がタバコを基準とする貨幣と比較しているのは
- (A) 金に基づく貨幣
- (B) 南部の植民地におけるお金
- (C) 開拓移民に使われた銀
- (D) 払い戻しの政府の約束

13. 筆者によれば南部の植民地は、時おり
- (A) 紙幣ではなくタバコを交換していた
- (B) 貨幣として銀と金の使用を禁じた
- (C) 国債手形への支払いを拒否した
- (D) 大量の貴金属を収集した

14. 4行目"deplored"に最も意味が近いのは
- (A) 妬んだ
- (B) 招待した
- (C) 受け入れた
- (D) 思いとどまらせた

15. 9行目"their"が指しているのは
- (A) ドル紙幣
- (B) 希少金属
- (C) 銀と金
- (D) 非正規軍兵士

16. 筆者は何の事例を示すためにサー・ウイリアム・フィップスの探検を取り上げたのか？
- (A) 植民地時代の愚かな軍事的試み
- (B) 初期の開拓移民の戦争参加への積極性
- (C) 初期政府の金への依存
- (D) 植民地がどのようにして紙幣発行を強要されたか

17. 16行目"eventual"に最も意味が近いのは
- (A) 完全な
- (B) 素早い
- (C) 後の
- (D) 信頼できる

18. おそらく筆者は次の意見のどれに最も同意しそうか。
- (A) 政府はどんな犠牲を払っても借金を避けるべきだ。
- (B) 借金の概念は正確に定義するのが難しい。
- (C) 借金を作ることは潜在的リスクがある。
- (D) あらゆる借金は何らかの具体的な資産により保証されるべきだ。

19. 22行目"with abandon"に最も意味が近いのは
- (A) 多くの
- (B) 無節操に
- (C) こっそりと
- (D) 定期的に

20. 最後の段落で筆者が暗に示しているのは
- (A) 多くの植民地が紙幣の使用をあきらめた
- (B) 金が最終的に貨幣の共通の形態になった
- (C) 時々、紙幣はその価値を完全に失った
- (D) 多くの植民地がロードアイランドの成功を実現しようと試みた

21. 筆者はおそらく次のどの意見に同意するか？
- (A) 債務は潜在的に危険だ。
- (B) 債務の概念は定義が困難だ。
- (C) 債務は是が非でも避けるべきだ。
- (D) あらゆる債務は具体的な資産により裏付けされるべきだ。

■ Questions 22-30

　アメリカの南北戦争の時、侵略者たちはミズーリ州南西部を一掃し、モーゼズ・カーヴァーの農場から奴隷の母親とその赤ん坊を奪った。モーゼズ・カーヴァーはその赤ん坊を300ドルの競走馬と交換して取り戻すことができたが、しかし、その子の母親はついに返されなかった。カーヴァーは母のない子に自分の家族の名である"カーヴァー"と、初代アメリカ大統領ジョージ・ワシントンの名を与えた。

　若きジョージ・ワシントン・カーヴァーは暑い平原で仕事ができるほど強くも屈強でもなかったが、家事はしっかりやった。さらに、庭での彼は、植物を育てる才能に恵まれているように見えた。やがて彼は教育を受けるためにカーヴァー家を去り、料理をしたり衣類を洗ったり雑多な仕事をしながらカンザス州で高校を終えた。高校を卒業しても彼は勉学をやめず、自分で働いて学費を稼いで大学に通い、そして農業学校に通い、1896年にアイオワ州立農業・機械工学大学から学位と修士号を受け取った。

　カーヴァーの植物の実験室と畑における業績のおかげで、彼はアラバマ州にあるタスキーギー・インスティチュートの創設者、ブッカー・T・ワシントンの目にとまることとなった。カーヴァーは1896年にタスキーギーの農学部長となる。そこでの47年間に、偉大な植物科学者として彼は科学的農業と農産化学（植物原料製品の産業利用）において顕著な業績を残した。彼はピーナツとサツマイモだけを原料に、数多くの役に立つ製品を作った。

22. この文章の主題は何か？
- (A) ジョージ・ワシントン・カーヴァーの科学的業績
- (B) ジョージ・ワシントン・カーヴァーのつつましい少年時代
- (C) ジョージ・ワシントン・カーヴァーの生涯
- (D) ジョージ・ワシントン・カーヴァーの成功への苦難

23. この文章によれば、モーゼズ・カーヴァーが赤ん坊のジョージ・ワシントン・カーヴァーを手に入れたのは
- (A) 300ドル支払って
- (B) 馬と交換して
- (C) 少年の母親を手放して
- (D) 良い父親になると約束して

24. 2行目"seized"に最も意味が近いのは
    (A) 救出した
    (B) さらった
    (C) 購入した
    (D) 襲撃した

25. 6行目"robust"に最も意味が近いのは
    (A) やる気がある
    (B) 従順な
    (C) 大きい
    (D) 健康な

26. この文章によれば、ジョージ・ワシントン・カーヴァーは、どのようにして高校時代に生計を立てたか？
    (A) 彼は植物を育て、畑で働いた。
    (B) 彼はモーゼズ・カーヴァーから援助してもらった。
    (C) 彼はちょっとした仕事をいろいろやった。
    (D) 彼は家々を掃除した。

27. この文章によれば、ジョージ・ワシントン・カーヴァーはどこの大学に通ったか？
    (A) ミズーリ州
    (B) アイオワ州
    (C) アラバマ州
    (D) カンザス州

28. 17行目"there"が指しているのは
    (A) 畑で
    (B) アラバマ
    (C) タスキーギーの農学部
    (D) 科学的農業

29. 17行目"notable"に最も意味が近いのは
    (A) 最初の
    (B) 重要な
    (C) 受賞した
    (D) 必要な

30. この文章からジョージ・ワシントン・カーヴァーについて何が結論付けられるか？
    (A) 自分の母親を知らなかった
    (B) モーゼズ家から粗末に扱われた
    (C) 素晴らしい教師だった
    (D) 独学で読み方を学んだ

■ Questions 31-40

　おとぎ話はまず子ども向けに作られ、そして主として子どもの領域のものだと一般的にみなされてきた。だが、真実からこれほどかけ離れたものはない。

　正に最初から、数千年も前から自然の強大な力に直面して共同体の繋がりを作るためにおとぎ話が語られた時代から、現在に至るまで、破局寸前のように見える世界に希望を提供すべくおとぎ話が書かれ、語られる時に至るまで、成熟した男性と女性はおとぎ話伝承の創造者であり養成者であった。おとぎ話が紹介されると、子どもたちはそれを歓迎するが、その主な理由はそれらが変化と独立への大いなる欲求を育んでくれるからだ。概して、西洋文学のおとぎ話はいつもの時代にも通じる西洋文明が進む中で確立されたひとつのジャンルになっている。数多くの批評家とシャーマン（呪術師）が、普遍的な典型を求める霊的探求もしくは宗教を通じて世界を救済する必要性のゆえに、おとぎ話を神秘化したり誤解したりしてきたが、口承ある

いは文学の形でのおとぎ話はどちらも史実に根ざしたものだ。それらは、私たちの心やコミュニティーを具体的な形で恐れさせ、自由意志と人間の思いやりを破壊しようとする野蛮で粗野な力を教化するための、固有の苦闘から生じている。それゆえ、おとぎ話は、この具体的な恐れを、主に隠喩の使用を通じて克服しようとしている。

　最初の"文学的"おとぎ話がいつ考え出されたのかを特定するのは困難であり、また、おとぎ話が何なのかを正確に定義することは難しいものの、不思議と驚きの要素が入った口承民話が数千年前からあり、主に大人が大人に語ってきたことを私たちは知っている。そうした話のモチーフが人々に記憶され、口伝えで継承され、聖書や西洋の古典作品となったのだ。文学的なおとぎ話の発展の基礎の役目を果たした初期の口承民話は、種族やコミュニティーや仲間の儀式や信仰と密接に結びついていた。それらが所属意識を育んだのだ。おとぎ話は、人々を指導し、楽しませ、警告し、手ほどきし、啓発した。それらは共有され、交換されるものであり、文学的なお話とは違い、その後それらは話者と聞き手の必要に応じて生まれ、使われ、修正されたのだ。

31. この文章の主題は何か？
(A) 文学的な民話と口承の民話の違い
(B) おとぎ話の起源と目的
(C) おとぎ話に対する現代のニーズ
(D) おとぎ話の普遍的テーマ

32. 筆者によれば、おとぎ話に共通する誤解とは何か？
(A) それらは書かれる前は、口頭によるものだった。
(B) それは信頼性の低い歴史案内だ。
(C) それらは子ども向けだ。
(D) それらは世代から世代へ受け継がれた。

33. おとぎ話の目的として述べられていないのは次のどれか？
(A) 暗闇と自然の力への恐れを克服するため
(B) 共有する人間の絆を創造するため
(C) 物質世界の起源を説明するため
(D) 手ほどきし、楽しませるため

34. 4行目"communal"に最も意味が近いのは
(A) 社会の
(B) 価値ある
(C) きつい
(D) 個々の

35. 6行目"catastrophe"に最も意味が近いのは
(A) 絶望
(B) 突破
(C) 啓示
(D) 大惨事

36. 第3段落で筆者が示唆しているのは
(A) 最初のおとぎ話は書き留められた
(B) 初期のおとぎ話のいくつかは、聖書の中に見出せるかもしれない
(C) 最初期の民話のテーマは失われてしまった
(D) 民話の語り部はおとぎ話の意味を巡って言い争う

37. おとぎ話の議論の中で、筆者が17行目の"metaphor"に触れたのはなぜか？
    (A) それは大人と子どもに同じように容易に理解される。
    (B) それは恐怖を克服するために用いられる主要なツールである。
    (C) それは普通の言語よりも概念をより明白に伝達する。
    (D) それは西洋文明におけるコミュニケーションの主要な手段である。

38. 19行目"conceived"に最も意味が近いのは
    (A) 考案された
    (B) 話された
    (C) 目撃された
    (D) 記録された

39. 22行目"these"が指しているのは
    (A) 文学的なおとぎ話
    (B) 口承民話
    (C) 諸要素
    (D) 大人たち

40. 筆者が最も同意しそうな一文は次のどれか？
    (A) 民話は最初期の美術の形式である。
    (B) おとぎ話は宗教的説法に不可欠である。
    (C) おとぎ話は固有の人間の事情から生まれた。
    (D) 民話は大半がその意味と価値を失った。

■ Questions 41-50

　アメリカだけでも250万人が苦しむ酷い精神障害、統合失調症の科学的理解に関し、劇的な変化が起こりつつある。この病気の最初の兆候は通常20代後半に現れるが、しかし、神経学者たちは現在、この病気の根源は実は脳が形成され、最初の神経細胞が成長し分割する時期の胎児の成長過程で起こるのではないかと考えている。

　多くの統合失調症患者の脳内の基本的な不備は、脳が最初に形作られる際に、ある神経細胞が間違った部分に移動し、脳の小さな部位が永続的にずれてしまう、あるいは間違って接続されてしまうためのようなのだ。位置のずれた神経細胞が見つかるのは特に神経系のサブプレートにおいてだ。これは他のニューロンをそれぞれ適切な場所に案内する構造である。サブプレートは妊娠4カ月頃に形成され、その子どもが生まれると間もなく消滅する。こうした神経構造における間違いにはひとつ、あるいはそれ以上の原因があるかもしれず、今後の発見が待たれている。しかし、ひとつの推測として、脳の接続ミスは母親が妊娠初期にウイルスに感染した時に起こるのかもしれない。

　統合失調症の主な症状には無関心、感情の鈍化、妄想、そして内面の声が聞こえる症状などがある。ひとたびこれらが顕在化すると、その人は生涯にわたって症状が一進一退するのが普通だ。この病気の原因は長い間謎だった。かつては家庭内でのコミュニケーションの乏しさが原因とされたが、この症状は現在、脳の病気であると認知されている。統合失調症への見方が変わりつつあるその根拠は、脳から採取した組織サンプルの実験室における分析に根ざしている。最近のある研究によれば、例えば、脳の解剖から、統合失調症患者20人のうち7人で前頭葉部のニューロンの位置がずれていたのに対し、通常の人々20人の脳ではそれがゼロだったことが明らかになっている。

　統合失調症の新概念の擁護者にとって厄介な疑問は、もしも脳の異常が誕生時から存在しているのなら、なぜそれが20年もの間顕在化しないのかという点だ。あり得る答えのひとつに、統合失調症患者は人生の初期段階から実は将来の問題の徴候があるのだが、それらはたいてい見逃されているというものがある。

41. この文章は主に何を論じているか？
- (A) 統合失調症の症状
- (B) 統合失調症の治療法
- (C) 統合失調症の新理論
- (D) 統合失調症の発見

42. この文章によると統合失調症の徴候が最初に現れるのはいつか？
- (A) 生誕時
- (B) 生まれる前
- (C) 子ども時代
- (D) 成人期の初め

43. 第2段落で詳しく論じられているのは？
- (A) 正常な人間の脳の構造
- (B) 神経細胞を配置換えする脳の能力
- (C) 統合失調症の脳の発達
- (D) 脳の形成における遺伝の役割

44. 14行目"speculation"に最も意味が近いのは
- (A) 結論
- (B) 仮説
- (C) 議論
- (D) 絵

45. 17行目"these"が指しているのは
- (A) 症状
- (B) 妄想
- (C) 声
- (D) 起源

46. 統合失調症の症状として筆者が述べていないのは？
- (A) 幻聴
- (B) 無関心
- (C) 暴力的な衝動
- (D) 妄想

47. 第3段落で何を説明するために、筆者は研究実験に言及したのか？
- (A) 統合失調症の原因は謎
- (B) 統合失調症の被害者は家庭生活に問題がある
- (C) 統合失調症は身体的な病気
- (D) 健康な人もまた統合失調症にかかることがある

48. 18行目"wax and wane"と入れ替えるのに最適なのは？
- (A) 増減する
- (B) 進む
- (C) 悪化する
- (D) 現れ、消える

49. 25行目"proponents"に最も意味が近いのは
- (A) 反対者
- (B) 批判者
- (C) 援護者
- (D) 犠牲者

50. 次の主張のうち、最も本文に近いのは？
    (A) 適切な治療をすれば、統合失調症患者は生産的な生活を送ることができる。
    (B) 研究者は現在、統合失調症の本当の原因を理解している。
    (C) 統合失調症は将来さらに一般的になる可能性が高い。
    (D) 母親たちは、いつか統合失調症の原因となる病気を持っているかどうか調べられるかもしれない。

1. **女性**：キャシーは心理学と経営学の両方を専攻しているの？
   男性：以前はそうだった。でも、心理学はあきらめたって聞いたよ。
   質問：男性はキャシーについて何をほのめかしているか？
   (A) 彼女は新しいビジネスを始める予定だ。
   (B) 彼女は学位を2つ得られればと願っている。
   (C) 彼女はもう心理学は勉強していない。
   (D) 彼女は大学をあきらめた。

2. **男性**：少しお金を貸してくれないかな？
   女性：先週借りたお金はどうしたの？
   質問：この会話から何が推測できるか？
   (A) 女性はすでに男性にお金を貸していた。
   (B) 女性は今週末はいない。
   (C) 男性は女性にお返ししたい。
   (D) 男性は自分の家計に非常に慎重である。

3. **女性**：申し込んだ仕事に受かったことが、ちょうどわかったわ。
   男性：ほんと！ すごいじゃないか。
   質問：男性の発言はどういう意味か？
   (A) 女性はそれについて今話すべきではない。
   (B) 女性は別の仕事に応募すべきだ。
   (C) 彼はそれについて後で女性に話してもらいたい。
   (D) 彼は女性が話した内容について喜んでいる。

4. **女性**：どうも、ピーターソン博士。私を探していたというのは本当ですか？
   男性：そう。君のリポートに関してちょっと話したいことがある。
   質問：男性は何を望んでいるか？
   (A) 新聞を見ること。
   (B) その女性と話すこと。
   (C) 女性が用紙に書き込むのを手伝うこと。
   (D) 女性の辞書を借りること。

5. **女性**：スーザンが奨学金を失ったって聞いた？
   男性：そうか、彼女がもうひとつアルバイトを得たのがそれで説明がつく。
   質問：スーザンについて男性は何をほのめかしているか？
   (A) 彼女は学校を退学することに決めた。
   (B) 彼女は以前よりも働いている。
   (C) 彼女はあまり熱心な学生ではない。
   (D) 彼女は別の奨学金に応募する予定だ。

6. **男性**：男子寮の新たな改築工事はどうなっているかな？
   女性：報告することは何もないわ。スタートしてもいないのよ。
   質問：女性の発言はどういう意味か？
   (A) 改築工事はまだ始まっていない。
   (B) 彼女は報告書を読んでいなかった。
   (C) その寮はまだ建設されていない。
   (D) 彼女は1階に引っ越した。

7. **女性**：学生レクリエーションセンターが日曜日何時に開くか知ってる？
   男性：1時だろ？
   質問：男性の発言はどういう意味か？
   (A) 学生レクリエーションセンターはひとつしかない。
   (B) 彼は質問する相手としてふさわ

しくない。
(C) センターはおそらく1時に開く。
(D) 日曜日に開いている娯楽センターはこれだけだ。

8. 女性：計画を進めて専攻を変えて幸せ？
   男性：幸せって？　有頂天さ！
   質問：男性の発言はどういう意味か？
   (A) 彼は講座のリーディングで先を行っている。
   (B) 彼は自分の決断に満足している。
   (C) 彼は自分の専攻を変えなかった。
   (D) 彼は自分がやったことを後悔している。

9. 女性：この冷蔵庫を私の部屋まで運ぶの手伝ってくれる？
   男性：メアリー、寮内で個人用冷蔵庫を使うのはルール違反だって知っているだろ？
   質問：男性は何をほのめかしているか？
   (A) 彼は喜んでその女性に手を貸すだろう。
   (B) 男性は女性寮に入れない。
   (C) 女性は居住規則に従うべきだ。
   (D) その冷蔵庫は重すぎて運べない。

10. 男性：ポケットとアパートのあらゆる場所を探したんだけれど、車の鍵が見つからないんだ。
    女性：車の中に置き忘れてないのは確かなの？
    質問：女性は何をほのめかしているか？
    (A) 男性はもう1度ポケットを調べるべきだ。
    (B) あの場所に駐車すべきでない。
    (C) 男性は車内に鍵を忘れた。
    (D) 彼女は男性の探し物を見つけるのを手伝うだろう。

11. 女性：ラルフ、今度の日曜日、ピクニックはどう？
    男性：ありがとう。残念だけど、それはこの週末には入れられないよ。
    質問：男性は何をほのめかしているか？
    (A) 彼はちょっと忙しい。
    (B) 彼はピクニックのことは忘れた。
    (C) 彼はその女性の招待を受け入れるだろう。
    (D) 彼は今週末は町にいない。

12. 男性：君の化学の授業には実験実習がたくさんあるみたいだね。
    女性：まったくよ。週に3回って信じられる？
    質問：女性は何をほのめかしているか？
    (A) その男性は彼女が化学実験室を持っているとは信じていない。
    (B) 彼女はすでにそのコースについてその男性に話した。
    (C) 彼女は化学のことは気にしていない。
    (D) 彼女の授業には多くの実験が求められている。

13. 男性：本当に遅れてる。もうちょっと速く運転できない？
    女性：この霧じゃあ無理。急がば回れよ。
    質問：女性の発言はどういう意味か？
    (A) 彼女はかなり注意深く運転し続けるだろう。
    (B) 彼らはそれでも時間までに到着するだろう。
    (C) 彼女はその男性に運転してもらいたい。
    (D) 天候は間もなく良くなるだろう。

14. 男性：ジャックがまだ具合よくないって本当？

女性：あんまりね。まだ熱があるわ。

質問：ジャックについて何が推測できるか？

(A) 彼はまだかなり腹を立てている。
(B) 彼は熱が出ている。
(C) 彼は最近仕事に行っていない。
(D) 彼はとても気分が良くなっている。

15. **女性**：ねえ、今日はあなたが掃除機をかけてくれない？　そうすれば私は勉強できるから。

男性：正直言ってね、デビー、君はどんな言い訳を使ってでも家事をさぼりたいんだろう。

質問：女性について、男性は何をほのめかしているか？

(A) 彼女はあまり家の周りの手伝いをしない。
(B) 彼女はあまりに周囲がうるさい時は勉強できない。
(C) 彼女は掃除機を修理してもらう必要がある。
(D) 彼女はその日の遅くに勉強できる。

16. **男性**：あれはたぶん僕がここで取った中で最悪の食事だった。

女性：私も同感。料理人を替えたか、いつものシェフの調子が本当に悪い日だったかどちらかね！

質問：女性の発言はどういう意味か？

(A) 彼女は一緒にそこに行くことに同意している。
(B) 彼女は普段、別のレストランで食事する。
(C) 彼女はその男性と意見を共有している。
(D) 彼女はいつものシェフは下手なコックだと思っている。

17. **女性**：この前貸したCD気に入った？

男性：気に入ってるかって？　出掛けて、あのアーティストが今まで出した全てのアルバムを買ったよ。

質問：男性の発言はどういう意味か？

(A) CDは全て売り切れていた。
(B) 彼はそのアーティストのファンになった。
(C) 彼は音楽を生で聞くのが好きだ。
(D) そのアーティストは新作を発表していない。

18. **男性**：この熱波、信じられる？

女性：ええ、温度があまりに高くて、歩道で目玉焼きができそうね。

質問：女性は何をほのめかしているか？

(A) 彼らはヒーターの温度を上げるべきだ。
(B) 今は朝食を食べる時間だ。
(C) 外はとても暑い。
(D) その男性はフライパンを確認するべきだ。

19. **女性**：あなたの講義ノートを見てもいいかしら？

男性：持っていればね。ティムに貸してあげたんだ。

質問：男性の講義ノートについて何が推測できるか？

(A) その女性はそれらを返すべきだ。
(B) 彼はそれらを見つけられないようだ。
(C) ティムのノートは彼のよりも良い。
(D) 別の生徒が今それらを使っている。

20. **女性**：ちょっと聞いてよ。結局、リチャードソン博士の心理学339のクラスが取れることになったの。

男性：せいぜい頑張って！　今学期の君は、あまり人と付き合えなくなるね。

質問：女性について、男性は何をほのめかしているか？
(A) その授業を取ることができて、彼女は幸運だ。
(B) 彼女は専攻を変えることを考えるべきだ。
(C) 彼女は並外れて難しいコースに入った。
(D) 彼女はもっと多くの人たちに会うようがんばるべきだ。

21. 男性：夕食には何がいい？　僕のおごりだ。

女性：あなたのおごり？　信じられないわ。宝くじか何か当たったの？

質問：男性について、女性は何をほのめかしているか？
(A) 彼は最近多額のお金を相続した。
(B) 彼は通常夕食代を払うとは申し出ない。
(C) 彼は彼女にあまり夕食を作らない。
(D) 彼は宝くじに多額のお金を使い過ぎている。

22. 女性：ねえ、私はあなたの母親じゃないけど、でも、その咳、本当に誰かに診てもらったほうがいいわ。

男性：ああ、君の言う通りかも。

質問：男性が最もやりそうなことは何か？
(A) 家にいて休む
(B) 彼の母に手紙を書く
(C) 彼の家族を訪問する
(D) 病院に行く

23. 女性：ベイリー教授が英語で私を落と

すと言ったのよ。ただ締め切りの2分後にエッセーを提出しただけでよ。

男性：彼女は、そんなことをして許されるべきではない！

質問：男性は何をほのめかしているか？
(A) その教授は不合理である。
(B) その女性はもっと時間を守るべきだった。
(C) その教授は締め切りを明言しなかった。
(D) その女性は実際にはその授業に落第はしないだろう。

24. 男性：どうしたんだい、アリス？　まるで親友を失ったような顔をして。

女性：論文を書くのにコンピューターを使っていて、書いたもの全てを誤って消してしまったのよ。

質問：女性が抱えている問題は何か？
(A) 彼女は友人とケンカした。
(B) 彼女のコンピューターは修理してもらう必要がある。
(C) 彼女は取り組んでいたファイルを失った。
(D) 彼女は論文のためのテーマを決められない。

25. 女性：この車の中にいて、（暑くて）うだってるわ。エアコンつけてくれる？

男性：いいとも。君には少し暑いんだね？

質問：おそらく男性は何をするか？
(A) エアコンをつける
(B) 車を点検に出す
(C) 車から出て歩く
(D) 窓を下げる

26. 男性：じゃあね、ジェーン。君に話し

たあの仕事の面接に行ってくる。
女性：そのネクタイでは行かないわよ
　　　ね。
質問：女性は何をほのめかしている
　　　か？
　(A) その男性はそれほどフォーマル
　　　な服装をする必要はない。
　(B) その男性の面接は今日ではない。
　(C) その男性は別のネクタイをする
　　　べきだ。
　(D) その男性はもっと良い仕事を見
　　　つけられた。

27. 女性：演劇部の秋の公演は本当に楽し
　　　　　かった。
　　男性：じゃあ見に行ったんだ、結局。
　　質問：男性はどう思い込んでいたか？
　　(A) その女性は劇を見に行かなかっ
　　　　た。
　　(B) その女性は演劇のクラスに遅刻
　　　　した。
　　(C) その部門の生産率が落ちた。
　　(D) 劇場の建築が予定より遅れてい
　　　　る。

28. 女性：私、メキシコ料理には目がない
　　　　　の。
　　男性：知ってるよ。だから君をここへ
　　　　　連れてきたんだ。
　　質問：この会話から男性と女性につい
　　　　　て何が推測できるか？
　　(A) 彼らはお互いに対し怒っている。
　　(B) 彼らはこれまで一度もこの場所
　　　　を訪れたことがない。
　　(C) 彼らはメキシコで休暇中だ。
　　(D) 彼らはレストランで食事中だ。

29. 男性：夏の終わりの山へのキャンプ旅
　　　　　行はどうだった？
　　女性：私たちがそこにいた間、毎日雪
　　　　　が降ったなんて信じられる？
　　質問：女性は何をほのめかしている

か？
　(A) 彼女はキャンプ旅行をキャンセ
　　　ルした。
　(B) 彼女が予想していたよりもかな
　　　り寒かった。
　(C) 彼女はキャンプよりスキーが好
　　　きだ。
　(D) その男性は彼らが本当に行った
　　　とは信じていない。

30. 女性：あれは私が今まで参加した中で
　　　　　最高の講演会だったわ。
　　男性：まったく同感だね。
　　質問：男性の発言はどういう意味か？
　　(A) 彼はその女性に同意していない。
　　(B) 彼はその講義に出席できないだ
　　　　ろう。
　　(C) 彼は彼らがもっと長く滞在して
　　　　くれたらと願った。
　　(D) 彼もまたその講義を楽しんだ。

■ Part B

学生選挙に関する次の会話を聞きなさい。

女性：学生自治会長に立候補するのでとてもワクワクしているの。

男性：わかるよ。でもやるべきことがたくさんあるよね、サリー。選挙活動には膨大な時間と労力がかかる。それに選挙戦の計画が必要だ。

女性：宣伝をして私の意見を広く知らしめる一番いい方法は何だと思う？

男性：まず、その2つは別個のことだと思う。学校新聞に広告を載せられるけど、でも、そこには考えを伝えるほど広いスペースはない。だから投票者と触れ合うための何らかの方法を考える必要があるね。

女性：もしかしたら大学のラジオ局で短いトークができるかも。ラジオ局長はいつもプログラムを求めているから。

男性：いい考えだ。それから選挙の前の週にカフェテリアの前にブースを置けるね。誰もがそこを通り過ぎなければならないだろうからね。

女性：その通りね。人と話すなら夕食後がいいわ。みんなあまり急いでいないから。そうするとやれることとして、学生新聞への広告、ラジオでのトーク、カフェテリアの外のブース、があるわね。注目を浴びるために何か他の方法はある？

男性：いくつかポスターを掲げる必要もあるね。たぶん、それの最適な場所は寮と学生会館の中だろう。それなら今晩にも始められるよ。

女性：わかったわ。私が紙を取ってくるから、大まかな下書きを描きましょう。

31. 女性が立候補しようとしているポジションは？
    (A) ディベートチームのキャプテン
    (B) 生徒代表
    (C) 学生自治会長
    (D) ラジオ局のディレクター

32. この男性と女性はどこに広告を載せようと計画しているか？
    (A) 大学ラジオで
    (B) カフェテリアで
    (C) 学生新聞で
    (D) 大学のテレビ局で

33. 女性はいつカフェテリアの外で学生たちに話をするか？
    (A) 朝食の前に
    (B) 昼食で
    (C) 午後の間に
    (D) 夕食の後に

34. この男性と女性はこの後どうするか？
    (A) 予算を立てる
    (B) ポスターを描く
    (C) 学生会館に立ち寄る
    (D) ラジオ局に電話する

Questions 35-38

学生寮に関する次の会話を聞きなさい。

男性：学生寮の主任とお話ししたいのですが。

女性：私が学生寮の主任です。私の名前はスタントンです。どんな用件ですか？

男性：私の名前はエドワード・ジョーンズです。この秋の新入生です。それで、大学の寮について少し情報が欲しいのですが。

女性：わかりました。この大学には4つの寮があります。1つは女子学生専用で、フランクリンホールです。1つは男子学生専用で、これはモリスホールです。寮の1つ、フェンネルホールは留学生のために用意されています。そして私たちの寮の1つは男女共用で、それがクーパーホールです。

男性：わかりました。クーパーホールについて教えてくださいますか？

女性：残念ですが、あの寮は上級生専用です。あそこに住むには、少なくとも2年生でなければなりません。

男性：では、モリスホールについて教えてくださいますか？

女性：モリスホールには特別規約があります。新入生は全員が3人部屋に入ります。上級生は2人部屋で暮らします。

男性：門限はありますか？

女性：いいえ、門限はありません。でも、深夜0時から午前8時までは静かにしておく時間です。この間、他の学生の迷惑にならないよう、ステレオは静かにかけなければなりません。

男性：どうやって申し込むのでしょう？

女性：住居申込用紙を送るだけでいいのです。ただし、あなたはすぐにそうすべきですね。この秋の学期にむけて寮はほぼ満員です。もし、申し込みが遅過ぎたら、大学敷地外の住居を探さないといけません。

35. 誰がクーパーホールに住んでいるか？
    (A) 女子学生だけ
    (B) 男子学生だけ
    (C) 留学生だけ
    (D) 2年生と3年生と4年生だけ

36. どんな特別規則がモリスホールでは施行されているか？
    (A) 訪問者は受付で記名しなければならない。
    (B) 学校がある平日の夜には門限がある。
    (C) 夜中を過ぎると静かな時間がある。
    (D) 寮内ではパーティーが禁止されている。

37. 学生寮の主任はどんなアドバイスを男性に与えたか？
    (A) 彼はできるだけ早く応募書類を送るべきだ。
    (B) 彼はキャンパス外にある住居を探すべきだ。
    (C) 彼は申し込む前に彼女のオフィスからの知らせを待つべきだ。
    (D) 彼はそれぞれの寮に申込用紙を送るべきだ。

38. この学生はどの寮に住む資格があるか？
    (A) フランクリンホール
    (B) モリスホール
    (C) フェンネルホール
    (D) クーパーホール

■ Part C

鉄道の駅に関する次の講義を聞きなさい。

　先週、私たちは19世紀後半のアメリカ経済の発展における鉄道が果たした役割に目を向けました。今日は、20世紀における鉄道の進化を検討したいと思います。そのために、私が指摘したいと思っている潮流の典型的な例として、ニューヨークのグランドセントラル駅に焦点を当てましょう。1913年に開業した時、グランドセントラル駅は鉄道産業にとっての神殿で、アメリカの工業力との成長のための動脈を提供し、またニューヨークシティそのものの活気の神殿でもありました。ここには長距離の大陸横断の旅に出発する乗客向けに食事を用意する巨大なキッチンと、トルコ風呂、個人用着替えルーム、それにシャワーがありました。疑問の余地なく、この頃はこの国における鉄道の全盛期でした。現在、グランドセントラルから最も遠い目的地はコネチカット州ニューヘイブンで、わずか90分の距離です。

　20世紀の大半、グランドセントラル駅とアメリカ東部のかつて立派だった鉄道駅の全てはないがしろにされたままになり、これは旅客鉄道の緩やかな排除を反映していました。まずは自動車に、そして飛行機によって。この変化により、駅を維持することに対しほとんどお金が投じられませんでした。それでもそれらは通勤客のために使われていましたが、もはや今世紀初頭にそうだったような快適で陽気な場所ではありませんでした。

　約10年前、都市計画者たちは市内に人々を呼び戻すために何かしなければならない、ということを理解しました。その結果、旧市街の鉄道の駅のかつての栄光を取り戻すことに多額の資金が投じられました。現在、そうした駅は近代的なショッピングモールのようになり、みんなに対し何かしら備えたものになっています。そして、ある程度、人々を再び電車に乗せることにも成功しています。たとえそれが週末に思い切って市街地に行ってみることに過ぎなくとも。グランドセントラル駅が再びかつてのようになることは決してないでしょう。しかし、鉄道旅行復活の兆しは現れ始めています。

39. 先週の講義の題材は何だったか？
- (A) 鉄道の駅の構造
- (B) 鉄道の旅の起源
- (C) 鉄道産業の未来の動向
- (D) 鉄道と経済の発展

40. 話者はアメリカの鉄道産業の最盛期としていつの時代に焦点を当てているか？
- (A) 20世紀初頭
- (B) 19世紀後半
- (C) 20世紀中盤
- (D) 20世紀後半

41. 話者によれば、なぜ鉄道が無視されるようになったか？
- (A) 大陸横断鉄道は経費が掛かり過ぎて運営できなかった。
- (B) 鉄道の駅が不快で危険だった。
- (C) 政府が経済的支援を打ち切った。
- (D) 他の交通手段のほうが魅力的だった。

42. 話者はアメリカの鉄道の将来をどう見ているか？
- (A) 主に悲観的
- (B) 基本的に中立
- (C) 注意深くも楽観視
- (D) 極度に熱狂的

Questions 43-46

大学生による次のアナウンスを聞きなさい。

おはようございます、みなさん。ブリクストン大学へようこそ。私はブレンダ・バークレーで、ここの2年生です。みなさんのオリエンテーションウィークの一部として、みなさんはさまざまなクラブのプレゼンを数多く聞くことになります。これからの学校での4年間、どんな活動に参加したいかを決める助けになるためです。私は、大学のオーケストラに加わることを考えてみるのをお勧めします。みなさんの多くに、音楽的な経歴があることを私は知っています。しかし、みなさんはまた、1年目にどれほど一生懸命勉強しなければならないかといううわさも聞いているかもしれません。そうしたうわさは本当です！ しかし、そのせいで私たちのオーケストラに入るのを恐れないでください。器材の購入から、リハーサルの時間を決めることまで、私たち学生がオーケストラ全ての責任を持ちます。でも、ついでですが、リハーサルは土曜日と日曜日にしか行われませんから、みなさんの忙しい授業スケジュールに支障は生じません。また、私たちは自分たちの音楽にとても真剣です。みなさんも世界的に有名な指揮者、マーク・スタインバーンの名をご存知かもしれません。そうです、そのマークは、ここブリクストンでの学生時代、私たちのオーケストラの一員だったのです。そして町にいる時はいつでも、今でも立ち寄って私たちを訪問してくれます。私たちは地元コミュニティーで年数回コンサートを行っています。もちろん、主に私たちは伝統的なクラシックの曲を演奏しますが、実際にはかなり幅広いレパートリーがあり、実は次のコンサートの大半は、アメリカ先住民の民族音楽のプログラムに捧げる予定です。これは私たちの大学の同窓生であるジェラルド・ハギング・ベアーがオーケストラのために特別にアレンジしてくれたものです。このオーケストラについてのさらなる詳細に関心がある場合には——そうだといいのですが——オリエンテーションの間、いつでも私に声を掛けてください。

43. このアナウンスは主に誰に向けられた
ものか？
(A) 高校3年生
(B) 大学1年生
(C) 大学2年生
(D) プロのミュージシャン

44. ブリクストン大学のオーケストラの特
徴は何か？
(A) 全て学生によって運営されている。
(B) 地域の人たちが参加できる。
(C) 世界的に有名な指揮者がいる。
(D) メンバーは大学の単位をもらえる。

45. オーケストラはどのくらいひんぱんに
リハーサルをするか？
(A) 毎日授業の後に
(B) 週末だけ
(C) 週に3回
(D) 1カ月に2回

46. 次のコンサートでオーケストラは主に
どんな音楽を演奏するか？
(A) 伝統的クラシック音楽
(B) イージーリスニングの曲
(C) ポップスのアレンジ
(D) 民族音楽

ハチに関する次の講義を聞きなさい。

　本日はミツバチに関する口頭発表を行いたいと思います。特に、女王バチがミツバチの巣に対して持つ影響について検討したいと思います。ただし、始める前に、豊富な情報を与えてくれたプロの養蜂家数名を紹介してくださったミラー教授にお礼を述べたいと思います。このプロジェクト開始前、私は博物館でハチの展示を見ましたが、私が知っていたのはハチが蜜を作るということだけでした。女王蜂は人間の女王と同じように部下を統制するわけではありませんが、しかし、女王バチは巣にいるあらゆるハチの生活に多大な影響力を持っています。女王バチの最も重要な務めは卵を産むことです。女王バチは夏の間、毎日1500〜2000個の卵を産みます。加えて、女王バチは継続的にフェロモンと呼ばれる性的な物質を分泌します。これは"社会性ホルモン"と呼ばれていますが、その理由は働きバチが口移しでこれを伝達し、ゆえに全ての働きバチが口でその一部を受け取るからです。このホルモンはハチの生活のほぼ全ての側面をコントロールしますが、特に繁殖の面でそうです。なぜならこれが別の女王が成長しないよう、通常の繁殖行動を阻害するからです。しかしながら、女王が年老いたり死んだりすると、そのフェロモン分泌がゆっくりになったり停止したりし、そしてこの女王バチからの物質の欠乏により、働きバチは自分たち自身で卵を産めるようになります。しかし、そうした働きバチは交尾していないため、全ての卵がオスのハチとなります。巣における女王バチの重要性は、もし殺されたり排除されたりした場合、あらゆる活動が阻害され、ハチたちが適切に作業しなくなるという事実に示されています。通常のフェロモンの供給が絶えるため、彼らはすぐに自分たちの女王バチの不在に気づくのです。

47. 誰が話をしているのか？

(A) プロの養蜂家
(B) 動物学の教授
(C) 生物のクラスの生徒
(D) 科学博物館のガイド

48. 話者によると、女王バチの最も重要な役割は何か？

(A) 卵を産むこと
(B) 他のミツバチを管理すること
(C) 巣を守ること
(D) 蜂蜜を作ること

49. フェロモンとは何か？

(A) 繁殖を抑制する物質
(B) 急速な成長を促進するホルモン
(C) 性行為の引き金になるホルモン
(D) 基本栄養素を提供する物質

50. 交尾しなかった働きバチはどうなるか？

(A) 通常のやり方で働くのをやめる。
(B) メスの子孫を作れない。
(C) 女王バチに攻撃を仕掛ける。
(D) それ以上卵を産むのをやめる。

Section 2 Structure and Written Expression 対訳

■ Structure

1. 生涯を通じて多作な発明家だったトーマス・エジソンは、アメリカの最も偉大な天才の一人とみなされている。

2. 造園において空間の印象は、樹木と岩と低木を注意深く配置することで形成される。

3. 明確に証明されてはいないものの、多くの歴史家はアメリカに初めて到達したヨーロッパ人はバイキングだったと考えている。

4. 奴隷として生まれたジョージ・ワシントン・カーヴァーは高校から大学へと進み、その後、植物学者として国際的な評価を得た。

5. アメリカ大陸の48州のうち、テキサス州は唯一、独立共和国としての地位を経験した。

6. トラは一般的にジャングルのネコ科動物と見なされているものの、1世紀にも満たない昔には、シベリアくらいはるか北の場所にも数多くいた。

7. 夕方の赤い空は、多くの場合、翌日の天候がおそらく良好であることを示している。

8. ウランは純粋な形で存在せず、ウランを多く含む鉱石から抽出しなければならない。

9. ガスは重ければ重いほど、容器全体によりゆっくりと拡散する。

10. 恐竜の大量絶滅の原因は、科学者たちの間であまり同意が得られていない事柄だ。

11. 連邦準備銀行がプライムレートを、つまり他の銀行に資金を貸し出す利率を上げると、経済全体の金利が上がる。

12. 人間に類似する巨大な霊長類は類人猿と呼ばれる。

13. 文章による議論は、それを支持する具体例が含まれていると、はるかに説得力を増すことができる。

14. ほとんどの州は、市民が合法的な居住者と見なされるためには、州の境界内に最低でも1年間居住することを求めている。

15. 寄生虫は主として、その宿主の状態に自らを適応させる驚異的な能力を持つ。

■ Written Expression

16. 日中にはわずかに変動するかもしれないものの、人間の体温は摂氏37.0度で比較的安定している。

17. パイナップルはブラックベリーやラズベリーがそうであるように、実は全体を形成するために集合した果実の固まりである。

18. アメリカの初期の写実主義者は、まるで写真よりも本物のように見えるような絵を描いた。

19. 政党の党大会は、リーダーを選んだり綱領を採択したりするのが目的の、政党所属会員による集会である。

20. ブロートーチ（バーナー）は、金属を溶かし融合させるために使う高温の炎である。

21. 色と透明度と重量が、磁器の質を判断する要素である。

22. インディアンの矢じりは、かつてアメリカ先住民が居住していた地域で今もよく見つかる。

23. スペイン語は、1980年代にヒスパニック系の住民たちが政治的に団結するための共通の土台を提供した。

24. ある種類のコイは、冷たく湿った泥に覆われても最長３カ月まで生き続けることができる。

25. エアロビクス運動は、筋肉の状態を向上させ、新陳代謝率を上げ、そして心臓を強くする。

26. 将来の収入の正確な予測がなければ、会社は固定費を支払う十分な資金すらなくなるなどのように、予算を使い果たしてしまいかねない。

27. 20世紀後半の50年で、高度に洗練された世界規模の通信網により広範囲に及ぶ情報が入手できるようになった。

28. 見事な現代美術コレクションで知られるボストン美術館は、所蔵する初期アメリカ絵画により多くの美術愛好家を引きつけている。

29. アーカンソー州の上院議員、ウイリアム・フルブライトは、アメリカの外交政策を批判した彼の世代の最初の人物の一人であった。

30. アメリカ東部の古代のアパラチア山脈は、ペルム紀の間、２億年以上前に初めて姿を現した。

31. そのリズムと音ゆえに、詩は伝統的に深い感情を表す最適な方法のひとつだと考えられてきた。

32. 南北戦争直前に発明された綿繰り機（綿の繊維と種を分ける装置）は、19世紀における最も重要な農業関連の大発見のひとつだった。

33. 火山が吹き出す3種類の物質として、溶岩、ガス、そして硬い岩の破片がある。

34. アメリカの西方への拡大の際に人気になったカウボーイ・バラードは、その起源を中世の歌に持つ。

35. 広く尊敬された裁判官、サーグッド・マーシャルは、最高裁判所に任命される前、公民権を先導する弁護士だった。

36. 綿や羊毛など天然繊維から作られる衣服は、合成繊維から作られたものよりも多くの場合より温かく、強く、安い。

37. 粒子加速器は不可欠な機器であり、これを使って現在量子力学の研究の大半が行われている。

38. ギルソナイトはアスファルトの極めて純粋な形であり、塗料と消去剤の両方の製造に用いられている。

39. 肌の専門家の多くは、肌の健康の最大の要因が食事であるという主張に懐疑的だ。

40. 科学的論議の顕著な特徴として、公平さ、客観性、抽象性がある。

Section 3 Reading Comprehension 対訳
■ Questions 1-8

　性差に関しての最近の調査でうそが暴かれた作り話は、痛みに耐える能力の違いだけではない。性別と犯罪に関する最も一般的に利用されている統計をざっと見てみるだけで、あらゆる先進国の刑務所における男性と女性の割合の不均衡が明らかになる。その結果、男性のほうが女性よりも犯罪を行う可能性がはるかに高いという意見が世間一般に受け入れられている。だが現実には、犯罪率に関する実際の性差は公的な統計が示しているよりも小さいかもしれない。

　"手紙の紛失"の実験は、性別と機会と犯罪について興味深い情報源を提供している。これらの実験では、お金を同封した手紙が公共の場に落とされた。異なる形式でさまざまな条件が変えられた――用いられた金額、現金かあるいは（郵便為替などの）別の形か、見かけ上の落とし主（老齢の女性か、裕福な男性か）など。手紙を拾った人物の特性が観察の対象となり、また、調査者はコード番号からそれが届けられたか、拾ったままになったかを判別可能だった。これらの研究では、お金の窃盗は見かけ上の被害者が裕福な男性で、しかもそれが現金の時に最も多かったが、しかし、女性の盗む可能性は男性と同じだった。例外として、金額がより大きかった場合、男性のほうがそのお金を懐に入れる割合が２倍だった。どうやら少額の現金を懐に入れるのは"盗み"と見なされていないが、大金の場合はそうなる、ということのようだ――そして男性のほうがより、そういう形で利得を手にする心づもりができているようだ。

　女性の有罪比率が男性のそれとほぼ同じである唯一の犯罪が万引きだ。このことは、女性は自分が公共の場にある時に、例えば家庭内ではなく買い物に出ている時に、犯罪行為に関わることを示している、と主張する者もいる。つまり、犯罪を行う機会がほぼ等しい場合、男性と女性は同じくらい違法行為をする可能性があるのだ。

　ただし、男性と女性が犯す犯罪の種類に関する重要な対比については異議を挟めない。というのも、報告されている女性の違法行為に暴力が絡むことはめったにないからだ。その結果として、警察やその他の役人はおそらく女性の犯罪者を男性の犯罪者よりも危険ではないと見なし、そして結果的に男性ならば逮捕されるかもしれないような女性の行為を見逃しているのかもしれない。

1. この文章の要点は何か？
   (A) 女性と男性では"盗み"となる概念が異なる。
   (B) 女性は男性よりも生まれながらに暴力の傾向が少ない。
   (C) 犯罪を行う傾向に関し、性別が決定的要因だ。
   (D) 犯罪を説明する際、性差が強調され過ぎることが多々ある。

2. ３行目"imbalance"に最も意味が近いのは
   (A) 不等
   (B) 不公平
   (C) 起こりそうにないこと
   (D) 矛盾

3. 筆者はなぜ１行目で"tolerate pain"という文言を使ったのか？
   (A) 痛みは容易に数量化できないものだ。
   (B) 男性は女性よりも、投獄の痛みによりうまく耐えることができる。
   (C) 男性は痛みをより感じやすいという考えは誤りであることが示されている。
   (D) 男性は先進工業国ではより痛みを受けやすい。

4. "手紙の紛失"実験でわかったことは次のうちどれか？
   (A) 男性と女性の犯罪傾向についての事前の考え方は基本的に正しかった。
   (B) 見かけ上の犠牲者の経済的地位が重要な役割を果たした。
   (C) 男性は女性よりも犯罪から多くの利得を得る傾向がある。
   (D) 女性は男性よりも万引きで捕まる可能性が高い。

5. 10行目の"altered"の意味に最も近いのは
   (A) 変更された
   (B) 変装された
   (C) 避けられた
   (D) 仮定された

6. 14行目"they"が指しているのは
   (A) 調査者
   (B) コード番号
   (C) 手紙
   (D) 個々人

7. 28行目"rarely"に最も意味が近いのは
   (A) ほとんど〜ない
   (B) まことしやかに
   (C) めったに〜ない
   (D) ありそうもない

8. 次の見解のうち、この文章でほのめかされているものはどれか？
   (A) 女性は家庭の外で罪を犯すことを避ける傾向がある。
   (B) 男性は女性よりも自分の違反行為を認める傾向が強い。
   (C) 女性は一般に推測されているよりも実はもっと暴力的だ。
   (D) 警察は女性が犯した罪に対してより寛容になる傾向がある。

■ Questions 9-19

　第二次世界大戦中、数多くのヨーロッパの画家がアメリカへ移民し、アメリカの若手画家たちに非常に大きな影響を与えた。戦後、そうした芸術家たちの集団があるムーブメントを起こし、それが世界の至る所で有名になり、あらゆる場所の芸術家たちにとってひとつの手本となった。抽象表現主義者（あるいは時には"アクションペインター"）と称された彼らは、スケールの大きい、活気にあふれた印象で、極めて個人的な性格の作品を作った。このムーブメントは、アメリカが大きな経済的・政治的な拡張期に入った1950年代において、特に隆盛を極めた。それゆえ、抽象表現主義者たちの作品は力強い国家の強さと自信を伝えるものになっているが、それにも関わらず、それらは画一性と没個性化へのプレッシャーに対する個人の重要性を宣言する私的声明でもある。抽象表現主義の出現はもうひとつ別の理由においても重要だ。アメリカはその歴史上初めて西洋芸術界の中心となったのだ。

　ジャクソン・ポロックは最初に台頭した抽象表現主義者の一人で、"ブルー・ポールズ"（青い柱）は彼の円熟した作品の一例である。巨大なキャンバス（長さが約5メートル）、それは8つの紺色の細くておよそ垂直の形状で強調されている。そのキャンバスのそれ以外の部分はさまざまな色彩の絡まった線からなり、それらは太かったり細かったり、明るかったり暗かったり、滑らかだったりギザギザだったり、あるいは温かだったり冷ややかだったりしている。ほとんどの伝統的な絵画とは異なり、この絵には関心の中心になるものがない。どの部分も

他の部分と同様に興味深く、また、キャンバスのぎりぎりの端まで力強さが弱まることなく形状が伸びている。ポロックは通常とは異なる手法で色彩を使っていた。彼は床にキャンバスを置き、その上に絵の具をたらし、製作を進めながら絵の具の色や種類や厚みを変えていった。従ってそうした色彩の線は彼が絵の具をたらす際の彼の腕と体の動きを反映している。すなわち、絵を描く行為が絵画そのものの一部となったのだ。それの印象とは、自発性ととてつもないエネルギーである。ポロックの絵画が初めて展示された時、彼の絵画手法には嘲笑が浴びせられた。しかし、彼には支持者もいたのだ。そして彼の影響は絶大であった。

9. 筆者の趣旨は何か？
    (A) アメリカの戦後の経済はアメリカの芸術にも反映された。
    (B) ジャクソン・ポロックは非常に才能豊かな画家になった。
    (C) 抽象表現主義は重要な芸術ムーブメントだった。
    (D) ジャクソン・ポロックが用いた絵画技法は明らかにオリジナルだった。

10. この文章によれば、抽象表現主義者ムーブメントの主な起源のひとつは
    (A) 第1次世界大戦
    (B) 移民の画家たち
    (C) 経済発展
    (D) 芸術的な反乱

11. 抽象表現主義ムーブメントが最も隆盛を極めたのはいつか？
    (A) 第二次世界大戦中
    (B) 第二次世界大戦前
    (C) 1960年代
    (D) 1950年代

12. 2行目"profound"に最も意味が近いのは
    (A) 息を飲むような
    (B) 深い
    (C) 束の間の
    (D) 突然の

13. 10行目"uniformity"に最も意味が近いのは
    (A) 同一性
    (B) 表現
    (C) 服従
    (D) 進展

14. 第1段落で筆者は何を示唆しているか？
    (A) 抽象表現主義は他の芸術ムーブメントよりも想像的であった
    (B) 芸術は寛大な資金援助なしではうまくいかない
    (C) 抽象表現主義の画家の大半はアメリカで生まれた
    (D) 経済と芸術は関連している

15. この文章によれば、抽象表現主義の影響で最も重要なのはどれか？
    (A) ジャクソン・ポロックの影響を制限した
    (B) 芸術の世界でアメリカを傑出した存在にした
    (C) 芸術を肖像から離れさせた
    (D) 全く新しい色彩の世界を創造した

16. 筆者が15行目で"Blue Poles"に触れているのはなぜか？
   (A) 抽象表現主義におけるポロックの初期の試みを例示するため
   (B) 抽象表現主義者の絵画の大きさを強調するため
   (C) 抽象表現芸術を代表する例を提供するため
   (D) ポロックが成熟するにつれ芸術家としてどれほど伸びたかを示すため

17. 17行目"vertical"に最も意味が近いのは
   (A) 輝いた
   (B) 目立つ
   (C) あいまいな
   (D) 縦長の

18. 伝統的な絵画とは対照的に、ジャクソン・ポロックの絵は
   (A) 色と形状の力強さが劣る
   (B) 視点の中心になるものがない
   (C) 新しい種類の塗料から作られた
   (D) はっきりした映像を含む

19. 筆者はどんな原理に基づいて論理を構成しているか？
   (A) 一連の例示によって指示された主張
   (B) いくつかのタイプの分類
   (C) 概説の後に例証を続ける
   (D) 解説してから要約する

■ Questions 20-31

　ブーントリングはその話者が人為的に作った方言に与えた名前で、1880年から1920年にかけてカリフォルニア州メンドシーノ郡アンダーソン・バレーの北部にて広く話された。この名前自体が、短縮された単語であり字面から意味がわかる複合語で、この方言の典型的な単語である。"ブーント"とはこの地域の語で"ブーンヴィル"を指す。ブーンヴィルはこの谷で最大の町で、また、"リング"はlingo（言語）を縮めたもの。従って、ブーントリングはブーンヴィルの特有の言語ということになる。

　この"地方の言語"は、20世紀初頭の10年の間にその発展の頂点に達し、1000以上の独特な基本語句の語彙を含み、また、地域の居住者とこの地域特有の地形的特徴を表わす数百の固有の名前もある。この言語は一時期、ブーンヴィルを中心とする孤立した地方の谷に住むほとんどの人々によって話され、理解されていた。ブーントリングの文法と音はほとんど英語と同一ではあるものの、世に知られない単語が多用されるため、この言葉にそうなじんでいない人たちにとっては事実上、ブーントリングは理解不能だった。当時この地域の人たちは、あえてアンダーソン・バレーに入ってきた数少ない外部の人間たちが言葉を全く理解できないという事実に大きな喜びを感じていた。実際、ブーントリングは彼らのアイデンティティーの象徴となり、密に結び付いているコミュニティーの会員バッジになった。アンダーソン・バレーでの生活において、この言語はかつてのような重要な役割を果たすことはなくなったものの、現在でも古い時代の人たちの間で記憶され、話されており、また、自分たちの谷の先祖の伝統を楽しみ、育んでいるより最近の世代の人たちによって研究と発展が進められている。

　ブーントリングでは、「文脈が全て」と言いたくなる。確かに、仮にそれが全てではないにしても、ほぼ全てに近い。この方言はこの谷そのものと話す人々にとても密に関連しているた

め、ある程度詳しく社会的な文脈を知らなくては、この特殊な言語を理解し、正しく評価することはできない。しかしながら、この社会学的背景に触れる前に、この地域の地形的な特徴を精査する必要がある。この地域社会の形成においてこの谷の独特な地勢が果たした役割を否定することはできない。急斜面の丘に囲まれたこの谷に行き来できる道は、1950年代まで1本しかなかった。

20. 第1段落の目的は何か？
(A) ブーントリングという名前の起源を示すこと
(B) ブーンヴィルの位置を示すこと
(C) アンダーソン・バレーを紹介すること
(D) ブーントリングの単語の一例を示すこと

21. 筆者が7行目に"local language"という表現を使っているのはブーントリングが何でないことを示すためか？
(A) 時には、理解が非常に難しい
(B) 一般的な意味での言語
(C) 一般に思われているようにその地域に固有のもの
(D) 一般的な英語と大きく異なる

22. 8行目"lexicon"に最も意味が近いのは？
(A) 語法
(B) 配列
(C) 補語
(D) 語彙

23. ブーントリングについて本文から推測されるのは？
(A) その地域で元から話されていた言語から自然に発展した
(B) 地元の居住者によって特別かつ意図的に作られた
(C) 興味を引かないため、消滅の危機に瀕している
(D) もはや尊重されない古い伝統の象徴

24. 14行目"virtually"に最も意味が近いのは
(A) 実質的に
(B) いく分
(C) 部分的に
(D) 確かに

25. この文章から推測されるブーントリングが最も広まったであろう時期は次のどれか？
(A) 1880年
(B) 1895年
(C) 1905年
(D) 1920年

26. 16行目"them"が指しているのは
(A) あいまいな語
(B) 地元の居住者
(C) 外部の人間
(D) 音

27. ブーントリングがこのような発展を遂げた主な理由として筆者がほのめかしているのは？
(A) アンダーソン・バレーそのものが行き難い場所だった
(B) アンダーソン・バレーの人たちが外部の人間を歓迎した
(C) アンダーソン・バレーにはほとんど人がいなかった
(D) アンダーソン・バレーの住民の大半は年配者だった

28. この文章によると、多くの人にブーントリングが難しいのはなぜか？
- (A) 数多くの標準的ではない音を含んでいる。
- (B) 数多くのなじみのない単語を使っている。
- (C) 間接的で文脈に基づいている。
- (D) 普通とは異なる文法構造を持つ。

29. 23行目"intimately"に最も意味が近いのは
- (A) 誤って
- (B) 感情的に
- (C) 密接に
- (D) 外見上

30. ブーントリングについて正しく述べているのは次のうちどれか？
- (A) ブーンヴィルの社会背景に関する深い知識が求められる。
- (B) 現在ではアンダーソン・バレー以外の人々ですら話している。
- (C) 元々のネイティブ・アメリカン居住者の言葉を含む。
- (D) これまでに一度も言語学者によって体系的に分析されたことがない。

31. アンダーソン・バレーの地形がブーントリングの初期の発展に寄与したと推測されるが、その理由は
- (A) 外部からの影響の量を制限した
- (B) 痩せた土地だったため、この地域の居住者たちは緊密に協力しあって働くことを余儀なくされた
- (C) 急斜面の丘のため、人々は互いの近くで生活することになった
- (D) この地域の居住者にとって外部からの物資を得ることは困難だった

■ Questions 32-41

　数千年にわたり、百万の人々による数十億の取引において、多くの物品が通貨として使われてきた。それらには石、塩、牛、貝殻などが含まれる。しかし金が使える場合にはいつも、それが他の交換手法に優る傾向にあった。うまく機能しているあらゆる貨幣と同じように、金は政府から"法的貨幣"であると規定される必要が決してなかった。金はその優れた性質ゆえに、最も理想的な貨幣だというのが共通認識だ。

　通貨のこのような資質は紀元前5世紀にアリストテレスによって早くも指摘されており、特に金に関しては、現在でも真実であり続けている。

　まず、通貨には耐久性がなければならない。蒸発したり、かびたり、さびたり、砕けたり、壊れたり、腐ったりしてはいけない。金は他のどんな固形物質以上に化学的に不活性である。食べ物や石油や手工芸品が通貨として使われないのはこのためだ。二つ目として、分割できなければならない。1オンスの金は——金塊であれ硬貨であれ金粉であれ——100オンスのピッタリ100分の1の価値がある。対照的に、ダイヤモンドが分割されるとその価値は崩壊するし、また、土地の一部を小銭にすることは容易ではない。三つ目として、通貨は便利でなければならない。金ならばその所有者は人生全てで得た富を物理的に持ち歩くことができる。不動産はその場所から動けない。また、同等の価値の銅、鉛、亜鉛、銀、そしてその他の金属の大

半は重すぎて持ち運べない。四つ目として、通貨または硬貨は不変でなければならない。24カラットの金にはひとつの等級しかない。従って、24カラットの金でありながら異質な等級のものを所有するという危険はない。金は宝石や手工芸品や土地や穀物やその他の商品と異なり、天然の元素であるため、24カラットの金はいつでもどこでも同じなのだ。五つ目として、少なくとも理想としては通貨は本来固有の価値を持っているべきだとされる。毎年、金の新しい産業利用法が登場する。あらゆる金属の中で、金は最も加工しやすく（形を変えやすい）、最も反応性が低い（海水、空気、酸に触れても損傷しない）。

　明らかにこうした特質が——過去5000年の間、宝飾品としての価値とはまた別に——金を非常に便利なものにしている。また、金は92種類の天然元素のひとつであり、いくつか独特な化学的特性を持っていることを覚えておくことも重要だ。ただし、それゆえにその価値は"謎めいている"などという主張は、ばかげているとしか、見なされない。

32. この文章の主な目的は何か？

(A) 金特有の性質を詳述すること
(B) さまざまな種類の通貨を定義すること
(C) 通貨の発展の概略を述べること
(D) 金に価値がある理由を説明すること

33. 通貨として使われた品で述べられていないものは次のうちどれか？

(A) 貝殻
(B) ビーズ
(C) 塩
(D) 家畜

34. 筆者によれば、金はなぜ公式通貨としての指定を受けずに相変わらずそのまま留まったのか？

(A) 全てのお金が伝統的に金を基本にしてきた。
(B) 金そのものが貴重であることに人々が同意している。
(C) 金の供給は需要より少ない。
(D) 金は常に良質な宝飾品を作るために必要とされてきた。

35. 3行目"surpass"に最も意味が近いのは

(A) 置き換える
(B) 価値を下げる
(C) 超える
(D) スピードを上げる

36. 11行目"it"が指しているのは

(A) 金
(B) 通貨
(C) 手工芸品
(D) 1オンス

37. 食物、石油、手工芸品などはなぜ通貨に適切でないのか？

(A) それらの価値は大きく変動する。
(B) すぐに使うことができない。
(C) 必ずしも長持ちしない。
(D) 輸送できない。

38. 第3段落で筆者がダイヤモンドと金を比べているのは、次のうちどの点を明らかにするためか？

(A) ダイヤモンドはたいてい過大評価されている。
(B) 金は少量に分割できる。
(C) 金はダイヤモンドよりも輸送が容易だ。
(D) ダイヤモンドは金ほど長持ちしない。

39. 20行目"gems"に最も意味が近いのは

(A) 宝飾品
(B) 珍しい鉱石
(C) 貨幣
(D) 貴石

**40. 21行目 "intrinsic" に最も意味が
近いのは**

(A) 本来の
(B) 異常な
(C) 明白な
(D) 実用的な

**41. 次の主張のうち、この文章が最も支持
するのはどれか？**

(A) 金の価値は他の貴金属の価値と密
接に関連している。
(B) 金の工業的利用は金の経済的使用
よりも重要だ。
(C) 金は信頼の置ける通貨としての役
割を現在でも果たし得る。
(D) 土地と金は最も価値が安定してい
る商品の2つだ。

■ Questions 42-50

　口腔健康管理専門の連邦機関、国立歯科研究所によると、アメリカの学童の半数は虫歯にな
ったことが一度もない。この主張は2010年に実施された口腔衛生の大規模調査に基づいてい
る。しかし、この主張は本当に真実だろうか。また、このように断言された発見は、親と健康
管理機関が、数百万人ものアメリカの子どもの実在して、しばしば深刻な歯の治療の必要性を
見過ごすことを後押ししていないだろうか。

　実際のところ、このデータを注意深く検証してみると、国立歯科研究所の結論とは別の結論
にたどり着く。この研究所の調査のデータを精査した専門家は、同研究所の50パーセントは
虫歯がないという主張は、最初の歯——一般に "乳歯" と呼ばれる——の虫歯を無視し、また5
〜17歳の子どもたちの永久歯の虫歯を平均化したことから生じた作り話だという立場を貫い
ている。もし最初の歯の虫歯が含まれたなら、幼稚園児の42パーセントが虫歯に見舞われ、
7歳児の半数が少なくとも1本の虫歯を持ち、9歳未満の子どもたちは平均して虫歯を4本持
つ。さらには、子ども時代を通じて虫歯の進行を追跡した場合、50パーセントではなく84パー
セントのアメリカの17歳は、永久歯の1本以上が虫歯である。正当に虫歯がないと言える
のは、17歳の人口の6人に一人だけである。

　国立研究所の "50パーセント虫歯なし" という統計は、少なくとも永久歯1本が虫歯になって
いる子どもたち全員の虫歯の経験を平均したことから生じたものだ。つまり、永久歯が生えた
ばかりで虫歯になるだけの時間をまだ経ていない就学前の子どもたちから、虫歯が生じるのに
十分な時間があった高校3年生までを平均したのだ。このデータを綿密に分析することが重要
な理由は、歯の疾患が少数の人々に限定されているのではなく、人々の間に大きく広まってい
ることをこれが示唆しているからだ。この事実の認識は、具体的な公衆衛生政策の必要性を指
し示している。というのも、虫歯の問題は親と社会がそれぞれの仕事を適切にやれば、ほぼ完
全に防ぐことが可能だからだ。

42. 筆者の趣旨は何か？
   (A) 国立歯科研究所の報告は信頼できない。
   (B) 良好な公衆衛生政策が次第に虫歯率を低下させている。
   (C) 子どもの虫歯は深刻かつ見落とされた問題だ。
   (D) 親は、歯の健康管理にもっと意識的になるべきだ。

43. 国立歯科研究所によるとアメリカの学生のうち虫歯にかかったことがないのは何パーセントか？
   (A) 17パーセント
   (B) 50パーセント
   (C) 42パーセント
   (D) 84パーセント

44. 研究で行う際に国立歯科研究所が冒した間違いは、次のうちどれと専門家は指摘しているか？
   (A) 人口における十分な事例を調査しなかった。
   (B) 十代の口腔衛生を考慮することを無視した。
   (C) "虫歯"を十分に明瞭に定義しなかった。
   (D) 第一生歯に見られる虫歯を含めなかった。

45. 3行目"extensive"に最も意味が近いのは
   (A) 重要な
   (B) 予備的な
   (C) 大きな
   (D) 進行中の

46. 8行目"inspected"に最も意味が近いのは
   (A) 編集した
   (B) 確認した
   (C) 計算した
   (D) 拒否した

47. 次の主張のうち、この文章が最も支持するのはどれか？
   (A) 歯の疾患の程度を立証するために、より正確な調査が役立つだろう。
   (B) 連邦機関は公衆衛生情報の情報源として当てにならないことが多々ある。
   (C) 歯の健診の費用を補うよう保険会社に要求されるべきだ。
   (D) 糖分豊富な食事は子どもたちの虫歯の主原因のひとつだ。

48. 15行目"tracked"に最も意味が近いのは
   (A) 抑制された
   (B) 増加した
   (C) 孤立した
   (D) 分析された

49. 22行目"they"が指しているのは
   (A) 結果
   (B) データ
   (C) 歯の疾患
   (D) 子どもたち

50. 筆者が16〜17行目で"17-year-olds"と述べているのはなぜか？
   (A) 歯の疾患の割合を測定する際、17歳という年齢が確立した基準とされている。
   (B) 青年後期の行動は大人の行動を高い確率で予測できる。
   (C) ティーンエージャーのわずか6分の1しか、元々の研究に含まれていなかった。
   (D) その年代の集団のうち、実際に虫歯のない人ははるかに少ない。

Answer Sheet

解答シート

Section 1

1 Ⓐ Ⓑ Ⓒ Ⓓ	11 Ⓐ Ⓑ Ⓒ Ⓓ	21 Ⓐ Ⓑ Ⓒ Ⓓ	31 Ⓐ Ⓑ Ⓒ Ⓓ	41 Ⓐ Ⓑ Ⓒ Ⓓ
2 Ⓐ Ⓑ Ⓒ Ⓓ	12 Ⓐ Ⓑ Ⓒ Ⓓ	22 Ⓐ Ⓑ Ⓒ Ⓓ	32 Ⓐ Ⓑ Ⓒ Ⓓ	42 Ⓐ Ⓑ Ⓒ Ⓓ
3 Ⓐ Ⓑ Ⓒ Ⓓ	13 Ⓐ Ⓑ Ⓒ Ⓓ	23 Ⓐ Ⓑ Ⓒ Ⓓ	33 Ⓐ Ⓑ Ⓒ Ⓓ	43 Ⓐ Ⓑ Ⓒ Ⓓ
4 Ⓐ Ⓑ Ⓒ Ⓓ	14 Ⓐ Ⓑ Ⓒ Ⓓ	24 Ⓐ Ⓑ Ⓒ Ⓓ	34 Ⓐ Ⓑ Ⓒ Ⓓ	44 Ⓐ Ⓑ Ⓒ Ⓓ
5 Ⓐ Ⓑ Ⓒ Ⓓ	15 Ⓐ Ⓑ Ⓒ Ⓓ	25 Ⓐ Ⓑ Ⓒ Ⓓ	35 Ⓐ Ⓑ Ⓒ Ⓓ	45 Ⓐ Ⓑ Ⓒ Ⓓ
6 Ⓐ Ⓑ Ⓒ Ⓓ	16 Ⓐ Ⓑ Ⓒ Ⓓ	26 Ⓐ Ⓑ Ⓒ Ⓓ	36 Ⓐ Ⓑ Ⓒ Ⓓ	46 Ⓐ Ⓑ Ⓒ Ⓓ
7 Ⓐ Ⓑ Ⓒ Ⓓ	17 Ⓐ Ⓑ Ⓒ Ⓓ	27 Ⓐ Ⓑ Ⓒ Ⓓ	37 Ⓐ Ⓑ Ⓒ Ⓓ	47 Ⓐ Ⓑ Ⓒ Ⓓ
8 Ⓐ Ⓑ Ⓒ Ⓓ	18 Ⓐ Ⓑ Ⓒ Ⓓ	28 Ⓐ Ⓑ Ⓒ Ⓓ	38 Ⓐ Ⓑ Ⓒ Ⓓ	48 Ⓐ Ⓑ Ⓒ Ⓓ
9 Ⓐ Ⓑ Ⓒ Ⓓ	19 Ⓐ Ⓑ Ⓒ Ⓓ	29 Ⓐ Ⓑ Ⓒ Ⓓ	39 Ⓐ Ⓑ Ⓒ Ⓓ	49 Ⓐ Ⓑ Ⓒ Ⓓ
10 Ⓐ Ⓑ Ⓒ Ⓓ	20 Ⓐ Ⓑ Ⓒ Ⓓ	30 Ⓐ Ⓑ Ⓒ Ⓓ	40 Ⓐ Ⓑ Ⓒ Ⓓ	50 Ⓐ Ⓑ Ⓒ Ⓓ

Section 2

1 Ⓐ Ⓑ Ⓒ Ⓓ	9 Ⓐ Ⓑ Ⓒ Ⓓ	17 Ⓐ Ⓑ Ⓒ Ⓓ	25 Ⓐ Ⓑ Ⓒ Ⓓ	33 Ⓐ Ⓑ Ⓒ Ⓓ
2 Ⓐ Ⓑ Ⓒ Ⓓ	10 Ⓐ Ⓑ Ⓒ Ⓓ	18 Ⓐ Ⓑ Ⓒ Ⓓ	26 Ⓐ Ⓑ Ⓒ Ⓓ	34 Ⓐ Ⓑ Ⓒ Ⓓ
3 Ⓐ Ⓑ Ⓒ Ⓓ	11 Ⓐ Ⓑ Ⓒ Ⓓ	19 Ⓐ Ⓑ Ⓒ Ⓓ	27 Ⓐ Ⓑ Ⓒ Ⓓ	35 Ⓐ Ⓑ Ⓒ Ⓓ
4 Ⓐ Ⓑ Ⓒ Ⓓ	12 Ⓐ Ⓑ Ⓒ Ⓓ	20 Ⓐ Ⓑ Ⓒ Ⓓ	28 Ⓐ Ⓑ Ⓒ Ⓓ	36 Ⓐ Ⓑ Ⓒ Ⓓ
5 Ⓐ Ⓑ Ⓒ Ⓓ	13 Ⓐ Ⓑ Ⓒ Ⓓ	21 Ⓐ Ⓑ Ⓒ Ⓓ	29 Ⓐ Ⓑ Ⓒ Ⓓ	37 Ⓐ Ⓑ Ⓒ Ⓓ
6 Ⓐ Ⓑ Ⓒ Ⓓ	14 Ⓐ Ⓑ Ⓒ Ⓓ	22 Ⓐ Ⓑ Ⓒ Ⓓ	30 Ⓐ Ⓑ Ⓒ Ⓓ	38 Ⓐ Ⓑ Ⓒ Ⓓ
7 Ⓐ Ⓑ Ⓒ Ⓓ	15 Ⓐ Ⓑ Ⓒ Ⓓ	23 Ⓐ Ⓑ Ⓒ Ⓓ	31 Ⓐ Ⓑ Ⓒ Ⓓ	39 Ⓐ Ⓑ Ⓒ Ⓓ
8 Ⓐ Ⓑ Ⓒ Ⓓ	16 Ⓐ Ⓑ Ⓒ Ⓓ	24 Ⓐ Ⓑ Ⓒ Ⓓ	32 Ⓐ Ⓑ Ⓒ Ⓓ	40 Ⓐ Ⓑ Ⓒ Ⓓ

Section 3

1 Ⓐ Ⓑ Ⓒ Ⓓ	11 Ⓐ Ⓑ Ⓒ Ⓓ	21 Ⓐ Ⓑ Ⓒ Ⓓ	31 Ⓐ Ⓑ Ⓒ Ⓓ	41 Ⓐ Ⓑ Ⓒ Ⓓ
2 Ⓐ Ⓑ Ⓒ Ⓓ	12 Ⓐ Ⓑ Ⓒ Ⓓ	22 Ⓐ Ⓑ Ⓒ Ⓓ	32 Ⓐ Ⓑ Ⓒ Ⓓ	42 Ⓐ Ⓑ Ⓒ Ⓓ
3 Ⓐ Ⓑ Ⓒ Ⓓ	13 Ⓐ Ⓑ Ⓒ Ⓓ	23 Ⓐ Ⓑ Ⓒ Ⓓ	33 Ⓐ Ⓑ Ⓒ Ⓓ	43 Ⓐ Ⓑ Ⓒ Ⓓ
4 Ⓐ Ⓑ Ⓒ Ⓓ	14 Ⓐ Ⓑ Ⓒ Ⓓ	24 Ⓐ Ⓑ Ⓒ Ⓓ	34 Ⓐ Ⓑ Ⓒ Ⓓ	44 Ⓐ Ⓑ Ⓒ Ⓓ
5 Ⓐ Ⓑ Ⓒ Ⓓ	15 Ⓐ Ⓑ Ⓒ Ⓓ	25 Ⓐ Ⓑ Ⓒ Ⓓ	35 Ⓐ Ⓑ Ⓒ Ⓓ	45 Ⓐ Ⓑ Ⓒ Ⓓ
6 Ⓐ Ⓑ Ⓒ Ⓓ	16 Ⓐ Ⓑ Ⓒ Ⓓ	26 Ⓐ Ⓑ Ⓒ Ⓓ	36 Ⓐ Ⓑ Ⓒ Ⓓ	46 Ⓐ Ⓑ Ⓒ Ⓓ
7 Ⓐ Ⓑ Ⓒ Ⓓ	17 Ⓐ Ⓑ Ⓒ Ⓓ	27 Ⓐ Ⓑ Ⓒ Ⓓ	37 Ⓐ Ⓑ Ⓒ Ⓓ	47 Ⓐ Ⓑ Ⓒ Ⓓ
8 Ⓐ Ⓑ Ⓒ Ⓓ	18 Ⓐ Ⓑ Ⓒ Ⓓ	28 Ⓐ Ⓑ Ⓒ Ⓓ	38 Ⓐ Ⓑ Ⓒ Ⓓ	48 Ⓐ Ⓑ Ⓒ Ⓓ
9 Ⓐ Ⓑ Ⓒ Ⓓ	19 Ⓐ Ⓑ Ⓒ Ⓓ	29 Ⓐ Ⓑ Ⓒ Ⓓ	39 Ⓐ Ⓑ Ⓒ Ⓓ	49 Ⓐ Ⓑ Ⓒ Ⓓ
10 Ⓐ Ⓑ Ⓒ Ⓓ	20 Ⓐ Ⓑ Ⓒ Ⓓ	30 Ⓐ Ⓑ Ⓒ Ⓓ	40 Ⓐ Ⓑ Ⓒ Ⓓ	50 Ⓐ Ⓑ Ⓒ Ⓓ

キリトリ

Answer Sheet

解答シート

Section 1

1 Ⓐ Ⓑ Ⓒ Ⓓ	11 Ⓐ Ⓑ Ⓒ Ⓓ	21 Ⓐ Ⓑ Ⓒ Ⓓ	31 Ⓐ Ⓑ Ⓒ Ⓓ	41 Ⓐ Ⓑ Ⓒ Ⓓ
2 Ⓐ Ⓑ Ⓒ Ⓓ	12 Ⓐ Ⓑ Ⓒ Ⓓ	22 Ⓐ Ⓑ Ⓒ Ⓓ	32 Ⓐ Ⓑ Ⓒ Ⓓ	42 Ⓐ Ⓑ Ⓒ Ⓓ
3 Ⓐ Ⓑ Ⓒ Ⓓ	13 Ⓐ Ⓑ Ⓒ Ⓓ	23 Ⓐ Ⓑ Ⓒ Ⓓ	33 Ⓐ Ⓑ Ⓒ Ⓓ	43 Ⓐ Ⓑ Ⓒ Ⓓ
4 Ⓐ Ⓑ Ⓒ Ⓓ	14 Ⓐ Ⓑ Ⓒ Ⓓ	24 Ⓐ Ⓑ Ⓒ Ⓓ	34 Ⓐ Ⓑ Ⓒ Ⓓ	44 Ⓐ Ⓑ Ⓒ Ⓓ
5 Ⓐ Ⓑ Ⓒ Ⓓ	15 Ⓐ Ⓑ Ⓒ Ⓓ	25 Ⓐ Ⓑ Ⓒ Ⓓ	35 Ⓐ Ⓑ Ⓒ Ⓓ	45 Ⓐ Ⓑ Ⓒ Ⓓ
6 Ⓐ Ⓑ Ⓒ Ⓓ	16 Ⓐ Ⓑ Ⓒ Ⓓ	26 Ⓐ Ⓑ Ⓒ Ⓓ	36 Ⓐ Ⓑ Ⓒ Ⓓ	46 Ⓐ Ⓑ Ⓒ Ⓓ
7 Ⓐ Ⓑ Ⓒ Ⓓ	17 Ⓐ Ⓑ Ⓒ Ⓓ	27 Ⓐ Ⓑ Ⓒ Ⓓ	37 Ⓐ Ⓑ Ⓒ Ⓓ	47 Ⓐ Ⓑ Ⓒ Ⓓ
8 Ⓐ Ⓑ Ⓒ Ⓓ	18 Ⓐ Ⓑ Ⓒ Ⓓ	28 Ⓐ Ⓑ Ⓒ Ⓓ	38 Ⓐ Ⓑ Ⓒ Ⓓ	48 Ⓐ Ⓑ Ⓒ Ⓓ
9 Ⓐ Ⓑ Ⓒ Ⓓ	19 Ⓐ Ⓑ Ⓒ Ⓓ	29 Ⓐ Ⓑ Ⓒ Ⓓ	39 Ⓐ Ⓑ Ⓒ Ⓓ	49 Ⓐ Ⓑ Ⓒ Ⓓ
10 Ⓐ Ⓑ Ⓒ Ⓓ	20 Ⓐ Ⓑ Ⓒ Ⓓ	30 Ⓐ Ⓑ Ⓒ Ⓓ	40 Ⓐ Ⓑ Ⓒ Ⓓ	50 Ⓐ Ⓑ Ⓒ Ⓓ

Section 2

1 Ⓐ Ⓑ Ⓒ Ⓓ	9 Ⓐ Ⓑ Ⓒ Ⓓ	17 Ⓐ Ⓑ Ⓒ Ⓓ	25 Ⓐ Ⓑ Ⓒ Ⓓ	33 Ⓐ Ⓑ Ⓒ Ⓓ
2 Ⓐ Ⓑ Ⓒ Ⓓ	10 Ⓐ Ⓑ Ⓒ Ⓓ	18 Ⓐ Ⓑ Ⓒ Ⓓ	26 Ⓐ Ⓑ Ⓒ Ⓓ	34 Ⓐ Ⓑ Ⓒ Ⓓ
3 Ⓐ Ⓑ Ⓒ Ⓓ	11 Ⓐ Ⓑ Ⓒ Ⓓ	19 Ⓐ Ⓑ Ⓒ Ⓓ	27 Ⓐ Ⓑ Ⓒ Ⓓ	35 Ⓐ Ⓑ Ⓒ Ⓓ
4 Ⓐ Ⓑ Ⓒ Ⓓ	12 Ⓐ Ⓑ Ⓒ Ⓓ	20 Ⓐ Ⓑ Ⓒ Ⓓ	28 Ⓐ Ⓑ Ⓒ Ⓓ	36 Ⓐ Ⓑ Ⓒ Ⓓ
5 Ⓐ Ⓑ Ⓒ Ⓓ	13 Ⓐ Ⓑ Ⓒ Ⓓ	21 Ⓐ Ⓑ Ⓒ Ⓓ	29 Ⓐ Ⓑ Ⓒ Ⓓ	37 Ⓐ Ⓑ Ⓒ Ⓓ
6 Ⓐ Ⓑ Ⓒ Ⓓ	14 Ⓐ Ⓑ Ⓒ Ⓓ	22 Ⓐ Ⓑ Ⓒ Ⓓ	30 Ⓐ Ⓑ Ⓒ Ⓓ	38 Ⓐ Ⓑ Ⓒ Ⓓ
7 Ⓐ Ⓑ Ⓒ Ⓓ	15 Ⓐ Ⓑ Ⓒ Ⓓ	23 Ⓐ Ⓑ Ⓒ Ⓓ	31 Ⓐ Ⓑ Ⓒ Ⓓ	39 Ⓐ Ⓑ Ⓒ Ⓓ
8 Ⓐ Ⓑ Ⓒ Ⓓ	16 Ⓐ Ⓑ Ⓒ Ⓓ	24 Ⓐ Ⓑ Ⓒ Ⓓ	32 Ⓐ Ⓑ Ⓒ Ⓓ	40 Ⓐ Ⓑ Ⓒ Ⓓ

Section 3

1 Ⓐ Ⓑ Ⓒ Ⓓ	11 Ⓐ Ⓑ Ⓒ Ⓓ	21 Ⓐ Ⓑ Ⓒ Ⓓ	31 Ⓐ Ⓑ Ⓒ Ⓓ	41 Ⓐ Ⓑ Ⓒ Ⓓ
2 Ⓐ Ⓑ Ⓒ Ⓓ	12 Ⓐ Ⓑ Ⓒ Ⓓ	22 Ⓐ Ⓑ Ⓒ Ⓓ	32 Ⓐ Ⓑ Ⓒ Ⓓ	42 Ⓐ Ⓑ Ⓒ Ⓓ
3 Ⓐ Ⓑ Ⓒ Ⓓ	13 Ⓐ Ⓑ Ⓒ Ⓓ	23 Ⓐ Ⓑ Ⓒ Ⓓ	33 Ⓐ Ⓑ Ⓒ Ⓓ	43 Ⓐ Ⓑ Ⓒ Ⓓ
4 Ⓐ Ⓑ Ⓒ Ⓓ	14 Ⓐ Ⓑ Ⓒ Ⓓ	24 Ⓐ Ⓑ Ⓒ Ⓓ	34 Ⓐ Ⓑ Ⓒ Ⓓ	44 Ⓐ Ⓑ Ⓒ Ⓓ
5 Ⓐ Ⓑ Ⓒ Ⓓ	15 Ⓐ Ⓑ Ⓒ Ⓓ	25 Ⓐ Ⓑ Ⓒ Ⓓ	35 Ⓐ Ⓑ Ⓒ Ⓓ	45 Ⓐ Ⓑ Ⓒ Ⓓ
6 Ⓐ Ⓑ Ⓒ Ⓓ	16 Ⓐ Ⓑ Ⓒ Ⓓ	26 Ⓐ Ⓑ Ⓒ Ⓓ	36 Ⓐ Ⓑ Ⓒ Ⓓ	46 Ⓐ Ⓑ Ⓒ Ⓓ
7 Ⓐ Ⓑ Ⓒ Ⓓ	17 Ⓐ Ⓑ Ⓒ Ⓓ	27 Ⓐ Ⓑ Ⓒ Ⓓ	37 Ⓐ Ⓑ Ⓒ Ⓓ	47 Ⓐ Ⓑ Ⓒ Ⓓ
8 Ⓐ Ⓑ Ⓒ Ⓓ	18 Ⓐ Ⓑ Ⓒ Ⓓ	28 Ⓐ Ⓑ Ⓒ Ⓓ	38 Ⓐ Ⓑ Ⓒ Ⓓ	48 Ⓐ Ⓑ Ⓒ Ⓓ
9 Ⓐ Ⓑ Ⓒ Ⓓ	19 Ⓐ Ⓑ Ⓒ Ⓓ	29 Ⓐ Ⓑ Ⓒ Ⓓ	39 Ⓐ Ⓑ Ⓒ Ⓓ	49 Ⓐ Ⓑ Ⓒ Ⓓ
10 Ⓐ Ⓑ Ⓒ Ⓓ	20 Ⓐ Ⓑ Ⓒ Ⓓ	30 Ⓐ Ⓑ Ⓒ Ⓓ	40 Ⓐ Ⓑ Ⓒ Ⓓ	50 Ⓐ Ⓑ Ⓒ Ⓓ

Answer Sheet

解答シート

Section 1

1 (A) (B) (C) (D)	11 (A) (B) (C) (D)	21 (A) (B) (C) (D)	31 (A) (B) (C) (D)	41 (A) (B) (C) (D)
2 (A) (B) (C) (D)	12 (A) (B) (C) (D)	22 (A) (B) (C) (D)	32 (A) (B) (C) (D)	42 (A) (B) (C) (D)
3 (A) (B) (C) (D)	13 (A) (B) (C) (D)	23 (A) (B) (C) (D)	33 (A) (B) (C) (D)	43 (A) (B) (C) (D)
4 (A) (B) (C) (D)	14 (A) (B) (C) (D)	24 (A) (B) (C) (D)	34 (A) (B) (C) (D)	44 (A) (B) (C) (D)
5 (A) (B) (C) (D)	15 (A) (B) (C) (D)	25 (A) (B) (C) (D)	35 (A) (B) (C) (D)	45 (A) (B) (C) (D)
6 (A) (B) (C) (D)	16 (A) (B) (C) (D)	26 (A) (B) (C) (D)	36 (A) (B) (C) (D)	46 (A) (B) (C) (D)
7 (A) (B) (C) (D)	17 (A) (B) (C) (D)	27 (A) (B) (C) (D)	37 (A) (B) (C) (D)	47 (A) (B) (C) (D)
8 (A) (B) (C) (D)	18 (A) (B) (C) (D)	28 (A) (B) (C) (D)	38 (A) (B) (C) (D)	48 (A) (B) (C) (D)
9 (A) (B) (C) (D)	19 (A) (B) (C) (D)	29 (A) (B) (C) (D)	39 (A) (B) (C) (D)	49 (A) (B) (C) (D)
10 (A) (B) (C) (D)	20 (A) (B) (C) (D)	30 (A) (B) (C) (D)	40 (A) (B) (C) (D)	50 (A) (B) (C) (D)

Section 2

1 (A) (B) (C) (D)	9 (A) (B) (C) (D)	17 (A) (B) (C) (D)	25 (A) (B) (C) (D)	33 (A) (B) (C) (D)
2 (A) (B) (C) (D)	10 (A) (B) (C) (D)	18 (A) (B) (C) (D)	26 (A) (B) (C) (D)	34 (A) (B) (C) (D)
3 (A) (B) (C) (D)	11 (A) (B) (C) (D)	19 (A) (B) (C) (D)	27 (A) (B) (C) (D)	35 (A) (B) (C) (D)
4 (A) (B) (C) (D)	12 (A) (B) (C) (D)	20 (A) (B) (C) (D)	28 (A) (B) (C) (D)	36 (A) (B) (C) (D)
5 (A) (B) (C) (D)	13 (A) (B) (C) (D)	21 (A) (B) (C) (D)	29 (A) (B) (C) (D)	37 (A) (B) (C) (D)
6 (A) (B) (C) (D)	14 (A) (B) (C) (D)	22 (A) (B) (C) (D)	30 (A) (B) (C) (D)	38 (A) (B) (C) (D)
7 (A) (B) (C) (D)	15 (A) (B) (C) (D)	23 (A) (B) (C) (D)	31 (A) (B) (C) (D)	39 (A) (B) (C) (D)
8 (A) (B) (C) (D)	16 (A) (B) (C) (D)	24 (A) (B) (C) (D)	32 (A) (B) (C) (D)	40 (A) (B) (C) (D)

Section 3

1 (A) (B) (C) (D)	11 (A) (B) (C) (D)	21 (A) (B) (C) (D)	31 (A) (B) (C) (D)	41 (A) (B) (C) (D)
2 (A) (B) (C) (D)	12 (A) (B) (C) (D)	22 (A) (B) (C) (D)	32 (A) (B) (C) (D)	42 (A) (B) (C) (D)
3 (A) (B) (C) (D)	13 (A) (B) (C) (D)	23 (A) (B) (C) (D)	33 (A) (B) (C) (D)	43 (A) (B) (C) (D)
4 (A) (B) (C) (D)	14 (A) (B) (C) (D)	24 (A) (B) (C) (D)	34 (A) (B) (C) (D)	44 (A) (B) (C) (D)
5 (A) (B) (C) (D)	15 (A) (B) (C) (D)	25 (A) (B) (C) (D)	35 (A) (B) (C) (D)	45 (A) (B) (C) (D)
6 (A) (B) (C) (D)	16 (A) (B) (C) (D)	26 (A) (B) (C) (D)	36 (A) (B) (C) (D)	46 (A) (B) (C) (D)
7 (A) (B) (C) (D)	17 (A) (B) (C) (D)	27 (A) (B) (C) (D)	37 (A) (B) (C) (D)	47 (A) (B) (C) (D)
8 (A) (B) (C) (D)	18 (A) (B) (C) (D)	28 (A) (B) (C) (D)	38 (A) (B) (C) (D)	48 (A) (B) (C) (D)
9 (A) (B) (C) (D)	19 (A) (B) (C) (D)	29 (A) (B) (C) (D)	39 (A) (B) (C) (D)	49 (A) (B) (C) (D)
10 (A) (B) (C) (D)	20 (A) (B) (C) (D)	30 (A) (B) (C) (D)	40 (A) (B) (C) (D)	50 (A) (B) (C) (D)

キリトリ

Answer Sheet

解答シート

Section 1

1 Ⓐ Ⓑ Ⓒ Ⓓ	11 Ⓐ Ⓑ Ⓒ Ⓓ	21 Ⓐ Ⓑ Ⓒ Ⓓ	31 Ⓐ Ⓑ Ⓒ Ⓓ	41 Ⓐ Ⓑ Ⓒ Ⓓ
2 Ⓐ Ⓑ Ⓒ Ⓓ	12 Ⓐ Ⓑ Ⓒ Ⓓ	22 Ⓐ Ⓑ Ⓒ Ⓓ	32 Ⓐ Ⓑ Ⓒ Ⓓ	42 Ⓐ Ⓑ Ⓒ Ⓓ
3 Ⓐ Ⓑ Ⓒ Ⓓ	13 Ⓐ Ⓑ Ⓒ Ⓓ	23 Ⓐ Ⓑ Ⓒ Ⓓ	33 Ⓐ Ⓑ Ⓒ Ⓓ	43 Ⓐ Ⓑ Ⓒ Ⓓ
4 Ⓐ Ⓑ Ⓒ Ⓓ	14 Ⓐ Ⓑ Ⓒ Ⓓ	24 Ⓐ Ⓑ Ⓒ Ⓓ	34 Ⓐ Ⓑ Ⓒ Ⓓ	44 Ⓐ Ⓑ Ⓒ Ⓓ
5 Ⓐ Ⓑ Ⓒ Ⓓ	15 Ⓐ Ⓑ Ⓒ Ⓓ	25 Ⓐ Ⓑ Ⓒ Ⓓ	35 Ⓐ Ⓑ Ⓒ Ⓓ	45 Ⓐ Ⓑ Ⓒ Ⓓ
6 Ⓐ Ⓑ Ⓒ Ⓓ	16 Ⓐ Ⓑ Ⓒ Ⓓ	26 Ⓐ Ⓑ Ⓒ Ⓓ	36 Ⓐ Ⓑ Ⓒ Ⓓ	46 Ⓐ Ⓑ Ⓒ Ⓓ
7 Ⓐ Ⓑ Ⓒ Ⓓ	17 Ⓐ Ⓑ Ⓒ Ⓓ	27 Ⓐ Ⓑ Ⓒ Ⓓ	37 Ⓐ Ⓑ Ⓒ Ⓓ	47 Ⓐ Ⓑ Ⓒ Ⓓ
8 Ⓐ Ⓑ Ⓒ Ⓓ	18 Ⓐ Ⓑ Ⓒ Ⓓ	28 Ⓐ Ⓑ Ⓒ Ⓓ	38 Ⓐ Ⓑ Ⓒ Ⓓ	48 Ⓐ Ⓑ Ⓒ Ⓓ
9 Ⓐ Ⓑ Ⓒ Ⓓ	19 Ⓐ Ⓑ Ⓒ Ⓓ	29 Ⓐ Ⓑ Ⓒ Ⓓ	39 Ⓐ Ⓑ Ⓒ Ⓓ	49 Ⓐ Ⓑ Ⓒ Ⓓ
10 Ⓐ Ⓑ Ⓒ Ⓓ	20 Ⓐ Ⓑ Ⓒ Ⓓ	30 Ⓐ Ⓑ Ⓒ Ⓓ	40 Ⓐ Ⓑ Ⓒ Ⓓ	50 Ⓐ Ⓑ Ⓒ Ⓓ

Section 2

1 Ⓐ Ⓑ Ⓒ Ⓓ	9 Ⓐ Ⓑ Ⓒ Ⓓ	17 Ⓐ Ⓑ Ⓒ Ⓓ	25 Ⓐ Ⓑ Ⓒ Ⓓ	33 Ⓐ Ⓑ Ⓒ Ⓓ
2 Ⓐ Ⓑ Ⓒ Ⓓ	10 Ⓐ Ⓑ Ⓒ Ⓓ	18 Ⓐ Ⓑ Ⓒ Ⓓ	26 Ⓐ Ⓑ Ⓒ Ⓓ	34 Ⓐ Ⓑ Ⓒ Ⓓ
3 Ⓐ Ⓑ Ⓒ Ⓓ	11 Ⓐ Ⓑ Ⓒ Ⓓ	19 Ⓐ Ⓑ Ⓒ Ⓓ	27 Ⓐ Ⓑ Ⓒ Ⓓ	35 Ⓐ Ⓑ Ⓒ Ⓓ
4 Ⓐ Ⓑ Ⓒ Ⓓ	12 Ⓐ Ⓑ Ⓒ Ⓓ	20 Ⓐ Ⓑ Ⓒ Ⓓ	28 Ⓐ Ⓑ Ⓒ Ⓓ	36 Ⓐ Ⓑ Ⓒ Ⓓ
5 Ⓐ Ⓑ Ⓒ Ⓓ	13 Ⓐ Ⓑ Ⓒ Ⓓ	21 Ⓐ Ⓑ Ⓒ Ⓓ	29 Ⓐ Ⓑ Ⓒ Ⓓ	37 Ⓐ Ⓑ Ⓒ Ⓓ
6 Ⓐ Ⓑ Ⓒ Ⓓ	14 Ⓐ Ⓑ Ⓒ Ⓓ	22 Ⓐ Ⓑ Ⓒ Ⓓ	30 Ⓐ Ⓑ Ⓒ Ⓓ	38 Ⓐ Ⓑ Ⓒ Ⓓ
7 Ⓐ Ⓑ Ⓒ Ⓓ	15 Ⓐ Ⓑ Ⓒ Ⓓ	23 Ⓐ Ⓑ Ⓒ Ⓓ	31 Ⓐ Ⓑ Ⓒ Ⓓ	39 Ⓐ Ⓑ Ⓒ Ⓓ
8 Ⓐ Ⓑ Ⓒ Ⓓ	16 Ⓐ Ⓑ Ⓒ Ⓓ	24 Ⓐ Ⓑ Ⓒ Ⓓ	32 Ⓐ Ⓑ Ⓒ Ⓓ	40 Ⓐ Ⓑ Ⓒ Ⓓ

Section 3

1 Ⓐ Ⓑ Ⓒ Ⓓ	11 Ⓐ Ⓑ Ⓒ Ⓓ	21 Ⓐ Ⓑ Ⓒ Ⓓ	31 Ⓐ Ⓑ Ⓒ Ⓓ	41 Ⓐ Ⓑ Ⓒ Ⓓ
2 Ⓐ Ⓑ Ⓒ Ⓓ	12 Ⓐ Ⓑ Ⓒ Ⓓ	22 Ⓐ Ⓑ Ⓒ Ⓓ	32 Ⓐ Ⓑ Ⓒ Ⓓ	42 Ⓐ Ⓑ Ⓒ Ⓓ
3 Ⓐ Ⓑ Ⓒ Ⓓ	13 Ⓐ Ⓑ Ⓒ Ⓓ	23 Ⓐ Ⓑ Ⓒ Ⓓ	33 Ⓐ Ⓑ Ⓒ Ⓓ	43 Ⓐ Ⓑ Ⓒ Ⓓ
4 Ⓐ Ⓑ Ⓒ Ⓓ	14 Ⓐ Ⓑ Ⓒ Ⓓ	24 Ⓐ Ⓑ Ⓒ Ⓓ	34 Ⓐ Ⓑ Ⓒ Ⓓ	44 Ⓐ Ⓑ Ⓒ Ⓓ
5 Ⓐ Ⓑ Ⓒ Ⓓ	15 Ⓐ Ⓑ Ⓒ Ⓓ	25 Ⓐ Ⓑ Ⓒ Ⓓ	35 Ⓐ Ⓑ Ⓒ Ⓓ	45 Ⓐ Ⓑ Ⓒ Ⓓ
6 Ⓐ Ⓑ Ⓒ Ⓓ	16 Ⓐ Ⓑ Ⓒ Ⓓ	26 Ⓐ Ⓑ Ⓒ Ⓓ	36 Ⓐ Ⓑ Ⓒ Ⓓ	46 Ⓐ Ⓑ Ⓒ Ⓓ
7 Ⓐ Ⓑ Ⓒ Ⓓ	17 Ⓐ Ⓑ Ⓒ Ⓓ	27 Ⓐ Ⓑ Ⓒ Ⓓ	37 Ⓐ Ⓑ Ⓒ Ⓓ	47 Ⓐ Ⓑ Ⓒ Ⓓ
8 Ⓐ Ⓑ Ⓒ Ⓓ	18 Ⓐ Ⓑ Ⓒ Ⓓ	28 Ⓐ Ⓑ Ⓒ Ⓓ	38 Ⓐ Ⓑ Ⓒ Ⓓ	48 Ⓐ Ⓑ Ⓒ Ⓓ
9 Ⓐ Ⓑ Ⓒ Ⓓ	19 Ⓐ Ⓑ Ⓒ Ⓓ	29 Ⓐ Ⓑ Ⓒ Ⓓ	39 Ⓐ Ⓑ Ⓒ Ⓓ	49 Ⓐ Ⓑ Ⓒ Ⓓ
10 Ⓐ Ⓑ Ⓒ Ⓓ	20 Ⓐ Ⓑ Ⓒ Ⓓ	30 Ⓐ Ⓑ Ⓒ Ⓓ	40 Ⓐ Ⓑ Ⓒ Ⓓ	50 Ⓐ Ⓑ Ⓒ Ⓓ

改訂版　完全攻略！ TOEFL ITP® テスト 模試4回分 [別冊]

発行日　2022年11月 4日（初版）
　　　　2024年 4月19日（第3刷）

編集　　株式会社アルク 文教編集部
編集協力・翻訳・マークシート制作　　五十嵐 哲
表紙デザイン　　早坂美香 (SHURIKEN Graphic)
本文デザイン・DTP　　新井田晃彦（有限会社共同制作社）、鳴島亮介
印刷・製本　　シナノ印刷株式会社

発行者　天野智之
発行所　株式会社アルク
　　　　〒141-0001　東京都品川区北品川6-7-29 ガーデンシティ品川御殿山
　　　　Website：https://www.alc.co.jp/

地球人ネットワークを創る

アルクのシンボル
「地球人マーク」です。